DAILY LIFE IN THE

BYZANTINE EMPIRE

The Greenwood Press "Daily Life Through History" Series

The Age of Charlemagne
John J. Butt

The Age of Sail
Dorothy Denneen Volo and James M. Volo

The American Revolution
Dorothy Denneen Volo and James M. Volo

The Ancient Egyptians
Bob Brier and Hoyt Hobbs

The Ancient Greeks
Robert Garland

Ancient Mesopotamia
Karen Rhea Nemet-Nejat

The Ancient Romans
David Matz

The Aztecs: People of the Sun and Earth
David Carrasco with Scott Sessions

Chaucer's England
Jeffrey L. Singman and Will McLean

Civil War America
Dorothy Denneen Volo and James M. Volo

Colonial New England
Claudia Durst Johnson

Early Modern Japan
Louis G. Perez

The Early American Republic, 1790–1820:
Creating a New Nation
David S. Heidler and Jeanne T. Heidler

18th-Century England
Kirstin Olsen

Elizabethan England
Jeffrey L. Singman

The Holocaust
Eve Nussbaum Soumerai and Carol D. Schulz

The Inca Empire
Michael A. Malpass

The Industrial United States, 1870–1900
Julie Husband and Jim O'Loughlin

Jews in the Middle Ages
Norman Roth

Maya Civilization
Robert J. Sharer

Medieval Europe
Jeffrey L. Singman

The Medieval Islamic World
James E. Lindsay

The Mongol Empire
George Lane

The Nineteenth Century American Frontier
Mary Ellen Jones

The Nubians
Robert S. Bianchi

The Old Colonial Frontier
James M. Volo and Dorothy Denneen Volo

Renaissance Italy
Elizabeth S. Cohen and Thomas V. Cohen

The Roman City: Rome, Pompeii, and Ostia
Gregory S. Aldrete

Science and Technology in Colonial America
William E. Burns

Science and Technology in the
Nineteenth-Century America
Todd Timmons

The Soviet Union
Katherine B. Eaton

The Spanish Inquisition
James M. Anderson

Traditional China: The Tang Dynasty
Charles Benn

The United States, 1920–1939: Decades of
Promise and Pain
David E. Kyvig

The United States, 1940–1959: Shifting
Worlds
Eugenia Kaledin

The United States, 1960–1990: Decades of
Discord
Myron A. Marty

Victorian England
Sally Mitchell

The Vikings
Kirsten Wolf

World War I
Neil M. Heyman

DAILY LIFE IN THE

BYZANTINE EMPIRE

Marcus Rautman

The Greenwood Press "Daily Life Through History" Series

GREENWOOD PRESS
Westport, Connecticut • London

Library of Congress Cataloging-in-Publication Data

Rautman, Marcus 1955–
    Daily life in the Byzantine Empire / Marcus Rautman.
        p. cm.—(The Greenwood Press "Daily life through history" series, ISSN 1080–4749)
    Includes bibliographical references and index.
    ISBN 0–313–32437–9 (alk. paper)
    1. Byzantine Empire—Social life and customs.   I. Title.   II. Series.

    DF521.R37   2006
    949.5'02—dc22   2005029687

British Library Cataloguing in Publication Data is available.

Library of Congress Catalog Card Number: 2005029687
ISBN: 0–313–32437–9
ISSN: 1080–4749

First published in 2006

Greenwood Press, 88 Post Road West, Westport, CT 06881
An imprint of Greenwood Publishing Group, Inc.
www.greenwood.com

Printed in the United States of America

The paper used in this book complies with the
Permanent Paper Standard issued by the National
Information Standards Organization (Z39.48–1984).

10   9   8   7   6   5   4   3   2   1

CONTENTS

Preface   vii

Exploring Byzantium   ix

Chronology   xxxi

1. Worldviews   1

2. Society and Economy   15

3. Family and Household   39

4. Constantinople   61

5. Cities and Towns   119

6. The Countryside   157

7. Military Life   199

8. The Monastery   233

9. Artistic Life   257

10. Life of the Mind   281

Rulers of Byzantium   313

Glossary   317

Some Byzantine and
Contemporary Writers   321

Selected Bibliography   325

Index   337

PREFACE

This book grows out of my long-standing interest in expanding the social setting of Byzantine history and bringing the subject before a wider public. In writing it I have been helped by many people. The suggestion of Alice-Mary Talbot first put me in touch with the project, although she is not responsible for the direction it eventually took. Kevin Ohe and Michael Hermann of Greenwood Press provided unwavering editorial support. My students over the years have been steady companions in exploring this fascinating world far removed from the American Midwest. And I owe a special debt to my two children for asking those obvious questions ("How did they brush their teeth?" "What about dog food?") I had never thought to ask.

Byzantium's chronological and geographic scope has forced me to be selective in this account. Rather than focus on a representative location and period, I have sketched the diversity of daily experiences as a way of respecting both what changed over the centuries and what did not. I have tried to keep the English-language reader in mind by using familiar geographic and personal names. I continue common practice in preferring Latin forms for people and titles through the seventh century, and Greek for the later medieval period. In transliteration I generally follow the *Oxford Dictionary of Byzantium*.

EXPLORING BYZANTIUM

This book looks at how people lived in the east Mediterranean during the Middle Ages. The subject is vast in place and time, spanning the distance separating western Europe and Asia and the long interval between classical antiquity and the early modern world. Today visitors to the area are struck by its many contrasts. The terrain ranges from high mountains in Italy and the Balkans to tiny Aegean islands, from the broad, sloping plateau of Anatolia to the deserts of Africa and the Near East. Local inhabitants speak Italian, Greek, Turkish, Arabic, or Slavic languages, often in combination or distinctive dialects. Major religious traditions include Judaism, Latin Catholicism, Orthodox Christianity, and Islam. Cities everywhere are crowded with cars, computers, and cell phones, but in remote villages people still tend crops and herd animals in ways little different from their medieval ancestors.

For over a thousand years this varied landscape made up what historians since the seventeenth century have been calling Byzantium, or the Byzantine empire. Those who lived back then would have been puzzled by the name. Most thought of themselves as later-day Romans (Rhomaioi), citizens of that epic multicultural state that in the first through third centuries of our era stretched across Europe, North Africa, and western Asia. In the early fourth century the emperor Constantine fatefully moved his capital from central Italy to the early Greek settlement of Byzantion at Europe's southeast tip. This New Rome soon became known as the city of Constantine, or Constantinople. Towering walls, marble streets, crowded markets, dazzling churches, and glittering palaces made this the largest

and most splendid city of the Middle Ages. Today *Byzantium* commonly
refers to the lands and peoples that made up the empire ruled from
Constantinople, from its founding in 324 to the arrival of the Ottoman
Turks in 1453.[1]

The Byzantines, to speak of them in this rather general way, saw
themselves as heirs of an ancient past, of living traditions that reached
back to the time of Constantine, or Augustus before him, or even back
to classical Athens. With hindsight it is clear that the medieval empire
played a key role in passing on many aspects of classical and Near Eastern
culture to Renaissance Italy and early modern Europe. Casual reference
to Byzantium emphasizes these elements of continuity and stability,
sometimes implying that it was a historical fossil preserving outmoded
social ways and political structures. The outsider's view of alien customs
survives in the pejorative English sense of *Byzantine* to denote unfathom-
able intricacy and intrigue. Yet the real Byzantium was a dynamic cultural
tradition that endured so long by adapting, on its own terms and with
greater or lesser success, to the world around it. Internal crises, shifting
borders, and contact with neighboring states meant that Byzantium was
neither static nor uniform but constantly exposed to new ideas from east,
west, and north, which it conveyed in turn to others. Byzantium was
also the first state to see Christianity established as the dominant form of
religion. Between the fourth and fifteenth centuries Orthodox Christianity
came to pervade almost all aspects of society, coloring thoughts, influenc-
ing behavior, and shaping the environment. Extended into the political
realm, religion promoted the idea of the emperor as God's earthly representative who ruled his people with divinely appointed authority, a
concept of Christian kingship that set a lasting precedent for later Europe.
Many aspects of the Byzantine legacy can still be found lying just beneath
the surface of our modern world.[2]

If the larger outlines of Byzantine culture can be broadly sketched, the
common, workaday experiences of its inhabitants are less well known.
The concept of "daily life" is a historian's abstraction that can only be
approached selectively.[3] As in other cultures, the social elites are relatively familiar to us through the letters they exchanged, the literature they
enjoyed, the clothes they wore, the houses they built, and the arts they
sponsored. Their lives intersected with other people about whom we
know much less: bureaucrats and scribes; lay clergy, monks, and nuns;
soldiers, shopkeepers, and traders; peasant farmers and slaves. Writers of
the period were generally men who made their home in Constantinople
and took every opportunity to praise its glamour and importance. Foreign
visitors were drawn to marvel at the city with its exotic imperial court.
Far fewer thought it worthwhile describing the humdrum routines of
provincial life, which were organized by the endless cycles of the agrarian
calendar. Most people within Byzantine borders lived in small towns and
rural villages, and it takes effort to imagine what their lives were like.

This book offers the general reader a glimpse of this fascinating part of the Middle Ages. The first chapters look at some of Byzantium's most characteristic features by asking how these people understood the world and their place within it. The middle chapters explore the material environment as a way of grasping the conditions that shaped daily routines. Common sights, sounds, smells, and tastes varied a great deal between capital and village, town and farmstead, and everywhere reflected one's personal wealth and social standing. Such circumstances were particularly important for two subsets of Byzantine society, the army and the monastery, whose members struggled to maintain the political and spiritual stability on which the empire depended. The final chapters touch on the creative legacy left by hand and mind in architecture, the visual arts, literature, and science.

Like any attempt at historical reconstruction, this account rests on the work of generations of scholars whose work has shaped our view of the past. In recent decades the pace of research has quickened as interest has grown in this part of the world. Byzantium's transnational scope is reflected in the breadth of its scholarship, with serious students routinely working with a half dozen medieval and modern languages. Fresh approaches to material culture and daily life have brought methods from other disciplines to bear on little-studied aspects of medieval society, while at the same time asking new questions of familiar monuments. It would be easy to overwhelm an introductory survey with scholarly documentation and tangential discussion. Every page mentions subjects for which one can find more information in the *Oxford Dictionary of Byzantium*, an indispensable scholarly guide to Byzantine culture and society. The bibliography at the end of this book provides a starting point for English-language readers who want a closer look at the Byzantine world. Some of the most exciting current research is available through online sources, which with time will offer an even more vivid bridge to the past.

SETTING AND ENVIRONMENT

Over the span of some 200 years Roman generals won control of almost all territories bordering the Mediterranean Sea, which since the late republic they proudly referred to as *mare nostrum* ("our sea"). Campaigns from the time of Caesar and Tiberius to Trajan and Marcus Aurelius were waged as far as the Rhine and Danube rivers, and for many years these marked the empire's northern boundary. The impossibility of maintaining this long, unstable frontier was a key reason why Constantine moved the imperial capital to Constantinople, whose early rulers controlled territories stretching from Italy and Africa in the west to the Balkans, Asia Minor, Egypt, and the Near East. Over the next thousand years borders shifted frequently as provinces were seized by competing rulers, retaken by imperial troops, and lost again to neighboring states. Regional inhabitants would have seen short-lived political fortunes as only one factor in their daily lives, which on a more basic level were shaped by local climate, topography, and natural resources.[4]

The Balkans and Asia Minor made up the heart of the Byzantine empire. The western territories included parts of modern Greece, Albania, the Former Yugoslav Republic of Macedonia, Bulgaria, and Turkey. Craggy mountains covered by dense forests divide much of this area into steep river valleys that drain into the Adriatic, Aegean, and Mediterranean seas. The most fertile areas are the broad plains along the Danube and the rivers of Thessaly and Thrace. Upland valleys are few, small, and lie far from the coast. The temperate climate that prevails in the north resembles much of continental Europe. Winds generally come from the north and west, becoming stronger and making sea travel difficult during the winter months. To the south the Aegean is a constant presence that provides a more moderate climate, with mild winters and warm summers tempered by cooling breezes. Coastal conditions generally favor the growing of cereals, vegetables, and fruit trees. Olives, which can survive on rocky soil with relatively little rainfall, are well suited to this terrain and have been raised here for thousands of years. Inland one finds terraced vineyards and orchards. Higher elevations are better for herding goats and sheep. Strong contrasts distinguish these mountainous inland regions. Travel and communication have always been hard, with the result that peoples with distinct languages and customs have long existed in close proximity. At the easternmost corner of the Balkans is Constantinople, the modern city of Istanbul.

High pastures and orchards in the mountains of central Greece. Courtesy of the author.

Across the narrow channel of the Bosphorus lies Anatolia or Asia Minor, a broad, peninsular landmass that roughly coincides with the borders of modern Turkey. In the west the terrain rises gently from the Aegean shore, forming fertile coastal plains that attracted Greek city-states to establish colonies in the first millennium B.C. By contrast, the north and south coasts are overshadowed by looming mountains that leave only a narrow strip along the water's edge. The Taurus mountains form a rocky, contested zone to the southeast, a barrier through which the famed Cilician Gates give access to Syria. At the middle of the subcontinent is a sloping plateau where long, hot summers alternate with cold, rainy winters. Unlike the western coastlands, this inland region has never been densely populated. Today cereals and specialty crops are widely grown here, but during the Middle Ages the land was mainly pasture and woodland, with sheep, goats, cattle, and horses among the most commonly raised animals. Medieval writers regularly mention the domains of Anatolian landowners and the great livestock herds they raised on their estates.

At one time or another several other regions belonged to Byzantium as well. Most of Italy and parts of southern Spain were subject to the early emperors, who resisted the advances of Vandals, Goths, and Langobards only to lose these provinces to the Franks in the eighth and ninth centuries. Byzantine authority once included parts of modern Syria, Lebanon, Israel, Jordan, and Egypt, as well as the North African coast from Libya to Tunisia. This area included some of the most productive lands of the

An inland valley of western Turkey. Courtesy of the author.

ancient Mediterranean, and was overtaken by the Umayyad Arabs in the seventh and eighth centuries. Byzantine campaigns regained control of parts of Syria and Palestine during the 900s, but were reversed by the Latin Crusaders in the twelfth century.

The landscapes and climates of the Mediterranean today do not much differ from those of the Middle Ages.[5] Several broad cycles of climatic fluctuation have taken place within the general stability of the recent Holocene era, which comprises the past 4,500 years. A relatively cool period during the Late Bronze Age (second millennium B.C.) was followed by warmer, more humid conditions lasting from the mid-first millennium B.C. through the mid-first millennium A.D. This span coincided with the maximum extent of Hellenistic and Roman settlement, a time when population and land use expanded on all fronts. By the sixth century consistently cooler temperatures seem to have settled over much of the region and may have prevailed globally as well. A general warming took place between the ninth and thirteenth centuries before another cool period set in, culminating in the "Little Ice Age" of the sixteenth century.

Briefer episodes of extreme weather certainly affected how people lived. Periods of low rainfall or prolonged frost devastated communities that depended on a narrow resource base. Earthquakes, plagues, and wars had even greater consequences. The impact of environmental factors on historical events has been much discussed. Balmy conditions combined with an expanding population would have encouraged people to move onto marginal lands, whose thin soils and steep slopes were vulnerable to drought and flood. Such expanding land use clearly took place in different areas in the fifth and sixth centuries. Conversely, prolonged warfare combined with recurring outbreaks of plague, cooler winters, and shorter growing seasons coincided with a time of crisis in the seventh and eighth centuries, before giving way to economic and political expansion during the medieval period. Critical in their immediate effects, such social changes appear characteristic of a delicate equilibrium maintained over the span of millennia.

THE HUMAN LANDSCAPE

The Byzantine empire's geographic diversity is paralleled by a cultural mosaic that appears most clearly in how people communicated with each other. The east Mediterranean includes several distinct linguistic zones. Ancient languages like Aramaic, Hebrew, and Egyptian continued to be used in different parts of the medieval Near East and North Africa. Syriac, or what has been called Christian Palestinian Aramaic, was recognized as a language of theological scholarship, while the late form of Egyptian known as Coptic was maintained by the church long after the arrival of Islam. The inhabitants of the Anatolian plateau and Caucasus mountains spoke a mixture of native Indo-European languages. Slavic peoples brought their language with them when they migrated into the Balkans in the fourth century. Italic languages dominated in Italy, and Latin strongly influenced the population of western Europe, the west Balkans, and coastal Africa. As the instrument of Roman government and culture, Latin also was spoken by civil and military officials and educated people across the Mediterranean. It served as the official court language in Constantinople through the time of Justinian, before finally giving way to Greek in the seventh century.

Greek had been the dominant language of the Aegean since the early Iron Age, and under the Hellenistic kings its classical form spread eastward to coastal Syria, Palestine, and Egypt. While Greek was widely used by administrators and city dwellers, in the countryside it coexisted with indigenous languages. Ways of expression depended on place and occasion, and it is not surprising to hear that church leaders like Epiphanius of Salamis could understand four or five regional languages. After losing the eastern provinces in the seventh and eighth centuries, the medieval empire became consolidated around a Hellenized heartland where Greek was the recognized language of religion, government, and commerce. It was widely spoken at home and taught by *grammatikoi* in almost every town and village. Most people would have had some basic skill in reading and writing it as well.

Different levels of fluency existed within this predominantly Greek milieu. The preferred language for courtly ritual and educated correspondence was a self-conscious confection based on Attic authors of the fourth and third centuries B.C. What people spoke at home or in the marketplace was more colloquial and informal. Altogether these styles made up a spectrum of dialects or *diglossia*, whose contrasts were still evident in the liturgical Greek, formal *katharevousa*, and spoken *demotike* used in twentieth-century Greece. This linguistic pluralism, preserved by official documents and personal letters, artfully composed epigrams and hurriedly scratched graffiti, reflects complex social hierarchies. For elite families in Constantinople the florid vocabulary and stilted syntax were ways to distinguish themselves from their rustic counterparts and economic inferiors. Most Byzantine authors were quite aware of their language's complexities. Technical writers in fields like engineering, medicine, and military affairs routinely apologize to the reader for not using a more sophisticated style. At the same time authors of saints' lives normally chose to record their edifying tales in as plain and straightforward a way as possible.

HISTORICAL OVERVIEW

Scholars disagree about the limits of Byzantine history, and particularly the point when Byzantium should be set apart from the Roman Empire. This book takes the broad view by focusing on the fortunes of

Constantinople and the territories it controlled between the fourth and fifteenth centuries. Two main periods can be distinguished within this millennium-long span.[6] Late antiquity extends from the new capital's foundation through the sixth-century reign of Justinian and his immediate successors. The period is marked especially by the continuation of Roman political institutions and social structures. Changes in daily routines were gradual and uneventful, often barely noticeable from one generation to the next. By contrast, the seventh and eighth centuries brought a series of military reversals and cultural crises that transformed every aspect of urban life. The restoration of political balance in the mid-ninth century marks the beginning of the empire's long medieval phase. The ninth to twelfth centuries were a time of military success and economic expansion when Byzantine culture attained its widest regard. After Latin Crusaders sacked its capital in 1204, Byzantium was reconstituted as a minor regional state that was eventually absorbed by the Turkish empire. Over these 11 centuries Byzantium changed in many important ways, yet throughout its life there endured a distinctive sense of cosmic order and social stability. For many people, especially those who spent their lives close to the land, this reassuring worldview was scarcely touched by political events of the day.

Late Antiquity   The foundation of Constantinople in the early fourth century was part of a continuing response by Roman rulers to problems they had faced for years. Many reasons underlie this turning point in ancient history, which generations of historians have characterized as the "decline" of classical civilization, foreshadowing its "fall" into barbarism. In one sense the empire can be seen as a victim of its success, having created a frontier too long to be effectively maintained. By the early third century Roman troops were garrisoned in fortresses from Britain to Mesopotamia, along the Rhine and Danube river banks and the desert fringe of Arabia and the Sahara. Soldiers of these outposts met varied local populations: tribes of Germanic peoples in the north, desert bedouin to the south, and Persians under the energetic Sasanian kings across the eastern frontier. Interaction across the border was often cooperative but required a continuing investment of attention and money. The growth of the Roman economy in the first and second centuries had been fueled in large part by the empire's rapid acquisition of new lands and trading zones, which now drained state resources. The increased authority of frontier generals resulted in their acclamation by troops under their command and a series of civil wars during the third century. Unable to govern this expanse successfully from Rome, in 284 the emperor Diocletian established a system of shared rule by a tetrarchy comprising two senior Augusti and two junior Caesars. His idea was not to partition the empire but to multiply the imperial presence. Each ruler built a permanent residence near the frontier, in Trier and Milan in the West, in Thessaloniki and Nikomedia in the East. The system scarcely survived Diocletian's retirement in 305 and collapsed amid competition among succeeding rulers. On October 28, 312, in a key battle fought before the gates of Rome, Constantine defeated his rival Augustus Maxentius. Within a dozen years he had dispatched his coruler, Licinius, and established himself as sole head of state.

The reign of Constantine (312–37) represents a defining moment in European history. This was a period of relative peace and stability after years of civil war, and the new emperor did much to rebuild Rome's cities and consolidate its borders. In 324 he established a new base for his government on the site of ancient Byzantion, which soon was known as Nova Roma Constantinopolitana: the New Rome, the city (*polis*) of Constantine. Outfitted with paved streets, plazas, public monuments, and expanded fortifications, it was well positioned to command military and economic affairs in the most prosperous part of the empire. Administrative reforms helped stabilize its economy and secure the place of the new capital.

Constantine is equally remembered for his proclamation of religious toleration, issued from Milan in 313. Medieval legend records how he had received a vision before his battle at the Milvian bridge, and was assured of victory if he fought *en toutoi nika*—under the sign of the cross or the *chrismon*, a monogram drawn from the initials of Christ's name. While Christianity had gained considerable following in the second and third centuries, the Edict of Milan opened the door to rapid growth by a church that clearly enjoyed official support. By setting up monumental basilicas in Rome and elsewhere, Constantine established an enduring example for his successors as patron of the church as well as restorer of the state. Moreover, he apparently saw himself as God's personal representative and earthly regent responsible for maintaining political order and divine favor. Understanding his duties to encompass religious affairs, Constantine summoned the first ecumenical church council to meet at Nicaea in 325.

Constantine's successor Constantius II (337–61), continued work on the new capital. He pressed on with construction of its main streets and harbors, as well as the cathedral. Decades of relative peace gave way to renewed military threats. Julian (361–63) died while organizing defenses against the Persians in the East, and Valens (364–78) was killed at Adrianople in Thrace while fighting the Goths. Stability was restored by Theodosius I (379–95), a forceful military leader who brokered peace with the Goths, recruiting many to serve in the late Roman army. Following Constantine's activist role in religious affairs, Theodosius issued an edict in 380 establishing Christianity as the state's official religion. In 381 he convened another church council, this time at Constantinople, which condemned the rising Arian heresy and promoted the status of the capital's patriarch over his peers at Alexandria and Antioch.

The fifth century was a time of growing contrasts between East and West. The eastern provinces benefited from Constantinople's rapid growth and the peace that prevailed across Asia Minor and the Near

East. Theodosius II (408–50) expanded the size of the capital by building another landward fortification west of Constantine's walls. This new barrier defined the full extent of the Byzantine capital and survives as one of its most impressive monuments. The city's expanding population soon became the largest in the east Mediterranean. Church leaders turned their attention to clarifying matters of doctrine and interpretation. Two more ecumenical councils were held to settle intense theological differences over the nature of Christ. The Council of Ephesus (431) condemned Nestorianism, a view of Christ that emphasized his human nature. It also advanced the special status of the Virgin Mary as the Theotokos, or "Bearer of God." The Council of Chalcedon (451) countered the Monophysite emphasis on Christ's pure divinity by emphasizing that his unique nature combined divine and human elements. The council also promoted the rank of the Constantinopolitan patriarch to parity with the pope in Rome. Such decisions effectively increased the capital's status at the expense of the provinces.

At the same time, the western provinces were experiencing serious difficulties. From the middle of the fourth century Gaul, Spain, and Italy were beset by internal clashes and pressure from neighboring Goths, Franks, and Alamanni. By 410 the Roman army had withdrawn from Britain. Germanic tribes crossed the Danube to raid towns and eventually settle in the Balkans. The Visigoths, led by their king Alaric, assaulted the cities of first Greece and then Italy before sacking Rome in 410—an event some people saw as marking the end of civilization itself. The Vandals next appeared in Italy before moving on to settle near Carthage in North Africa. Imperial diplomacy in the West increasingly aimed at granting land and status in return for the cooperation of neighboring peoples. By the end of the century the Ostrogoths had established themselves in Italy under their king Theodoric, who ruled from Ravenna in the name of the emperor in Constantinople. Such circumstances led to the redistribution of land and reshaping of cities into smaller, less populous centers. The abdication of the last Western Roman emperor in 476 recognized what in fact had occurred much earlier.

This first phase of Byzantine history culminated in the long reign of Justinian (527–65). Like his uncle Justin I (518–27), Justinian was born in Illyricum and rose rapidly through army ranks. In Constantinople he met and married Theodora, a woman of modest origins who would became the best known of all Byzantine empresses. Justinian consolidated the accomplishments of his predecessors by building fortifications, roads, and bridges across the empire. He won key victories against the Persians in the East and mounted a major campaign to regain the western provinces. His general Belisarius took Carthage in 533 and with Narses reestablished Byzantine control over most of Italy. Justinian's court historian, Procopius, records in great detail these campaigns and the triumphs won by imperial forces.

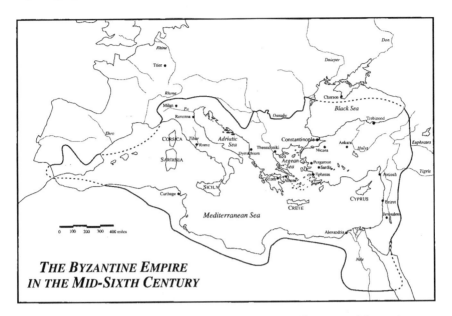

Map of the Byzantine empire in the mid-sixth century. Courtesy of the author.

Justinian also initiated a broad cultural revival. He personally intervened in the most divisive religious controversies of his day, and convened the fifth ecumenical council at Constantinople in 553 in an effort to establish Christian orthodoxy. He revised the accumulated hodgepodge of Roman law into a unified *Corpus juris civilis,* a compilation of legal codes that remains the foundation of Western law. He began an unprecedented series of public building projects, of which the most spectacular was the capital's new cathedral of Hagia Sophia. Remarkably, all these successes were won against a background of mounting civil strife, recurring droughts, earthquakes, and a devastating plague that arrived in Egypt in 541 and spread through the empire during the following years.[7]

Depleted resources and overextended borders left the empire in a state of nearly continuous crisis and upheaval. By 568 the Langobards had crossed from Hungary into Italy and claimed most of the countryside. The Avars and Slavs advanced into the southern Balkans and settled throughout the peninsula. In the early seventh century the Sasanians swept out of Persia and seized Antioch, Jerusalem, and Alexandria. Avars and Persians pressed into the Aegean and in 626 laid siege to Constantinople. The emperor Heraclius (610–41) won victories along the eastern frontier and even retook the major cities. Yet within a generation these gains had been reversed by the Umayyad Arabs under the unifying banner of an expansionist Islam. The Arab advance redrew the geopolitical map by taking Syria, Palestine, and Egypt, moving rapidly across North Africa, and in the early eighth century crossing into southern Spain. Arab generals even took their campaign to Constantinople, besieging it unsuccessfully in 674–78 and again in 717–18. By the ninth century Arab rule encompassed all of the Near East and North Africa, as well as the large islands of Crete and Rhodes. A precarious frontier was established in the Taurus mountains while an uneasy neutrality prevailed in Cyprus. In Italy the Franks replaced the Langobards as the dominant power. The pope's coronation of Charlemagne in 800 increased religious tensions between East and West and precipitated the ninth-century Photian schism between Constantinople and Rome.

These reverses marked a turning point in Byzantium's history. Within a couple of generations the empire's total area had been reduced by half. Italy now was controlled by Germanic peoples, while the Slavs occupied much of the Balkans. The rich agricultural lands of Syria, Egypt, and North Africa had been permanently lost to the Arabs, and Anatolia itself had come under attack. This dramatic redrawing of Byzantine borders brought about a fundamental reorganization of government, with the creation of military districts or themes administered by generals who reported directly to the emperor. Concentrated about its Greek-speaking core, the territory remaining to Byzantium was far more homogeneous than the empire of late antiquity.

This time of retrenchment coincided with the centrally important controversy of iconoclasm. This was on its face a theological dispute concerning pictorial representations of religious figures: Could a painted image of Christ or other holy figures be a true image of higher reality, or was it an idolatrous violation of the second commandment? The question had been posed by early church leaders but never satisfactorily resolved. It was revived in the early eighth century by those who interpreted the empire's misfortunes as divine punishment for its transgressions. Such views reflected the state's pragmatic interests in consolidating authority in the provinces; more fundamentally, they were part of the step-by-step shaping of doctrine through church councils and imperial policy. Energetic rulers from Leo III (717–41) and Constantine V (741–75) to Leo V (813–20) and Theophilos (829–42) won significant military victories at the same time that they enforced a ban on religious art. Apart from a brief interlude under Irene (780–802) and Nikephoros I (802–11), iconoclasm remained in place from 730 until 843. Written records preserve the arguments of both adherents (iconophiles) and opponents (iconoclasts) of image worship, which retained its popular appeal through years of official sanction. Iconoclasm's ultimate repeal is still celebrated on the first Sunday of Easter Lent as the Triumph of Orthodoxy.

Medieval Byzantium Resolution of political and religious strife inaugurated a sustained period of stability and cultural achievement. During the reign of Michael III (842–67) the church's central offices were reorganized by Patriarch Photios (858–67, 877–86).

In addition to stimulating fresh interest in classical culture, Photios supported the mission of the monks Constantine and Methodios to spread the gospel among the western Slavs in Moravia. Constantine adopted the Slavic name of Cyril and around 860 invented the Cyrillic alphabet to translate the Bible into this northern language. Other missions met with success among the Bulgars and later the Rus of Kiev. The growing influence Byzantium had on its northern neighbors around this time was paralleled by a widening gap with the Latin church in Rome.

The first part of the medieval period was dominated by the so-called Macedonian dynasty founded by Basil I (867–86) and continued during the reigns of Leo VI ("the Wise," 886–912) and Constantine VII (Porphyrogennitos, 913–59). Byzantine dominance of the east Mediterranean was maintained through intermittent wars with the Bulgars and Arab Abbasids. Successful generals like Romanos I Lekapenos (920–44), Nikephoros II Phokas (963–69), and John I Tzimiskes (969–76) asserted power during their regencies for minor heirs to the throne. Basil II (976–1025) accomplished the conversion of the Kievan Rus in the late tenth century and by 1018 had vanquished the Bulgaria state. These victories opened a period of renewed building activity across the empire.

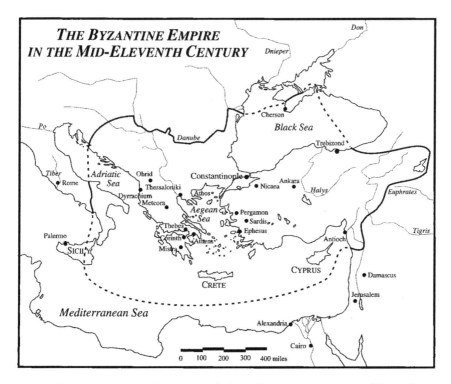

Map of the Byzantine empire in the mid-eleventh century. Courtesy of the author.

The Macedonian dynasty gave way to a succession of emperors drawn from wealthy landowning families, including Alexios I Komnenos (1081–1118), his son John II (1118–43), and his grandson Manuel I (1143–80). The growth of Constantinople and the centralization of imperial power favored the development of an aristocratic class of property owners and senior government officials. The power of provincial elites was clear in the growth of rural estates and interregional commerce. Most families stayed in the capital, where they were able to shape legislation to their advantage. The state's bureaucratic complexity also fostered a professional civil service. Both factions exerted increasing influence on the emperor and wielded power in their own name. The later eleventh and twelfth centuries were times of cultural brilliance. Some of the best-known examples of Byzantine art were commissioned by these affluent families: monasteries and churches filled with icons, paintings, and mosaics; gold and silver liturgical equipment; decorated liturgical books; and devotional objects. Such patronage increasingly focused on workshops based in Constantinople.[8]

At the same time, the frontier was coming under pressure by neighboring states. The Bulgars and Serbs rebelled against Byzantine rule and won short-lived independence. Many Armenians left their mountain homeland for new lands in Asia Minor. More fatefully, Turkic tribes pressed into eastern Anatolia and in 1071 defeated Romanos IV Diogenes at the battle of Manzikert. New challenges appeared in Italy. Western Europe's economic expansion fueled the growth of city-states like Amalfi, Genoa, Pisa, and Venice. North Italian merchants prospered as middlemen between northern Europe and the East. They soon established themselves in busy ports along the coast, where they won favorable trading and customs arrangements through bilateral treaties. The Normans occupied captured Byzantine territories in south Italy before expanding into Sicily, Corfu, and Albania around 1100. These changes coincided with rising instability in Constantinople, which saw a series of short-lived emperors in the late twelfth century.

Western interest in the east Mediterranean culminated in the mounting of four major crusades between the late eleventh and early thirteenth centuries. The first expedition, launched by Pope Urban II in 1096, assembled a multinational consortium of Latin knights to reclaim the Christian holy sites of the Near East. Individual crusaders were motivated by chivalric ideals, the promise of worldly and spiritual privileges, and the chance to win land and power. The first three crusades were organized with the cooperation of the Byzantine emperor, who provided support and access to eastern ports. Leaders of the Fourth Crusade, preached by Pope Innocent III in 1198 and substantially underwritten by Venice, took advantage of weak imperial leadership and seized the Byzantine capital on April 12, 1204. Untouched by enemies for nearly 700 years, the city's houses, markets, palaces, and churches were pillaged over the course of three days. Much of the surviving population fled the city, whose devastation by the Latins left deep enmity between Eastern and Western Christianity. Provincial territories were divided among the conquerors under the leadership of a Frankish emperor in Constantinople.[9]

The history of the late Middle Ages centers on the reconstitution and gradual disintegration of a reduced Byzantine power. The Latins claimed scattered holdings in Thessaloniki, Euboea, south Greece, and along the Near Eastern coast, yet their control of the countryside was tenuous and they were unable to administer all their possessions. Neighboring peoples took advantage of the situation and acquired new territories in the Balkans and central Anatolia. The more powerful Byzantine families set up rival splinter states on ancestral lands outside Latin control. The Angeloi family established its base at Arta in the mountains of northwest Greece. The Komenoi retreated to the south shore of the Black Sea, where they secured the region around Trebizond. Theodore Laskaris set himself up at the ancient city of Nicaea, from which he controlled much of western Asia Minor. These three regimes became rallying points for anti-Latin sentiment, which ultimately coalesced around the Nicaean state. Using diplomatic means as much as military force, the usurping leader Michael Palaiologos regained Constantinople on July 25, 1261.

The dynasty founded by Michael VIII (1259–82) survived until the end of the Byzantine empire nearly 200 years later. The capital's repair was only one of many urgent tasks facing the new rulers. The Latins had lacked resources to run the city and left it impoverished, its population dispersed, buildings damaged, archives lost, and treasury empty. Territories effectively controlled by Constantinople at this time were limited to south Greece and the Aegean coast, with the Italian states continuing to hold a number of islands. Bulgarian and Serbian leaders pressed back the Balkan frontier while the Ottoman Turks advanced westward across Anatolia. Unable to raise a viable army, the Palaiologan emperors were forced to renew relations with Venice while simultaneously negotiating short-term alliances with Genoa, Aragon, and even Rome. Mercenaries hired to counter these powers soon proved equally threatening to the faltering state. Internal clashes fueled by religious controversy and socioeconomic tensions led to civil wars that raged through much of the fourteenth century. This only distracted attention from the steady advance of the Ottomans into Thrace and Serbia, where Murad I met the Serbs at Kosovo in 1389. For the rest of its days, Byzantium consisted of isolated fortresses and walled towns along the coast. Attempts by John V (1341–91) and Manuel II (1391–1425) to rally Western support against the Turkish advance recalled deep anti-Latin sentiment and divided the Greek population. In the end, many Byzantines may have agreed with the admiral Loukas Notaras that Constantinople would fare better under the Turkish turban than the Latin tiara. The Mongels under Timur (Tamerlane) briefly checked the Ottomans at Ankara, but in 1453 the youthful Mehmet II besieged the Byzantine capital and on May 29 breached its walls. The last emperor, Constantine XI (1448–53), died in the city's defense, embodying a heroic resistance that echoes in Greek folklore.

Despite its geographic and military limitations, Byzantium in the late Middle Ages saw intense activity in the arts, literature, and science. A circle of scholars developed fresh interest in classical mathematics, philosophy, and natural science. Renewed ties with Italian and Arab scholars reestablished the capital as a formidable intellectual center. The revival of learning and the arts went together with the copying of works of classical literature for private and monastic libraries. Churches and monasteries were repaired or built anew in Constantinople, Thessaloniki, and Mistra. Orthodox monastic enclaves like Mount Athos prospered with the support of the imperial family as well as Bulgarian, Russian, and Serbian rulers. Sustained over the span of generations, this cultural flourishing reflected a tradition that would outlast the loss of the capital.[10]

EXPLORING DAILY LIFE

Recovering the routines of everyday life depends on many kinds of evidence. Serious study of Byzantium began only in the late nineteenth century, and for years focused primarily on written documents and the arts of the church. By the end of the twentieth century scholars had expanded the traditional scope of historical narrative to gain a fuller sense of Byzantine society. They also recognized the problems involved in writing social history, which stem from both the scarcity of surviving material and the difficulty of interpreting it. Recent scholarship is pursuing a number of new directions, including the family and domestic routines, health, science, technology, the countryside, and the environment. Such studies draw on a broad base of information.

Material remains offer an essential complement to written sources when approaching Byzantium. These encompass the totality of tangible objects surviving from the period, from decorated churches and devotional objects to the clothing and jewelry, tools and coins, and pots and dishes everyone used on a daily basis. Different methods are needed to deal with the variety of available evidence.

Literary Sources Written documents provide our clearest view of urban life. While almost all civil, fiscal, and military records are lost, some 2,000 documents can be consulted in their original form or later copies. Some of the most informative documents are chronicles, histories, religious tracts, imperial edicts, law codes, scientific treatises, guidebooks, letters, and saints' lives. Most writers had a strong sense of historical precedent, with the result that texts always need to be read with caution. Historical authors, writing mainly in Latin in late antiquity and in Greek in the medieval period, give year-by-year coverage of important events, often betraying personal views along the way. Military campaigns typically are described in the language of classical warfare, while one witness of the sixth-century plague patterned his report after the famous account of Thucydides. Classical ideals also underlie the composition of *ekphraseis,* formal rhetorical descriptions of a work of art, building, or city. Hagiography, or writing about the lives of saints, became an important category of literature in the seventh and eighth centuries. While varying widely in their composition and circumstance, most saints' lives tell the remarkable stories of their subject in an unadorned style suggesting they may once have been read aloud. In all these settings writers tried to make sense of their lives within the framework of Orthodox Christianity.[11]

Most Byzantines received some basic level of schooling and were able to read and write at least a little. The prestige **Epigraphy** of language, famously apparent in the Bible (Genesis 1:1), appears in the variety of objects that were inscribed with words. Building inscriptions and tombstones can provide information about a person's life, family, and values. In the decorative arts formulaic texts or abbreviations accompany familiar images of Christ or the saints, providing no new information but functioning as a kind of invocation or prayer. Similar formulas were commonly built into fortifications, chiseled into paving stones, and scratched into plates and dishes. Such examples betray great confidence in the power of words in public and private life, especially during the formative period of late antiquity.[12]

Coins provide a special perspective of Byzantine life. Numismatics concerns the production of coins by state **Numismatics** authorities at mints in Constantinople and several provincial cities. Stamped images and texts usually identify the reigning emperor and his coruler, permitting individual coins to be assigned to a specific date and place of production. Widely distributed to civil officials, soldiers, and neighboring states, these tiny imperial portraits were an effective way of announcing a change in administration or policy. Coins bearing religious symbols or figures helped reinforce the emperor's distinctive view of his office and the divine protection it enjoyed. Most of our information about Byzantine numismatics comes from large collections held by museums and private individuals. Each year hundreds of additional coins are found by accident and excavation across Europe, North Africa, and Asia. This abundance reflects Byzantium's wide-ranging commercial and political contacts and attests to the importance of coins in everyday affairs.[13]

Many medieval buildings still stand in the cities and countryside of the east Mediterranean. Most are churches **Architecture** that continue to be used for worship by Orthodox communities. Other have been modified to meet the need for mosques, museums, public buildings, or private residences. Some of the best-preserved structures belong to remote monasteries that have maintained their facilities and routines to the present day. While generally not as well preserved, extensive fortifications still surround cities like Nicaea, Thessaloniki, and Istanbul, as well as remote military outposts and hilltop castles. Most surviving examples of Byzantine architecture were built of stone and brick, and were covered with tiled roofs supported by wooden beams or brick vaults. Study of standing buildings can reconstruct their original form and decoration across centuries of use or neglect. Even the smallest structure represents someone's decision to invest land, materials, and labor in its construction. The permanence of these buildings played an important part in organizing the medieval landscape.[14]

Art Byzantine culture may be best known today by works of art displayed in museums around the world. Many of these objects were brought to western Europe as cultural trophies during the time of the Crusades. Kept for centuries in medieval treasuries, these celebrated examples represented Byzantium as a culture of overwhelming splendor and confident spirituality. Certainly most examples of Byzantine art were created for spiritual purposes. The church provided a frame for religious art to be filled with images for veneration. Public worship required a specific setting, ceremony, and equipment: chalices and patens for celebrating the Eucharist, liturgical books for readings, and reliquaries to protect sacred artifacts. Religious texts, icons, and devotional objects also were used at home by families on different social levels, in town and country. Spiritual interests ran deep yet coexisted with other concerns. Well-to-do houses were decorated with historical wall paintings and ornamental hangings. Classical manuscripts were studied, copied, and illustrated. Many people tended their personal appearance by wearing clothes and jewelry reflecting their social identity and status. Buckles, combs, earrings, and pins were ornamented with images and patterns carrying historical and cultural overtones. Even these modest objects add a great deal to our view of Byzantium.[15]

Archaeology Archaeological evidence constitutes an even broader variety of material culture with special potential for understanding daily life. Archaeologists are concerned with the full range of historical artifacts regardless of their intrinsic quality or value. Objects commonly found by excavators include tools, weapons, pottery, glass, and jewelry, as well as coins and works of luxury art. As informative as the objects themselves are the controlled circumstances of their discovery, usually by field survey or excavation. In recent years archaeological surveys have provided a wealth of information about the Byzantine countryside, including the expansion of rural settlement during late antiquity, a period of retrenchment in the seventh to ninth centuries, and a slow medieval recovery. Stratified excavations have focused on churches but also public buildings, houses, fortified sites, and cemeteries. Study of shipwrecks, harbors, and underwater sites is producing fresh information about sailing and maritime trade. Unlike many museum objects, these artifacts usually have a known context that gives information about their original use. Human remains from intact burials similarly have little intrinsic value, yet are of great importance for exploring questions of family structure, health, mortality, and mortuary customs. Excavated animal bones and shells offer details about livestock raising, butchering techniques, and diet. Environmental studies, including the analysis of ancient pollens, surface soils, and alluvial corings, provide information about farming practices, hydrology, earthquakes, and climate.[16]

Postmedieval settlement patterns, social structures, and beliefs make up a final category of information. The tradi- **Ethnography** tions and fashions that typified life in Constantinople were grounded in a distinctive worldview that pervaded the empire. The fundamental conservatism of this outlook only increased with distance from the capital, with the result that the more remote regions saw the fewest changes over time. Especially in isolated, mountainous areas, the daily experiences of most people changed little from the Byzantine millennium through the Ottoman centuries. Between the eighteenth and early twentieth centuries a steady stream of travelers from western Europe published books describing the landscapes and people they observed. Some of these accounts offer vivid reminiscences of personal adventures; others purposely compare current beliefs and customs with classical antiquity. Modern ethnographers and folklorists have equally been drawn to explore the complex structure of traditional Greek village life. For all that has changed over the years, regional lifeways still preserve much of the legacy of the past.[17]

Returning from working in the fields of south Greece in the 1930s. Photo courtesy of Department of Art History and Archaeology, University of Missouri-Columbia.

NOTES

1. For the classical background see Tim Cornell and John Matthews, *Atlas of the Roman World* (Oxford: Facts on File, 1982); Michael Grant and Rachel Kitzinger, eds., *Civilization of the Ancient Mediterranean: Greece and Rome*, 3 vols. (New York: Charles Scribner's Sons, 1988); Charles Freeman, *The World of the Romans* (Oxford: Oxford University Press, 1993); John Boardman, Jasper Griffin, and Oswyn Murray, eds., *The Oxford Illustrated History of the Roman World* (New York: Oxford University Press, 2001); and John Wacher, ed., *The Roman World*, 2 vols. (New York: Routledge, 2002).

2. See Nikos Svoronos, "Towards Nationhood: The Survival of the Hellenic Spirit," and Richard Clogg, "Eclipse and Rebirth: From the Ottoman Period to Modern Greece," in *The Greek World: Classical, Byzantine, and Modern*, ed. Robert Browning (New York: Thames and Hudson, 1985); and David Ricks and Paul Magdalino, eds., *Byzantium and the Modern Greek Identity* (Brookfield, Vt.: Ashgate, 1998).

3. Classical Rome has attracted a number of such approaches; see recently Lesley Adkins and Roy A. Adkins, *Handbook to Life in Ancient Rome* (New York: Oxford University Press, 1998); Lionel Casson, *Everyday Life in Ancient Rome*, rev. ed. (Baltimore: Johns Hopkins University Press, 1998); Jérome Carcopino, *Daily Life in Ancient Rome*, 2nd ed. (New Haven, Conn.: Yale University Press, 2003); and Gregory S. Aldrete, *Daily Life in the Roman City: Rome, Pompeii, and Ostia* (Westport, Conn.: Greenwood Press, 2004). Among the few attempts to take on the Eastern Middle Ages are Gérard Walter, *La vie quotidienne à Byzance au siècle des Comnènes (1081–1180)* (Paris: Hachette, 1966); and Tamara Talbot Rice, *Everyday Life in Byzantium* (London: B. T. Batsford; New York: G. P. Putnam's Sons, 1967). See bibliography for other ways of looking at the problem.

4. Accessible introductions to the area include Michael Grant, *The Ancient Mediterranean*, 2nd ed. (New York: New American Library, 1988); and J. Donald Hughes, "Land and Sea," in Grant and Kitzinger, *Civilization of the Ancient Mediterranean*, 1:89–133.

5. Bernard Geyer, "Physical Factors in the Evolution of the Landscape and Land Use," in *The Economic History of Byzantium from the Seventh through the Fifteenth Century*, ed. Angeliki E. Laiou (Washington, D.C.: Dumbarton Oaks, 2002), 1:31–45.

6. Scholars conventionally divide Byzantine history into three or more phases depending on their interests and sources. Medieval authors typically emphasize continuity despite the fundamental changes that took place in the seventh and eight centuries. See bibliography for representative surveys.

7. For overviews see Peter Brown, *The World of Late Antiquity A.D. 150–750* (London: Thames and Hudson, 1971; reprint, New York: Norton, 1989); and Averil Cameron, *The Mediterranean World in Late Antiquity, A.D. 395–600* (New York: Routledge, 1993). The reign of Justinian is one of the most extensively discussed periods of Byzantine history; see Michael Maas, ed., *The Cambridge Companion to the Age of Justinian* (Cambridge: Cambridge University Press, 2005).

8. General surveys include Arnold Toynbee, *Constantine Porphyrogenitus and His World* (London: Oxford University Press, 1973); Mark Whittow, *The Making of Byzantium, 600–1025* (Berkeley: University of California Press, 1996); and the comprehensive exhibition catalog edited by Helen C. Evans and William D. Wixom,

The Glory of Byzantium: Art and Culture of the Middle Byzantine Era, A.D. 843–1261 (New York: Metropolitan Museum of Art, 1997).

9. The crusades have a complicated literature of their own. Recent views are collected in Thomas F. Madden, ed., *The Crusades: The Essential Readings* (Oxford: Blackwell, 2003).

10. John R. Melville Jones, *The Siege of Constantinople 1453: Seven Contemporary Accounts* (Amsterdam: Adolf M. Hakkert, 1972); Donald M. Nicol, *The End of the Byzantine Empire* (London: E. Arnold, 1979). For the late period in general, see the exhibition catalog edited by Helen C. Evans, *Byzantium: Faith and Power (1261–1557)* (New Haven, Conn.: Yale University Press, 2004).

11. Useful anthologies of Byzantine writings include Charles M. Brand, ed., *Icon and Minaret: Sources of Byzantine and Islamic Civilization* (Englewood Cliffs, N.J.: Prentice Hall, 1969); Cyril Mango, *The Art of the Byzantine Empire, 312–1453* (Englewood Cliffs, N.J.: Prentice Hall, 1972; reprint, Toronto: Medieval Academy Reprints for Teaching, 1986); and Deno John Geanakoplos, *Byzantium: Church, Society, and Civilization Seen through Contemporary Eyes* (Chicago: University of Chicago Press, 1984). Published volumes in the Dumbarton Oaks *Byzantine Saints' Lives in Translation* series include Alice-Mary Talbot, ed., *Holy Women of Byzantium: Ten Saints' Lives in English Translation* (Washington, D.C.: Dumbarton Oaks, 1996); and idem, *Byzantine Defenders of Images: Eight Saints' Lives in English Translation* (Washington, D.C.: Dumbarton Oaks, 1998). Online sources include both old and new editions: see the Medieval Sourcebook for Byzantium, edited by Paul Halsall, http://www.fordham.edu/halsall/sbook1c.html.

12. An accessible introduction to Byzantine inscriptions is needed. Lawrence Keppie, *Understanding Roman Inscriptions* (Baltimore: Johns Hopkins University Press, 1991), provides background and touches the threshold of late antiquity.

13. Philip D. Whitting, *Byzantine Coins* (New York: G. P. Putnam's Sons, 1973); Philip Grierson, *Byzantine Coins* (Berkeley: University of California Press, 1982).

14. Cyril Mango, *Byzantine Architecture* (New York: Harry N. Abrams, 1976; reprint, New York: Rizzoli, 1991); Richard Krautheimer, *Early Christian and Byzantine Architecture,* 4th ed. (Harmondsworth, England: Penguin Books, 1986); Robert G. Outsterhout, *Master Builders of Byzantium* (Princeton, N.J.: Princeton University Press, 1999).

15. See bibliography for representative surveys and exhibition catalogs.

16. Recent work is surveyed by Michael Grünbart and Dionysios Stathakopoulos, "Sticks and Stones: Byzantine Material Culture," *Byzantine and Modern Greek Studies* 26 (2002): 298–327.

17. For an introduction to the Turkish sources see Raphaela Lewis, *Everyday Life in Ottoman Turkey* (New York: G. P. Putnam's Sons, 1971); Suraiya Faroqhi, *Subjects of the Sultan: Culture and Daily Life in the Ottoman Empire* (London: I. B. Tauris and Company, 2000); and John Freely, *Istanbul: The Imperial City* (New York: Penguin Books, 1998).

CHRONOLOGY

312 C.E.	Constantine defeats Maxentius at the Milvian bridge near Rome
313	Constantine and Licinius issue Edict of Milan proclaiming religious toleration
325	First ecumenical church council meets at Nicaea, condemns Arian heresy
330	Constantine presides at the dedication of Constantinople
378	Goths defeat Valens at Adrianople in Thrace
381	Second ecumenical church council meets at Constantinople
391–93	Theodosius outlaws classical cults, suppresses games at Olympia
410	Visigoths under Alaric sack Rome
431	Third ecumenical church council meets at Ephesus, condemns Nestorianism and proclaims Mary's divine motherhood
451	Fourth ecumenical church council meets at Chalcedon, condemns Monophysite heresy
476	Romulus Augustus, last emperor in the West, deposed by Odoacer

493	Ostrogoths under Theodoric enter Ravenna
529	Justinian closes the Academy in Athens and other philosophical schools
532	Nika riot in Constantinople; Justinian begins work on the Great Church of Hagia Sophia
533–54	Reconquest of north Africa, Sicily, and Italy by Belisarius, Narses
540–72	War with Persia
541	Plague breaks out in Egypt, sweeps across empire with recurrences through mid eighth century
553	Fifth ecumenical church council meets at Constantinople
568	Langobards arrive in Italy
586	Avars and Slavs press into the Balkans
602–28	War with Persia
614	Persians capture Jerusalem
622–32	Muhammed, founder of Islam, leaves Mecca for Medina
626	Avars and Persians besiege Constantinople
633–42	Arab conquest of Mesopotamia, Palestine, Syria, and Egypt
674–78	Arabs besiege Constantinople, repulsed by "Greek fire"
680–81	Sixth ecumenical church council meets at Constantinople
692	Quinisext council meets at Constantinople
717–18	Arabs besiege Constantinople
726/30	Leo III proclaims iconoclasm
751	Langobards take Ravenna, ending Byzantine rule in Italy
754	Church council at Hiereia palace ratifies iconoclasm
787	Seventh ecumenical church council meets at Nicaea, condemns iconoclasm
800	Pope Leo III crowns Charlemagne emperor in the West
815	Second iconoclast church council meets at Constantinople
827–965	Arabs capture Crete, Sicily
843	Iconoclasm repealed under Michael III
860	Kievan Rus attack Constantinople

863	Constantine (Cyril) and Methodios sent to Moravia to begin mission to the Slavs
875–902	Byzantine reconquest of Sicily and southern Italy
961–69	Nikephoros II Phokas retakes Crete, Cyprus, Palestine, and Syria
996–1018	Basil II conquers Bulgarian empire
1054	Great Schism between Patriarch of Constantinople and Pope in Rome
1060–c. 1100	Norman conquest of Sicily, Corfu, Albania
1071	Seljuk Turks under Alp Arslan defeat Romanos IV Diogenes at Manzikert in eastern Anatolia
1096–99	First Crusade, culminating in the capture of Jerusalem
1147–49	Second Crusade
1180	Stephen Nemanja establishes Serbian empire
1187	Arabs under Saladin take Jerusalem
1189–92	Third Crusade
1201–1204	Fourth Crusade, culminating in the capture of Constantinople by Baldwin of Flanders
1261	Michael VIII Palaiologos expels Latins from Constantinople
1321–28	Civil war between partisans of Andronikos II and Andronikos III
1329	Ottoman Turks capture Nicaea
1341–47	Civil war over regency of John V Palaiologos
1389	Murad I defeats Serbs at Kosovo
1394–1402	Bayezid I besieges Constantinople
1402	Timur (Tamerlane) defeats Turks at Ankara
1430	Murad II takes Thessaloniki
1448	Russian church establishes independence of Constantinople
1453	Mehmet II enters Constantinople
1461	Fall of Trebizond

1

WORLDVIEWS

The Byzantine empire was the medieval continuation of the Roman Empire, a highly centralized state that at its greatest extent reached from Spain to the Near East, from the broad Danube plain to the fertile Nile valley. For over a thousand years the empire was a link of political and cultural continuity that reached back to Roman antiquity. It preserved a rich heritage of classical art and learning, especially in geography, literature, philosophy, and science. Squeezed between the expanding Islamic states of the Near East and the emerging kingdoms of northern Europe, the Byzantines developed a distinctive view of themselves while mediating between their neighbors to the east and west.

COSMOLOGY AND RELIGION

Byzantium was a predominantly Christian state whose inhabitants shared a profoundly religious view of the world. Most people saw their culture as fitting into an interrupted historical development stretching from the Old Testament kingdoms to the prophesized return of Christ at the end of worldly time. The culmination of this long process was the Roman Empire, particularly its conversion to Christianity under Constantine and its preservation by his successors. The empire was understood as an imperfect reflection of the kingdom of heaven, the only enduring reality beyond the transitory visible world. As had David, Solomon, and other biblical kings, the Byzantine emperor ruled in this temporal world like Christ presiding in his eternal kingdom. His chief duties were to protect his people from threats both internal, in the form of doctrinal heresy, and external. The principal responsibilities of the church were to interpret this orthodox view and apply it to current events. Dissent and disagreement were resolved through formal gatherings of religious leaders, synods, convocations, and the seven ecumenical councils that met between 325 and 787. The last of the great controversies, which concerned iconoclasm or the prohibition of religious images, took up much of the eighth and ninth centuries until its final rejection in 843. Maintaining centralized imperial and religious authority in later centuries was an effective way of preserving uniform doctrine.

The Byzantine outlook underlies the concept of the universal chronicle, a popular type of writing sometimes known as the "chronicle from Adam." Universal chronicles were drawn up as both a historical record of humanity and a conceptual representation of that view. The format is a synchronized compilation of events dating from the creation of the world, as recorded in the Bible and understood from Assyrian, Egyptian, Greek, and Roman sources. Most Byzantines saw their lives as fitting into this historical continuum through which God revealed his moral purpose. This sequence began with the moment of Creation, usually put in the sixth millennium B.C., and would close with Christ's return sometime in the near future. This terminus or omega point was anticipated with any number of strong emotions.

Most early Christian writers believed that the end of the world was close at hand. The view is expressed by Old Testament prophets and underlies the gospel accounts of Jesus' ministry. It is elaborated by eschatological texts of noncanonical standing in the Orthodox church. The events of the Parousia, or Second Coming, were understood to take place in several stages. First, wars would rage between nations of the world, to be followed by a time of famines, plagues, and upheavals. An interlude of human testing would see widespread suffering and iniquity. False prophets would rise up, culminating in the arrival of the Antichrist, who would afflict humanity with his special mischief. Ultimately the sun, moon, and stars would fall as Christ returned in glory to usher in the kingdom of heaven. The individual soul, judged on the basis of one's moral deeds or failings, could look forward to eternal life with God or endless perdition.

This somber view of human history persisted through the Byzantine period. The simple language and wide circulation of universal chronicles, almanacs, and similar handbooks reflect their popularity among all levels of readers. Early church writers like Eusebius of Caesarea and Origen looked on these accounts guardedly, and Augustine expressly rejected the literalism of the apocalyptic vision presented in the book of Revelation. Later scholars searched current events for clues about their place in this universal reckoning. The view of immanence was stressed by the gospel writers, who clearly felt the kingdom of heaven was at hand. A particularly intense period of apocalyptic speculation took place in the early sixth century, which was estimated to fall 6,000 years from Creation. The understanding that a thousand years are but a day in the sight of God (Psalm 90:4) led to the view of a 6,000-year interval foreshadowing the millennium of Christ. Together with frequent earthquakes and the devastating plague that reached the Mediterranean in 541, the constant military campaigns waged by Justinian seemed ominous to many contemporary observers, a few of whom saw the emperor as a demon if not the Antichrist himself. Later commentators found signs of the Second Coming in catastrophic events of their own day: Islam's rapid spread across the eastern provinces, the sack of Constantinople by the Crusaders in 1204, the millennial anniversary of the city's foundation in 1324, its fall to the Ottomans in 1453, or even the turn of the seventh millennium since Creation in 1492. The common thread of such prophecies is the immanence of the end, when all humankind will face its final testing. Their currency in plain language reflects the earnestness with which they were held by all parts of Byzantine society.[1]

TIME

The reckoning of time is a distinctive aspect of any culture. The choice of calendar systems, administrative cycles, and religious festivals reveals how people understand the world and their relationship to it. Several traditional ways of recording time were continued in the Byzantine period, while new ones were also devised.

The day was divided into two 12-hour cycles fixed by the rising and setting of the sun. Following Roman civil custom, the Byzantines began their calendrical day *(nychthemeron)* at midnight with the first hour of day *(hemera)* coming at dawn. **Hours of the Day** The third hour marked midmorning, the sixth hour noon, and the ninth hour midafternoon. Evening *(hespera)* began at the 11th hour, and with sunset came the first hour of night *(apodeipnon)*. The interval between sunset and sunrise *(nyx)* was similarly divided into 12 hours as well as the traditional "watches" *(vigiliae)* of Roman times. The length of these units varied through the year: daylight hours of about 45 minutes were observed around the winter solstice, lengthening to nearly 75 minutes by the summer solstice. The biannual equinox, the only day with an hour of exactly 60 minutes, offered astronomers, military leaders, and scientists a chance to calibrate water clocks and other timekeeping devices. Most people were content to refer to the primary, half, and quarter hours of the day.

Activities took place mainly during the daylight hours. Farming, hunting, fishing, traveling, shopping, building, manufacturing, writing, and similar pursuits naturally took advantage of the clarity and safety of daytime. Military planners preferred to stage maneuvers and battlefield engagements during the day. Meals were prepared before sunset even if the evening meal was served after dusk. Taverns in Constantinople were not supposed to open their doors before the second hour of the day on Sundays, nor to stay open after the second hour of the night. Safety concerns and limited interior lighting contributed to the lack of nightlife. The main streets of the capital were lit by torches, although one rarely went out unaccompanied in the dark. Palaces, houses, and churches might be adequately illuminated by candles and lamps made of terra-cotta and glass, but a great many lamps were needed to give enough light for entertainment or work. The candles and lamps used in most homes were better suited to solitary reading.

The sun was the most reliable means of marking time. Sundials *(horologia)* gave a good sense of the daytime hours. Public sundials had been conspicuous features in many Roman cities. In the early first century the emperor Augustus had set up a huge *horologium* in the Campus Martius in Rome, bringing a 72-foot-high obelisk from Egypt to serve as the needle *(gnomon)*. In Constantinople a monumental sundial stood for a while near the southwest corner of Hagia Sophia. Portable sundials seem to have been used by traveling merchants and soldiers; several surviving examples include complex gearing to make calendrical calculations as well. Water clocks *(klepsydra)* offered another way of tracking time. A water clock typically consisted of a basin or jar from which water was allowed to drain over a specified time. By observing the dropping water level one could get a reasonable sense of the passage of hours, which was needed especially for astronomical observations. Byzantine astronomers used the "Handy Tables" of Ptolemy, together with the commentary of Theon of Alexandria, to calculate differences in local time across the empire—an expanse that stretches across three modern time zones.

The liturgical day was organized into a similar cycle of hours or services that developed over the Byzantine period. The main occasions were matins *(orthros)* held at sunrise and vespers *(hesperinos)* celebrated at sunset. Services were held at regular intervals during the monastic day, with the first, third, sixth, and ninth hours corresponding to prime, terce, sext, and none in the Latin schedule. Compline *(apodeipnon)* normally marked the end of the day in the monastery. Nighttime vigils accompanied Nativity (Christougennos), Epiphany, and Easter (Pascha). Special liturgies with additional observations were scheduled for Hagia Sophia, churches in the Great Palace, and monasteries across the empire.

Days of the Week The seven-day week was known throughout the ancient world. The Roman calendar had assigned one of the planetary deities to each day of the week, beginning with the sun and continuing with the moon, Mars, Mercury, Jupiter, Venus, and Saturn. Like the Sabbath observed in the Jewish calendar, the Romans had long recognized the seventh day (dedicated to the aged Saturn, so *Saturni dies* or Saturday) as a time for rest and worship. Constantine drew on gospel accounts of Christ's crucifixion on the sixth day of the Jewish week, and his resurrection on the third day following, to establish the concept of a weekend with the sun's day *(dies Solis)* reserved for markets and relaxation. The Byzantines naturally avoided using these Latin names with their pagan echoes. They began their week with the "Lord's day" (Kyriake), followed by an orderly succession of numbered days (Deutera, Trite, Tetarte, and Pempte), a day of "preparation" (Paraskeve), and finally Sabbaton.

Each day was devoted to remembering one or more martyrs or saints, whose observed feast days gradually eclipsed traditional festivals. Kyriake was seen as both the first and eighth day of the week, in the same way that Christ was the alpha and omega of the cosmos, existing both before and after time. The second day of the week recognized angels, "the secondary luminaries as the first reflections of the primal outpouring of light,"[2] just as the sun and the moon had been observed during the Roman week. John the Baptist, the forerunner (Prodromos) of Christ, was honored on the third day. Both the second and third days were viewed as occasions for penitence. The fourth and sixth days were dedicated to the Cross with holy songs sung in remembrance of the Crucifixion. The Virgin Mary was honored on the fifth day of the week, while the seventh day was set aside for the martyrs of the church.

The succession of distinct seasons was widely recognized in antiquity and since the time of Hesiod had been much discussed **Seasons** by classical authors. The meteorological character of the seasons varied from the temperate continental climate of north Italy, the Balkans, and the Black Sea to the more Mediterranean environment of North Africa and the Near East. Across much of this region spring and summer are only brief interludes between winter and summer. Some agrarian authorities made further refinements to include as many seasons as planets in the sky or days in the week: *sporetos* or seed-time preceding the solstice, winter, *phytalia* or tree-planting lasting until the equinox, spring, summer, *opora* or fruit-harvest, and autumn. Fixed calendar dates were less reliable guides to changing seasons than the solstice and equinox, which could be observed by city dwellers as well as farmers and pastoralists everywhere. Nature provided clues to the passing of days in the appearance of spring plants and the migration of birds; in Greece, the arrival of spring still coincides with the return of swallows from wintering grounds in Africa.

Awareness of the seasons had always been vital for Roman farmers, with the vernal equinox coming after the last killing frost. The *Geoponika*, a tenth-century collection of agricultural writings, provides a month-by-month planting guide for the environs of the capital. The return of westerly winds and the summer solstice announced the beginning of the sailing season for merchant ships and naval expeditions. Seasonal rhythms provided a general basis for predicting the weather. Classical writers and oral tradition told how one could forecast by watching the winds, shapes of clouds, flights of birds, and the clarity of stars at night. In most areas rainfall could be predicted by the formation of clouds in the mountains or along the coast. The appearance of flocks of cranes and other birds continues to be a good sign of fair weather. For all these indicators dawn was the best time to foretell the day ahead.[3]

Calendar

The Byzantines did not have a universally accepted chronological system. Archivists, chroniclers, historians, and other writers kept track of dates in different ways. This inconsistency reflects an unresolved ambivalence about the purposefulness of history and the possibility of human progress while awaiting the Second Coming.

The Julian calendar was the most widely used way of recording years over the Byzantine millennium. Faced by the need to devise a uniform method of reckoning time across an expanded Roman Empire, Julius Caesar in 46 B.C. introduced the concept of a year lasting 365 days, with an extra day to be added every fourth February. The year began on January 1 and was divided into 12 months of uneven lengths, which left an error of 11 minutes and 14 seconds each solar year. By 325 the discrepancy had shifted the Julian calendar 3 days awry of the solar year; by 1582 the accumulated error had grown to 10 days, which prompted the great calendrical reform of Pope Gregory XIII. Long-standing differences between the Latin and Orthodox churches slowed the Gregorian calendar's acceptance in the East, however, and only in 1923 did Meletios, patriarch of Constantinople, recommend its adoption. Many Greek families and most monasteries on Mount Athos still observe the ancient Julian calendar.[4]

Official dates were generally recorded by the cycle of tax assessments, known as *indictions,* which were introduced by Constantine in the early fourth century. These established the tax to be paid on land holdings and occurred once every 15 years. For administrative purposes each fiscal year began on September 1 and ran through the following August. As a result, many dates given by Byzantine writers need to be adjusted to conform with the modern calendar.

There were other ways to record years as well. The most common was to date an event to the reign of a specific emperor, or patriarch when recording church affairs. In late antiquity regnal years were commonly stamped in Roman numerals on coinage. Sometimes the year was given the name of the presiding consul or praetorian prefect of Constantinople. Traditional systems continued in different provinces. Many Greek writers went on dating events in terms of Olympiads, which occurred every four years from the first Olympic games in 776 B.C. until their suppression by Theodosius in the late fourth century. In Syria the Seleucid calendar began on October 1, 312 B.C., although different systems were preferred in Antioch and some other cities. The Alexandrian calendar used in Egypt began with the age of Augustus on August 30 in the year 30 B.C. Other eastern communities marked the elevation of Diocletian in A.D. 284 as beginning the "Era of the Martyrs." The monk Dionysius Exiguus, working in Italy in the sixth century, calculated that the birth of Jesus occurred on March 25 in the 754th year after the founding of Rome. This "Dionysian Era" was widely used in western Europe during the early Middle Ages, and foreshadows the *anno Domini* system of modern times.

The liturgical schedule was based on the civil calendar, and for most of the Middle Ages began with the feast of the birth of the Virgin on September 8. Key festivals included Nativity or Christmas (Christougennos, December 25), Epiphany (January 6), Presentation in the Temple (Hypapante, February 2), and Ascension of the Virgin (Koimesis, August 15). Most festivals and saints' days are given fixed dates in the *Synaxarion of Constantinople,* a list of religious observances in the capital that was assembled before the tenth century. The main exception is Easter (Pascha) and the related feasts of the Lenten season. Christ's crucifixion and resurrection were believed to have taken place during the Jewish Passover month of Nisan, which was based on lunar phases. When the first ecumenical council met at Nicaea in 325 it determined that Easter should be linked to the spring equinox of the solar year. Briefly put, Easter was assigned to the first Sunday after the first full moon following the equinox. The use of different calendars and different traditions of computing the date of Easter continue to divide the Latin and Orthodox churches.

These short temporal cycles were fitted with some difficulty into a universal cycle that was calculated in the number of years since Creation— a date known in the West as *annus mundi.* A number of early scholars tried to determine of the date of Creation based on study of the Septuagint, the Greek translation of the Hebrew Bible made during the Hellenistic period. In the late second century A.D. Theophilus of Antioch estimated the date of Creation at 5515 B.C., and a little later Julius Africanus began his world chronicle with 5500 B.C. In the early fourth century Eusebius of Caesarea reckoned that the ministry of Jesus began in the 5228th year after Creation, and so dated the Constantinian era to the mid-sixth millennium. Eastern consensus eventually departed from Western authorities and settled on a date we know as Sunday, March 25, of the year 5508 B.C. Complex calculations of 19-year lunar and 28-year solar cycles within this world era allowed scholars to discover the cosmic significance of certain historical dates, such as the birth of Christ or the Crucifixion. Similar calculations of the paths of the seven known planets among the constellations were useful for casting astrological horoscopes.[5]

The many possible ways of recording time meant that Byzantine sources often give conflicting dates for specific events. Sometimes Jewish, Persian, or Arab records provide confirmation or refinement. The Jewish calendar was based on the 12-month lunisolar Babylonian year, which began in the fall and required the intercalation of an extra month every third year. Each month began at sundown when the new moon was sighted in Jerusalem. The destruction of the Temple in A.D. 70 and the resulting diaspora of Jews across the empire led to the creation of a theoretical lunar cycle that is still used for religious purposes. The Islamic calendar is based on years of 12 lunar months beginning with the Hegira, when Mohammed (ca. A.D. 570–632) left Mecca to spend the last 10 years of his life in Medina. Each year has 354 or 355 days arranged in alternating months of 29 or 30 days, with an extra day added 11 times in every 30-year cycle. Dates are given by the year following the Hegira (1 A.H. = A.D. 622). Ambiguities among these different recording systems may have disconcerted Byzantine officials and chroniclers but mattered little to most people, who marked time by the orderly progression of agricultural seasons and church festivals. Tombstones of the early period reflect an interest in recording little more than the name, age, and day of death. The regularity of holidays, weather cycles, and years revealed the divine order *(taxis)* underlying the world.

LIFE CYCLE

The human life span provided a more basic and much less abstract measure of time. Classical authors had understood human lives as passing through a succession of distinct stages, each with its own blessings and liabilities. Pythagoras, writing in the sixth or fifth century B.C., had proposed an orderly model consisting of four phases of 20 years. Hippocrates and his followers identified six or seven developmental phases of uneven duration, beginning with infancy and childhood, progressing through adolescence and maturity, and declining through old age. Ptolemy, in his first-century astrological *Tetrabiblos,* connected these seven life stages with the visible planetary bodies. The first 4 years of restless lunar infancy, according to Ptolemy, are followed by 10 fleeting years of childhood under Mercury (ages 4 to 14) and 8 years of youthful passion under Venus (14 to 22). The ambitions and achievements of maturity are governed by 20 years under the sun (ages 22 to 42) and 15 years under Mars (42 to 55), followed by 12 years of contemplative wisdom under Jupiter (55 to 67) and the cold silence of old age brought by Saturn. While later scholars knew of this theorizing, most Byzantines only distinguished infancy and childhood, on the one hand, from maturity and old age, on the other.

From Infancy to Maturity   The centrality of the family emphasized the important place of children, even though few sources speak directly of their experiences. The practice of infant baptism brought early recognition of children as full spiritual members of the Christian community, despite the fact that only half of all newborns survived to the age of five. Childhood experiences varied according to social status, with poorer children enduring a limited diet, accidents, physical punishment and abuse, and the demands of working in shops or fields, especially if one of the parents died early. Most children soon learned parental expectations, from helping with domestic chores or in the fields to doing well at one's lessons.[6]

Byzantine adulthood began when one reached the threshold of social responsibility at about 15 to 17 years of age. Some boys and girls may have left home to be married as early as 13 or 15, but most older children remained part of their parents' household while they learned domestic and professional skills. Young men became eligible for military service around the age of 20, and might campaign over several seasons before reaching the legal age of majority at 25.

The average Byzantine life span was relatively brief, and even allowing for a high rate of childhood mortality may have been only 35 to 40 years. A recent survey of late-antique grave markers found that fully half of all men died before reaching the age of 40 to 45. Naturally women suffered greater risks and infirmities, with most dying during the prime childbearing years of 15 to 24. Excavated remains from cemeteries in Greece give an average span of about 35 years for the medieval period, with men surviving women by 5 to 6 years. Comparable figures have been reported by archaeologists working in Italy, Turkey, Cyprus, and across the Near East. The fact that such numbers come from permanent settlements during stable times should not disguise the greater risks experienced by the poor, soldiers, and rural inhabitants, whose burials are rarely discovered. Monastic burials are among the best documented for the medieval period, and it is not surprising that monks, nuns, and aristocrats generally lived longer than city dwellers and farmers. The average medieval life span was significantly shorter than that known in classical Greece.[7]

Old Age Perhaps 10 percent of the Byzantine population survived the hazards of childhood, reproduction, accident, and war and made it to old age. The final stage of life for Pythagoras was 60 to 80 years; for Ptolemy old age began in the late 60s. Byzantine writers often looked to the biblical milestone of threescore and 10 mentioned in the Psalms (90:10), while acknowledging that few people actually attained this goal. The demands of running the empire may explain why medieval emperors lived to an average age of 60. Senior citizens were widely respected for their experience and wisdom. In the countryside, where written records were less systematically kept, older inhabitants were counted on to remember family histories and relationships, local traditions, and even the location of property boundaries. In many cases the aura of advanced age shaded into degrees of holiness. Byzantine saints are routinely reported as living into their 80s and 90s.

The infirmities of age led to concerns about care and welfare. After the death of a spouse a surviving parent might move into the home of an adult sibling or child, or take monastic vows. Some couples chose to separate after their children had married and enter different monasteries. In either case a substantial donation of money or property was needed to underwrite the costs of physical and spiritual support during one's final years. Less fortunate survivors who lacked family or tangible assets might relocate to special retirement communities *(gerokomeia)*. Some of these were set up as urban charities by lay patrons while others were supported by nearby monasteries. Both kinds of facilities provided their inhabitants with shelter, food, clothing, and personal care. Some, like the *gerokomeion* mentioned in the charter of the Pantokrator monastery in Constantinople, were affiliated with a hospital with trained physicians. Similar living conditions combined a restricted, mostly vegetarian diet with the rudimentary sanitation and health care of a secluded, stable environment.[8]

Death and Burial   In the same way that the imperial court was only a pale reflection of an enduring heavenly kingdom, so the Byzantines saw life as a brief interlude in the soul's progress toward the Last Judgment. The distinction between the physical body and its inhabiting spirit had been widely taught by classical philosophers, although most were uncertain about what happened to the soul after death. Church leaders saw death as an awkward moment of transition in which the soul was freed from earthly bondage and returned to a state of pure spirituality. While all humans were thought sinful by nature, one's conduct in life was a way of testing the goodness of the individual spirit. The existence of an afterlife was not doubted, but its nature was subject to varying interpretation. Many believed that after leaving the body, the naked, genderless soul was escorted heavenward by an angel, passing through as many as 21 toll stations *(teloneia)*, where its shortcomings were paid for by earthly good works. Along the way malevolent demons tried to waylay these vulnerable spirits, just as they afflicted the living while on earth. The surest protection one had from such mortal dangers was to maintain spiritual purity by leading a virtuous life. Death was not to be feared but welcomed as one's birthday *(dies natalis)* to eternal life. There was, after all, comfort in knowing that the life course was well traveled. Writing in the early ninth century, Theodore of Stoudios reminds us that we all "will proceed along the same road which our parents have traveled before us."[9]

Funerary customs were highly ritualized. Most people looked forward to dying at home, comforted by the presence of family members, friends, and a priest to administer the final sacraments. The first concern of those attending was to close the eyes and mouth of the deceased to keep demons as well as the liberated soul from inhabiting the body. Death *(thanatos)* and sleep *(koimesis)* were closely related in Greek thought, and it was important to arrange the arms, legs, and head of the deceased as though sleeping. The body was washed with clean water; anointed with wine mixed with aloes, myrrh, or perfumed oils; and wrapped in a plain linen shroud with the hands tied across the chest and the feet bound. Only under exceptional circumstances was the body embalmed before burial. Clothing reflected the social standing of both deceased and community: monks and nuns were buried in their monastic habit, clergy in their official vestments, civil and military leaders with their cloaks of office, and ordinary people in their finest garb. Sandals, scarves, and other head coverings were regularly included. Church leaders spoke against the giving of funerary wreathes, but the ancient tradition of placing a coin in the deceased's hand or mouth ("Charon's obol," to pay the mythic ferryman for transporting the soul across the river Styx to the land of the dead) continued in some places throughout the Middle Ages.

The *prothesis* or final display of the deceased took place at home the next day. The body was laid out in the main room with the head facing east and an icon placed on the chest. Beginning in the early morning, visitors came to pay respects and offer condolences to the family. Late in the afternoon a funerary procession was organized, led by torches and icons and sometimes accompanied by hired singers and mourners, to carry the deceased through the streets to the cemetery or other place of burial. Long centuries of tradition encouraged the development of cemeteries apart from inhabited areas and outside the city walls.[10]

The classical practice of cremation had been widely abandoned in the second and third centuries, and almost all Byzantine burials were inhumations. Some of the earliest known Christian burials took place in subterranean catacombs, of which the best known are those surrounding Rome. The wealthy were usually buried in carved stone sarcophagi placed in aboveground tombs and mausoleums. Much more common were shallow graves *(areae)* lined with bricks and covered with tiles. Such open-air cemeteries (*koimeteria*, or sleeping areas) grew up around cities in the fourth and fifth centuries, usually together with a special funerary church. The traditional distance between living and dead narrowed during the medieval period as cemeteries developed closer to residential neighborhoods, often being established on the grounds of churches or monasteries. Even in death there was competition for space close to the grave of a local martyr or holy place. Higher-ranking individuals were commonly interred in special tombs inside a funerary chapel or church. Founders of monasteries made elaborate arrangements for their own burial and future commemoration by monastic residents. By contrast, soldiers who died while on campaign were placed in mass graves near the battlefield or along the road.

Medieval burials generally took place in shallow brick-lined graves oriented to the west and covered by roof tiles or stone slabs. A priest was called to preside over the actual interment and sprinkle the deceased with oil, wine, and earth. A piece of pottery or tile scratched with a traditional formula like IC XC NIKA ("Jesus Christ conquers") might be placed next to the body. Church leaders tried to restrain public grieving and discouraged the giving of grave goods, yet excavated burials not infrequently contain a coin, a piece of jewelry, or a pottery flask. Mourners might leave the remains of a simple meal and a burning lamp at the gravesite before returning home for a funerary banquet *(syndeipnon)*. Family members generally returned to the cemetery on the 3rd, 9th, and 40th days after burial to offer prayers and share a handful of *kollyba,* a mixture of boiled wheat with dried fruits and nuts, with the deceased. Later observances marked birthdays and household anniversaries.[11]

ATTITUDES TOWARD NATURE

The complexities of medieval worldviews are clear in attitudes toward the natural world. From a theological standpoint the Byzantines saw themselves as an integral yet special part of nature *(physis)*, which God had created for human benefit. The earth's fertility and abundance are common themes for writers; birds, dogs, bears, lions, and even ants and spiders could serve as metaphors of virtue or industry, or just objects of idle wonder.[12] Agricultural treatises, based on Roman authors and collected in the *Geoponika,* reflect centuries of firsthand experience dealing with the Mediterranean terrain, climate, plants, and animals. Like their Roman predecessors, the elites of late antiquity cultivated an idealized view of beneficent nature. They generally lived at least part of the year in grand rural houses or villas, which they consciously arranged for viewing vineyards, orchards, mountains, and lakes. The palaces of the emperors were set amid beautifully landscaped gardens and looked out on the Sea of Marmara. For such families the world of nature offered a respite from the crowded urban conditions, a restorative escape from city life.

Such views were profoundly affected by the crises of the seventh and eighth centuries. Confronted by external threat and internal upheaval, most families retreated to fortified cities or hilltop villages. Those who lived close to the land were little inclined to romanticize it. Saints' lives stress the constant hazards of rural life, with its unpredictable droughts, infestations of locusts, hot dry summers, and relentlessly bleak winters. Houses in town and country were surrounded by high walls that sheltered private gardens. Medieval writers describe such cultivated spaces in flowery language and usually were less interested in their practical kitchen uses than in their allegorical potential. Private retreats were stocked with flowers, fruit trees, fountains, and ponds. Luxurious yards, exotic plants, and animals of every stripe were featured in the decoration of the Great Palace. Flowers like the rose, violet, narcissus, lily, and crocus were prized for their color and beauty, fragrance, and even touch. Wild birds were drawn to such gardens, and peacocks were kept for their rare beauty. Parks of cultivated wilderness lay just outside the walls of the capital for the emperor to display his hunting skill and authority. In every case nature to be enjoyed was safely enclosed and tamed, clearly separate from the hazardous outside world. The four biblical rivers that once flowed from paradise to sustain the world now were seen as an insuperable barrier separating humanity from its lost origin. Return, like personal redemption, lay out of one's reach, hoped for but beyond the worldly horizon.[13]

NOTES

1. For a comprehensive overview see "The Conceptual World of Byzantium," in Cyril Mango, *Byzantium: The Empire of New Rome* (New York: Charles Scribner's Sons, 1980), 149–229.

2. Kenneth Snipes, "An Unedited Treatise of Michael Psellos on the Iconography of Angels and on the Religious Festivals Celebrated on Each Day of the Week," in *Gonimos: Neoplatonic and Byzantine Studies Presented to Leendert G. Westerink at 75,* ed. John Duffy and John Peradotto (Buffalo: State University of New York, Department of Classics, 1988), 203.

3. Classical sources for the seasons include Aristotle's *Meteorologica,* Aratos's *Phaenomena,* Pliny's *Natural History,* and Theophrastos's *On Weather Signs.* Still informative is Martin P. Nilsson, *Primitive Time Reckoning* (Lund, Sweden: C.W.K. Gleerup, 1920). For weather forecasting see Jamie Morton, *The Role of the Physical Environment in Ancient Greek Seafaring* (Leiden, the Netherlands: Brill, 2001), 284–309.

4. E.G. Richards, *Mapping Time: The Calendar and Its History* (Oxford: Oxford University Press, 1988); David Ewing Duncan, *Calendar: Humanity's Epic Struggle to Determine a True and Accurate Year* (New York: Avon Books, 1998). For the classical background see E.J. Bickerman, *Chronology of the Ancient World,* 2nd ed. (Ithaca, N.Y.: Cornell University Press, 1980).

5. The rather complicated figuring of the date of Creation is summarized by Mango, *Byzantium,* 189–200.

6. For early life experiences in Rome and late antiquity see Thomas Wiedemann, *Adults and Children in the Roman Empire* (New Haven, Conn.: Yale University Press, 1989); and Nikos Kalogeras, "What Do They Think about Children? Perceptions of Childhood in Early Byzantine Literature," *Byzantine and Modern Greek Studies* 25 (2001): 2–19. For the medieval period see Ann Moffatt, "The Byzantine Child," *Social Research* 53 (1986): 705–23.

7. Alice-Mary Talbot, "Old Age in Byzantium," *Byzantinische Zeitschrift* 77 (1984): 267–78; George T. Dennis, "Death in Byzantium," *Dumbarton Oaks Papers* 55 (2001): 1–7.

8. Talbot, "Old Age in Byzantium," 268–69; Alexander P. Kazhdan and Giles Constable, *People and Power in Byzantium: An Introduction to Modern Byzantine Studies* (Washington, D.C.: Dumbarton Oaks, 1982), 52–53. For retirement communities see Demetrios J. Constantelos, *Byzantine Philanthropy and Social Welfare* (New Brunswick, N.J.: Rutgers University Press, 1968), 222–40.

9. Quoted in Dennis, "Death in Byzantium," 6, who adds that as in life, so in dying "if you had packed the necessary provisions and if your documents were in order, then you had nothing to fear and you would arrive safely at your new destination."

10. Byzantine funerary practices continue many aspects of earlier Near Eastern, Jewish, and classical traditions. For background see Alfred C. Rush, *Death and Burial in Christian Antiquity* (Washington, D.C.: Catholic University of America Press, 1941); and Jocelyn M.C. Toynbee, *Death and Burial in the Roman World* (Ithaca, N.Y.: Cornell University Press, 1971). For medieval and later Greek

traditions see James Kyriakakis, "Byzantine Burial Customs: Care of the Deceased from Death to the Prothesis," *Greek Orthodox Theological Review* 19 (1974): 37–72; Dorothy Abrahamse, "Rituals of Death in the Middle Byzantine Period," *Greek Orthodox Theological Review* 25 (1984): 125–34; and for popular beliefs Michael Angold, *Church and Society in Byzantium under the Comneni, 1081–1261* (Cambridge: Cambridge University Press, 1995), 442–57.

11. Traditional Greek funerary practices are an important source for understanding Byzantine customs. Foremost among several important studies are Loring M. Danforth, *The Death Rituals of Rural Greece* (Princeton, N.J.: Princeton University Press, 1982); and Margaret Alexiou, *The Ritual Lament in Greek Tradition*, 2nd ed. (Lanham, Mass.: Rowman and Littlefield, 2002).

12. From late antiquity to the end of the Middle Ages, Greek epigrams and poems reflect a sympathetic relationship with nature; see examples in Constantine A. Trypanis, ed., *The Penguin Book of Greek Verse* (Harmondsworth, England: Penguin Books, 1971).

13. For changing attitudes toward nature see Henry Maguire, *Earth and Ocean: The Terrestrial World in Early Byzantine Art* (University Park: Pennsylvania State University, 1987); Antony R. Littlewood, "Gardens of Byzantium," *Journal of Garden History* 12 (1992): 126–53; and in general Antony Littlewood, Henry Maguire, and Joachim Wolschke-Bulmahn, eds., *Byzantine Garden Culture* (Washington, D.C.: Dumbarton Oaks, 2002)

2

SOCIETY AND ECONOMY

PEOPLE

Byzantium, like classical Rome before it, was the home of so many different peoples that one can speak of a distinct Byzantine society only in general terms. Over the course of centuries the Roman Empire had accumulated territories reaching from Britain to the Near East, yet all the while maintained its ancient capital in central Italy. The foundation of Constantinople in 324 abruptly and permanently shifted the seat of government to the east Mediterranean, a region of great cultural complexity. The sight of Roman armies was perfectly familiar to inhabitants of the East. The fertile coastlands of Asia Minor, Syria, Palestine, and North Africa supported hundreds of cities whose residents had prospered under Hellenistic and Roman rule. Yet beyond this urbanized fringe lived other peoples who had adjusted to the presence of foreign rulers while continuing their own customs on an everyday basis. The new capital's location at the intersection of Europe and Asia reflects the urgency of communicating readily with all parts of its territory as well as with surrounding states. The diversity of ethnicities, languages, and cultural traditions was apparent across the empire, in its provincial cities as well as in the capital. Byzantium was never a unified nation in the modern sense of the term.[1]

The loss of Italy, Africa, and the eastern provinces in the seventh century left the Balkans and western Asia Minor as Byzantium's geographic center. This had always been the most thoroughly Hellenized part of the empire, a region long familiar with the sedentary patterns of classical life. For centuries Greek had been spoken throughout the countryside as well as in towns. At the same time the uplands of northern Greece and the Anatolian plateau were home to nomadic pastoralists and transhumant farmers who continued using their ancestral languages. Between the fourth and sixth centuries large numbers of Illyrians, Goths, Avars, and Slavs moved into the lower Balkans. These were followed by Turkic-speaking Bulgars, who settled along the Danube in the sixth and seventh centuries and soon developed a formidable rival state. Farther east, Armenians, Caucasians, and Turkic groups expanded their presence in Anatolia. Years of cooperation, exchange, and intermarriage created highly colored provincial societies that influenced the life and politics of Constantinople. The medieval epic of Digenis Akritis, that celebrated hero of the eastern frontier, preserves the adventure and romance of this exotic margin. The development of archaizing language, distinctive costumes, and elaborate ceremonies at court reflects this interchange with frontier cultures while reinforcing the capital's sense of its own superiority.[2]

The later Middle Ages saw growing interaction between Byzantium and its neighbors. Proselytizing missions to the Slavs in the ninth and tenth centuries led to close ties with the Kievan Rus and expanded contacts with Scandinavia. These distant peoples, far removed from the capital, soon became valued sources of mercenaries for the Byzantine army. Relations with the Arabs, who now controlled much of Rome's earlier territories in North Africa and the Near East, alternated between open hostility and wary cooperation. The growth of powerful states in Italy—the Normans in the south, the maritime cities of Amalfi, Genoa, and Venice in the north—brought increasing contact and competition with western Europe. Economic opportunities and diplomatic assignments attracted foreigners to live in the cities of south Greece and coastal Asia Minor, and especially in Constantinople. Trading concessions granted to Western merchants in the eleventh and twelfth centuries encouraged them to build commercial warehouses along the Golden Horn. Ambassadors like Liudprand of Cremona, the Ottonian court's personal representative, stayed in special apartments near the palace. Latin churches and Islamic mosques served their own congregations in the late-medieval capital.

Jews occupied a special place in Byzantium. Roman law as well as rabbinic custom had always held the Jews to be a separate people (*ethnos*). The Orthodox church recognized their religious rights, even during times of political persecution and cultural discrimination. Jewish communities, synagogues, and cemeteries are known to have existed in many cities, particularly during late antiquity. There must have been a sizable population at Sardis in western Asia Minor, for example, where excavations have identified a large synagogue of the fourth or fifth century. Each community had its rabbi who acted as chief administrator and judge. While some Jews sided with Byzantium's opponents in Palestine and the Balkans, others came from across the Mediterranean to live in

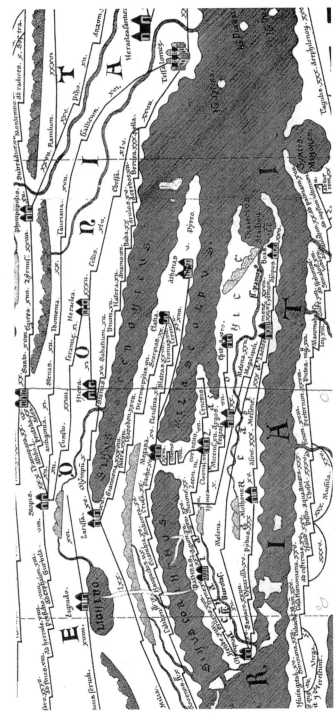

The area of present-day Greece as shown on the Peutinger Table, a late-medieval copy of a fifth-century itinerary. Major cities are indicated by paired towers. The importance of Thessaloniki is clear from its five towers. From Konrad Miller, *Weltkarte des Castorius genannt die Peutinger'sche Tafel* (Ravensburg, Germany: Otto Maier, 1888).

cosmopolitan centers like Thessaloniki and Constantinople. Byzantine Jews forged close ties with the court of the Khazars, who controlled a vast area north of the Caucasus and officially adopted Judaism around 864. The Sephardic Benjamin of Tudela visited about 25 Jewish communities while traveling in the twelfth century, and found that the largest numbers were concentrated in Thebes and the capital. Other writers tell us that many Jews occupied separate quarters (Hebraike), often located near administrative or commercial regions. The Jews of Constantinople are known to have lived along the banks of the Golden Horn and in the Chalkoprateia district near Hagia Sophia and the Great Palace. Many of these people were involved in the textile trades or worked as glassmakers, smiths, and tanners. Others found employment as scribes, translators, and physicians.[3]

SOCIAL STRUCTURE

Byzantine society consisted of many small groups that were joined by ties of kinship or occupation. At the top of the social pyramid was the emperor *(basileus Rhomaion)*, a remote and infrequently seen individual who was regarded as the divinely anointed lord and father of the empire. The broad foundation was the nuclear family and its near relations. Between these extremes existed a variety of groups whose overlapping boundaries and interconnections were constantly changing and not always clear. Social relations were mainly vertical, with most people taking a pragmatic view of relationships outside the family. The absence of strong horizontal associations may be one reason why Byzantium remained a society of families united by a centralized, autocratic state.

Over the years a man would belong to a succession of social units or microstructures, ranging from his immediate family to a military cohort, trade group, or confraternity. Each of these situations—the domestic household, professional guild, school, church, or monastery—provided a structured setting for peer relations. Disinterested friendships in most other circumstances were viewed with suspicion. The eleventh-century provincial administrator and moralist Kekaumenos, looking back on a life of personal experience, gives plenty of reasons for avoiding unnecessary entanglements. The classical idea of mutual friendship was discussed on a philosophical level and is preserved in letters exchanged by churchmen, civic leaders, and scholars. Leo of Synada, writing in the tenth century, likens a friendship without the exchange of letters to a lamp without oil. Conventional views of gender roles had a significant bearing on voluntary associations, especially for women and eunuchs, whose options for friendships were more limited. The most enduring of all these groups was the family, yet even ties of birth and marriage were transformed upon entering a monastery.[4]

The family's centrality generally discouraged the for-
mation of wider kinship networks. By the sixth century a   **Kinship and**
body of civil and religious law had shaped a new under-   **Family**
standing of the family as a spiritual and socioeconomic
entity. The consensual marriage of man and woman formed a "golden
team" that served as the basic unit of landownership, production, and
taxation. Legislation gave women specific rights and divided property
equally among surviving children. Such concerns were clearly different
from western Europe, where clan ties were reinforced by the tradition of
primogeniture. There the territorial integrity of hereditary domains was
maintained by awarding the largest part of an estate to the eldest son.

The family's importance at the expense of wider kin groups can be
seen in the use of Byzantine names. Naming traditions have always
been an effective way of establishing social identities and relationships.
Roman custom had combined a given name (*praenomen*, usually passed
from father to son), with the name of the family (*nomen*) and one or more
distinguishing surnames (*cognomena*). In late antiquity this practice was
simplified to identifying just one's father or place of origin. A typical
fifth-century name, for example, might identify Alexander simply as
the son of Demetrius (Alexandros Demetriou). Such formulas, found on
grave markers across the empire, span at most two or three generations.
Many men were known only by their given name together with their rank
or hometown. Sixth-century civil appointees range from the ruthlessly
efficient praetorian prefect John the Cappadocian to the scholarly career
officer John the Lydian. Chroniclers of the sixth and seventh centuries
include John of Antioch, John of Ephesus, and John of Epiphaneia. Major
theologians of the period were John (the Grammarian) of Caesarea, John
of Damascus, and John (Scholastikos) of Scythopolis.

The consolidation of rural properties in the hands of larger clan units
revived the popularity of family names in the medieval period. In some
cases a descriptive patronymic originated in a profession or moral characteristic, as seen in the emperors Romanos III Argyros ("silver"), Michael V
Kalaphates ("the caulker"), or Constantine IX Monomachos ("warrior").
The names of military families often can be traced to an ancestral village
or region, social rank, or personal attribute, such as the Angelos, Doukos,
Komnenos (apparently derived from a village of Komne), Laskaris (perhaps derived from the Persian word for "warrior"), Palaiologos (a venerable name meaning "junkman"), Pediasmos ("inhabitant of a valley"),
and Phrangopoulos ("son of a Frank"). Villagers commonly were called
by their trade: Chalkeos (metalworker), Gounaras (furrier), Kalligas
(shoemaker), Kerouras (gardener), Mylonas (miller), Raptes (tailor),
Tzykalas (potter). A son usually took the family name of his father, but in
some cases might adopt his mother's name. A daughter was expected to
assume the name of her husband, yet might retain her own if she came
from a well-known landed family. Passed down over many generations,

such venerable patronymics were a hallmark of later Byzantine society. Many are still used today.[5]

Government
The main branches of imperial service were the court, the military, and the civil bureaucracy. All of these came under the emperor's direct authority. The emperor rose to his office by varied paths, from being born *porphyrogennitos* into the reigning family or named as coruler by the current emperor to seizing power with the support of the army. The senate, an advisory and largely ceremonial body made up of members of the upper classes, validated the new emperor's claim, and the patriarch crowned him in the cathedral. The imperial household included members of the ruler's immediate family together with a large number of palace officials. Many of these carried titles reflecting their onetime roles as personal attendants: bodyguard *(parakoimomenos)*, chamberlain *(koubikoularios)*, sword bearer *(spatharios)*, and so on. For much of the Middle Ages the crucial positions were filled by eunuchs, loyal confidants who advised the emperor, protected his family, and organized the ceremonial life of the palace.

The most visible aspects of government were the military and civil service. The military consisted of an elite imperial guard and a series of provincial field armies, all of which were commanded by generals *(strategoi)* who reported to the emperor. The navy, less consistently supported over the years, was organized into several fleets based in the maritime provinces. The imperial guard was staffed by professional soldiers and commanded by career officers. The provincial army's rank and file consisted of young farmers, laborers, and merchants recruited from the general population or conscripted in times of crisis. By contrast, the civil bureaucracy was staffed by skilled, literate men who ran the state's complicated fiscal and judicial machinery. Administration, record keeping, and legal work took place mainly in the capital, supported by taxes raised through a network of provincial officials.[6]

Social Classes
Rigid class boundaries in the modern sense did not exist in Byzantium, but most people knew they belonged to one of three broad socioeconomic tiers. The small number of elites consisted of high-ranking government officials, military leaders, and major landowners. Almost all of these were men who came from established families that controlled significant estates and urban commercial properties. Honors and titles were handed out by the emperor in a mutually beneficial arrangement that brought status and opportunities for enrichment in exchange for political support. Titles were conferred for the life of the recipient but did not remain with his family, which slowed the formation of a hereditary aristocracy as in western Europe. The frequent invention of new honors meant that constant negotiation was needed to maintain status at court. In the later Middle Ages these powerful families were sometimes referred to as the *dynatoi,* or "powerful ones."[7]

The middle classes *(mesoi)* were made up of smaller property owners and well-to-do merchants. The largest number were farmers who lived in provincial towns near lands they owned. Successful families were distinguished by their diversified holdings and drew a reliable surplus from fields, vineyards, and livestock. Over time many families also established workshops to process their own commodities. The production and exchange of crafts and services concentrated in provincial towns and especially the capital, with some families specializing in long-distance trade. Small producers and merchants were hard hit by the political crises of the seventh and eighth centuries, but grew in numbers during the late-medieval period.[8]

By far the largest number of people belonged to the lower classes, comprising the rural peasantry and urban poor. Medieval writers use similar words *(aporoi, ptochoi)* when referring to free tenant farmers and destitute town dwellers. A rural family normally lived on the land it worked, small fields and orchards that it either owned outright or leased from others. The main task of family members was to raise enough food to feed themselves as well as pay rents and taxes. This relentless subsistence cycle allowed few opportunities for surplus production or entrepreneurial activity, with the result that most of the peasantry were effectively tied to the land. The city poor, by contrast, existed as a distinct social group that relied on official, religious, and private charity. Concern for the poor began with the emperor, who supervised the state's many philanthropic operations. In late antiquity this took the form of free bread distributed from state-run bakeries to residents of the capital. Throughout the Middle Ages the emperor dispensed alms at civic and religious festivals, setting an example for court members and private citizens. Church leaders cited the gospels (Matthew 6:2–4) in strongly endorsing almsgiving, both as an expression of Christian philanthropy and in anticipation of divine judgment. Most of this private aid was funneled through churches and monasteries to orphanages; homes for the poor, homeless, and aged; and hospitals.[9]

Slavery *(douleia)* was a persistent feature of Byzantine society. Slaves were considered a special class of property and had few **Slaves** legal rights. They could not themselves hold ownership nor give evidence in court. Owners were responsible for the conduct of their slaves and were allowed to discipline them with lethal force. At the same time church leaders stressed that slavery placed mutual obligations on both parties, including obedience by the enslaved and good treatment by their owners.

Slaves came from several sources. A child born to enslaved parents or a mother of slave status became the property of the owner, who might choose to abandon the infant, sell it, or raise it within his household. The decision was largely economic and varied with local circumstances. A second main source was enemy captives taken during battle. Some prisoners of war were executed, but most were exchanged, ransomed, or kept as slaves. Captured Byzantine citizens retained some rights, and courts recognized as valid existing marriages and wills. Foreign slaves also could be acquired by piracy or bought in the marketplace, which was regulated by imperial decree. Byzantine law forbade selling oneself into slavery as a way of escaping financial burdens, even though some forms of agricultural dependency may not have significantly differentiated slaves from free peasants and tenant farmers.

Slaves were given various economic and social assignments. Some of the most affluent landowners kept hundreds of slaves. The wealthy widow Danelis of Patras is said to have brought 3,000 slaves to Constantinople in the ninth century as a gift for Basil I. Such huge, plantation-like operations were not common, however, since most rural families could not afford to hire servants, much less own slaves. Byzantine slavery was mainly an urban phenomenon, with the largest number of slaves toiling in private households and workshops in the capital. Slaves were most efficiently put to work processing crops, weaving baskets and textiles, and making bricks and pottery. Skilled artisans were always needed to make jewelry and luxuries. The Great Palace engaged large numbers of slaves as well as hired servants; the many eunuchs who worked there represented a special category of involuntary servitude. In larger urban households slaves cleaned, prepared meals, and raised the children. Some owners leased their slaves to other families for pay.

Slavery's status declined in the medieval period. Early church teachings generally recognized the legacy of slavery even while discouraging it in practice (1 Timothy 6:1; Colossians 3:22). Well-treated slaves in a large household probably were better off than the urban poor. Their legal standing gradually improved, and by the ninth century slaves had gained limited property rights. During the eleventh and twelfth centuries they were granted the right to receive the basic sacraments of baptism, the Eucharist, and funeral rites, which increased their status as individuals and improved their general living conditions. Under Alexios I Komnenos slaves were allowed to marry. Freedom was often granted in recognition of long years of faithful service, usually after the death of the owner. A typical case was the eleventh-century slave Maria, who when freed by the widow Gemma was given her late owner's bed together with an allotment of grain. In his will the provincial magnate Eustathios Boilas bestowed freedom and legacies on his remaining slaves, while leaving directions for the education and employment of their children. So common was the practice that a special church service was developed for the manumission of slaves. By the end of the Middle Ages slavery was relatively uncommon and had little economic significance. The few remaining slaves were scarcely distinguishable from household servants.[10]

More than any other institution, the church was responsi-
ble for holding together the disparate elements of Byzantine   **The Church**
society. Unity was not easily achieved but emerged out of
intense discussions about the nature of Christ, which culminated in the
eighth and early ninth centuries in the policies of iconoclasm. The shaping of an Orthodox worldview with consistent doctrine and practice did
not take place within a vacuum but was linked with other concerns: the
role of the emperor, the relation of secular and religious authority, the pre-
eminence of the capital, and relations with Latin Christianity. Many of the
most contentious issues had been settled by the tenth century, by which
time Byzantium had closed ranks around its Aegean base. Growing contact with western Europe in the thirteenth and fourteenth centuries stirred
fresh controversies that would outlive the Middle Ages.

The church's hierarchical structure paralleled the main lines of imperial authority. By the early fifth century the patriarch of Constantinople
was recognized as the highest-ranking of the four eastern patriarchates
and of equal status with the pope in Rome. The empire's ecclesiastical provinces *(eparchia)* were headed by archbishops or metropolitans
who supervised their subordinate bishops *(episkopoi)*. Each bishop
officially resided near his episcopal church or cathedral, although he
might choose to stay for a time in the capital. Most people worshipped
in local churches *(paroikia)* served by an assigned priest *(papas)*. Lower
clergy included deacons, subdeacons, and readers *(anagnostes)*. The staff
attached to a church depended on its location, size, and importance.
Hundreds of priests and other clergymen were engaged in celebrating daily services at Hagia Sophia. Village churches, by contrast, were
served by a single priest.[11]

While priests in western Europe were clearly distinguished from ordinary people, the Byzantine clergy remained in close contact with the rest of
society. Readers and subdeacons were drawn from the laity and expected
to be 20 years old. Deacons had to be 25, priests and bishops at least 30.
In larger congregations women were able to find positions as readers and
deaconesses. One the sharpest differences with the Latin church was over
clerical celibacy, which Byzantium treated with greater flexibility. Lower
clergy were allowed to marry, and married deacons and priests could
serve if they had wed before being ordained. A newly appointed bishop
was installed only if his wife volunteered to enter a nunnery. Even though
celibacy was an essential part of monastic life, monks and nuns often
remained in touch with relatives and friends.

Byzantium's religious hierarchy mirrored its administrative structure in
many ways, yet for most people the church was a more immediate presence than the state. One encountered secular officialdom when paying
taxes or drawing up legal documents, but outside of the capital one
rarely saw the emperor or his representatives. By contrast, churchmen,
priests, monks, and nuns were everywhere. They lived in houses, official

The medieval seal of the cathedral clergy of Constantinople. The sealing, impressed in lead, shows the sixth-century emperor Justinian offering a model of the domed church of Hagia Sophia to the Virgin. From Gustave Schlumberger, *Sigillographie de l'empire byzantin* (Paris: Ernest Leroux, 1884).

residences, and monasteries throughout the empire. They appeared daily in the streets, shops, and markets. Most importantly, this extensive clergy led regular services in thousands of churches and chapels. Varying in size and organization yet united in their liturgical essentials, these buildings formed a vital sanctuary in which all parts of medieval society—rich and poor, free and slave—gathered for the drama of Orthodox worship.

Liturgy   Over the centuries the Byzantine church developed a complicated schedule of services for different settings, times of year, and special occasions. The most important of these was the order of worship established in the fourth century by Basil of Caesarea and John Chrysostomos. Local variations were gradually standardized, and by the twelfth century the present form of the liturgy was used throughout the empire. Similar services were found in Bulgaria, Russia, Serbia, and other states that acknowledged the patriarch of Constantinople as their spiritual leader. The standard ceremony involved a symbolic reenactment of Christ's Passion along with chanted or sung commentary. It lasted about an hour and a half and had four essential parts. The opening *prothesis* or offertory set the stage by assembling the elements of bread and wine. The *enarxis* introduced one or more psalms that were sung antiphonally, together with litanies, prayers, and the doxology. The Liturgy of the Word began with the "Lesser Entrance" of the Gospels (Evangelion) and singing of the Trisagion (the three repeated "holies" of the Latin Sanctus). Worship culminated in the "Greater Entrance" and the sharing of the Eucharist, followed by blessings and dismissal. The officiating priest, attendant clergy, and lay members were actively involved at different times during the service, whether reading lessons, singing psalms, or offering chanted responses. All music was voiced without instrumental accompaniment. Lay members regularly received the Eucharist in late antiquity, but for most of the medieval period communion was limited to major feast days.

This elaborate ceremony took place at an altar set within a clearly organized space and surrounded by religious images. Architecture and liturgy changed in important ways over time: churches generally became smaller and more compact, processions were simplified, and participation narrowed to prescribed responses to readings and psalms. Painted icons of religious figures were such an important part of the service that some of them were mounted on a screen *(templon)* in front of the sanctuary. By the late Middle Ages this screen had developed into the *iconostasis*, a high barrier that hid the altar from the congregation's view with a tall, central doorway that admitted the clergy's two ceremonial entrances. The icons on the *iconostasis* remained directly accessible by individual worshippers, who approached them with a deep bow *(proskynesis)* and venerated them by touching and kissing their painted surface. Prayer services were held throughout the day, especially in monastic churches, and marked the transitional moments of baptism, marriage, and death. Prayed, sung, and acted according to long-established tradition, the liturgy reinforced the concept of a timeless Orthodox community whose members knew the feelings expressed by John of Damascus, who wrote of entering the church weighted down by the cares of the world, "the prickles of thorny thoughts," but amid the brilliance of its images is "refreshed as if in a verdant meadow, and my soul is led to the glory of God."[12]

GENDER ROLES

The different expectations a culture has of men and women say a lot about itself, and it is unsurprising that public life in Byzantium was disproportionately male. Social conventions at all levels were modeled on the nuclear family, which looked to the divinely sanctioned emperor as the remote father of his people. Apart from an occasional empress or regent who ruled on behalf of a child, men occupied all official posts in the imperial court, civil bureaucracy, and military. Women were excluded from the priesthood and church hierarchy as well, yet found a special place in female monastic houses. Many nunneries in Constantinople were run by female abbots and assistants, even if they needed male priests to lead them in worship. Secular urban life held greater opportunities for women at all levels, from managing household affairs and making crafts to selling market goods and working as public entertainers. Life in the provinces was less bound by conventional roles.

Women
Views of women were complex and contradictory. Women formed the center of any family, and the household was seen as their proper place. Bearing and caring for children were celebrated as any woman's highest achievements; infertility was thought to be a source of great shame. At the same time individual women aroused deep suspicion. They could appear irresolute and weak in their daily lives, yet threatened men with dangerous sexual distractions. This ambiguous view of women as both virgin and temptress, Mary and Eve, comes from documents written almost entirely by men. One of the few sources by a woman, the *Alexiad* of Anna Komnene, offers unique insight into one imperial household but has little to say about broader gender roles, especially at nonelite social levels. How most Byzantine women understood their place in the world remains unclear.[13]

Expectations changed over the Byzantine millennium. In late antiquity women regularly shared in public life. They went to chariot races and performances in the theater, visited the public baths at designated hours, cheered imperial and religious processions in the streets, and attended public executions of criminals. In elite families they actively managed large households and supported the arts. All went to church services and many took monastic vows. Women are said to have been among the main opponents of iconoclasm in the eighth and early ninth centuries. The medieval period saw family life turn sharply inward, with the public, male world more clearly separated from the enclosed, domestic sphere of women and children. Kekaumenos, writing in the eleventh century, saw his family as a defensive outpost whose women were under constant threat. In the home they had to be kept apart from male visitors. He thought women should go outdoors only with heads covered by a shawl or veil *(maphorion)* and accompanied by other women, servants, or family members. They should not attend games, exhibitions, and performances. Limitations on public appearance became more restrictive for women of higher social rank. Not everyone followed such strict guidelines, yet for many women the church was their main chance for socializing outside the home.

Career prospects were limited but not insignificant. Spinning and weaving were honorable crafts long practiced at home. Industrious weavers produced clothes for their families as well as a surplus to sell in the market. Medieval women were active in the cloth-making trades, and in Constantinople even had their own festival, the Agathe, to recognize their activities. Female physicians and midwives treated women patients in hospitals and at home. Women are known to have run boutiques and shops. Some found employment as attendants helping other women in the baths. Women prepared and served simple meals in guest houses and tavernas, which fairly or not were disparaged as places of prostitution. Others sold produce in open-air markets and street-side stands. Fewer restrictions applied in the countryside, where women worked in family gardens and orchards, sold market crops, wove cloth and baskets, and made pottery to sell to their neighbors.

Sometimes it was necessary to follow less respected paths. Some girls and young women were abducted or lured from the countryside to work as urban prostitutes. A few established themselves as courtesans and mistresses for prominent men, which on rare occasions led to marriage. Others found work as domestic servants in elite households. The world of public entertainment offered unconventional opportunities for fame and wealth. The classical stage had long since degenerated into raucous performances of mime and pantomime, which were condemned by churchmen and social commentators. Women acrobats, dancers, and performers were seen as little different from prostitutes, concubines, and other subverters of family morals. Apart from such impersonal public spectacles, dancing remained an important part of festivals throughout the Byzantine period. Musicians and dancers were hired to perform in homes for banquets, weddings, and other occasions.

Religion offered many women significant opportunities for social engagement. Attending church services and religious festivals was one of the few unquestioned reasons for going out in public. Accompanied by children, servants, or friends, women of all ages made frequent visits to neighborhood churches, healing shrines, and monasteries. Well-to-do families supported these places with gifts of money and property. Wealthy widows founded a large number of monasteries, especially in the later Middle Ages. The attractions of religious life drew many women to leave their families, usually after the children were grown or upon the death of a spouse, and permanently enter a convent. Religious charities provided opportunities for fellowship and volunteer work. The pervasive poverty found in all medieval cities meant there was a constant need for help in orphanages, shelters, soup kitchens, hospitals, and old-age homes. Such activities brought personal satisfaction as well as spiritual reward. It was in the convent that many women felt most at home.[14]

Eunuchs constitute one of the most distinctive features of Byzantium. The Orthodox worldview entailed strict hierar- **Eunuchs** chies of gender roles, political rank, and spiritual status. The definition of these social categories in late antiquity was a major concern of both court and church, which shaped popular perceptions in later years as well. The central place that eunuchs claimed in Constantinople between the fourth and twelfth centuries reflects the persistent need to bridge the gaps—between men and women, emperor and subjects, patriarch and laity—that were fundamental to Byzantine society.

Eunuchs had been retained as servants at the imperial palace in Rome and filled many important positions at the Byzantine court. Since the castration of males was officially forbidden, many eunuchs were brought as slaves from neighboring states to the north and east. The second-century physician Galen describes the surgical options, which involved crushing or excising the testicles, while admitting his own reluctance to perform such operations. When castrated as infants or children, eunuchs developed a peculiar adult physique, comportment, and voice. By contrast, adult castrates normally retained their mature physical characteristics, including sexual desire. In all cases the eunuch's sterility set him outside conventional gender roles, which were based on procreation as the key to social stability. The steady demand for eunuchs in Constantinople was recognized outside the city. Castrated slaves were brought as diplomatic gifts by ambassadors from Italy, Persia, the Slavic north, and the Caucasus. Aristocratic families are known to have sent such offerings; the widow Danielis dispatched a hundred eunuchs to the emperor Basil I in the late ninth century. Such ready availability suggests that the practice was not unknown in the provinces.

Eunuchs occupied positions outside the imperial palace as well. Military commanders like the sixth-century general Narses were celebrated as clever field strategists. Others served as regional administrators and in aristocratic houses. Their equal, presumably deferential familiarity with men, women, and children suited them for work as doctors and teachers. Many pursued careers as musicians, singers, actors, and prostitutes.

In a society that stressed external appearance and social rank, eunuchs were viewed with mixed feelings by many observers. Their supposed lack of sexual distraction allowed some to develop formidable intellectual and rhetorical skills. In addition to their distinctive body language, voice, and lack of beard and body hair, eunuchs were said to have less stable temperaments and to resemble women in their lack of discipline and self-control. Michael Psellos, writing in the late eleventh century, praises individual eunuchs as loyal, shrewd, and hardworking, yet remained wary of their ambiguous, changeable, and haughty nature. Conspicuous in appearance and manner and versed in esoteric palace routines, eunuchs were sometimes suspected of possessing supernatural skills.

Eunuchs came to occupy a special place in the church. Early Christian authors regarded them as not fully male and condemned the practice of castration, whether done for punitive or spiritual reasons, while nevertheless praising the result. The emerging emphasis on celibacy as a desirable moral goal opened new opportunities for eunuchs as monks, priests, bishops, and patriarchs. Monasteries for them were set up in Constantinople and at Mount Athos; this segregation may reflect lingering suspicions of both their sexuality and their unfair advantage at attaining physical celibacy. Theophylaktos, archbishop of Ohrid in the early twelfth century, wrote a rhetorical dialogue in defense of eunuchs in which he compares them to early ascetics in seeking spiritual fulfillment by leading a "life beyond nature." The wider celebration of the celibate ideal helped erode their special status in the late Middle Ages.[15]

LAW AND ORDER

The cosmic order underlying the Byzantine worldview was apparent in the structure of human society. The emperor was held to be God's earthly representative and his laws essential for maintaining stability. Conformity to sanctioned patterns of belief and conduct supported this sense of order. Antisocial behavior called it into question.

Noncriminal departures from prevailing standards reflected the absence of personal qualities like godliness, honor, and shame. Such fundamental virtues characterized one's everyday relationships with family members, neighbors, coworkers, and the church. The state was a remote concept far less intimately involved in daily affairs than was the community of saints. Social stability rested on interpersonal relationships and loyalties. As a result, criminal laws mainly addressed specific instances of theft, damage, or injury to another person or property.

With its occasional statuary revisions, standing secular courts, and uninterrupted imperial authority, the Byzantine legal system continued an unbroken tradition from classical Rome. Justinian's compilation of the *Corpus juris civilis* in 534 still forms the basis of Western jurisprudence. Important Greek editions include the eighth-century *Ecloga* issued by Leo III and the tenth-century compilation of civil law known as the *Basilika*. The so-called *Farmer's Law (Nomos georgikos)* and *Rhodian Sea Law (Nomos nautikos)* are private collections of codes pertaining to rural life and maritime affairs. An expanding body of canon or church law reflects changing attitudes as well as the church's growing authority in the later Middle Ages. Such sources enumerate the most common infractions, the general outlines of trial procedure, and punishments meted by the state.[16]

Crimes generally were classified by the victim, who sought redress privately or in court. The integrity of the family was underscored by Constantine's laws on abortion, prostitution, and adultery, which frequently mandated maiming or execution. **Crime and Punishment** Offenses against property ranged from damage through accident or negligence to intentional burglary and theft. The *Farmer's Law* documents the petty grievances of village life, paying particular attention to pilferage of crops and havoc caused by wandering animals. City dwellers constantly watched for pickpockets, street thieves, and domestic burglars. Urban cemeteries sometimes posted guards to prevent the looting of clothing and jewelry from fresh burials. Outbursts of violence were an inescapable part of medieval life that often resulted in injury and death. Abduction and rape were seen as violations of both property and person, and always merited harsh penalties. Physical assault and sexual offenses figure prominently in the *Ecloga*, which prescribes financial compensation, imprisonment, and exile. Injuries inflicted by robbers and brigands commonly resulted in death, as did angry blows exchanged at work or in the marketplace. In such cases courts focused on discovering the intention of the accused, which was best gauged by the object or weapon used. An accidental killing was treated as negligence and remedied by monetary reparation. Drunkenness was considered an aggravating circumstance that merited short-term exile. Premeditated assault with a lethal weapon, by contrast, could earn the death penalty even if no fatality occurred.

Criminal offenses were not prosecuted by a state attorney but by advocates for the plaintiff, who personally filed claim in court. Similar procedures were followed in civil and criminal trials. Charges were brought before the magistrate, whose authority and competence had to be established. Witnesses were called and gave evidence, testifying under torture or undergoing ordeal if necessary. As many as five witnesses were needed when dealing with serious crimes. The court was required to issue its judgment within two years of the trial. Defendants in capital cases might be imprisoned throughout the process. Frivolous lawsuits were discouraged by subjecting the losing plaintiff to the same penalty as the accused. Revenge killings were relatively uncommon.

As in many societies, criminal penalties varied with the status of plaintiff and defendant. Ranking officials were in the best position to defend themselves or settle out of court. Elites convicted in capital cases other than treason faced losing their titles, personal property, and being banished to a monastery or remote province. Confiscated assets typically were divided into thirds among the family of the victim, the condemned man's own children, and the monastery to which he was to be confined. Public flogging, mutilation, and execution were remedies applied mainly to members of the lower classes. The *Farmer's Law* and *Book of the Eparch* recommend scourging, head shaving, and other humiliations in cases of willful negligence, theft, or using false measures and weights. Slaves were considered private property and could lawfully be disciplined with corporal or even lethal force. State prisons were notoriously dismal places intended more for temporary confinement than long-term incarceration.

Byzantium inherited from Rome a long list of capital crimes, which by the eighth century had been pared to willful murder, high treason, military desertion, heresy, and sexual deviation. In Constantinople condemned prisoners were detained by the urban *eparch* at the Praetorium before being paraded through the streets to their place of execution. Forcing male prisoners to wear women's clothing or ride backward a donkey or camel clearly set them outside the normal social order as a prelude to permanent exile by disfigurement or death. Most state killings took the form of public spectacles in the Amastrianum plaza or the hippodrome. Customary methods included burning at the stake, beheading by sword, hanging, and impaling; crucifixion was forbidden. By the eighth century physical mutilation—blinding, cutting off a hand or foot, or slitting the tongue or nose—had been introduced as an alternative to death. In all cases the public humiliation of the condemned emphasized his rejection by society and set an example for others. A full month was supposed to pass between sentencing and execution to allow time for judicial appeal and imperial clemency. Application of the death penalty waned over time as successive legal revisions restricted its use. John II Komnenos was widely praised for having permitted no executions during his long reign (1118–43).

The church played a significant role in tempering attitudes to crime and punishment. As early as the fourth century state authorities recognized the right of the church to grant asylum to Christians fleeing civil prosecution. By the tenth century even adulterers and murderers were seeking sanctuary in the cathedral of Hagia Sophia, which turned away only traitors and defaulting taxpayers. Petitioners pleaded their case before an ecclesiastical court that was guided by a separate body of canon law. The authority of these courts extended to clergy who were charged with civil crimes as well as offenses like apostasy, heresy, schism, simony, and sacrilege. The church saw asylum as an opportunity for personal repentance and spiritual healing. Public confession was followed by a regimen of penance, which included compensating the victims, prolonged fasting, and exclusion from communion. Blinding or maiming drew on scriptural basis (Matthew 18:8–9) as a way of enforcing social exile and focusing attention on repentance. The most common recourse for serious offenders was confinement in a monastery. The emphasis on restitution and banishment meant that capital punishment was rarely used in the late Middle Ages.[17]

ECONOMY

The Byzantine economy was based on a combination of monetary and nonmonetary activity. Monetary exchange took the form of coins that were issued by the state, and prevailed in Constantinople and places with which it had close contact. Nonmonetary exchange of goods and services through barter was more typical of remote areas. The two systems were to some extent complementary, with payment in kind practiced in parts of the capital and coins circulating far into the countryside. Wealth generally took the form of landownership; civil, military, and ecclesiastical offices; and imperial awards and honors. The potential of land was realized by exploiting its agricultural, pastoral, or natural-resource productivity, of which a significant part was taxed by the state. Official titles normally carried an annual stipend that was paid in cash, luxury goods, grants of land, or commercial concessions. Imperial recognitions by the emperor brought similar possibilities for generating wealth. Few other aspects of Byzantine culture exerted as great an influence on daily life.[18]

One of Byzantium's chief institutional features is that it
Coins and always maintained a coherent monetary system. Reforms
Monetary initiated by Diocletian and Constantine laid the foundations
Exchange for the Byzantine economy by replacing the gold *aureus* with
the *solidus* and introducing the *follis* in bronze. Most later
emperors continued issuing coins in gold, silver, and bronze. Gold and
silver were intrinsically valuable, and coins minted in Constantinople
were known throughout the medieval world for their exceptionally
high purity. The state required that taxes be paid in gold coins, even if it
sometimes requisitioned materials as well. In turn, gold was the primary
means of paying civil and military employees and maintaining the public
infrastructure. Gold coins were used for charitable distributions within
the empire as well as bribes, gifts, and tribute sent to foreign powers.
Bronze coins had little value as metal but functioned as authorized tokens
that could be exchanged for gold or silver.[19]

Metal for minting coins came from different sources: foreign trade,
tribute from neighboring states, and state-run mines within the empire.
Domestic mines were the main supplier of gold, silver, and copper, but
also produced great quantities of iron, lead, and other industrial metals.
A large number of mines had operated within Roman borders, particularly in Spain, the north Balkans, eastern Asia Minor, Cyprus, and Egypt.
By the seventh century many of these source areas had been lost to
Byzantium, which increasingly relied on operations closer to the Aegean.
Greece remained an important source of gold, silver, lead, copper, and
iron. Silver, lead, and iron came from Attica, while Asia Minor, Armenia,
and Cyprus produced silver, copper, and iron. The Taurus mountains
remain an especially rich source of materials.

Strabo, Pliny, and other Roman authors identify the mineral resources
found in all these areas and describe how different kinds of ore were
taken together. Gold usually occurs with silver and copper or iron, and
can be found in surface deposits of river alluvium or deep mines. The
largest Roman mines had been run by the state. These were notoriously
harsh places and usually were worked by criminals, prisoners of war,
and slaves. State-owned mines continued through late antiquity together
with smaller operations leased to private entrepreneurs. Most medieval
mines seem to have been privately run and employed area inhabitants
on a seasonal basis. Ores were smelted near their source before undergoing further refinement in urban workshops. Traditional gold-refining
methods involved liquidation under intense heat and amalgamation with
mercury to remove base metals and separate the silver. Silver was more
commonly obtained by smelting lead ores like galena (lead sulfide). State
officials supervised the final stage of refining gold and silver, and certified
their purity.[20]

The state kept its minting authority under tight control, never permitting local rulers or bishops to issue coins, as happened in western Europe.

Coins were struck in both the capital and the provinces. About a dozen imperial mints operated in late antiquity, with the greatest number located in large Eastern cities like Alexandria, Antioch, Constantinople, Kyzikos, Nikomedia, and Thessaloniki. Important Western mints included Carthage, Ravenna, and Rome. Short-lived operations were set up in other provincial towns, especially in south Italy, in response to changing military needs. The empire's loss of territory in the sixth and seventh centuries led to consolidation of minting in Constantinople, which by the tenth century had become the only source of Byzantine coins.

Mint operations are not well understood. The main requirements were a secure location, ready access to the sea, a reliable labor force, and strict supervision. Official dies were cut with the name and image of the reigning emperor, year in office, and monetary denomination. Religious figures or symbols became prominent after the seventh century. Additional markings identified the supervising authority. Blank disks were made by pouring the molten metal into molds. These were pressed or "struck" between facing dies mounted on a pliers-like clamp or press, one forming the obverse ("heads") and the other the reverse ("tails") of the finished coin

Byzantine coinage—particularly the gold solidus or *nomisma*—was the most widely accepted form of wealth throughout medieval Europe and the Near East. Early historians describe the extravagant donations of gold and silver coins and plate to early churches in Rome, Milan, and Constantinople. The emperor Anastasius reportedly left the imperial treasury with a balance of 23,040,000 gold solidi (320,000 pounds) in the early sixth century, a time when the empire's total monetary budget was about 7 million solidi. A few years later Justinian spent nearly two million solidi building his new church of Hagia Sophia. Such wealth was not limited to the imperial family. Court officials received an annual stipend supplemented by silks and other costume needed for palace ceremonies. Beyond the borders solidi were used to hire mercenaries,

Gold solidi of Justin I (early sixth century) and Theophilos (early ninth century). The solidus remained the basic unit of currency through much of the Middle Ages. From Ivan Tolstoy, *Vizantiiskiia Monety* (St. Petersburg: R. Galiksi, 1912–14).

pay ransoms, safeguard trading routes, and secure the cooperation of neighboring rulers. Byzantium's seemingly insatiable demand for gold may have been responsible for a general shortage in western Europe in the eighth through tenth centuries. The rising power of the Arab court and other medieval states led to the devaluation of the solidus in the eleventh century.

For most of this period the solidus effectively functioned as the "dollar of the Middle Ages," and was "admired by all men and in all kingdoms because no kingdom has a currency that can be compared to it." Seventy-two gold solidi (at ~4.5 g) were struck to the pound (six to the ounce), and purity was maintained at close to 98 percent (24 carets) as late as the seventh century. (The weight of a caret at 0.189 g was based on a single carob seed at 1/1,728 of a Roman pound. The modern use of *24 caret* to mean pure gold preserves the original value of the Byzantine solidus.) Fractional coinage in gold included the *semissis* (~2.25 g) and *tremisis* (~1.5 g), as well as the silver hexagram (~6.7 g), whose purity in the seventh century was about 96 percent. Smaller denominations—the small change used for daily transactions—took the form of bronze (copper alloy) and were based on the follis. The relative value of copper varied over time, falling from 180 large folles under Justinian to 288 folles (576 half-folles, 1,152 *dekanoumia*) for much of the Middle Ages. Each of these denominations was of a different size and clearly marked by a letter: the large follis (worth 40 *noummi*) carried the letter *M*, the half-follis a *K*, the *dekanoumium* an *I*, and the *pentanoumium* an *E*. Like the solidus, the follis was for over 500 years one of the principal coins of the medieval Mediterranean. Debased during the eleventh century, the purity of gold coinage was restabilized in 1092 when Alexios Komnenos introduced the *hyperpyron* (~4.3 g) with a purity of about 85.4 percent (20 1/2 carets). Around the time of the Fourth Crusade, *trikephala* struck in electrum (a natural gold-silver alloy found in Asia Minor) and *trachea* of billon (less than half silver in content) replaced bronze coinage altogether. These late denominations were not flat but very thin, concave or cupped discs, sometimes called *scyphate*. The silver *basilikon*, introduced in the early fourteenth century, was based on the Venetian ducat.[21]

The value of individual issues varied a great deal over the years, with the result that Byzantine prices and their modern equivalents are hard to establish. Most people obtained gold to pay taxes from private money changers. Civil and military salaries were paid in gold, land, and other high-value commodities. Real estate was transacted in solidi. Slaves were priced according to age, health, and skill. Infants were discounted at a couple solidi; a youth over the age of 10 might cost 10 to 20 solidi. In the sixth century a musician was worth 100 solidi, but a *grammatikos* cost twice as much. Hand-lettered books were in short supply and commanded high prices; a decorated gospel book might cost as much as 30 or 40 hyperpyra in the late Middle Ages. Routine purchases were made in fractional coinage. The large number of bronze coins required for even minor purchases presented the shopper with certain practical difficulties. In the sixth century, when 40 small coins (noummi) were being struck to the follis, a sizable bag of bronze was needed to buy a loaf of bread or mug of wine. For even the cheapest meals one needed at least a follis or two. A simple cloak might cost 50 folles, a heavy dalmatic up to 2,000. Large quantities of coins were weighed on a balance scales rather than individually counted. The innumerable small bronze coins found on archaeological sites today represent only a small part of the personal savings, purchases, and losses of early inhabitants of the region.

NOTES

1. Cyril Mango, *Byzantium: The Empire of New Rome* (New York: Charles Scribner's Sons, 1980), 11–31.

2. See Henry Maguire, ed., *Byzantine Court Culture from 829 to 1204* (Washington, D.C.: Dumbarton Oaks, 1997). For Digenis see most recently Elizabeth Jeffreys, ed. and trans., *Digenis Akritis: The Grottaferrata and Escorial Versions* (Cambridge: Cambridge University Press, 1998).

3. Andrew Sharf, *Byzantine Jewry from Justinian to the Fourth Crusade* (New York: Schocken Books, 1971); idem, *Jews and Other Minorities in Byzantium* (Tel Aviv: Bar-Ilan University Press, 1995). For the account of Benjamin of Tudela (1160–73) see Manuel Komroff, ed., *Contemporaries of Marco Polo* (New York: Boni and Liveright, 1928), 251–322.

4. Margaret E. Mullett, "Byzantium: A Friendly Society?" *Past and Present* 118 (1988): 3–24; Charles Barber, "Homo Byzantinus?" in *Women, Men and Eunuchs: Gender in Byzantium,* ed. Liz James (New York: Routledge, 1997), 185–99.

5. For medieval village names see Angeliki E. Laiou-Thomadakis, *Peasant Society in the Late Byzantine Empire* (Princeton, N.J.: Princeton University Press, 1977), 108–41.

6. Michael McCormick, "Emperors," in *The Byzantines,* ed. Guglielmo Cavallo (Chicago: University of Chicago Press, 1997), 230–54; André Guillou, "Functionaries," in Cavallo, *The Byzantines,* 197–229.

7. Michael Angold, ed., *The Byzantine Aristocracy, IX–XIII Centuries* (Oxford: British Archaeological Reports, 1984), 92–111.

8. Nicolas Oikonomides, "Entrepreneurs," in Cavallo, *The Byzantines,* 144–71.

9. Demetrios J. Constantelos, *Byzantine Philanthropy and Social Welfare* (New Brunswick, N.J.: Rutgers University Press, 1988); Evelyne Patlagean, "The Poor," in Cavallo, *The Byzantines,* 15–42; Alexander Kazhdan, "The Peasantry," in Cavallo, *The Byzantines,* 43–73.

10. Speros Vryonis, "The Will of a Provincial Magnate, Eustathius Boilas (1059)," *Dumbarton Oaks Papers* 11 (1957): 263–77. For slavery see Demetrios J. Constantelos, *Poverty, Society, and Philanthropy in the Late Mediaeval Greek World* (New Rochelle, N.Y.: Aristide D. Caratzas, 1992), 103–14.

11. Vera von Falkenhausen, "Bishops," in Cavallo, *The Byzantines,* 172–96.

12. Adapted from John of Damascus, *On the Divine Images,* trans. David Anderson (Crestwood, N.Y.: St. Vladimir's Seminary Press, 1980), 1.47. For introductions to the Byzantine liturgy see Glanville Downey, *Constantinople in the Age of Justinian* (Norman: Oklahoma University Press, 1960), 114–35; and Thomas F. Mathews, *The Early Churches of Constantinople: Architecture and Liturgy* (University Park: Pennsylvania State University Press, 1971), 138–76.

13. See Judith Herrin, "In Search of Byzantine Women: Three Avenues of Approach," in *Images of Women in Antiquity,* ed. Averil Cameron and Amélie Kuhrt, rev. ed. (New York: Routledge, 1993), 167–89; Alice-Mary Talbot, "Women," in Cavallo, *The Byzantines,* 117–43; the recent exhibition catalog by Ioli Kalavrezou, *Byzantine Women and Their World* (New Haven, Conn.: Harvard University Press, 2003); and Carolyn L. Conner, *Women of Byzantium* (New Haven, Conn.: Yale University Press, 2004).

14. Angeliki E. Laiou, "Women in the Marketplace of Constantinople (10th–14th Centuries)," in *Byzantine Constantinople: Monuments, Topography and Everyday Life,* ed. Nevra Necipoğlu (Leiden, the Netherlands: Brill, 2001), 261–73. For social contributions see Alice-Mary Talbot, "Byzantine Women, Saints' Lives, and Social Welfare," in *Through the Eye of a Needle: Judeo-Christian Roots of Social Welfare,* ed. Emily Albu Hanawalt and Carter Lindberg (Kirksville, Mo.: Thomas Jefferson University Press, 1994), 105–22.

15. Recent studies include Shaun F. Tougher, "Byzantine Eunuchs: An Overview, with Special Reference to Their Creation and Origin," in James, *Women, Men and Eunuchs,* 168–84; and Kathryn M. Ringrose, *The Perfect Servant: Eunuchs and the Social Construction of Gender in Byzantium* (Chicago: University of Chicago Press, 2003).

16. English translations include Walter Ashburner, "The Farmer's Law," *Journal of Hellenic Studies* 32 (1912): 68–95; A.E.R. Boak, "The Book of the Prefect," *Journal of Economic and Business History* 1 (1929): 597–618; Edwin Hanson Freshfield, *A Manual of Later Roman Law* (Cambridge: Cambridge University Press, 1927); and excerpts in Deno John Geanakoplos, *Byzantium: Church, Society, and Civilization Seen through Contemporary Eyes* (Chicago: University of Chicago Press, 1984). In general see Angeliki E. Laiou and Dieter Simon, eds., *Law and Society in Byzantium: Ninth–Twelfth Centuries* (Washington, D.C.: Dumbarton Oaks, 1994).

17. Ruth J. Macrides, "Killing, Asylum, and the Law in Byzantium," *Speculum* 63 (1988): 509–38; idem, *Kinship and Justice in Byzantium, 11th–15th Centuries* (Brookfield, Vt.: Aldershot, 2000).

18. For summaries of recent research on the Byzantine economy see Angeliki E. Laiou, ed., *The Economic History of Byzantium from the Seventh through the Fifteenth Century* (Washington, D.C.: Dumbarton Oaks, 2002).

19. Cécile Morrisson, "Byzantine Money: Its Production and Circulation," in Laiou, *Economic History of Byzantium,* 3:909–66.

20. For the geological background see Michael Denis Higgins and Reynold Higgins, *A Geological Companion to Greece and the Aegean* (Ithaca, N.Y.: Cornell University Press, 1996); and Bernard Geyer, "Physical Factors in the Evolution of the Landscape and Land Use," in Laiou, *Economic History of Byzantium,* 1:31–45. The evidence for medieval mines is reviewed by Speros Vryonis, "The Question of the Byzantine Mines," *Speculum* 37 (1962): 1–17; and Kaus-Peter Matschke, "Mining," in Laiou, *Economic History of Byzantium,* 1:115–20.

21. Robert Sabatino Lopez, "The Dollar of the Middle Ages," *Journal of Economic History* 11 (1951): 209–34, quoting at 209 the world traveler Cosmas Indikopleustes, who certainly would have known the reputation of the sixth-century solidus; see also Geanakoplos, *Byzantium*, 298–99. For well-illustrated surveys of coinage see Philip D. Whitting, *Byzantine Coins* (New York: G. P. Putnam's Sons, 1973); and Philip Grierson, *Byzantine Coins* (Berkeley: University of California Press, 1982).

3

FAMILY AND HOUSEHOLD

The family, from the Great Palace down to the smallest village, was Byzantium's basic social unit. The concept of voluntary marriage between man and woman, consented to and supported by both sets of parents, was recognized by the church and sanctioned by civil law. At the same time, the new assurance of rights for women and children encouraged the inward focus of domestic life and fostered a society of independent households very different from classical Rome. The social identity of members and their place in the extended family were affirmed at the transitional moments of birth, marriage, and death. More than any other circumstance, it was the family that shaped one's experience of daily life.

FAMILY STRUCTURE

Individual families were changing constantly in number, composition, and age, and any "typical" family unit varied with place and time. The empire's growing population between the fourth and sixth centuries suggests that late-antique households were larger than those of the later Middle Ages. Saints' lives tell us that in the ninth and tenth centuries most families included two or three children. Late-medieval village families in north Greece had an average of three or four children. It is unsurprising that prosperous rural families tended to raise more offspring than did the urban poor. With childhood mortality approaching 50 percent, the goal of demographic stability was not always realized.

In the traditional Roman family the authority of the man *(pater familias)* was paramount. Marriages were contracted by the fathers of the couple. This arrangement left the woman with few protections. Any children born to the couple had to be recognized by the father as his legal heirs or were abandoned. Kinship networks were expanded by strategic adoptions, often of adults. This hierarchical ideal was modified in the fourth century. Recognizing that population growth and social stability depended on the structure of the Roman *familia,* Constantine issued legislation guaranteeing the rights of spouses and children, and by so doing established a new precedent for the state's involvement in domestic behavior. The man remained the head of the household but the woman was given a substantially greater role. Her betrothal was still arranged but now involved the consent of her mother. As a wife she retained a stake in the dowry she brought to the marriage and could no longer be divorced without cause. In many cases the woman took control of domestic affairs, from raising children to managing servants and financial assets. She typically assumed responsibility for the family's religious observances. In most cases the family remained the focus of her public as well as private life.

Marriage   The Byzantine family was based on the joining of a man and a woman in a new legal entity. Civil and religious laws reflect the state's interest in maintaining social stability. Marriages could not be contracted between close biological or spiritual relations, which generally extended to the seventh degree of consanguinity. Betrothals could take place at an early age, sometimes even in infancy. The minimal statutory age for marriage was set at 15 years for boys and 12 or 13 years for girls, but these thresholds were overlooked when convenient. Both sets of parents took a hand in arranging the union, with the mothers assuming an active role in planning the wedding and setting up the new household. There were many considerations in negotiating a marriage. Such relationships usually involved members of similar background and social status, and often reflected the parents' interests in forming useful alliances and preserving ancestral property. Chastity was expected, and a midwife might be asked to verify the girl's virginity.

The financial investment of both families took the form of an exchange of money and property. The bride's parents offered a wedding dowry *(proika)* that was matched by a gift from the family of the groom. In most cases the dowry included the practical necessities for setting up the new household, such as the woman's personal trousseau, with linens, furniture, and domestic utensils. More importantly, the dowry functioned as long-term insurance against financial troubles for the couple and any future children. Depending on the family's status, this might include land, houses, shops, jewelry, or other tangible assets that could not be easily squandered. Village families contributed gardens, orchards, wooded groves, and livestock. Details were negotiated before the wedding and

A medieval incised and glazed dish depicts an elegantly dressed couple. The man holds a sword; the woman wears a long headdress and floor-length garment. The embroidered costumes and heraldic shields reflect the Western presence in Cyprus in the late Middle Ages. Photo courtesy of the Pierides Foundation, Larnaca.

spelled out in a written contract signed by both parties. Even families of modest means provided a dowry for their daughters. A respectable marriage was nearly impossible without one.

The wedding day was a defining moment in the lives of most people. The bride underwent an elaborate process of bathing and dressing before receiving the groom in the home of her parents. The couple formalized their marriage with the clasping of hands and the exchange of rings and other jewelry. Several well-known gold rings carry a brief inscription invoking the blessing of peaceful harmony *(concordia* or *homonoia)* on the new couple; others depict the husband and wife joined by Christ.

Some newlyweds surely recalled the ancient belief in a special nerve that ran from the ring finger directly to the heart. Such formalities were followed by a noisy procession to the couple's new house, where family and friends celebrated through the night with feasting, singing, and dancing. More elaborate wedding ceremonies developed over time. By the tenth century marriages were being sanctified by a priest, usually in a church. Later weddings continued to involve the joining of hands, exchange of rings, and sacramental crowning of the couple. They were invariably accompanied by celebrations at home.[1]

Marriage brought the new wife certain protections. Medieval divorce was restricted to circumstances like female adultery, leprosy, murderous assault, or male impotence. Byzantine law characteristically recognized adultery and madness as grounds for separation only on the part of the wife. In case of annulment or divorce the man kept his wedding gift while the woman retained her dowry. Upon the death of the husband the family's assets were assigned to the widow, who was responsible for raising and arranging marriages for her children. A young divorced woman might feel pressured by her neighbors to take a second husband, but for an older widow remaining single had clear advantages: neither virgin nor spouse, she stood outside normative expectations of women. Widowhood, moreover, often brought financial independence, with new opportunities to support the church and its charitable activities. In the case of remarriage the woman retained only her dowry and wedding gift, with the rest of the estate reverting to the husband's family. If there were older children the estate was divided between them and the widow. Subsequent marriages were discouraged with lesser or greater force by civil and canon law.

Late-antique and medieval marriage rings. The alternating male and female busts on the earlier example have been replaced by scenes from the life of Christ. On the bezel Christ and the Virgin crown the married couple with *homonoia*. From O. M. Dalton, *Catalogue of Early Christian Antiquities and Objects from the Christian East* (London: British Museum, 1901).

Bearing and raising children were essential parts of Byzantine family life. No household was considered complete **Children** without children, preferably boys, and infertility was seen as cause for shame. Childless couples might seek out holy men or women, pray to certain saints, or pursue folk remedies when trying to conceive a male child. Pregnant mothers were particularly vulnerable to Gylou, a much-feared female demon believed to cause miscarriages or stillbirths. The state's interest in reproduction is clear from the legal protection it granted children. The use of contraceptives was discouraged by the church, and abortion was denounced as an offense against the husband. While unwanted children had been routinely given away or abandoned in earlier times, Byzantine tradition condemned both practices. In the case of second marriages the adoption of stepchildren was required.

Birth and christening brought much celebrating. Nearly all children were born at home with the assistance of a family member, neighbor, or midwife. Within the first week the infant was taken to a local church to be baptized and named by a priest. Naming traditions changed over time. Children often were called after parents, grandparents, or other family members. Classical names like Alexander and Marcellus remained popular in the fourth and fifth centuries, but were increasingly rivaled by biblical names. During the medieval period it was common to name a child after the saint on whose feast day he or she was born. John, Peter, Paul, Demetrius, George, Nicholas, and Theodore were frequently used for boys; Anna, Chryse, Eleni, Kale, Maria, Zoe, and derivative names like Georgia, Ioanno, Theodora, and Theophano were common among girls. The imperial family helped popularize such names as Alexios, Basil, Constantine, Leo, and Manuel. In late antiquity clan names were less important than establishing the identity of the father. Distinctive family names based on a trade or place of origin became widespread in the late period. These usually but not always came from the father's side.

The mother invariably took charge of raising and educating her children, emphasizing basic communication skills and proper behavior. At the age of six or seven most boys and some girls were sent during the day to study reading and writing with a tutor (*didaskalos*) outside the home. Betrothals might be contracted between neighboring families at an early age, especially when significant amounts of property were involved. Most children had married and left the their parents' home before turning 20.

The nuclear family was the heart of the Byzantine household (*oikos*). Around this was a network of other **The Extended** relatives who visited regularly even if not actually **Family** residing under the same roof. Grandparents took an active interest in the welfare of parents and children. Uncles and aunts were frequent guests in the home, as were their own children. Most members of this extended family spent their lives in the same village, town, or valley.

Adoptive godparents were a special part of the extended family. At the time of baptism the parents identified an adult sponsor to look after their child's spiritual interests and upbringing. This could be either a man or a woman; he or she might be a relative or come from another family. The choice of a godparent was influenced by any number of practical concerns, including the desire to build alliances with neighbors or business associates. Either way, the new relationship represented a significant expansion of the family and created a bond of supportive friendship and coparenthood *(synteknia)* among the adults. The godparent had different but equally important responsibilities: to watch out for the youngster's well-being, to provide religious instruction and counseling, and to offer lifelong moral guidance. If the parents died the godparent assumed full responsibility for raising, educating, and arranging a marriage for the child. This durable institution of adoptive kinship survives in the figure of the *koumbaros* still found in Greek and Cypriot families.[2]

LIFE OF THE HOUSEHOLD

The *oikos* often included more than parents and children. A large, well-established family might involve grandparents, other relatives, servants, slaves, and sometimes close friends. Both parents, two or three children, a grandparent, and a servant or slave could be found in prosperous rural households.

The physical setting varied widely. Wealthy urban families lived in spacious mansions with running water and special rooms for receiving visitors and dining. Most city dwellers occupied a few rooms in a multistoried tenement, where they dealt with cramped, noisy conditions and competed for the landlord's attention to address needed repairs. Craftsmen and merchants usually rented small street-level shops and lived upstairs with their families. Village houses ranged from elegant suburban retreats to a couple rooms looking onto a small yard.

Private and public concerns came together in all these places. The outer threshold marked the formal boundary separating the household from the world beyond, but this line was crossed repeatedly in both directions. Men spent most of their lives in public view, whether distinguishing themselves in military or civil affairs or tending shops, orchards, or livestock. The lives of married women looked inward, centering on the home but involving frequent expeditions to support it, from shopping in the market and visiting with relatives and friends to representing the family at church. Visitors included business colleagues, political allies, domestic contractors, and friends, as well as members of the extended family. A main room near the entrance was preferred for entertaining guests. In most cases this room also served for banquets marking religious holidays and other events in the life of the *oikos,* such as the birth of a child, the marriage of a daughter, or the death of a family member. Medieval moralists spoke of the importance of keeping women and girls apart from visitors: they should be seated separately, were not allowed to drink, and were urged to keep to their own quarters (the *gynaikeion*). Writing in the eleventh century, the stern-minded retiree Kekaumenos makes clear his views of household management: "Do not let your wife, daughter or daughter-in-law leave their rooms and look into the house proper. If it were to happen that they should have to come out then your friend would immediately notice and fix his eyes upon them." The suspicion and severity of such guidelines reflect public expectations of Byzantine gender roles, but also suggest that many families disregarded them.[3]

Women clearly claimed a key position in domestic life despite such restrictions. The chief responsibilities were supervising household affairs, managing finances, and raising the children. Each day's routines saw fetching water, food, and fuel, cooking, and serving meals. Mothers taught their sons and daughters to speak and modeled social roles. Girls and women handled the essential tasks of spinning, weaving, mending, and washing clothes. They were instrumental in maintaining the health of family members and negotiating key life transitions. At the same time theirs was a world rarely recorded by male observers.[4]

A death in the family brought duties that were handled mainly by women. Preparations began with a ritual sweeping of the house. Immediately after death the eyes of the deceased were closed and the mouth tied shut with a band to prevent entry by the departed soul or evil spirits. The body was laid out on a cot or litter with the head and limbs arranged to suggest sleep. Warm water was mixed with wine, herbs, perfumes, or scented oils for washing the body, which was wrapped in a plain linen winding-sheet. It was important to dress the deceased in the best available clothing, invariably white to reflect the new purity of the body. A child might be dressed in a simple tunic, a bride in her wedding dress with a wreath of flowers. Branches and garlands of laurel, olive, myrtle, and cypress were scattered on the floor of the main room of the house for the public lying-in-state *(prothesis)*. This period of reception began early in the day, so that friends had a chance to say farewell to the deceased and console family members. The end of household preparations might be signaled by breaking pots and dishes to drive evil spirits from the house. Family members accompanied the body to the cemetery where women led the ritual display of grief at the graveside, weeping and sometimes covering the body with freshly cut locks of hair. In the evening the women prepared a funerary banquet *(syndeipnon)* at the home for relatives, friends, and clergy. Established mourning rituals, ineffectively discouraged by the church, included visiting the grave on the 3rd, 9th, and 40th days after burial. Prayers and handfuls of *kollyba* made of boiled wheat mixed with dried fruits and nuts were shared by family members with the deceased. Many women chose to wear black, neglect their personal appearance, and confine themselves to the house and cemetery throughout the period of mourning, which could last a year or more.[5]

Diet and Dining   Most Byzantine families observed what can be called a traditional Mediterranean diet made up mainly of grains, pulses, vegetables, olives, wild greens, and fruit. Cereals were the foundation of this menu and took the form of freshly baked bread *(artos)*, long-lasting biscuits *(paximadia)*, and porridge *(traganos)*. Asiatic rice was not widely available in the east Mediterranean until the late Middle Ages. Pulses and vegetables varied with place and season but typically included beans, lentils, chickpeas, and greens. Olives and olive oil were used generously in cooking and made up about a third of the total dietary intake. Animal products were consumed in more limited quantities, if not just on special occasions. The main kinds of meat came from sheep, goat, poultry, and pigs, with cattle and wild game considered relative luxuries. Fresh fish and other seafood were available near the coast, along rivers, and around mountain lakes. A few chickens, sheep, and goats generally kept rural families supplied with eggs and milk, which could be stored in the form of butter and cheese. Fresh fruit was often hard to find and always highly prized. Wine of varying quality accompanied most meals. The broad outlines of this culinary regimen had been in place since the second millennium B.C. and still prevail across much of the Mediterranean and Near East. Recent research has shown the dietary benefits of these basic foods and the moderation, whether for economic or religious reasons, with which they were consumed.[6]

There were two main meals during the day: a light breakfast *(ariston)*, and a main meal *(deipnon)* served toward evening. Some writers also mention an early *prophagion* taken at dawn. Family members sat on benches or chairs gathered around a small table, or shared their meals while seated on the floor in traditional Near Eastern fashion. Meals often were served as small portions of different prepared dishes *(opsa,* the modern *meze)*, which were presented in a variety of vessels. Late-antique tableware generally consisted of broad ceramic bowls and shallow dishes. Wine was poured from flagons into glass goblets and ceramic cups. Tall-footed bowls and goblets became more popular over time. Some families continued the Roman custom of reclining and using table napkins when dining, wearing one tied around the neck and wiping one's hands with another.

Depictions of banquets in manuscripts and wall paintings suggest how dishes might be arranged and what utensils were available. Early dining customs involved eating with the hands directly from a shared platter. Small loaves or pieces of bread would have been universally available for arranging portions and dipping in sauces. Knives had been used for eating since Roman times and are often shown resting on the table or held in the hand. Iron and bronze cutting blades with bone handles are regularly found during excavation of early Byzantine sites. Spoons were almost as familiar and are frequently listed in household inventories.

Carved wood spoons were used for cooking and sometimes at the table, especially by village families. The origin of the dining fork is less clearly understood. The Romans used large forks with paired tines for spearing roasts and lifting food from the fire. Large metal spoons with forked handles were helpful for slicing and serving meats, but were not intended for personal use. Table forks are first mentioned by Western observers in the tenth and eleventh centuries. The appearance of forks in late-medieval wall paintings probably reflects their currency among higher social levels. A well-known legend tells how an eleventh-century Byzantine bride took a case of two-tined table forks to Italy as part of her dowry when she married the heir to the doge of Venice. The forks seem to have been a novelty to the Venetians, who were offended when she refused to eat with her hands. Italian society was slow to take up their use, and not until the sixteenth century were forks widely found in western Europe.

Personal appearance and public comportment were vital concerns of most people, whether performing official functions, walking down the street, or receiving visitors at home. The ancient custom of regular public bathing declined in late antiquity, and after the seventh **Grooming and Personal Appearance** century people washed less frequently, either in the house or at private baths. In tenth-century Constantinople one young, wellborn woman is known to have made weekly visits to the baths for the express purpose of maintaining cleanliness and beauty. By contrast, monks may have bathed no more than once a month. Any well-equipped townhouse would have kept mirrors, combs, tweezers, and similar implements for personal grooming. Luxury soaps, salves, powders, perfumes, and cosmetic preparations could be bought in the shops of Constantinople.

Following the example set by Constantine, men generally went clean-shaven in late antiquity. Beards do not seem to have been common in secular society before emperors took them up in the seventh century. From this time on beards were a universally respected sign of maturity and power. Monks and priests wore beards as a sign of spiritual authority. Most men had dark brown or black hair that they cut hair short out of convenience and respect for church teachings against personal vanity. Infrequent fashions swept through court circles and provincial elites. During the fifth and sixth centuries many young men wore their hair long at the back, as was the custom among the empire's Germanic military allies. The tenth and later centuries brought longer hair styles and occasional fads for shaving, probably reflecting contact with visitors from western Europe and the Arab states. Some residents of the capital were known to dye their hair or wear wigs.

For women long hair was a much admired attribute, but only when it was kept well tended and, paradoxically, concealed from public view. Most women parted their hair in the center and pinned it in place with bone or ivory combs, pins, or bands. Hairnets set with beads, gems, or pearls were especially popular in the capital. Contrary to the advice of church leaders, some women enhanced their hair with powders, tints, and extensions. Respectable postadolescent women were expected to cover their heads with a veil *(maphorion)* when appearing outside the home, a convention observed more strictly in towns than in villages. Exposed, flowing hair was seen as a sign of bad behavior and loose morals. During the late Middle Ages complicated headdresses and turbans were favored by courtly men as well as women.[7]

Clothing and jewelry were the most obvious outward expressions of social standing and occupation. The main article of clothing for most people was a tunic (sometimes called a *kamision*) of varying length made of plain cotton, linen, or wool. Embroidered emblems, stripes, and cuffs could be stitched to the fabric for decoration. Men and women of the working classes wore tunics belted at the waist with a wool outer cloak for warmth during the winter months. The tunic served as an undergarment for members of the aristocracy, for whom multilayered costume was an essential part of urban apparel. So important was clothing to courtly life that the emperor routinely distributed silk cloth and finished garments to palace officials as part of their annual stipend. Standard elite dress for men included a tunic with long sleeves and the traditional cloak *(chlamys)*. An outer tunic or dalmatic was introduced later. Military officers sometimes wore a cloak known as a *paludamentum*. Such clothing became longer and more colorful with time, and typically was decorated with embroidered collars, armbands, cuffs, and hems. A belt was cinched by a buckle, whose material and decoration advertised the wearer's social status if not courtly rank. A decorative brooch fastened the front or side of the cloak. During the later Middle Ages a long, belted, caftanlike garment became fashionable, worn with or without an outer cloak. Aristocrats and court officials wore felt or fur headdresses of increasingly exotic design. All of these garments were made of different grades of finely woven fabrics, which after the ninth century were mainly silk.[8]

Women's fashions are less well known The basic elements included a long dress or gown worn with an outer cloak. Women of the sixth-century court, as depicted in the famous mosaics in the church of San Vitale in Ravenna, wore long undergarments with tight sleeves, fitted gowns with full sleeves, and loose cloaks of elaborately woven design. Later fashions involved decorative collars, armbands, hems, and broad sleeves with wide embroidered cuffs. Most garments were of silk embroidered with silver and gold threads and attached gems. Outer cloaks were circular, semicircular, and trapezoidal in shape. Silk scarves, complicated hats, and simple crowns were work for headdresses. Jewelry included rings, earrings, pendants, buckles, brooches, and belts made of gold and silver, set with pearls, precious gems, and semiprecious stones. Particularly important were *enkolpia* ("on the breast"), pendants worn around the neck that carried a Christian image, inscription, or relic. Surviving examples of

Late-antique linen tunic with applied embroidered ornament, including figured medallions. The basic tunic, also known as a *chiton* or *kamision,* was worn across the social spectrum. From O.M. Dalton, *Catalogue of Early Christian Antiquities and Objects from the Christian East* (London: British Museum, 1901).

Byzantine jewelry preserve our clearest view of the original splendor of the court.[9]

Standards of personal cleanliness changed a great deal over the centuries. In late antiquity city dwellers regularly visited public baths, a custom that was replaced in the medieval period by less frequent washing at home. Neighborhood baths continued to function, but on a much smaller scale and using far less water than before. Different kinds of soap were sold by vendors or could be produced at home. One of the most widely used cleaning agents of antiquity was *nitron,* a kind of soda (sodium carbonate) that would foam when combined with ammonia or vinegar. Pliny indicates the different colors and sources of nitron and lists its many domestic and industrial applications. It removed dirt when bathing, could be combined with honey, oil, or wine as a skin conditioner, and was recommended as a paste for cleaning teeth. Other kinds of soap *(saponion),* as discussed by Roman naturalists and medical writers, were made by boiling animal or vegetable fats with caustic lye. Most personal laundry was washed at home using water

Hygiene

mixed with nitron and other materials acting as detergent. Drawing on Roman experience, Byzantine families found different kinds of earth, plants, wood ash, and stale urine useful for cleaning clothes. Fullers and launderers met the needs of elite urban households.[10]

Household Medicine
The family was the first line of defense against common ailments and when dealing with accident or illness. Without ready access to medical care, even minor problems could easily become chronic or life-threatening. Most people were aware of the potential effects, either beneficial or hazardous, posed by animals, plants, and minerals. Detailed knowledge of medical authorities like Hippocrates, Dioscorides, and Galen was limited to scholars and trained physicians, but the traditional remedies of Mediterranean plant lore were practiced in both town and village. In many places only a fine line separated classically recognized treatments from less orthodox remedies, which might be condemned by priests as evidence of superstition or witchcraft.

Women, as primary nurturers of the family, were instrumental in maintaining these traditions. Reproductive health issues were a constant concern that lasted from the beginning of menstruation around the age of 12 into old age. Emotional as well as physical afflictions often were attributed to the behavior of the womb (*hystera,* once believed the cause of hysteria). Traditional Greek medicine taught that the womb was a freewheeling, octopus-like organ that wandered throughout the body, causing headaches, emotional outbursts, and erratic behavior. Placating a "wandering womb" required one to wear an amulet (*phylakterion*), often carved of bloodstone (hematite), which was believed to have magical properties. Similar measures were needed to counter the threats of Gylou, a serpentlike female demon who threatened the health of infants, both *in utero* and newborn. Medieval amulets depict this as a Medusa head surrounded by snakelike rays. Such experiences were passed down from mother to daughter and shared among groups of neighborhood women. Larger households could afford to keep slaves who were specially trained in the healing arts. Eunuchs were presumed to threaten neither male authority nor female purity, and so could tend the needs of both sexes. At the time of death it was left to women to wash the deceased and prepare the body for burial.[11]

Sex
Attitudes on sexual matters are not easy to reconstruct. Most writers deferred to religious authority in defining the boundaries of acceptable behavior. Church leaders stressed the importance of chastity and viewed sexuality as an impediment to spiritual growth. Virginity was seen as the ideal human state and an expectation of marriageable girls. Female public dress was held to the same high standard of modesty and included long, flowing clothes and head scarves; the epitome of chaste attire, of course, was the monastic habit. Sexual relations were sanctioned only between married men and women for the

purpose of producing children. Intercourse without the intention of conceiving a child was likened to prostitution. The church mandated that couples refrain from sexual contact on Saturdays, Sundays, and during times of Lent. Women were considered impure while menstruating and for 40 days after giving birth; only in life-threatening circumstances could such a woman receive communion. Popular belief held that sexual intercourse during menstruation could produce deformed children.

Of course the reality of human behavior was another matter. Emperors and high court officials were widely known to keep concubines and mistresses, often within the palace itself. Unaccompanied virgins and nuns ran the risk of assault in the streets of Constantinople. Prostitution was prevalent among public entertainers and tavern workers, from the theaters and shops of the capital to remote roadhouses along state highways. Monasteries and churches were not immune from sexual tensions, and administrators went to great lengths to separate the sexes and protect younger residents. Erotic epigrams, poems, and romances reflect amorous feelings of the period. Writing in sixth-century Constantinople, Paul the Silentiary urges, "Let us throw off these cloaks, my pretty one, and lie naked, knotted in each other's embrace. Let nothing be between us; even that thin tissue you wear seems thick to me as the wall of Babylon." Dream books were used to interpret the complex imagery of suppressed longing. Aphrodisiacs, amulets, and magical spells were available to stimulate affection, maintain potency, and suppress one's own desire as well as the unwanted advances of others. As with other medieval peoples, the greatest liberties were permitted at opposite social extremes, with sexual license considered the prerogative of elites and the affliction of the lower classes.[12]

The discrepancy between public attitudes and private practice extended also to same-sex relations. These were expected to remain within the bounds of dispassionate friendship *(philia)*. Homosexual relations had been widely tolerated in classical Greek and Roman society, primarily as a temporary association of an older man with a youth. From the beginning the church had strongly condemned such contact. Monastic regulations make clear the widespread suspicion of homosexuality among groups of cloistered men and women, especially when young adults or eunuchs were present. Such liaisons ran counter to biblical tradition and posed serious distraction from the individual's spiritual quest. A medieval ceremony acknowledging ritual brotherhood *(adelphopoiesis)* provided an acceptable framework for cultivating close spiritual friendships between friends of the same sex.[13]

The state encouraged large families, and church leaders forbade almost all methods of preventing **Family Planning** pregnancy, yet many parents felt the need to limit the number of children they raised for economic or health reasons. Classical doctors knew contraceptive methods that had long been practiced by women across the Mediterranean. Dioscorides and Galen mention plants that were helpful in preventing pregnancy. The most common of these were asafetida *(assa)*, juniper, pennyroyal, squirting cucumber, and the wild carrot known as Queen Anne's lace. Most of these grew in the wild and could be readily gathered by knowledgeable peasants. Soranus of Ephesus recommends applying astringent, fatty ointments to close the opening of the womb before intercourse. Later authorities describe the contraceptive properties of different materials, including olive oil, honey, cedar resin, alum, balsam gum, and white lead. Wool plugs soaked in herbal and mineral preparations were used as vaginal sponges. The sap of the domestic cedar could be applied by men as a contraceptive. Less risky, if generally ineffective, folk measures included observing phases of the moon, the rhythm method, wearing protective amulets (Aetius of Amida recommends one containing a cat's liver), or holding one's breath during intercourse.[14]

The uneven success of contraceptive techniques meant that some women needed to end their pregnancies by other means. Abortion was strongly condemned by leaders of church and state, who did not hesitate to compare it to murder. Official prohibitions aside, the hazards of abortion seem to have been well known and were chanced mainly when there were questions of legitimacy, particularly among unfaithful spouses, entertainers, and prostitutes. Medical writers describe several ways of inducing abortion, which ranged from soaking in hot baths, performing strenuous exercises, and placing a heavy weight on the abdomen to undergoing harrowing surgical procedures. Several authorities list herbal abortifacients that were effective through the third month of pregnancy. Most women may have lacked theoretical knowledge of such matters but knew where to turn in times of need.[15]

The abandonment of unwanted children was widely known in ancient society and continued through the Middle Ages. Illegitimacy, health, and poverty were the main reasons for giving up an infant. In most cases the child was not deliberately exposed but left in a public place where he or she could be claimed by others. Inevitably the church came to play a significant role in caring for foundlings. Eastern bishops, emperors, and lay patrons established group homes for infants *(brephotropheia)* and older children *(orphanotropheia)*. Municipal asylums like the famous Ospedale degli Innocenti in Florence were founded throughout Italy. Orphans who survived might eventually be taken in by foster parents, adopted by lay families, or remain in a monastic setting all their lives. Church leaders and emperors consistently condemned parents for abandoning their children, equating it with murder in legal terms. At the same time their well-meaning, institutionalized philanthropy may have encouraged the practice.[16]

Childbirth Women were the chief facilitators of childbirth. Greek and Roman doctors received some obstetrical training but normally left delivery to the family and a neighborhood midwife. Competent midwifery had a long tradition in the classical world and was seen as a respectable profession for Roman and Byzantine women. Family members prepared for the occasion by providing the woman's bedroom with a supply of warm water, oil, ointments, aromatic herbs, and bandages. Delivery was supposed to take place while the mother lay on a hard bed or sat in a special birthing chair that speeded the process. The midwife helped by providing cervical massage, pressing on the abdomen, and encouraging deep, rhythmical breathing. Immediately after birth the infant was washed with water mixed with salt or nitron and swaddled in clean linen cloths. The mother was left to rest on a mattress for a weeklong period of lying-in *(locheia)*. Protective folk traditions, amulets, incense, icons, and prayers all had their place at the time of delivery, yet even routine childbirth presented risks. Comparative data suggest that without the benefits of modern hygiene, maternal mortality

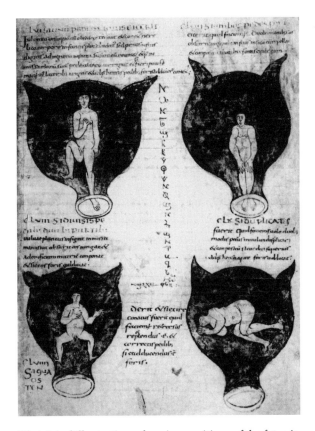

Obstetrical illustrations showing positions of the fetus in the womb. From a medieval Latin copy of late-antique edition of the *Gynaikeia* of Soronos of Ephesus. Photo copyright Bibliothèque royale de Belgique, Brussels (ms. 3701.15).

may have averaged two to three percent, with levels of neonatal death reaching five to eight percent. Both infant and mother were thought to be especially vulnerable for the first 40 days after childbirth, a period when physical and spiritual threats were believed to be at their peak.

Growing Up   Early childhood was thought to last from birth until around the age of six or seven.[17] Baptism and naming took place within the first week, and brought social recognition by family and community. Infancy lasted two or three years, until the child was weaned and began to talk. Guiding this crucial developmental phase was the responsibility of parents, siblings, and other members of the household, including the adoptive godparent. Boys and girls were not treated very differently during their early years. Most authorities followed the guidelines suggested by Plato and Aristotle, for whom the main goals of early life were to learn family rules and develop social skills by playing with others. Children occupied themselves with dolls, minia-ture clay pots, pull-toys, balls, hoops, board games with dice and knuckle-bones, and all kinds of found objects. Common games included leapfrog, wrestling, and swinging from trees. Imaginative role-playing was patterned after the world of adults. Team games like cops-and-robbers could take the form of monks-and-demons or Romans-and-Goths.[18] Household pets were frequent companions.

Like adults, the health of children reflected above all position in society. The distinctive maladies of youth were well known to classical medical writers but were not systematically treated by doctors. As a rule the same healing methods were used with youngsters and grownups. Childhood mortality rates were high, and only half of all children survived past the age of five. While baptized children were presumed to be full members of the Christian community, their marginal status often resulted in less formal burial practices. In late antiquity infant burials sometimes took place within a settlement, even under the floor of a house, and at night.

Crossing the nominal threshold of reason at the age of seven introduced the next phase of childhood. Most boys of this age began the serious business of studying with the neighborhood teacher *(didaskalos)*. Classes were brief and held in small groups, sometimes within the home, with girls occasionally joining as well. The main objectives were to learn the letters of the Greek alphabet and acquire a basic ability to read and write. Essential texts included psalms, parts of the Bible, and Homer, which were memorized at length. The precocious Michael Psellos says that he began reading Homer at the age of eight and finished the *Iliad* within a year. The books of Ecclesiastes and Proverbs were seen as good sources of concise ethical advice. Alert parents and teachers leavened the drudg-ery of memorization by making up rhymes and songs, staging contests, and awarding prizes. There was no literature written expressly for chil-dren, yet animal stories, fables, adventures, and saints' lives made good lessons. Games at this age had more complicated rules and heightened risks; they also made greater intellectual and physical demands. Older children spent increasingly more time with their peers and gradually formed identities of their own.

Reaching age seven usually brought greater responsibilities as well. In addition to studying outside the home, children were expected to run errands and help with the family garden and orchard. Between seven and twelve boys were instructed in handcrafts and manual skills by their fathers, while girls learned from their mothers how to clean, cook, spin, and weave. A late epigram in the Greek Anthology echoes Paul's admonition (1 Corinthians 13:11) to put childhood behind: "Today, dear God, I am seven years old, and must play no more. Here is my top, my hoop, and my ball: keep them all, my Lord." Children of this age also were subject to betrothals arranged by their parents. Marriage was not supposed to take place until the groom was 15 and the bride at least 12 years old. Sometimes the arrangements were rejected by the young people involved, who might flee to a monastery rather than marry. Most accepted their family responsibilities, however, postponing their departure for celibate life until they had produced an heir to continue the family line.[19]

Parents at all levels of society played a pivotal role in shaping the interests and career prospects of their offspring. Most children followed the vocations and opportunities of the families into which they were born. The structure of the imperial family and the importance put on proper succession illustrate this well. During the medieval period aristocratic families amassed huge fortunes that they passed on to their children. Skillfully negotiated marriages provided strategic opportunities for both boys and girls while protecting the interests of the wider families. Anna Komnene pursued the intellectual and literary advantages open to her as a daughter of the emperor. Professional parents could provide special options for their children. One sixth-century family of Tralles in western Asia Minor is remembered for the accomplishments of its five sons: the architect Anthemius, author of a famous mathematical treatise and codesigner of the great church of Hagia Sophia; Alexander, a doctor and author of medical treatises; Olympius, a legal authority; Metrodorus, a grammar teacher in the capital; and Dioscorus, like his father a physician in Tralles. Fathers in town and country normally passed on knowledge of a particular craft or trade to their sons. By far the greatest number of children simply continued to practice the agricultural traditions of their ancestors on inherited village lands.

Some parents chose to have their infant boys castrated in order to pursue specialized career paths open only to eunuchs. Castration was illegal in the empire and strongly condemned by the church, yet the harsh realities of provincial life compelled more than a few parents to take this drastic step toward placing their sons in good jobs. The practice seems to have been especially prevalent in the eastern provinces; many influential eunuchs are known to have come from Paphlagonia in northern Asia

Minor. In Constantinople eunuchs occupied key positions in the palace bureaucracy as well as the church. Lacking progeny and normal family ties, castrates were presumed (often erroneously) to be without personal ambition and sexual drive. They were particularly valued as supervisors of aristocratic households and rural estates. Bypassing traditional gender barriers, they freely associated with women as well as men as doctors, domestic managers, and servants.

Companion Animals

The role of household pets must have been much greater than Byzantine writers allow. Dogs have been an important part of pastoral communities in the Near East since their domestication in the late-Paleolithic period. In Greece, Rome, and Persia they performed valuable services by hunting game, herding livestock, and guarding the home. Roman authors describe how dogs were specially bred to suit their tasks: quick and agile for hunting and herding, large and loud for patrolling house and vineyard. Household dogs needed to be vigilant and not wander. Some were tethered with collars and muzzles during the day but let loose at sundown; stealthy dark dogs were preferred for camouflage at night. Other dogs were trained to accompany family members when running errands in town. Service dogs assisted the blind, while others were taught to perform tricks in public spectacles. The faithfulness of dogs is a theme often stressed by Roman and Byzantine writers. As the first-century agriculturalist Columella asks, "What servant is more attached to his master than is a dog? What companion more faithful? What guardian more incorruptible?" On several occasions a dog is said to have identified its dead master's assailant. Martial memorably recorded his fondness for his dogs in two heartfelt epigrams; it seems likely that many Byzantine people shared his feelings as well. Roman families are known also to have kept cats, hedgehogs, birds, and other creatures in the home. Such companions, like children, servants, and slaves, lived on the household's social margin and for this reason spent considerable time together. Their constant presence went unremarked by adult observers but probably changed little over the years.[20]

Entertainment and Games

The inward orientation of Byzantine society ensured that social milestones were celebrated mainly at home. Wedding celebrations included a banquet at the house of the groom, which was accompanied by drinking, singing, and dancing that lasted until dawn. The birth of a child was invariably welcomed with gifts to the parents and prolonged feasting. Such special occasions usually brought crowds of family members and friends into the home. In aristocratic circles the festivities could continue for weeks at a time.

Games offered recreational pastimes for the family. Young children seem to have been left to devise their own amusements. Boys and girls played with balls and hoops, rode on carts and swings, and picnicked with dolls and tiny clay vessels. Role-playing was based on the adult activities they observed.

No doubt the most popular games were those that had been around for centuries. Simple games of chance called for tossing common objects like potsherds and pebbles. Medieval writers mention dice *(kyboi)*, checkers *(petteia)*, and backgammon *(tablia)*, although the equipment and rules are not always clear. Gaming boards were idly scratched onto roof tiles and deliberately carved onto the steps of courtyards, porticos, and stairs. Games of three-in-a-row (like tic-tac-toe) were played on a square surface with nine shallow holes or an incised nine-spot. The more challenging mill game, also called *mereles,* took place on a pattern of inscribed squares. The most popular, judging from the number of recorded examples, was the variant known as "nine mens morris." The playing surface consists of three nested squares joined at the middle of each side by four radiating lines. Two players alternate arranging their nine markers at corners and intersections with the goal of placing three in a row, so completing a "mill." Once all 18 markers are on the board, they can only be moved to an adjacent corner or intersection. Upon completing a mill a player can remove any of his or her opponent's markers. A player loses when he or she is reduced to two markers or cannot make any further moves. The appearance of such gaming boards in everyday places makes clear their popularity as casual diversions within and outside the home.[21]

The game of chess *(zatrikion)* apparently was invented in Persia and spread to Byzantium in the medieval period. Excavation of an early eleventh-century shipwreck has recovered carved wooden chessmen, including figures of a king *(shaw)*, minister *(firz,* the modern queen), chariot *(rukh,* or rook), and foot soldiers *(fara* and *baidaz,* or pawns). By the twelfth century the game had caught on with the Byzantine nobility. Anna Komnene says that her father, the emperor Alexios I, escaped the cares of office by playing *zatrikion* with family members in the palace.

While only pebbles, potsherds, or pinecones were needed for many games, elite families played *tablia* and *zatrikion* on special boards with markers carved of horn or cast in silver or gold. Players of both high and low social standing commonly read special meaning into the outcome, believing that victory at the table foretold success in personal, business, or military affairs. The throwing of knucklebones *(astragaloi)*, lots, and other kinds of gambling had long been known across the Mediterranean and the Near East. The popularity of gambling in Byzantium, as in other cultures, betrays a deeply superstitious view of the world and the hope of at least temporarily controlling one's fate.[22]

NOTES

1. Gary Vikan, "Art and Marriage in Early Byzantium," *Dumbarton Oaks Papers* 44 (1990): 145–63; Ioli Kalavrezou, *Byzantine Women and Their World* (New Haven, Conn.: Yale University Press, 2003), especially 215–31.

2. For aspects of ritual kinship see Ruth Macrides, "The Byzantine Godfather," *Byzantine and Modern Greek Studies* 11 (1987): 139–62; and Margaret E. Mullett, "Byzantium: A Friendly Society?" *Past and Present* 118 (1988): 3–24.

3. The well-known passage from Kekaumenos is quoted in Charles Barber, "Homo Byzantinus?" in *Women, Men and Eunuchs: Gender in Byzantium,* ed. Liz James (New York: Routledge, 1997), 185–99; and also in Mullett, "Byzantium: A Friendly Society?" 11; and Deno John Geanakoplos, *Byzantium: Church, Society, and Civilization Seen through Contemporary Eyes* (Chicago: University of Chicago Press, 1984), 236–37.

4. Alice-Mary Talbot, "Women," in *The Byzantines,* ed. Guglielmo Cavallo (Chicago: University of Chicago Press, 1997), 117–43; Kalavrezou, *Byzantine Women and Their World;* Carolyn L. Conner, *Women of Byzantium* (New Haven, Conn.: Yale University Press, 2004).

5. James Kyriakakis, "Byzantine Burial Customs: Care of the Deceased from Death to the Prothesis," *Greek Orthodox Theological Review* 19 (1974): 37–72; Dorothy Abrahamse, "Rituals of Death in the Middle Byzantine Period," *Greek Orthodox Theological Review* 25 (1984): 125–34. For an introduction to traditional Greek practices see Margaret Alexiou, *The Ritual Lament in Greek Tradition,* 2nd ed. (Lanham, Mass.: Rowman and Littlefield, 2002).

6. An illustrated introduction to traditional fare is Dario Giugliano, Michael Sedge, and Joseph Sepe, *The Mediterranean Diet: Origins and Myths* (Naples: Idelson-Gnocchi, 2000). For the East see Andrew Dalby, *Siren Feasts: A History of Food and Gastronomy in Greece* (London: Routledge, 1996); and idem, *Flavours of Byzantium* (Totnes, England: Prospect Books, 2003).

7. Judith Herrin, "In Search of Byzantine Women: Three Avenues of Approach," in *Images of Women in Antiquity,* ed. Averil Cameron and Amélie Kuhrt, rev. ed. (New York: Routledge, 1993), 169; and Kalavrezou, *Byzantine Women and Their World,* especially 333–39 on attitudes to feminine appearance.

8. See Maria G. Parani, *Reconstructing the Reality of Images: Byzantine Material Culture and Religious Iconography (11th–15th Centuries)* (Leiden, the Netherlands: Brill, 2003), 51–80, for a survey of elite costume in the later Middle Ages. The classical background is reviewed by Judith Lynn Sebesta and Larissa Bonfante, *The World of Roman Costume* (Madison: University of Wisconsin Press, 1994). See also illustrations in the early study by Mary G. Houston, *Ancient Greek, Roman and Byzantine Costume and Decoration,* 2nd ed. (London: Adam and Charles Black, 1947; reprint, New York: Dover Publications, 2003).

9. Jewelry has been featured in several important exhibitions, including Kurt Weitzmann, ed., *Age of Spirituality: Late Antique and Early Christian Art, Third to Seventh Century* (New York: Metropolitan Museum of Art, 1979); Helen C. Evans and William D. Wixom, eds., *The Glory of Byzantium: Art and Culture of the Middle Byzantine Era, A.D. 843–1261* (New York: Metropolitan Museum of Art, 1997); and Helen C. Evans, ed., *Byzantium: Faith and Power (1261–1557)* (New Haven, Conn.: Yale University Press, 2004).

10. Nitron and soap are discussed by R. J. Forbes, *Studies in Ancient Technology* (Leiden, the Netherlands: Brill, 1955), 3:174–82; and J.R. Partington, *A History of Greek Fire and Gunpowder* (Cambridge: Cambridge University Press, 1960), 298–309.

11. For background see Jean-Jacques Aubert, "Threatened Wombs: Aspects of Ancient Uterine Magic," *Greek, Roman, and Byzantine Studies* 30 (1989): 421–49.

For Byzantium see Gary Vikan, "Art, Medicine, and Magic in Early Byzantium," *Dumbarton Oaks Papers* 38 (1984): 65–86; Gillian Clark, *Women in Late Antiquity: Pagan and Christian Lifestyles* (Oxford: Oxford University Press, 1993); and Kalavrezou, *Byzantine Women and Their World.*

12. Paul the Silentiary, in *The Greek Anthology,* vol. 1, trans. W.R. Paton (New York: G.P. Putnam's Sons, 1916), 5.252. Byzantine epigrams are included in many editions of the Greek (or Palatine) Anthology; for a collection of verse translations see Peter Jan, ed., *The Greek Anthology and Other Ancient Greek Epigrams* (London: Allen Lane, 1973).

13. For difficulties interpreting the formal language of medieval friendship see John Boswell, *Same Sex Unions in Premodern Europe* (New York: Villard Books, 1994); and Claudia Rapp, "Ritual Brotherhood in Byzantium," *Traditio* 52 (1997): 285–326.

14. The classical background is reviewed by Valerie French, "Birth Control, Childbirth, and Early Childhood," in *Civilization of the Ancient Mediterranean: Greece and Rome,* ed. Michael Grant and Rachel Kitzinger (New York: Charles Scribner's Sons, 1988), 3:1355–62.

15. Anna L. McClanan, "'Weapons to Probe the Womb': The Material Culture of Abortion and Contraception in the Early Byzantine Period," in *The Material Culture of Sex, Procreation, and Marriage in Premodern Europe,* ed. Anne L. McClanan and Karen Rosoff Encarnación (New York: Palgrave, 2001), 33–57.

16. John Boswell, *The Kindness of Strangers: The Abandonment of Children in Western Europe from Late Antiquity to the Renaissance* (New York: Pantheon, 1988); Timothy S. Miller, *The Orphans of Byzantium: Child Welfare in the Christian Empire* (Washington, D.C.: Catholic University of American Press, 2003).

17. For the first years of life see Dorothy Abrahamse, "Images of Childhood in Early Byzantine Hagiography," *Journal of Psychohistory* 6, no. 4 (1979): 497–517; Ann Moffatt, "The Byzantine Child," *Social Research* 53 (1986): 705–23; and Nikos Kalogeras, "What Do They Think about Children? Perceptions of Childhood in Early Byzantine Literature," *Byzantine and Modern Greek Studies* 25 (2001): 2–19.

18. In fourth-century Syria "one little girl, dressed in rags, puts her friends into stitches of laughter by exorcising them." Quoted in Thomas Wiedemann, *Adults and Children in the Roman Empire* (New Haven, Conn.: Yale University Press, 1989), 151.

19. For the epigram see ibid., 153; and similar dedications in book 6 of the Greek Anthology.

20. For Roman views of dogs see Columella, *On Agriculture,* trans. Harrison Boyd Ash, E.S. Forster, and Edward H. Heffner (Cambridge: Harvard University Press, 1941–55), 7.12–13; Martial, *Epigrams* 1.109, 11.69. The best modern sources are Jocelyn M.C. Toynbee, *Animals in Roman Life and Art* (London: Thames and Hudson, 1973; reprint, Baltimore: Johns Hopkins University Press, 1996), 121–22; and Douglas Brewer, Terence Clark, and Adrian Phillips, *Dogs in Antiquity: Anubis to Cerberus; The Origins of the Domestic Dog* (Warminster, England: Aris and Phillips, 2001). We know of hundreds of personal names—descriptive, playful, endearing—that Roman owners gave their animals, including dogs that were kept for hunting, for herding sheep, as sentries, and as household companions. A talented dog of the sixth century appears in Geanakoplos, *Byzantium,* 321. A special empathy for wildlife appears in Agathias's sixth-century lament on a dead partridge; see the Greek Anthology, 7.204; and Constantine A. Trypanis, ed.,

The Penguin Book of Greek Verse (Harmondsworth, England: Penguin Books, 1971), 390. At the same time, the traditional wariness of unknown dogs lingers in their frequent demonization in religious art and sermons.

21. H.J.R. Murray, *A History of Board Games Other than Chess* (Oxford: Clarendon Press, 1952), 37–48. There are several online versions of nine mens morris.

22. Anna Komnene, *Alexiad,* trans. E.R.A. Sewter (as *The Alexiad of Anna Comnena*) (Harmondsworth, England: Penguin Classics, 1969), 12.6; Anthony Bryer, "Byzantine Games," *History Today* 17, no. 7 (July 1967): 453. The nonrepresentational chessmen from the shipwreck at Serçe Limani were found together with a backgammon mat and a bronze cube with 5 to 14 holes on its six faces.

4

CONSTANTINOPLE

The history of Constantinople, the greatest city of medieval Europe, is in many ways the story of Byzantium. Founded as a strategic base in the early fourth century, the new settlement grew rapidly as imperial and religious power became concentrated inside its walls. Within a hundred years the emperor was staying year round in a grand palace that had become a potent symbol of empire. Nearby stood the home church and residence of the city's religious leader, the patriarch. To the west was the hippodrome, an enormous open-air arena for public assembly and spectacle. Through recurring cycles of growth, decline, and reconstruction the city and its monuments remained the foremost embodiment of Byzantine culture.

Constantinople served for over a thousand years as Byzantium's capital, its administrative and ceremonial focus as well as its largest urban center. With the arrival of Mehmet II in 1453 it became the capital of the even vaster Ottoman Empire, whose domains stretched from North Africa to the Near East. The Topkapi Sarayi replaced the Great Palace on the promontory and most churches were converted into mosques, yet the streets, markets, and neighborhoods remained those of a cosmopolitan center of wealth and beauty. For the past century Istanbul has flourished as the largest city of the Turkish Republic, with a population today exceeding 12 million. The location, size, and splendor of ancient Byzantium have always held a special place between East and West.[1]

This complex history presents special challenges when trying to understand how people lived from day to day. Centuries of continuous habitation have taken their toll of the urban fabric, and no Byzantine buildings

survive in their original form. As in other long-occupied cities, the more
deeply buried remains of early periods often are better known than less
substantial traces of medieval times. Archaeological research is difficult
to conduct in any urban setting, and the busy pace of modern Istanbul
makes this particularly problematic. Byzantine Constantinople survives
as well in written documents, ranging from carved inscriptions and historical accounts to letters, guidebooks, and legends. Native residents and
foreign visitors alike recorded their impressions of this dazzling and con-
fusing place. These tangled sources allow us to glimpse the people who
once lived and worked here.[2]

"THE ACROPOLIS OF THE WORLD"

Constantinople lies at the southeast corner of Europe, at the end of
a triangular peninsula pointing across the narrow Bosphorus strait
toward Asia Minor. The site was occupied long before the time of
Constantine. Local archaeologists have found pottery dating as early as
the sixth millennium B.C. Legend records that in the mid-seventh century B.C. Byzas, ruler of Megara in south Greece, established a colony at
the peninsula's seaward tip. Having first consulted the famous oracle at
Delphi about a likely location, Byzas settled on a projecting spur of land
facing the earlier colony of Chalcedon. His new settlement, soon known
as Byzantium, came with natural advantages. The low promontory was
defensible by land and water. There was access to the sea for fishing,
and to the west stretched the fertile plain of Thrace. The location, moreover, was ideal for commerce. It took advantage of sea passage between
the Mediterranean and the Black Sea as well as the land route joining
Europe and Asia. The settlement founded here prospered as both a
Greek colony and Roman city before coming to Constantine's attention
in the early fourth century A.D.

Constantinople's unique situation is still apparent. It is surrounded
on three sides by water, with no part lying far from the sea. To the
south is the Sea of Marmara or Propontis, a watery expanse that ends
in a long coast with narrow beaches and deep harbors. Ships leaving
here pass through the Dardanelles strait, the ancient Hellespont, before
reaching the Aegean Sea. To the east is the Bosphorus, a swift-flowing
channel that drains the Black Sea 20 miles farther north. In places only
half a mile wide, the Bosphorus forms a clear physical barrier separating Europe from Asia, the Ottoman continents known as Rumeli and
Anadolu. The deep inlet called the Golden Horn (Chrysokeras) lies
between the north coast of Constantinople and the facing shore of
Sykae, the late-medieval city of Galata. For centuries bustling commercial districts have crowded both sides of this naturally sheltered
harbor. No less than in antiquity, the setting remains strategically vital
and scenically splendid.

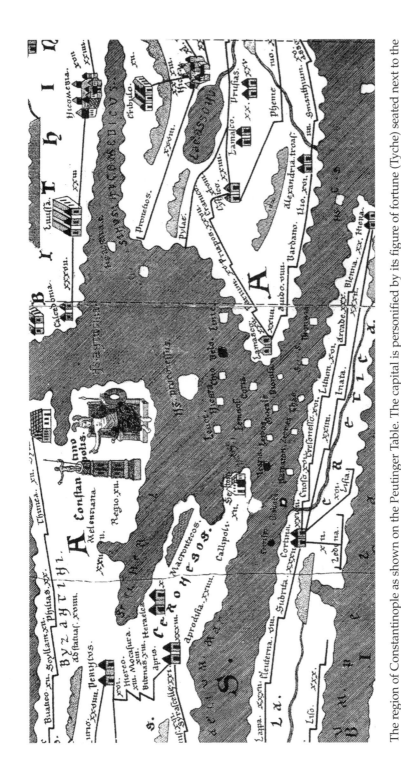

The region of Constantinople as shown on the Peutinger Table. The capital is personified by its figure of fortune (Tyche) seated next to the Column of Constantine. Nikomedia and Nicaea appear as walled cities across the Bosphorus. The largest of the Aegean islands is Crete. From Konrad Miller, *Weltkarte des Castorius genannt die Peutinger'sche Tafel* (Ravensburg, Germany: Otto Maier, 1888).

The Bosphorus north of Constantinople, from Anadolu Hissar in Asia looking west to Rumeli Hissar in Europe, in the early nineteenth century. Both fortifications date to the Ottoman campaigns against the Byzantine capital. Drawing by William H. Bartlett, in Julia Pardoe, *The Beauties of the Bosphorus* (London: George Virtue, 1839).

CITY OF CONSTANTINES

It takes effort to visualize the topography of ancient Byzantium beneath the sprawl of the modern city. The most prominent landform is a low ridge that stretches down the middle of the peninsula, from the outer walls to the Saray Burnu point overlooking the Bosphorus. A small river, the Lykos, once originated on the south side of this central ridge and emptied into a swampy estuary on the Marmara shore. Natural springs drained in narrow channels to north and south. At the tip of the peninsula is a low hill, the Promentorium Bosphorium, that served early inhabitants as an acropolis. The area's appearance changed dramatically during the fourth and fifth centuries. Large-scale earthmoving operations regularized the terrain, the shoreline was pushed outward by draining marshes and dredging harbors, and whole neighborhoods were established on previously unoccupied land. Medieval writers liked to mention that Constantinople, like the old Rome in Italy, was founded on seven hills and divided into 14 populous regions. The administrative districts are well documented but the hills, while providing useful reference points, rose as much in popular imagination as on the ground. At the same time the new

The promontory of Constantinople–Istanbul today as seen when crossing the Bosphorus by boat. The cathedral of Hagia Sophia appears at the center next to the church of Hagia Eirene. The grounds of the Great Palace stretched toward the "Blue Mosque" of Sultan Ahmet to the left. Courtesy of the author.

capital looked very much like other east Mediterranean cities, with large plazas and grandiose monuments connected by colonnaded streets. Over time development spread westward from the old urban center. New walls enclosed a mixture of crowded neighborhoods and undeveloped areas filled with gardens, orchards, and decaying buildings. Today as throughout the Middle Ages, one's awareness of the past is never far away.

Constantinople's key urban features were established in three main phases in the second, fourth, and early fifth centuries. The Roman city, like its Greek predecessor, occupied the peninsula's eastern tip. The early settlement was fortified under Hadrian and expanded by Septimius Severus to include a forum, temples, baths, hippodrome, and other public buildings. Two harbors faced north onto the Golden Horn. Houses would have occupied most of the remaining area. In the late Middle Ages the Ottoman sultans also were drawn to the promontory with its commanding view on all sides, and arranged Topkapi Palace looking across the Bosphorus.

Urban Development

The city expanded considerably after Constantine built a two-mile-long wall stretching from the Golden Horn to the Marmara, about two miles west of the Severan wall. At the east end of the peninsula, atop the first hill, work began on a palace that would serve as the emperor's residence. Official buildings were set up nearby: a large public square (the Augustaion) built in honor of Constantine's mother, the Augusta Helena, the senate house (Curia), the Stoa Basilica with its law courts, and two large churches. The hippodrome was expanded southward onto a tall hillside terrace. A main paved street known as the Mese, or "Middle Way," the present Divanyolu, led west from this imperial quarter to the new Forum of Constantine, an enormous circular plaza surrounded by a two-storied portico that was built atop the second hill. The main road continued west to the Forum of the Bulls (Forum Tauri, later the Forum of Theodosius) on the third hill. Farther along was another plaza known as the Philadelpheion, which stood near the city's geographic center. Two branching streets continued to the walls. One headed past the emperor's mausoleum and the church of the Holy Apostles atop the fourth hill and on toward the Danube frontier. The other ran through the Amastrianum plaza as far as the Golden Gate, where the Via Egnatia began its westerly course across Thrace. Intersecting roads to either side of this main artery reached into commercial and residential quarters. By the end of the fourth

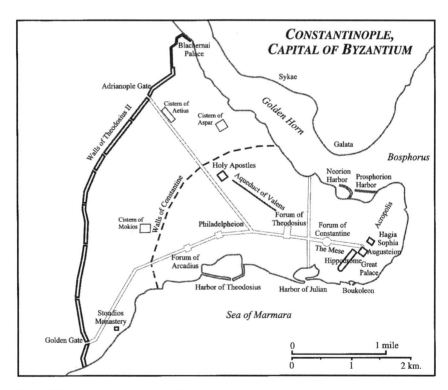

Plan of Byzantine Constantinople showing its major urban features. The city probably reached its greatest extent in the sixth century. Courtesy of the author.

century as many as 200,000 people may have walked these streets on a daily basis.

The city grew rapidly and by the early fifth century Theodosius II felt it necessary to expand its defended area. A second line of fortifications was built about a mile west of Constantine's land walls and incorporated the fifth, sixth, and seventh hills. The two branches of the main street were extended to reach new gates in this outer circuit, which now enclosed as great an area as the old Rome in Italy. Despite all this activity, much of the new land continued to be used for gardens, pastures, and suburban estates. Urban life revolved around business and housing districts along the Mese and especially the palace quarter at its eastern end. Embraced by water and sheltered by massive walls, Constantinople was becoming a monumental statement of late Roman urbanism.

Around 425 an official inventory was drawn up listing the city's major features. This document, the *Notitia urbis Constantinopolitanae*, lists 14 administrative districts together with the most important buildings found in each one. Altogether there were five imperial palaces, including the large residence known as the Great Palace. Public structures included four forums, two basilicas, and two theaters. Fourteen churches were in service, including the cathedral next to the patriarch's residence. The four harbors had 17 docks and five warehouses. The aqueduct supplied four cisterns and many bathhouses, of which 8 were open to the public and 153 were privately run. Fifty-two porticoes stood along the sides of 322 streets. The city's elites presumably occupied the 4,388 substantial townhouses *(domi)* that made the list. Most residents lived in multistoried tenements *(insulae)* or modest hovels that went unmentioned by the compilers of the *Notitia*. Such figures give an idea of the capital's rapid growth in the years following its foundation.

Constantinople probably reached its greatest extent in the early sixth century. By the time of Justinian most of its infrastructure was in place. The imperial residence encompassed an assortment of official offices, reception rooms, residential quarters, chapels, and gardens stretching from the hippodrome down to the water's edge. A network of paved streets organized public and private buildings. Many churches had been built by the emperor and others by leading local families. About 80 monasteries stood in different quarters. As many as half a million people lived here around this time.

Over the following centuries this urban framework saw successive periods of stress, damage, and consolidation. Earthquakes regularly shook the area and often brought down buildings. Crowded conditions and social tensions led to fires and riots. The worst of these was the Nika revolt of January 532, which began in the hippodrome and destroyed much of the civic center. Justinian's ambitious new church of Hagia Sophia, begun soon afterward, needed frequent repairs as foundations settled and earthquakes rattled its vaults. Up to half the population may have died or fled during the plagues of the mid-sixth and mid-eighth centuries. Others left as a result of Arab and Slavic attacks between 626 and 718. Most public buildings were abandoned during these years, with only 70,000 inhabitants remaining in town.

Constantinople's later development followed a very different course that reflected different needs, primarily those of the court and church. The palace complex was expanded to accommodate new facilities and a larger staff. The patriarch's offices were repaired, churches and monasteries rebuilt, and charitable foundations set up anew. The empire's recovering economy supported a thriving international marketplace. Artisans and merchants worked in street-side shops under the watchful eye of local officials. Eventually traders from Italy, Spain, and the Islamic states were allowed to settle in commercial enclaves along the Golden Horn. At the same time the consolidation of provincial wealth in the hands of a few families led to the rise of new social elites who installed themselves in grand houses. The mansions and monasteries they founded were Constantinople's most visible signs of medieval splendor. Most of these vanished during the Latin occupation of the thirteenth century, when shops were vandalized, houses burned, churches looted, and whole neighborhoods left in ruins. The reconstituted empire of the Palaiologan rulers lacked resources to repair more than isolated parts of the palace and a few monasteries. Western visitors describe the general dilapidation of the area. As few as 50,000 residents remained in the fifteenth-century city ruled by Constantine XI.

ADMINISTRATION AND AMENITIES

Any settlement the size and complexity of Constantinople needed considerable administrative support. Municipal affairs were supervised by the *eparch* or prefect *(eparchos)*, a key appointee of the emperor. This powerful official held sway throughout the city and its environs. Working out of the Praetorium, a large office building on the Mese not far from the Great Palace, the eparch and his staff of ministers, magistrates, and exarchs were responsible for maintaining public facilities and services. Fortifications and harbors demanded constant attention, streets needed frequent cleaning, baths had to be maintained and repaired. The water supply depended on an extended network of aqueducts, pipes, cisterns, and reservoirs. The hippodrome suffered wear and tear from its large crowds. As late as the sixth century the eparch was the chief sponsor of commemorative arches, public forums, markets, and churches. He enforced building regulations and supervised construction guilds. Vital foodstuffs had to be assembled and distributed to the population. Manufacturing and commerce received close supervision. Urban ceremonies needed to be planned and staged.

Public safety was a primary concern. As head of the police force, the eparch was instrumental in maintaining law and order. Like any large city, Constantinople saw its share of criminal behavior. Among the most commonly reported misdeeds were pickpocketing, domestic burglaries, theft from churches and monasteries, arson, riots, assaults, and murders. Cemeteries were subject to looting, even in relatively stable times. Cases of bribery, extortion, and forgery routinely appeared in the courts and were an inevitable part of conducting business and government. The main police station was at the Praetorium, which stood close to law courts and had an attached prison. Armed officers *(collegiati)* patrolled the streets, especially at night, and intervened with clubs and maces when needed. Fires, whether accidental or deliberately set, were among the most serious afflictions. As in Rome, teams of firefighters were drawn from local guilds and posted to guard each administrative region. The most common firefighting materials were water, sand, earth, manure, urine, and vinegar. Even with the sea so close, buckets, jars, and hand pumps were inadequate when combating a large-scale outbreak. By the eighth century soldiers had learned that special clothing offered protection against incendiary weapons. Heavy cloaks cut from raw animal hides were soaked in vinegar and urine and coated with alum, talc, and gypsum. Similar protective garb was probably worn by auxiliaries when contending with urban fires.

Protecting the capital was of paramount importance for the emperor. At an early date the Virgin was identified as the **Defense** city's special patron, and by safeguarding religious orthodoxy the emperor ensured her spiritual protection. On a more practical level, military defense began with the army's control of the frontier, which for most of the Middle Ages lay far beyond the city's walls. Several military units were based in Constantinople or its environs. The emperor's bodyguard occupied barracks on the palace grounds. At different times the palace guard included elite mercenaries like Goths, Slavs, and Varangians, who unfailingly impressed visitors to the court. Five cavalry regiments were stationed near the capital while not accompanying the emperor in the field.

Constantinople's exposed location on the Thracian plain led the emperor Anastasius to establish an advance line of defense some 40 miles to the west. The Long Walls of Thrace ran 28 miles from the Black Sea coast to the Propontis. Half of this length survives in some form. The original barrier consisted of a low forward wall with a deep ditch and a main wall built of brick and stone. Projecting towers of semicircular and polygonal plan stood at distances of 150–400 feet, depending on the terrain. Supporting camps and forts were located along the main roads. The entire system can be compared with the Hadrian's Wall, which stretches 73 miles across northern England. For over 200 years this forward defense guaranteed the capital's water supply and agricultural base. No longer maintained after the eighth century, the Long Walls continued to impress medieval travelers approaching from the west.[3]

Fortifications

The land walls of Constantinople are one of the greatest surviving monuments of antiquity. This massive three-and-a-half-mile-long barrier was built under Theodosius II in response to recent attacks by the Goths along the Danube frontier. The Gothic threat soon turned westward, but the walls proved invaluable in later centuries. Much newly enclosed area served for gardens and pastures, in this way supporting the population in times of siege. Huge open-air cisterns were built on undeveloped tracts. The walls were regularly maintained, and apart from a small expansion at the north end to include the Blachernai area were left in their original place. They withstood at least 17 sieges by the Avars, Bulgars, Arabs, Rus, and other hostile armies before the Latins took the city in 1204. Repaired in the late thirteenth century, the walls resisted the Ottoman advance until 1453. The strength of the walls and belief in their divine protection were key reasons for the empire's longevity.

The Theodosian land walls presented a triple line of defense some 200 feet wide. Approaching from the west, one first met a 60- to 65-foot-wide stone-lined moat, behind which a thick, outer wall rose to a height of 30 feet. About 65 feet farther on was a second wall, 16 to 20 feet thick at its base and 35 to 40 feet high. Both walls were defended by more than 90 projecting towers of square and octagonal plan. Walls and towers were built in a distinctive

The landward fortifications of Constantinople built under Theodosius II. Drawing by Thomas Allom, in *Constantinople and the Scenery of the Seven Churches of Asia Minor Illustrated* (London: Fisher, Son and Company, 1838).

local style with alternating bands of red bricks and limestone blocks. Their monumental appearance embodied Byzantium's strength and permanence throughout the Middle Ages.[4]

Six main gates and four minor portals opened through this landward defense. The Charisios (Adrianople) Gate served one branch of the main street leading to the Capitolium, near the Philadelpheion. Farther south was the famous Via Egnatia, which ended at the Golden Gate (Porta Aurea). This was the city's most imposing entrance and looked like a reinforced gateway combined with a Roman triumphal arch. Statues of emperors, sculptural reliefs, painted religious icons, and a quadriga of colossal elephants decorated the gate and an inner court. Over the centuries the Golden

The land walls of Constantinople today. A low forward wall and moat stood in front of the two main lines of defense. Much of the area was used for gardens and grazing. Courtesy of the author.

The most southerly part of the land walls, from the Golden Gate to the sea walls along the Marmara shore. From Gustave Schlumberger, *Un empereur byzantin aux dixième siècle, Nicéphore Phocas* (Paris: Firmin Didot, 1890).

Gate remained a key setting for ceremonial occasions, especially when the emperor left the city or returned from campaigns. Michael VIII Palaiologos entered Constantinople through the Golden Gate after expelling the Latins in 1261. In the late Middle Ages the area was turned into a fortified castle, known in Ottoman times as the Castle of Seven Towers (Yediküle).

East of this defense work Constantinople had nearly eight miles of shoreline. Low walls with occasional towers guarded the most important coastal stretches. The Great Palace reached as far as the shore in several places along the Promentorium Bosphorium. A small harbor known as the Boukoleon allowed the emperor to board ship or receive visitors directly at the palace. Nowhere were the sea walls very substantial, and few traces of them survive. Clearly the navy carried the main burden of defending the city. Battle fleets were based in nearby ports. On the Marmara side were two large harbors built in the fourth century by Julian and Theodosius I. To the north the Neorion and Prosphorion harbors opened onto the lower Golden Horn. During the medieval period the entire estuary with its exposed coastline could be sealed from the Bosphorus by a huge iron chain suspended on boats.

Water Supply Water for drinking and bathing was a perennial concern, especially during the long, dry months of summer. The capital's many advantages of location did not include fresh water. The only natural resources—the small Lykos river and some

Section of the aqueduct of Valens between the third and fourth hills. Maintained throughout the Middle Ages, the city's water supply system was one of the great achievements of ancient engineering. Drawing by William H. Bartlett, in Julia Pardoe, *The Beauties of the Bosphorus* (London: George Virtue, 1839).

minor springs—were unable to sustain a population of any size. The problem was long-standing and had prompted the Roman emperor Hadrian to build a gravity-fed aqueduct originating in the region of Halkali, about 10 miles to the northwest. This vital conduit was restored by Valens in the later fourth century and soon needed expanding to cope with the growing population. By the time of Justinian a complex network of pipes drew on sources more than 150 miles west of the city. Roman water engineers relied on centuries of hydrological experience when designing this system, which reflected a sophisticated understanding of lifting devices, inverted siphons, and fluid mechanics. Thirty stone bridges and miles of underground tunnels still survive in the forested hills of Thrace. At least two subterranean channels carried the main supply into the city. The best-known part of the aqueduct is a half-mile-long section between the third and fourth hills. The twin water channels run at a one percent grade and are supported by more than 80 two-tiered arches to a height of 100 feet. Frequently repaired during Byzantine and Ottoman times, the entire system constituted the longest aqueduct of the ancient Mediterranean.

Exposed sections of the aqueduct were an obvious weakness in times of siege. Between the fourth and seventh centuries many cisterns and tanks were built to address this defect. Most were located on hilltops in the

The Philoxenus cistern in the nineteenth century. The many underground cisterns supported the city in times of siege. Drawing by William H. Bartlett, in Julia Pardoe, *The Beauties of the Bosphorus* (London: George Virtue, 1839).

western city and were fed by the aqueduct and surface runoff. The *Notitia* mentions four main cisterns. One of these was the huge uncovered reservoir built in 421 by Aetius, probably acting in his role as eparch. This vast space measured about 800 by 280 feet in plan and was cut into the sixth hill, near the land walls. The slightly later cistern of Aspar, measuring some 500 feet on each side, was on the nearby fifth hill, and the so-called cistern of Saint Mocius, 560 by 480 feet in plan, lay farther south on the seventh hill. These open-air holding tanks were 30 to 50 feet deep and together held almost a million cubic meters. Scores of smaller, vaulted cisterns also have been identified, especially in the palace quarter. Forty of these are believed to underlie Topkapi Palace. The largest vaulted reservoir is the Basilica cistern, built by Justinian as the substructure of the Stoa Basilica. Known today as the "underground palace" (Yerebatansaray), the Basilica cistern is covered by a brick canopy supported on 336 columns and has a capacity of 78,000 cubic meters. The nearby Philoxenus (Binbirdirek, or "thousand-and-one-column") cistern has 224 columns and holds 40,000 cubic meters. No less than the fortifications, these reservoirs were a key factor in Byzantium's long-term survival.[5]

High-pressure plumbing served many needs. Terra-cotta and lead pipes ran beneath cobbled roads and sidewalks. Settling tanks for waterborne sediment were located at critical junctures for frequent cleaning.

As in Rome, the main consumers of water were the imperial palaces, public baths, and general population. Water managers used automatic distribution stations, supplemented by manual valves, to maintain the supply and shut down less essential services in times of shortage. The first to benefit were fountains, baths, and latrines in the palace, followed by houses of well-connected families. General needs were met by public bathhouses and fountains *(nymphaeae)*, with the steady flow of water flushing latrines and drains. The *Notitia* lists four principal fountains, including a *nymphaeum maius* that stood at the end of the main aqueduct in the Forum of Theodosius. Small fountains with basins and multiple taps were found in plazas and on street corners in all parts of town. People visited these places daily, filling and carrying home heavy amphorae and jars. Enterprising vendors sold water by the cup in the streets. Many people dug wells and cisterns to supplement their supply at home.

Feeding Constantinople's huge population was a matter of critical importance. Shortages in supply and distribution **Provisions** could lead to riots, while a crop failure or prolonged siege resulted in famine. For centuries the emperor had provided the citizens of Rome with the free distribution of bread, known as the *annona civica*. This costly, state-sponsored entitlement depended on the distant province of Egypt, where the Nile river's reliable annual flooding yielded a bountiful crop of wheat. Every year in late summer a fleet of ships had taken this harvest to granaries in Ostia, which supplied state-run bakeries in Rome. In the early fourth century Constantine diverted this supply to his new capital. Granaries were built on the island of Tenedos beyond the Dardanelles and along the Marmara shore. For nearly 300 years the eparch oversaw the baking of bread in municipal ovens and its allocation on the streets. The loss of the eastern provinces in the seventh century brought an end to these distributions, and for grain the city's reduced population turned to nearby Thrace and Bithynia. Olive oil, which had come mainly from Cilicia, Palestine, and Syria, was nearly as important a commodity and was subsidized to a lesser extent by the state.

Wheat and barley were dietary mainstays, and most official attention was directed to managing their supply. Fish was an important source of protein, and the fishing industry was closely supervised. Most residents ate fresh or preserved fish on a regular basis. Meat, eggs, and cheese were regulated and remained fairly expensive. Fresh produce could not travel any great distance and so was grown nearby. Almost everyone kept a garden or raised herbs and vegetables in earthenware pots. A single tree offered fruit as well as shade. There was a full square mile of arable land within the city, while another four to five square miles were worked just beyond the Theodosian walls, where the twelfth-century French monk Odo of Deuil saw "gardens that furnish the citizens all kinds of vegetables." More agricultural land lay across the Bosphorus. Farmers brought produce to market by donkey, oxcart, or boat, visited with friends, and returned home the same afternoon. In times of scarcity the city had to draw on a much wider geographic area.

We know a great deal about local farming thanks to the *Geoponika*, a tenth-century collection of traditional agricultural writings. In addition to listing crops that were grown near the capital, the *Geoponika* also gives planting instructions for different times of year. Constantinople has a typically Balkan climate with cool, wet winters and an average midwinter temperature of 41 degrees Fahrenheit (5 degrees Celsius). This is the best time for planting hardy greens and vegetables like cress, endive, lettuce, mangold, and orache, which can be brought to market by March. Summers are mild with markedly less rainfall. Spring and summer gardens should include kohlrabi, carrots, leeks, sea kale, and chicory. Cabbage, mangold root, radishes, and white cabbage grow well into the fall. Common herbs are basil, marjoram, rosemary, savory, coriander, saffron, dill, rue, fenugreek, cress, fennel, and mint. All crops suffer from unpredictable weather, and drought, hail, and extreme heat are not unusual. Winters normally bring 8 to 10 days of freezing temperatures, but in 927–28 the city experienced 120 days of damaging frost. To get through the winter months many people relied on stored cabbages, turnips, and other vegetables, which they kept in dark cellars or pickled in salt or vinegar.[6]

Public Health The eparch also was responsible for maintaining public health. Water was essential for drinking and for bathing and sanitation as well. Public and private latrines drained into underground sewers that emptied into the sea. Palaces, townhouses, and apartment blocks had latrines that were flushed with running water or by buckets drawn from wells or cisterns. In more modest homes waste was collected in a recessed pit in the courtyard. At regular intervals these pits would be cleaned out and hauled off to fertilize nearby gardens and fields. Garbage removal and sanitation were among the main tasks assigned to household servants and slaves.

Baths Public bathing was one of the most distinctive features of classical culture. The Romans saw baths as an essential urban amenity. Such buildings tangibly embodied the benefits of Roman rule by meeting social and hygienic needs in an opulent setting. The eight public baths *(thermae)* mentioned by the *Notitia* clearly played such a role in the early life of Constantinople. The most famous were the Baths of Zeuxippus, built by Septimius Severus and restored by Justinian, which stood in the palace district. The Baths of Constantius II were located near the center of town. The sixth-century Baths of Dagistheus were found along the Mese near the Forum of Constantine. In addition to these large public facilities, hundreds of private baths served the needs of elite households and ordinary citizens.

Large or small, bathhouses were complex assemblages of specially designed spaces that were vaulted and lit by small, high windows. Like their classical predecessors, Byzantine baths offered a bathing experience with three main stages. One began by disrobing in a changing room *(apodyterium)* and washing in the warm bath *(tepidarium)*. From here one moved on to the sauna-like hot room *(caldarium)* followed by the cold-water bath *(frigidarium)*. The entire building was organized around furnaces for heating water and pumping hot air through floors and the walls. In late antiquity visual luxury was as essential as physical comfort. Visitors describe how the great baths of the capital were outfitted with wall paintings, floor mosaics, classical statuary, and marble revetment. The Baths of Zeuxippus resembled an art museum with scores of historical and mythological statues arranged within its halls. For a minimal fee one could enter these cavernous, multifunctional complexes and find a comfortable, even luxurious setting for bathing, exercise, and meeting friends for conversation, business, readings, and lectures. Paid attendants were supposed to enforce hours, procedures, and conduct. Men and women bathed in separate rooms or at different times. Clergy and monks were regular visitors to the baths, even while their leaders railed against them as places of licentious behavior.

The baths of Constantinople, while extremely popular, were ruinously expensive to keep up. They were costly to build, needed frequent repairs, and consumed much water and fuel. During the sixth and seventh centuries the perception of bathing shifted from urban necessity to infrequent luxury. Most public facilities were closed or turned to other uses. The Baths of Zeuxippus became a military barracks and later a prison. Medieval renewal went little further than building small baths in the imperial palace, elite homes, and monasteries. Most people washed far less often in small neighborhood bathhouses.

Constantinople had several distinctive institutions that served public needs, especially among the poor and home- **Charitable** less. Among the most prominent were the state-supported **Institutions** orphanages *(orphanotropheia)* that were founded in late antiquity and operated throughout the Byzantine period. The largest of these stood on the acropolis north of the Great Palace and was run by palace officials; by the ninth century the director *(orphanotrophos)* was one of the highest ranking members of the imperial court. The *orphanotropheion* of Constantinople was known to take in infants and children of all ages. It included a school and was considered a lively center for culture and music, with a children's choir that performed on special occasions in the palace. Similar charities served the poor *(ptocheia)*, the homeless *(xenones)*, and the aged *(gerokomeia)*. Sick and injured residents received treatment at hospitals *(xenodocheia)*, of which the largest was attached to the imperial monastery of Christ Pantokrator. Justinian and Theodora founded convents for the city's prostitutes. Such philanthropic undertakings were much more highly developed in Constantinople than in medieval Europe, and were studied with interest by churchmen from the West.[7]

Burial practices were guided by tradition and law. Family
Burials   members prepared the deceased for burial and led the procession from house to cemetery. In late antiquity wealthy families
might build a subterranean tomb *(hypogaion)* outside the city walls or pay
for the carving of a stone sarcophagus. Most people were simply interred
in a shallow grave lined with bricks or tiles and marked by an inscribed or
painted tombstone. Wardens were posted to guard against looting fresh
graves and stripping corpses of their garments.

The ancient ban on urban burial began to break down after construction
of the Theodosian walls brought several existing cemeteries inside the
city. The necessity of prompt interment in a warm climate was especially
acute in summer and times of plague, most critically in the mid-sixth
and mid-eighth centuries. In 542–43 epidemic decimated the population and led to a general breakdown of local customs. Eyewitnesses like
Procopius and John of Ephesus describe how the outbreak led to bodies
being dumped in plague pits, cisterns, and the sea. Later burials took
place in the less densely occupied western quarters and across the Golden
Horn in Sykae. Social standing normally dictated practice. Elite families
designed private mortuary chapels as part of their self-endowed monasteries. Burial associations, confraternities, and trade guilds helped make
arrangements for their subscribers. It commonly fell to the church to bury
the poor and destitute.

PUBLIC PLACES

The people of Constantinople generally spent their days outside in the
streets and plazas. The most important of these open spaces was the Mese,
the grand boulevard that was the axis of both city and empire. Originating
at the Milion, the official milestone that stood in front of the Great Palace,
this broad corridor stretched west as far as the Philadelpheion. From
here two main roads continued to gates in the city walls. Throughout
its length the Mese was paved with blocks of marble, dazzling white in
sunshine and slippery gray when wet. On both sides rose porticoes with
sidewalks and shops. At regular intervals one found open-air forums or
plazas with freestanding triumphal arches, monumental columns, and
life-size statues. A large tetrapylon, an arched structure supported by
four piers, marked the Mese's intersection with the main north–south
street, the Portico of Domninos, which ran from the Golden Horn to the
Julian harbor. This imposing urban framework set the stage for public life
throughout the Middle Ages.

Not only the Mese but most major streets were flanked
Streets and   by porticoes and sidewalks paved with marble or mosaics.
Porticoes   This system of colonnaded thoroughfares was one of the
city's most distinctive features. Residents and visitors alike
remarked how streets and plazas were used by everyone for routine traffic,

commerce, assemblies, and parades. Underground sewers kept public areas free of trash and passable when raining. Municipal authorities saw the need to maintain a minimum road width of 12 feet as well as a 15-foot clearance below balconies. They also insisted that shop owners keep the walkways clear and decorated with marble as a way of ornamenting the city and pleasing pedestrians. On important occasions the streets would be strewn with flowers and the porticoes hung with garlands of laurel, rosemary, and myrtle, with silk banners and hangings suspended from the walls. Proprietors were obliged to keep torches in front of their shops to light the streets at night.

Streets and sidewalks were busy places during daylight hours. Horses, carts, and wagons traveled the main corridors along with porters carrying heavy loads on their backs. Strolling through the porticoes one came across all kinds of commercial activity, from craft shops and retail stores to tavernas and baths. Shops belonged to carpenters, cobblers, and smiths; makers of baskets, harnesses, and sausages; and sellers of dried produce, soaps, and textiles. Some specialty trades occupied designated districts, like the perfume dealers outside the Great Palace and the copper workers near Hagia Sophia. Sellers of baked goods and cooked foods set up temporary stands between the columns. People paused for conversation while venders sold water, fresh fish, fruits, and vegetables from carts. Scribes and money changers sat at their tables and gossiped with friends and passersby. Pimps and prostitutes solicited customers. Loiterers gambled, threw dice, and played on game boards scratched on the steps of the colonnades. With sunset the crowds cleared. Flickering lamps and torches lit the empty streets, which now became dangerous for the solitary traveler. Bands of *collegiati* patrolled the main thoroughfares alert to burglars and thieves. One was well advised not to venture outside after dark without the company of servants or slaves.

An intricate network of secondary roads and alleyways reached into the neighborhoods where most people lived. Unlike the main streets, these irregular, winding paths followed the uneven terrain. Many were unpaved, abruptly rising and falling with steps cut out of bedrock, occasionally widening into a small plaza with a fountain. Individual quarters might be named after a local mansion or other landmark, often an old church or monastery. Tall tenements and modest houses were built of stone, brick, and wood, and in some cases were accessible only by animals or on foot. Odo of Deuil warily describes such parts of the twelfth-century city as "squalid and fetid and in many places harmed by permanent darkness, for the wealthy overshadow the streets with buildings and leave these dirty, dark places to the poor and travelers; there murders and robberies and other crimes which love the darkness are committed."[8]

Residents shared their streets with animals. On certain days of the week one could expect to meet sheep, goats, pigs, and cattle being herded from the gates to the main livestock market in the Forum of Theodosius, or to small neighborhood markets throughout the city. Elite citizens and visiting dignitaries used horses for getting around town. Street performers appeared with trained bears, birds, and dogs, while exotic creatures were exhibited at festivals. Dogs accompanied their masters on errands and served as guides for blind beggars. No doubt the famous stray dogs that roamed Ottoman Istanbul were descended from Byzantine ancestors. Nineteenth-century travelers described them as forming "a great free vagabond republic, collarless, nameless, houseless, and lawless. The street is their abode, there they dig little dens, where they sleep, eat, are born, brought up, and die; and no one, at least at Stamboul, ever thinks of disturbing their occupations or their repose."[9]

Plazas
Key points of the city plan were marked by broad plazas, with small open areas formed by intersecting secondary streets.

The most imposing of these public spaces were the forums built by the early emperors. These were paved with marble, surrounded by porticoes, and decorated with statues. In especially important places an honorific column towered above surrounding buildings. The focus of the Forum of Constantine was a 115-foot-tall shaft of purple marble, raised on a high, stepped platform and crowned by a colossal statue of the emperor. The column was reinforced by iron hoops in the fifth century and by the tenth century had become the focus of ceremonies honoring the sainted emperor and his mother, Helena. A large statue of the empress once stood atop a tall column in the Augustaion. The Forum of Theodosius featured a monumental fountain, a pair of triumphal arches, and a column covered with spiraling battle reliefs. A similar monument stood in the Forum of Arcadius, recording victorious campaigns like the famous columns of Trajan and Marcus Aurelius in Rome. A statue of Marcian once topped the 35-foot-high granite column that still stands on the fourth hill. A column with a mounted statue of Justinian dominated the square in front of the Great Palace. Such monuments would have been conspicuous landmarks for local residents. Other public spaces were filled with gardens and fountains.

Sights
Constantinople was one of the preeminent tourist attractions of the medieval world. Places of cultural interest, historical importance, and popular curiosity were everywhere. The heroic fortifications, the sprawling imperial palace, and the immense cathedral of Hagia Sophia were not just functional buildings but reassuring symbols of permanence and divine grace. The hippodrome was a trophy case honoring victorious charioteers and generals. The successful exploits of emperors lived on in commemorative columns, arches, wall paintings, and mosaics. Famous works of Greek sculpture, like Pheidias's gold-and-ivory Zeus from Olympia and the Aphrodite of Knidos by Praxiteles, could be seen in public baths and private mansions. Mythological and historical figures populated city squares and porticoes. Life-size statues

The Column of Constantine, originally crowned by a colossal statue of the emperor, stood at the center of an open forum along the Mese. Imperial and religious ceremonies took place here throughout the Middle Ages. Courtesy of the author.

were rarely made by Byzantine sculptors and for this reason drew keen interest. As their original identities faded with time, these images took on mysterious powers in the popular imagination. Some monuments, like the fabled Serpent Column in the hippodrome, were thought to offer protection from snake bites. Other statues were known to be inhabited by demons, who caused them to speak, move, seduce women, or injure people. Commoners, elites, and even the emperor's family approached statues in order to identify a faithless spouse, restore sexual potency, or foretell future events. A ninth-century guidebook to local marvels warned its reader, "Take care when you look at old statues, especially pagan ones."[10]

CHURCHES AND MONASTERIES

Constantinople was a city of churches, and the signs of Christianity were visible everywhere. Two of the most important religious buildings had been begun by Constantine or his immediate followers: the Great Church near the acropolis, and the Holy Apostles with the imperial mausoleum close to the outer walls. By the sixth century places of worship could be found in every corner of the city. Most of these were small and attracted people who lived nearby. Others were built by imperial or private donors, sometimes in a spirit of competitive display. Foundations ranged from minor shrines honoring local martyrs to enormous buildings that covered an entire block. In the fifth century the wealthy widow Olympias established a women's monastery near Hagia Sophia. Around the same time the former consul Sporacius built a church of Saint Theodore next to his house on the Mese. In the early sixth century Anicia Juliana, a direct descendant of Theodosius I, set up a vaulted basilica in honor of Saint Polyeuktos near the center of town. Local quarters were called after these patrons for centuries to come. Many churches and monasteries were surrounded by gardens and orchards that symbolized the heavenly *paradeisos* their visitors hoped to attain. The suburban shrine of the Virgin Zoodochos Pege, for example, was found in "a dense grove of cypresses and a meadow abounding in flowers in the midst of soft glebe, a park abounding in beautiful shrubs, and a spring bubbling silently forth with a gentle stream of sweet water." Not infrequently touched by earthquakes, riots, and fires, the surviving churches were maintained by local patrons, led by members of the imperial family, who endowed monasteries sheltering hundreds of monks and nuns.[11]

After the seventh century and the loss of the Christian Holy Land, Constantinople became the empire's main pilgrimage destination. Pious rulers and citizens worked hard to locate sacred relics, ranging from the bones of early martyrs to such instruments of the Passion as fragments of the cross, sponge, lance, crown of thorns, and stone from the tomb. Many of these objects, whether simply displayed or encased in bejeweled reliquaries, were kept in the Great Palace; others were held by local churches. The miracle-working robe, girdle, and shroud of the Virgin, for example, could be seen at the famous church of the Virgin Chalkoprateia in the copper workers' district below Hagia Sophia. Several monasteries claimed the head of John the Baptist. Not everyone took their authenticity for granted. The eleventh-century bureaucrat and sometime-poet Christopher of Mytilene scoffs at incredulous believers who purchase "as real relics the bones of plain people and who find acceptable the existence of too many limbs belonging to one and the same saint." Over time painted icons became equally potent devotional objects. Certain icons representing holy figures, particularly images of the Virgin kept at the Blachernai and Hodegon monasteries, claimed a prominent role in urban ceremonies. The icon of the Virgin Blachernitissa was credited with saving the capital from the Avars in the seventh century, an event long commemorated by the Akathistos liturgy during the fifth week of Easter Lent. On several occasions the icon of the Virgin Hodegetria was carried along the walls as part of the city's defense.[12]

Some miracle-working relics and icons became the focus of healing shrines that played a unique role in promoting public health. Sites of religious therapies were sought out by all levels of urban society. Among the best known were the shrines of the doctor saints Cosmas and Damian, Saint Therapon, and the Virgin *ta Kyrou*. Some cults were quite specialized. Saint Panteleimon (feast day observed July 27) was known to cure cases of demonic possession. The relics of Saint Photeine (feast day March 20), found in her church in the Chalkoprateia district, could reverse blindness and other eye afflictions. One visited the chapel of Saint Artemios (feast day October 20) in the church of Saint John Prodromos ("the forerunner," John the Baptist) to be treated for hernias and genital diseases; the related cult of Saint Febronia focused on helping women.[13] The usual way of seeking aid was to buy a votive candle or lamp to accompany prayers to the saint. In other cases one attended a service and received a token, oil, salve, or holy water from a sacred spring *(ayiasma)*. Treatment of more serious afflictions required incubation. After purifying themselves, patients slept within the halls of the church in hopes of being visited by the healing saint in a dream. Some religious centers maintained facilities for caring for the sick and aged. The Pantokrator monastery, founded by the imperial family in the twelfth century, supported the city's largest hospital together with a staff of trained doctors.

The greatest church of Constantinople, and indeed the empire as a whole, was the cathedral that came to be **Hagia Sophia** known as Hagia Sophia. This enormous structure stood in the old city center, next to the patriarchal residence and not far from the Great Palace, a location that ensured its centrality in civic and religious affairs. An earlier church on the site, planned if not actually begun by Constantine, was destroyed during the Nike riot of 532. Within weeks Justinian began work on a much larger and more ambitious building, which on December 27, 537, was dedicated to the holy wisdom *(sophia)* of Christ. Despite occasional damage and frequent repairs, Justinian's church still stands as one of the great triumphs of world architecture. It was designed by two mathematicians and engineers, Anthemius of Tralles and Isidorus of Miletus, and completed in only five years. The original structure was a broad, three-aisled basilica crowned by a 100-foot-wide dome at a total height of 180 feet—the largest interior space surviving from antiquity. Massive outer piers reinforce this central unit while decorative marbles and shining mosaics once enlivened the interior: huge columns of green and purple marble flanking the nave, gray slabs paving the floor, multicolor revetment lining the walls, and fields of

The cathedral of Hagia Sophia as seen from the south in the nineteenth century. Built in 532–37 atop the ruins of its fourth- and fifth-century predecessors, the colossal church was the medieval city's most prominent landmark. From Gustave Schlumberger, *Un empereur byzantin aux dixième siècle, Nicéphore Phocas* (Paris: Firmin Didot, 1890).

The interior of Hagia Sophia as seen from the upper gallery. The vaulted building was the largest covered space of antiquity and the scene of Byzantium's most important ceremonies. Courtesy of the author.

gold covering the vaults. The immense building could be seen throughout Constantinople and across the Bosphorus. Breathtaking in design and scale, the church soon came to symbolize both city and empire. Medieval visitors marveled at the structure. Popular legend called it the work of thousands of master masons guided by angels, fulfilling a vision revealed to Justinian in a dream. The words of Procopius preserve the wonderment with which observers first beheld this miraculous space, "a spectacle of great beauty, stupendous to those who see it and altogether incredible to those who hear of it.[14]

CONSTANTINOPOLITAN SOCIETY

Over the course of its thousand-year history, Constantinople was home to several million people drawn from across the medieval world. Imperial, civil, and ecclesiastical elites claimed center stage in the palace quarter, while lesser officials lived and worked throughout the city. The presence of the court attracted wealthy families who held large tracts in town as well as in the provinces. Merchants and traders were drawn by local harbors and markets. Others came for the countless opportunities and diversions of metropolitan life. The population fluctuated over the Byzantine millennium, from a peak of nearly half a million in the early sixth century to perhaps 50,000 after the Fourth Crusade. By the fourteenth century many foreigners from northern Europe, Italy, and the Near East had taken up permanent residence. After all these changes one wonders whether Justinian would still have recognized the late-medieval city. Yet writers of each generation continued to express admiration for the capital and their deep satisfaction with living there.

The entire east Mediterranean was represented in the city's population. In late antiquity there were Greek-speakers from the Balkans, western Asia Minor, and Cyprus; Latin-speaking Italians, Illyrians, and North Africans; Germanic-speaking Gepids, Goths, and Herules from northern Europe; Armenians from the high eastern plateau; Aramaic-speaking Palestinians and Syrians; Jews; and Coptic Egyptians. Latin was the official language of court, law, and the army through the sixth century, but the most widely used language of the Hellenized East was Greek.

While the emperors needed to defend the purity of the faith and protect its true believers, cultural differences were apparent and usually tolerated. Jews were considered a separate people *(ethnos)* and a protected minority, even though subject to discrimination and occasional persecution. An early Jewish community was established in the copper makers' quarter near Hagia Sophia, where a synagogue was built in the fifth century. Jews pursued sundry vocations like medicine, clerical trades, tanning, and long-distance commerce. A number of Jews emigrated to Constantinople to avoid persecution in their homelands as well as to pursue military and commercial opportunities. Byzantium's medieval revival encouraged Italian and Arab merchants to establish commercial colonies along the

Golden Horn. Jewish synagogues, Latin churches, and Islamic mosques were all found in the fifteenth-century city.

Palace Life   The house of the emperor was the focus of the city and indeed the empire as a whole. Over the centuries several official residences were built for members of the imperial family. The main facility was the Great or Sacred Palace, which included the Daphne built by Constantine, the Magnaura, the seaside Boukoleion, and related buildings on the first hill. The hippodrome stretched along the west side of the palace, physically separating it from the city while providing a meeting space for citizens and emperor. Later residences stood elsewhere in town. The Komnenoi favored the Blachernai palace, a fortified complex near the church of the Virgin Blachernitissa at the north end of the Theodosian walls, overlooking the Golden Horn. Altogether the sources mention 11 imperial palaces within the walls and as many suburban retreats along the Marmara and Bosphorus shore. Accompanied by family members, bodyguards, church leaders, and court officials, the emperor moved from place to place with the changing seasons and for ceremonial occasions.

The Great Palace was virtually a city in itself, a vast complex covering more terrain than many towns. Very little survives of the buildings apart from official protocols and the breathless accounts of medieval visitors. These speak of a tangle of domestic quarters, reception halls, dining rooms, churches, and recreation areas. The loosely related components occupied a landscape that was both urban and rural. The palace faced the most densely occupied part of town, yet had space for fishponds and water courses; gardens with flowers, herbs, and vegetables; and groves of fruit and nut trees. Sporting fields occupied narrow terraces reaching from the Augustaion and hippodrome down to the Marmara shore. The Boukoleion with its small harbor stood at the water's edge with a balcony looking out to sea. Other gardens and apartments were reserved for the personal retreat of the emperor's family. Visitors frequently remark on the luxurious, paradiselike setting. Such elaborate facilities needed endless maintenance, and already by the sixth century parts were falling into disrepair. The medieval residence must always have balanced splendor with dilapidation.

The Great Palace served as center stage for the daily drama of life at court. Citizens most often saw their emperor in the hippodrome when he presided over games and celebrated military triumphs. Visitors entered the palace itself through a vestibule known as the Bronze Gate (Chalke). Justinian and later emperors decorated this entryway with religious icons as well as mosaics depicting successful field campaigns. Corridors led to rooms for formal meetings and ceremonial dining. Excavations have identified one apsidal reception room together with a large court paved with mosaics of rural scenes. The most famous of these imposing spaces was the throne room, an octagonal chamber known as the Golden Hall

(Chrysotriklinos), where the emperor appeared before a large mosaic of Christ. An inscription running around the mosaic made clear the symbolism linking Byzantium with the kingdom of heaven: "behold, once again the image of Christ shines above the imperial throne and confounds the murky heresies; while above the entrance is represented the Virgin as divine gate and guardian." As described by Constantine VII in the *Book of Ceremonies*, this is where the emperor received foreign ambassadors, promoted military officers, and awarded court dignities. Formal banquets were held as well, with high-ranking diners arranged at tables according to strict protocol. Another famous reception room was the Hall of the Nineteen Couches (Dekanneakubita), where the emperor and his guests reclined while dining in classical Roman style. The Ottonian ambassador, Liudprand of Cremona, tells of being served from golden vessels so heavy that they had to be suspended from the ceiling. Several chapels were available for the emperor's use, the most famous being the church of the Virgin of the Pharos and the New Church (Nea Ekklesia) built by Basil I in the ninth century. Witnesses describe these buildings as wonders of their time, "in which art, riches, an ardent faith and a bountiful zeal were all combined and the most beautiful materials were gathered together from every quarter." Elsewhere the walls were decorated with colorful tapestries, silks, paintings, and mosaics. Statues of emperors, saints, and mythological characters were still displayed in the tenth century. Libraries, records offices, and workrooms for preparing state documents were nearby.[15]

The emperor and his family were attended by myriad officials and their assistants, with the result that almost all daily routines were ceremonial in some sense. Most palace operations, including access to the emperor, were run by a powerful staff of household chamberlains or *koubikoularioi*, mainly eunuchs. The imperial apartment (*sacrum cubiculum* or *koiton*) was supervised by the grand chamberlain (*parakoimomenos*, "the one who lies beside"), who was personally responsible for the emperor's safety. The empress shared the same room but also maintained separate quarters with her own staff. Nearby was the famed purple-lined chamber (Porphyra) reserved for giving birth. The special status of a child born to a reigning couple was known as *porphyrogennitos*, or "born in the purple." Both Basil I and Leo VI were credited with building luxurious bathhouses within the palace. Such facilities show that the most intimate routines were an integral part of imperial pageantry.

Courtly society was organized by strict rules of hierarchy and precedent. The *Book of Ceremonies* provides a glimpse of official routines during the tenth century, and stresses the importance of setting and decorum. The patriarch of Constantinople always occupied a unique position close to (and sometimes at odds with) the emperor. Secular bureaucracies supervised military, fiscal, and judicial affairs. Each of these was headed by a senior official who reported to the emperor and was assisted by various subordinates. Generals, landowners, civil officers, and other individuals were recognized by the award of imperial dignities and titles like *strator* ("groom"), *spatharios* ("sword bearer"), *vestiarios* ("wardrobe keeper"), and *kouropalates.* These awards, which were combined and revised over the centuries, brought the recipient closer access to the emperor and opportunities for greater wealth and status. Security was provided by a rotating staff of palace guards, of which the axe-wielding Varangian guards were the best known.

Costume was an essential part of palace life. The imperial couple wore robes with many layers of fine silk embroidered with silver and gold threads and embellished with semiprecious gems and pearls. Military commanders and other officers wore a heavy cloak *(paludamentum)* that varied with the branch of service. Bright, vibrant colors were preferred for fabrics woven in delicate patterns. Scarlet slippers or boots were a sign of highest rank. Both the emperor and his coruler wore heavy crowns with large pearl pendants. This complicated language of costume was maintained throughout the Byzantine period, both within the palace and on field campaigns. The production of court finery accounted for a significant part of the household budget.[16]

Eunuchs Many key positions were filled by eunuchs. These were either foreign captives or young castrates who had been groomed for a palace career. Eunuchs were completely dependent on the emperor and were presumed to be loyal to him. Since they could not themselves occupy the throne, they were believed to pose no threat to the imperial family's power and purity. New arrivals were trained by experienced veterans in court protocols. As a result, palace eunuchs formed an interconnected network stretching across civil and clerical boundaries. Official garb included a white tunic trimmed with gold decoration and a red doublet with gold edging. Eunuchs of the *protospatharios* ("first sword bearer") rank were distinguished by pearls set in a special neck decoration. Others are known to have worn earrings. Their lack of beards and altered voices set them apart from other men and confirmed their place outside the normal social order.

Eunuchs occupied the highest ranks of personal assistants to the emperor. The chief responsibilities of the koubikoularioi involved activities that in other households were managed by women: cooking, serving meals, tending the wardrobe, writing letters, and managing finances. The highest-ranking eunuch was the parakoimomenos, who supervised the personal safety of the emperor by locking himself within his bedchamber at night. Others functioned as policy advisors, physicians, and barbers. Eunuchs conducted marriage negotiations, assisted the birth and education of imperial children, and arranged burials. Their intermediate gender gave them free access to the restricted women's quarters. The ambiguous status of eunuchs allowed them to cross freely the boundaries of personal and institutional etiquette, which made them valued intermediaries between the palace bureaucracy and the outside world. At one point in the eleventh century eunuchs held more than 30 administrative posts in the palace. Their status declined during the twelfth century when the Komnene dynasty brought to court a new masculine ideal.

Christianity was fundamental to Byzantium, and clergy occupied a prominent place in society. The highly centralized structure of the church reflects its origins in late antiquity. **The Church** Individual churches across the empire were organized by diocese. Each diocese was supervised by a bishop, who came under the authority of the regional metropolitan. Metropolitan bishops belonged to a council that reported directly to the patriarch of Constantinople. Independent archbishops or patriarchs supervised affairs in the great cities of Alexandria, Antioch, and Jerusalem, and Rome. By the late fourth century Constantinople ranked first in precedence among the Eastern patriarchs. The long struggle over primacy with Rome seriously divided the Latin and Orthodox churches.

The patriarch lived in a complex of buildings that faced onto the Augusteion opposite the Great Palace. Corridors communicated directly with Hagia Sophia. Written sources mention living quarters for the cathedral's extensive clergy, meeting rooms, records archives, and library. The patriarch employed his own staff of deacons, priests, and monks, and sponsored a school to instruct clergy and monks in theology. His close relationship with the emperor is one of the most distinctive features of Byzantine culture.

Orthodox clergy appeared regularly in the streets of Constantinople. Parish churches were found in every neighborhood and were tended by assigned deacons, subdeacons, and priests, who usually lived nearby. Private chapels, healing shrines, and *martyria* had their own caretakers and clergy. Thousands of monks and nuns lived in the city's many monasteries. They were easily recognized by their distinctive clothing and widely admired for their spiritual dedication.

The state was run by a secular bureaucracy that employed thousands of men in the capital and throughout the empire. **Government** The late Roman system of prefectures survived until the **Service** seventh century, when provincial government was consolidated into a smaller number of military *themes (themata)*, initially 7 and eventually more than 20, each coming under the command of a thematic general *(strategos)*. During the medieval period civil authority increasingly was assigned to male relatives of the emperor. Considered together with the church, the Byzantine bureaucracy was the largest and most elaborate system known in the Middle Ages. Officials were regularly promoted in rank and kept records in triplicate to guard against misappropriation of funds. Career bureaucrats maintained stability through imperial regime changes and helped ensure the state's long-term survival.

The three main branches reporting to the emperor were the military, fiscal, and judicial authorities. In late antiquity the praetorian prefect commanded the army based outside the city and so served as the senior civil functionary. After the seventh century the military was supervised by the generals of the provincial armies. Urban affairs were managed by the eparch of Constantinople. The fiscal branch, known as the Sacred Largesse, controlled the central treasury and minted coins. Income came mainly from taxes levied on land, state-owned mines, and customs duties. Major expenditures included maintaining the imperial family, the military, and the civil bureaucracy. During the medieval period most fiscal departments *(sekreta)* were headed by officials known as *logothetes*. The judicial branch supervised legislation and local tribunals, and took on increasing responsibilities for provincial government. It is unsurprising to find overlapping roles within this complex system, with individuals frequently moving among different departments and holding multiple offices.

The civil service was an attractive career option for young men. Well-off parents sent their sons to established schools in the Chalkoprateia and Sphorakiou districts in hopes of finding an entry-level position. The emperor subsidized some of these schools, and teachers like Michael Psellos worked hard to win imperial stipends. One needed to be literate to hold most clerical positions, but many appointments did not require advanced education. Family connections were equally useful, especially for sons of current officeholders. Eunuchs were highly valued in many departments. Competent performance brought a steady salary *(roga)*, relatively modest at entry levels, and opportunities for advancement. The emperor regularly distributed gifts of money, land, and privileges to higher officials. Individual departments developed their own loyalties and rivalries. Rising through the ranks brought increased occasions for personal enrichment through bribes and fees. This kind of discretionary patronage was so widespread, especially in the provinces, that it was regulated by the state. Officials understandably held onto their posts as long as possible.

Elite Society

The presence of the court encouraged the formation of a local class of social elites, commonly called the *dynatoi*, or "empowered ones." In late antiquity this consisted mainly of wealthy men who held honorary titles and seats in the senate, an advisory assembly whose power was largely symbolic. Provincial landowners were increasingly influential powerbrokers during the medieval period, often holding court appointments that they used to press for favorable legislation and policies. Most of these landed magnates resided for long periods in the capital, where they kept up fine mansions for their families. Members of this well-to-do class rarely went out unaccompanied by a couple of servants or slaves. Men generally rode on horseback and women traveled in closed carriages or sedan chairs. Travel at night was always a risky undertaking.

Better Gardens and Homes

Housing was an obvious hallmark of social status, especially for the wealthy families that built grand homes throughout the city. Some of the oldest, most powerful names were found living in the region of the

A well-preserved late-medieval palace, the Tekfur Sarayi, located near the Theodosian land walls and the Blachernai palace. Tall windows on the upper floor gave residents a view of their city. Much of the neighborhood consisted of gardens and grazing land. Drawing by William H. Bartlett, in Julia Pardoe, *The Beauties of the Bosphorus* (London: George Virtue, 1839).

first hill, not far from the Great Palace. Especially prestigious addresses were on the main colonnaded streets. The wealthy fourth-century widow Olympias kept a house near the Baths of Constantius in the central part of town, but also owned shops, a bakery, and a private bath close to Hagia Sophia. Excavations near the hippodrome have found houses of high-ranking officials of the fifth and sixth centuries. Visible remains include curving porticoes and vaulted halls that advertised the owners' wealth and influence. Well-connected citizens favored the city's south slopes, where they built terraced houses with balconies overlooking the Marmara—a view that was protected by local laws. Writing in the sixth century, Paul the Silentiary describes how three sides of his house looked over "the pleasant expanse of the sea, struck by the sunlight from all quarters." Others turned to undeveloped land between the walls of Constantine and Theodosius, where there was space for sprawling complexes with reception halls, chapels, courtyards, and gardens. Such mansions stood in sharp contrast to the city's dilapidation in the later Middle Ages.[17]

The largest properties were set back from the street behind high walls of brick and stone. After passing through the gateway visitors found themselves in a carefully arranged courtyard crowded with plants, fountains, and shade trees. Wealthy residents prided themselves on raising exotic flowers and fruit trees; solidly middle-class homes had at least a few tall cypresses as well. The tenth-century imperial functionary John Geometres proudly distinguished his house by the large bay and fruit trees that overhang the street wall. The fourteenth-century residence of the prime minister Theodore Metochites included a chapel, bathhouse, and other buildings set amid gardens with fountains, water channels, statuary, and porticoes. Smaller courts would have included at least a few potted plants and flowers. As in the countryside, urban families realized the importance of maintaining a kitchen garden and some fruit and nut trees. In his letters John Geometres claims that he grew vegetables year round next to his house. Eustathios, who lived in Constantinople in the twelfth century before becoming metropolitan of Thessaloniki, sent his friends fruit picked from his own trees. Such writers often use agricultural metaphors in their letters. They prized flowers highly. Roses were planted in baskets, ceramic pots, and organized beds, and were trained to climb trellises, trees, and garden walls. Raising garlic nearby was thought to increase their natural fragrance.

Large residences in the eastern neighborhoods included street-side shops and tavernas leased out to private entrepreneurs. Security was always a concern. Urban properties could not be left alone but had to be watched by a porter who kept doors locked and windows barred. Many houses were organized around an interior court. This often was the busiest part of the residence, the place where women and servants gathered during the day. Guests were received in a single large room. Some writers recommend that women retire to separate apartments *(gynaikonitis)* when outside visitors are present. Domestic quarters were on the upper floors with separate rooms for dining and sleeping. Windows looked across the city and balconies projected over the street. Walls were covered with paintings or ceramic tiles and hung with textiles. Curtains were used to close windows and separate rooms. Water came from a courtyard fountain or cistern. Larger homes had private latrines and sometimes small baths. City ordinances dictated that houses be set 10 feet apart with balconies at least 15 feet high.

Not much is known about how houses were furnished. One common type of dining table in late antiquity was a semicircular marble surface supported by a wood or masonry stand, around which diners reclined on a cushioned bench. Such tables were small and accommodated at most seven or eight diners, which meant that banquets were intimate affairs. Most medieval tables were rectangular and made of wood. Some meals may have been shared on a tray or carpet spread on the floor. Chairs and folding stools seem to have been replaced by simple benches, sometimes with high backs. Wood-frame beds used rope-supported mattresses together with cotton and linen sheets and pillows. Mattresses were stuffed with straw, cotton, or wool. Pillows and coverings were woven of

Ottoman timber-frame houses in Izmir, which preserve many
characteristics of medieval houses in Constantinople. The
width of streets and height of balconies were regulated by
local ordinance. Drawing by Thomas Allom, in *Constantinople
and the Scenery of the Seven Churches of Asia Minor Illustrated*
(London: Fisher, Son and Company, 1838).

cotton, wool, and silk and filled with batting or goose down. Valuables
were locked away in cupboards and chests.

Some elite houses had a private chapel with its own clergy. Private services always ran the risk of heresy and needed permission from the local
bishop. Like other churches, such chapels would have been decorated with
paintings of saints and other religious figures. Bronze or silver vessels were
used to celebrate the Eucharist. Devotional objects included painted icons,
ivory triptychs and chests, bejeweled reliquaries, and liturgical books.

Fine Dining

Eating was an everyday activity that grew increasingly ritualized with social rank. Most families shared food twice a day, with the main meal occurring in late afternoon or early evening. While breakfast *(ariston)* was taken informally, the evening meal *(deipnon)* could be a significant occasion with guests from outside the family, an elaborate menu, and hired entertainment. The Roman practice of staging formal meals in designated rooms, often known as *triklinia,* continued through late antiquity. Diners on cushioned benches reclined around the semicircular-shaped table with the host seated at the right. Banquets were for the benefit of men and reinforced the social networks of public life. Women might be present but usually sat at a separate table. Meals were served on broad ceramic or silver dishes and were accompanied by wine poured into stemmed glassware. Customs changed over time, and while some writers describe elaborate banquets, most medieval families dined with less ceremony. By the tenth century meals generally took place in a room that served many purposes. Diners sat upright at a rectangular table laid with a different kind of service. Silver plate continued to be used by the wealthier families but was supplemented by colorfully glazed bowls and cups. Illuminated manuscripts and wall paintings regularly show a large serving bowl in the center of the table, with small, deep dishes, goblets, mugs, knives, and forks nearby. Dinner entertainment still included recitations of poetry or stories, mime, music, and dance.

Ten diners and a well-mannered dog gather for a late-medieval banquet. The table is set with platters, flagon, goblets, and other utensils for eating and drinking. The figure style and costume reflect Western influence at the time. From an illustrated paper edition of the *Book of Job with Commentaries,* dated 1362 and signed by Manuel Tzykandyles of Mistra. Photo courtesy of the Bibliothèque Nationale de France, Paris (ms. grec 135).

These usually followed the meal and were accompanied by more or less drinking of wine, as at the *symposiai* of classical times. Women were excused from the more dubious postdinner festivities. A woman's presence at drinking parties could be considered grounds for divorce.

Constantinople was always a city of fine dining. While the classical tradition of writing cookbooks did not continue into the Middle Ages, Byzantine menus can be pieced together from other sources. Historians sometimes mention the elaborately set table as the scene of important conversations. Dietary treatises clearly describe the benefits of a moderate, healthful diet. Byzantine moralists make clear that food reflects different levels of prestige yet scorn the extravagant tastes of social climbers. Arab and Western travelers report on local dining customs and the tremendous range of European and Asian cuisine they found in the capital.[18]

Fresh meat was the surest sign of rank. Lamb and beef became increasingly popular over time, and were supplied by large herds raised on the estates of Anatolia. Wild game from Thrace and Bithynia included gazelles, wild asses, sparrows, and other birds. Poultry and pork were generally looked down on as country fare. The city's most important source of protein was fish. Fishermen of the Bosphorus reliably netted tuna, mullet, turbot, mackerel, bass, lobsters, crabs, crawfish, shrimp, oysters, mussels, scallops, and shellfish. In the later medieval period anchovy, salt roe, and caviar were brought from the Black Sea, with pickled herring coming from northern Europe. Fish sauces mentioned by medieval visitors continue more or less directly the well-known, aromatic *garum* favored by classical epicures. The *Geoponika* gives an updated recipe: "Prepare a brine salty enough that an egg will float in it ... Put the fish in the brine in a new earthenware pot, add oregano, and place it over a flame sufficient for the liquid to reduce gradually ... Then let it cook, and filter it several times until it become clear." Meats preserved by salting, smoking, and drying were a necessary, if less highly regarded option. Butter and cheese were medieval staples with different kinds available in the market. Cretan, Paphlagonian, and Vlach cheeses were especially prized in the capital.[19]

Like all Byzantines, elite families preferred the finest grades of wheat bread and ate darker grains only under duress. Vegetables were an important if underappreciated part of the menu, and usually were served cut up and cooked with meat. Fresh cabbage, beans, lentils, carrots, and greens were the most widely consumed; garlic, leeks, and onions were used for seasoning. Byzantine cooks prepared meals with native and imported spices like caraway, cardamom, cinnamon, clove, coriander, cumin, ginger, juniper, marjoram, mustard, nutmeg, pepper, poppy, rosemary, and saffron. Ground cumin and its relative ajowan had long appeared in Mesopotamian, Greek, and Roman cooking. Spicy coriander berries and leaves were favored in stews. Dark red sumac berries made a seasoning both colorful and pungent. Typical menu items included roast meats and casseroles prepared with meat or fish, cooked in oil with eggs or cheese, cabbage, garlic, onions, and pepper. The growing taste for meat was accompanied by the greater use of butter and animal fat in cooking. Fresh fruit did not travel well and was always in demand. Citrus, figs, and pomegranates came from the Aegean coastlands, while Anatolian apples, pears, cherries, and grapes were highly prized. Fruit, puddings, and honey-sweetened pastries, the ancestors of modern baklava and halva, were favored deserts. Special dishes were prepared for the Lenten fast and other holidays.[20]

Meals were accompanied by wine mixed with water. Distinct vintages came from all parts of the empire. Syrian and Palestinian wines were especially popular in late antiquity. A well-stocked medieval cellar would have included wines from around the Aegean. Clear, fresh water was always appreciated. Fennel, sage, and other herbs steeped in hot water gave a delicately flavored beverage known today in Greece as "mountain tea" (*vouno tsai*) or in Turkey as "island tea" (*adaçay*). Coffee beans, while grown in Ethiopia and Yemen in late antiquity, were not available in the Mediterranean before commercial cultivation began in Arabia in the fifteenth century. Turkish *kahve*, today sometimes fancifully called "Byzantine coffee" in Greece and Cyprus, was not introduced before the sixteenth century.[21]

Urban Crowds Most urban lives went unrecorded. We can imagine members of the lower and middle classes experiencing conditions that were cramped, crowded, and uncomfortable. As in other cities, houses in Constantinople often consisted of two or three levels of small rooms arranged around a central court. A sturdy door stood between street and court, which was paved with brick or stone and had a covered portico on one or more sides. This open, multipurpose space was where the family spent much of the day, the women spinning and weaving, watching their children, and preparing the evening meal. Rooms were separated by movable screens and curtains, and served for winter dining, sleeping quarters, and household storage. The availability of water indicated social status. Better-off residents tapped into the municipal supply or drew rainwater from a cistern. Others had to fetch water from a neighborhood fountain. A small latrine would have been flushed by roof drains into the public sewer, more reliably in winter than during the warm, dry summer. Most families made do with septic pits that they emptied regularly. Frequent earthquakes and fires hit hardest the crowded, poorly built houses of the central neighborhoods, which needed rebuilding every few generations. The dwindling population left more space for this modest level of housing in the later Middle Ages. Over time many parts of town came to resemble villages, with animals stabled on the ground floor and living quarters removed to an upper level.

Many people rented space in multistoried tenements resembling those of imperial Rome. Written sources tell us such buildings were tall and set close to each other, often separated by only a narrow alley. Walls were built of mortared brick and stone. Floors and roofs were made of tiles supported on timber beams. Official decrees recognized persistent fire hazards by limiting their height to 100 feet. The twelfth-century poet John Tzetzes had a second-story apartment in such a building. In one of his letters he describes the inconveniences in familiar terms: uncut weeds surround his building, the street floods when it rains, his front door is blocked by road building, the plumbing does not work, and his neighbor keeps livestock as well as a dozen children of his own.

Such conditions were still better than those endured by the truly destitute. The nominal poverty level stood at the possession of 50 gold coins (nomismata), an arbitrary amount that remained on the books for centuries. Writers had several terms for the poor (*aporos, penes, ptochos*), but give little sense of the challenges they faced on a daily basis. Looking for odd jobs must have been an ongoing concern for many city dwellers. The more able-bodied carried heavy loads of dry goods, building materials, and garbage on their backs. Others survived by begging or scavenging in the streets. Saints' lives from the sixth and seventh centuries suggest that a beggar in the capital could scrape together 10 to 20 bronze folles in the course of a day. A basic meal at a street-side taverna might cost a follis or two and include salted mackerel or tuna, beans, and coarse dark bread washed down with cheap wine or vinegar. Other needs were met by exchanging found or stolen items. Life for the homeless must have been especially miserable during the damp winter months. Throughout the Middle Ages street people sought shelter in porticoes, plazas, and public buildings.

Attitudes toward the poor changed over time. The long-standing Roman concern for supporting the urban citizenry and maintaining social order survived in the distribution of free bread as late as the sixth century. State entitlements stopped with the loss of the eastern provinces and the sharp population decline of the seventh and eighth centuries. During the medieval period the church was the main source of public charity. The emperor and leading citizens helped the poor by giving alms, especially during religious festivals, but a more effective approach was their support of churches and monasteries with their missions, including hospices for the aged, sick, and destitute. Widespread philanthropy reflects ethical and spiritual motivations on the part of the donors, who were encouraged by Christian tradition and their hopes for the afterlife.[22]

ECONOMIC LIFE

The economies of classical antiquity were dominated by the cities of Greece and Rome, where urban crowds provided markets for the exchange of specialized goods and services. Constantinople's rapid growth created a dynamic new center in the east Mediterranean. This was encouraged above all by the needs of government: to support the imperial palace, maintain its many bureaucracies, and subsidize living costs by distributing flour and oil to residents. The capital was ideally situated for long-distance exchange, and a stable political environment encouraged merchants to bring commodities from far away. By the sixth century local markets featured amber, furs, and slaves from northern Europe, gold and incense from the Red Sea coast, precious gemstones from central Asia, and ivory, pepper, spices, and silk from India and China. The crises that interrupted exchange routes in the seventh and eighth centuries only strengthened the city's unique place in the medieval Mediterranean economy.

Local manufacturing and commerce were overseen by the eparch. The state had an obvious interest in maintaining the economic welfare of its citizens and supporting its own activities. This supervision was carried out through a complex system of trade guilds, associations of craftsmen, merchants, and other professionals that are enumerated in the tenth-century *Book of the Eparch*. Designated assessors, inspectors, and deputies monitored the membership of guilds; the location of shops; the accuracy of weights, measures, and currency used in the marketplace; and especially the activities of foreign merchants. Prices were closely regulated to maintain economic stability.[23]

Trades covered by the *Book of the Eparch*

1. Notaries
2. Jewelers
3. Bankers
4. Silk-garment merchants
5. Dealers in Syrian silks
6. Dealers in raw silk
7. Silk spinners
8. Silk weavers
9. Linen merchants
10. Perfume dealers
11. Candle makers
12. Soap makers
13. Victualers
14. Leatherworkers
15. Butchers
16. Pork dealers
17. Fishmongers
18. Bakers
19. Tavern keepers
20. Deputies
21. Cattle-market inspectors
22. Contractors, including joiners, plasterers, marble workers, locksmiths, and painters

Selections from the *Book of the Eparch*[24]

1. Notaries
   1. Whoever wishes to be appointed a notary must be elected by a vote and decision both of the *primikerios* and the notaries acting with him to ensure that he has a knowledge and understanding of the laws, that he excels in handwriting, and that he is not garrulous, nor insolent, and does not lead a corrupt life, but on the contrary is serious in his habits, guileless in his thoughts, eloquent, intelligent, a polished reader, and accurate in his diction ...
   2. The candidate must know by heart the forty titles of the *Manual of Law* and must also know the six books of the *Basilika*. He shall also have received a general education so that he may not make mistakes in formulating his documents and be guilty of errors in his reading ...
2. Jewelers
   1. We ordain that the jewelers may, if any one invites them, buy the things that pertain to them, such as gold, silver, pearls, or precious stones; but not bronze and woven linens or any other materials which others should purchase rather than they ...
   3. Following the old custom, on the regular market days the jewelers shall take their seats in their shops along with their statores or attendants in charge of their sales tables ...
   7. If any jeweler is found to have bought a sacred object, whether damaged or intact, without having shown it to the eparch, both he and the seller shall suffer confiscation.
3. Bankers
   1. Anyone who wishes to be nominated as a banker must be vouched for by respected and honest men who will guarantee that he will do nothing contrary to the ordinances; to wit, that he will not pare down, or cut, or put false inscriptions on nomismata or miliarisia, or set one of his own slaves in his place at his bank if he should happen to be occupied with some temporary duties, so that no trickery may thereby enter into the business of the profession ...
   2. The moneychangers shall report to the eparch the forgers who station themselves in the squares and streets in order to prevent them from indulging in illegal practices ...
10. Perfume dealers
    1. Each perfume dealer shall have his own station and try not to overreach his fellows. They shall watch one another to prevent any from lowering their prices or selling unreasonably small quantities, or keeping in stock victualers' wares or any other sort of common goods, for an unpleasant odor does not harmonize with a pleasant one. They shall sell pepper, nard, cinnamon, wood of aloes, ambergris, musk, incense, myrrh, balsam, wild beet, balm, assafoetida, thapsia, hyssop, and all other things of use in the trade of perfumers and dyers. They shall place their show tables with the containers in a line extending from the sacred image of Christ our Lord which is by the Chalke up to the Milion, so that these may send forth a savory aroma befitting the image and make pleasant the porches of the palace ...

17. Fishmongers
    1. The fishmongers shall take their stand in the so-called Greatest Vaults of the city to sell their fish. Each vault shall have an overseer whose duty it is to observe the cost of the fish at sea and the resale price, so that he may receive a commission of one miliarision on the nomisma.
    2. Those who sell fish shall not pickle them or sell them to strangers for export, unless there is a surplus, when they may do so to prevent their spoiling.
19. Tavern keepers
    3. Tavern keepers are forbidden to open their shops and sell wine or food before the second hour of the day (7 a.m.) on high festivals or on Sundays. At night they shall close their shops and put out the fires when the second hour arrives (7 p.m.), in order to prevent the habitual daytime patrons, if they have the opportunity of returning at night, from becoming intoxicated and shamelessly engaging in fights, acts of violence, and brawls.
22. Contractors
    1. All craftsmen, such as joiners and marble-workers, plasterers and others, who make an agreement and receive a deposit for the performance of any piece of work, shall not abandon this and undertake another before they have finished it ...
    4. Those who build walls and large domes or vaults shall exercise all care and skill to prevent the foundation from becoming weak and the structure crooked or uneven. For if it should collapse within ten years, unless by act of God, the builder must replace it at his own expense. If the undertaking is a large one, involving more than a pound of gold, the contractor who built it shall replace it with his fellow workmen without pay, with the employer furnishing the material. Clay structures shall be under observation for six years, and if a work collapses within this period through negligence on the part of the builder, he shall renew it without pay ...

Money and Banking

Byzantium's monetary economy was based on bronze, silver, and gold coinage. The law generally required taxes to be paid with gold, and state employees took most of their salaries in the same form. The supply of coins contracted sharply in the seventh century, however, and in later times many people simply swapped homemade crafts and services for things they needed. Informal exchange by barter became widespread in the provinces, particularly in remote towns and villages. Bargaining in kind surely went on in Constantinople, but coins remained integral to the local economy.

The mint of Constantinople was the only issuing authority for most of the Middle Ages. The workshop itself was in a secure part in the palace. Copper and bullion were brought from state-owned mines and cast in small blank disks. Mint officials supervised the cutting of metal dies with images of the current emperor and coruler, Christ or the Virgin, and an identifying text and date. Freshly struck coins entered circulation mainly as wages paid to civil servants and soldiers. With each transaction the emperor's image and authority were recognized by the Byzantine shopper.[25]

What we today call the financial-services industry occupied a marginal place in Byzantium. State policies discouraged the growth of an independent financial sector by actively regulating the economy and limiting entrepreneurial initiative. Like other professions, membership in the guild of bankers *(trapezetai)* was hereditary, an arrangement that ensured steady employment while limiting opportunities for horizontal movement. Standardized prices and exchange rates stabilized the market yet allowed for moderate growth.

Acquiring coins to pay taxes and other debts meant selling goods or visiting a money changer. Medieval money changers kept shops in key commercial districts near the city gates, close to the harbor, and along the Mese. Even routine transactions posed obvious potential for abuse and were closely watched. Strict rules governed the lending of money for profit, with a maximum of 4 to 12 percent payable as interest during the sixth century. Public attitudes were further influenced by church teachings that cast usury and financial exploitation in an unfavorable light. This cautionary outlook shaped an economy that was internally stable but in the end could not successfully compete with merchants from Italy and the West. The presence of professional financiers and moneylenders in the fourteenth-century capital shows how much the Byzantine economy had changed.[26]

The main commercial areas were concentrated along the north and south coasts. Two large harbors faced the Sea of Marmara: one built by Julian near the palace quarter, the other by Theodosius near the mouth of the Lykos river. **Markets and Trades** Huge warehouses and bakeries were set up nearby to handle the annual grain shipment from Egypt. To the north were two smaller harbors, the Prosphorion and the Neorion, as well as a long, naturally sheltered shoreline. With the loss of the eastern provinces most commercial activity shifted to the banks of the Golden Horn. Business thrived as docks, warehouses, and workshops were built from the Bosphorus as far west as the city walls. Concessions granted to the Italian republics encouraged the growth of trading centers on both sides of the Golden Horn in the eleventh and twelfth centuries.

Hundreds of small establishments—workshops, retail stores, tavernas, and restaurants—were scattered throughout the city. The most desirable locations lay along the Mese and major intersecting streets, with the central business district between the forums of Constantine and Theodosius. Certain professions congregated in different parts of town. Fish was sold at seaside wharves, while fresh produce could be found near the city gates. Butchers gathered around the Forum of Theodosius. West of Hagia Sophia the streets were filled with the hammering of copper workers. The quieter, sweet-smelling shops of perfume dealers lined the Mese next to the imperial palace. Shops faced directly onto the street or sidewalk, preferably under a sheltering portico. Most were small, with the ground floor serving as retail space for the proprietor who lived upstairs.[27]

Merchants used different instruments for weighing their goods. One of the most common kinds of scales was the steelyard *(kampanos)*, a horizontal metal bar with calibrated intervals. The bar was asymmetrically suspended by a chain and had a small lead-filled bust of an empress that served as a sliding counterweight. Equal-arm balances *(zyga)* had two pans attached by chains to a suspended beam. Large balances were used for weighing goods like dried meat and fish, vegetables, oil, butter, and cheese. Smaller sets were needed to assay coins, spices, silks, and precious metals. Sets of certified weights were stamped by the issuing authority and kept in special boxes. Small glass weights were used when assessing the value of individual gold coins. Agents of the eparch regularly checked the accuracy of balances and scales.

Bakers   Bakeries were found in all parts of town. Palaces and larger monasteries had their own ovens, but most citizens depended on public bakers. The *Notitia* suggests the fifth-century bread supply was processed by some 20 state bakers and given away at 107 distribution points. Many of these operations were located in the bakers' district (Artopoleia) near the Julian harbor. By the early sixth century local bakers must have been turning out thousands of loaves on a daily basis. At the same time more than a hundred private establishments served neighborhood needs. The smaller size of the medieval population did not lessen the importance of bread for local inhabitants. Bakers remained a privileged part of society and were excused from other public duties.

A typical bakery included rooms for storing flour, fuel, and water, a wide counter for kneading dough, and a permanent hearth or oven. Grain was sorted and milled in the countryside and carried as flour in woven bags or baskets. Keeping flour in large earthenware jars helped protect it from damp, mold, insects, and rodents. Separate pots were needed for yeast, which the *Geoponika* recommends making from ground millet. Ovens stood in a corner of the shop or an outer yard; either way, they posed a fire hazard and could be no closer than 10 feet from other buildings. Large ovens were built of bricks and had a separate firing chamber below the baking surface. Baking began very early in the morning and continued throughout the day. Neighborhood residents brought casseroles for warming in the afternoons.

Different kinds of bread were sold by weight at fixed prices. The highest quality was made of carefully sifted, hard-shelled durum wheat and was known as white or "clean" bread *(artos katharos)*. Less expensive bread of intermediate quality *(mesokatharos)* consisted of wheat blended with other grains. Darker, heavier grains—summer wheat, barley, rye, and millet—were used to make less expensive "dirty" bread *(ryparos)* for the poor. While shunned by most people, these darker cereals could be stored for long periods and were appreciated in times of drought or siege. Local bakers also produced specialty confections and cakes.

The meat supply was closely watched by the eparch. Most animals came from farms in Thrace and Bithynia or large **Butchers** estates in Asia Minor. On certain days of the week sheep, goats, pigs, and cattle were brought by ship or land and herded through the streets to local markets. The centrally located Forum of Theodosius was known as the main livestock center for most of the Middle Ages. Sheep from Asia were brought to the Prosphorion harbor and the nearby Strategion. Animals from Thrace were herded to the Amastrianum plaza. Poultry and game were sold near gates in the city walls. Animals were slaughtered and butchered in these markets or in street-side shops. Local regulations reflected popular prejudice in differentiating sheep and cattle dealers from those who worked with poultry and swine. Sophisticated urban palates had little taste for pork, which usually was smoked or made into sausage for the lower classes.

The seasonal migration of fish through the Bosphorus provided residents with a reliable source of seafood, even **Fishmongers** in times of siege. The most abundant species were bonito, mackerel, and tuna. Crustaceans, mollusks, and shellfish were sold locally. The lighter-flesh species were more highly regarded, and luxury products included bass and sturgeon as well as Black Sea caviar and roe. Most fish were sold in seaside markets, with the busiest found along the Golden Horn. Agents of the eparch inspected these markets and regulated prices on a daily basis. Independent fishmongers also carried their wares through the streets and sold fish door to door. Fresh seafood commanded a premium since it could not be stored. Each day's surplus was preserved by drying or salting, and then sold at a discount to local merchants or exporters. Preserved fish was an inexpensive mainstay of the common diet.

Local wine shops stocked products from across the Mediterranean. Most wines were shipped from their **Wine Dealers** source in sturdy ceramic amphorae. Varieties could be identified by a vessel's shape, size, or painted label. Large amphorae held up to seven or eight gallons and were kept cool and sealed as long as possible. The continued fermentation of unsold wine led to higher levels of acetic acid and lowered alcohol content, resulting in a kind of vinegar that was destined for tavernas and domestic use. Large households bought wine in bulk, but many people brought home smaller quantities in flasks and jars. At any given time a typical wine shop had several amphorae for decanting and sale. Wine of varying quality also accompanied simple meals in tavernas. Standard prices were fixed by the eparch and were nominally uniform across the city.

Excavated amphorae and literary sources tell us a great deal about the wine trade. In late antiquity much wine was imported from Egypt and Palestine, with products of the Gaza region enjoying an especially good reputation. Later authors praise the wines of Crete, Euboea, and the eastern islands of Lesbos, Chios, Samos, and Rhodes. Celebrated varieties came from the region of Mount Ganos in Thrace, western Asia Minor, and south Greece. In later centuries wines also were imported from Italy. Many Greek wines tasted sweet and heavy, and were commonly mixed with water before drinking. Popular tastes ran to vintages like muscat and malmsey, which were shipped to western Europe in the late Middle Ages. As in Roman times, some wines like *konditon* were flavored with pepper, cinnamon, cloves, aromatic herbs, honey, and minerals. Medieval authors recommend combining one part honey with four parts wine to make fermented *mulsum* to accompany appetizers. Vintners in south Greece tempered strong local wines with pine resin, either added directly or by storing in fresh pine barrels. Pliny and Dioscorides note that resinated wines were produced in classical times. Byzantine writers indicate that these products, like the modern retsina, were very much an acquired taste. Liudprand of Cremona, for one, did not care for it. Medieval distillers also continued the Roman practice of favoring liqueurs with anise, the pungent, licorice-flavored spice that originated in western Asia Minor and spread across the Aegean.[28]

Tavernas   Small drinking and eating establishments *(tabernai)* were found throughout town, in back-street neighborhoods as well as along the Mese. Taverna owners *(kapeloi)* sold wine with appetizers and simple meals to be eaten on the premises or taken away. All but the smallest places had a separate room for storing and preparing food. Customers sat on benches at a long table. A typical working-class meal might include an omelet, salted pork with garlic, and a heated side dish. Eating usually went together with conversation, singing, and gambling.

Affordable wine was the main attraction of most tavernas. Even the poorest customers could afford the cheap, acidic drinks that were always on hand. Most wines were cut with water before drinking and during the winter months were served warm. Some tavernas, known as *phouskaria*, sold specialty drinks flavored with cumin, fennel, anise, and thyme. Such beverages *(phouska)* might be made from mead or beer as well as wine or vinegar. Mead, a form of fermented honey, was said to be well suited to the cold, damp climate of northern Europe, where it was widely consumed. Beers made from roasted barley and millet had a long history in the Near East. Soldiers and mercenaries from the Balkan frontier may have been the main consumers of these specialties in the capital. Fruit liqueurs made of dates, pears, and plums are also known.

Naturally these places were extremely popular. The combination of fast food, cheap wine, easy conversation, and lowbrow entertainment drew people day and night. Diversions included dancing, singing, mime plays, fights, and sexual encounters. Gambling was a favorite pastime. Dice, checkers, backgammon, and other games of chance were played at the table and on the steps outside the front door. Drunkenness was a common occurrence and sometimes led to brawling and debauchery. Legislation tried to limit taverna hours, especially on Sundays and during Lent. The eparch could close tavernas altogether in times of crisis to keep soldiers from becoming incapacitated. Church leaders lamented the bad reputation of tavernas, calling them places of fornication and discouraging priests from visiting them. Saints' lives vividly describe both the attractions and moral hazards they posed.

Many small, privately managed shops carried food and dry goods for household use. Like the ubiquitous *pantapoleia* of modern Greece, these little stores *(saldamarioi)* were scattered among different neighborhoods so that, as the eparch decreed, "the populace may have at hand that which it needs to live." The most commonly stocked items were dried meat and sausage, olive oil, butter, cheese, and honey. Vegetables included dried legumes like broad beans, chickpeas, and lentils; pulses; and fresh greens. Some stores also sold wine, cloth, soap, pine oils, pots, and nails.[29] **Grocers**

Istanbul's famous Spice Bazaar continues a long tradition of local dealing in exotic goods. The Byzantine spice market was located near the palace quarter in the Portico of Achilles. Special vendors *(myrepsoi)* sold native and imported herbs for cooking and medicinal purposes, dispensing advice and offering a kind of pharmacy for city residents. Some of the best known domestic spices were ajowan, anise, caraway, coriander (cilantro), cumin, mustard, saffron, silphium, and sumac. Many of these plants had been used since prehistory and are still widely grown in the region. The *Book of the Eparch* mentions various aloes, hyssop, and asafetida *(assa)* as products of the Black Sea coast. The greatest demand was for exotic spices, which came overland from China and central Asia, and by sea from the Islamic ports of the Near East. Cinnamon (cassia) came from Sri Lanka and southeast Asia, and was a valued ingredient in medicines and perfumes. Cardamom was brought from southeast India. Ginger, with its beneficial digestive properties, was imported in dried and pickled forms from Eritrea, Sri Lanka, and south China. Pepper, which came mainly from India, had been the single most important trading spice since Roman times. When pepper was in short supply, domestic juniper berries were used as a substitute. The sixth-century monk Cosmas Indikopleustes names southern India and Sri Lanka as important sources of clove, pepper, musk, and aromatic mountain roots like costus *(putchuk)*, and nard (spikenard). Nutmeg and mace, which originated in the Banda Islands of the west Pacific, first reached the Mediterranean around the eighth century. Byzantine merchants prospered by fetching these treasured commodities and exporting them to western Europe in the late Middle Ages.[30] **Spices**

Professional groups of chandlers *(keroularioi)* are known as early as the seventh century, a time when candles began to replace oil-fueled terra-cotta lamps **Candle Makers** for domestic lighting. Wax and olive oil were the most common materials for making candles. The *Book of the Eparch* forbids using beef or sheep tallow, perhaps out of concern for fire hazard or air quality. Tapers were formed by dipping, casting in slender molds, or rolling flat sheets of wax around a string wick. Some candles were formed by repeatedly dipping both ends of a long wick and were sold in pairs. Candle makers were required to work out of shops and not sell their goods in the street or market. They often sold their wares by weight and with separate holders; broken candles might also be brought to them for repair. Candles and torches accompanied all kinds of ceremonies, from street processions to neighborhood worship services. The palace alone burned thousands of large candles each year. Several local monasteries and churches, including Hagia Sophia, maintained workshops that supplied their own needs. Torches were used for street lighting, but oil lamps and especially candles were the main sources of artificial light at home.

Textiles   Spinning and weaving were important activities in almost every household, but commercial cloth production and retailing were special concerns of the eparch. Linen and cotton, sometimes blended with wool for extra strength, came from different parts of the empire as well as neighboring states as both bulk fabric and finished articles of clothing. Linen products were bleached or left in their natural condition and finished in urban workshops. Weaving and clothes making could be done in large *ergasteria* or small shops with only a counter and space for a wood-frame loom. The treadle loom, which by the sixth century was known across the Near East, was three times more productive than the traditional warp-weighted looms used at home. The eparch grouped textile workers into several professional organizations. Women engaged in carding, spinning, and weaving cloth had their own holiday, the festival of Agathe, which they marked with a procession, church service, and dancing.

Linen and cotton clothing was lightweight and comfortable, and was worn by most people on a daily basis. Tunics were loosely fitted and came in various lengths. These were worn with trousers and an outer cloak, often made of wool. Good-quality wool was always in demand, with the best kind of angora and cashmere (so named after Ankara and Kashmir) coming from the eastern provinces. Dyeing and laundering woven fabrics required large vats, special detergents, and lots of heated water. Such tasks were the responsibility of a different group of guild workers, who operated small, neighborhood laundries.

Silk   The importance of costume is especially clear in the case of silk (*metaxa*), which was worn by all members of the court and aristocracy. Before the sixth century silk cloth was a luxury imported from China and India, either by sea or overland through the steppes of central Asia. The historian Procopius relates how in 554 two monks returning from the Far East smuggled with them the eggs of silk moths, and so introduced their cultivation to the Mediterranean. Both silk moths and the white mulberry trees they feed on proved well suited to the Aegean coastlands. Domestic production came to constitute a significant part of the medieval economy.

The commercial potential of silk making was realized in medieval Athens, Corinth, and Thebes, but large-scale production always centered on the capital. Court and church officials needed a great deal of silk for ceremonial garments, wall hangings, furniture covers, and diplomatic gifts. The state's economic interest is clear from the eparch's supervision of five distinct silk-related professions. Separate guilds oversaw acquiring raw materials, spinning and weaving, dyeing, distributing and retailing, and importing silk from abroad. The quality of state-run workshops was carefully regulated, with women specifically mentioned as among the most highly skilled workers. Foreign trade was strictly limited by the state.[31]

Leather goods were an integral part of classical life that only grew in importance in Byzantine times. For centuries **Leather** Mediterranean craftsmen had made flat sandals, lace shoes, and work boots out of tough animal hides. The workshops of Constantinople also turned out special fashions for court society, including elegant dyed shoes and high, fur-lined boots. Leather belts and fur cloaks became increasingly popular features of urban costume. In addition to such personal apparel, a great deal of leather was needed to furnish soldiers with armor, shields, tents, and cavalry fittings. Palace bureaucrats, churchmen, and writers, moreover, demanded a growing supply of parchment made from the hides of calves and sheep. In late antiquity most of the empire's official needs for leather goods were met by state-run factories, but by the tenth century the leatherworkers in Constantinople had been organized into several different guilds. Large livestock herds kept on Anatolian estates were important suppliers of the capital. Hides usually were cleaned and tanned in the villages, before being brought to town for specialized processing. Jews and Italian merchants were active participants in the leather trade during the late years of the empire.

Many area residents were involved in the building trades. No doubt military engineers designed the forti- **Construction** fications, aqueduct, and harbors, but most of the urban fabric—streets and plazas, shops and houses, churches and monasteries— was the result of local effort. The Great Palace, the church of Hagia Sophia, and other major projects were undertaken by teams of trained workers supervised by professional engineers. By contrast, most medieval construction was done by local builders perhaps advised by a master mason (*protomaistor*). Brick makers, stonemasons, carpenters, and ironworkers probably belonged to separate guilds. A project of any size employed crowds of unskilled laborers as well.

Most materials came from the city's environs. Bricks and roof tiles were made in suburban brickyards along the coast of Thrace and Bithynia.

The same forests that fueled the kilns also supplied timber for scaffold-ing and roofs. Stone came from local quarries, particularly the island of Prokonnesos in the Sea of Marmara. This was the empire's best-known source of marble in late antiquity. Generations of skilled stoneworkers carved columns, bases, capitals, and cornices out of the fine, gray island marble. Heavy architectural blocks were carried by ship to Constantinople and other eastern cities. Colored marbles were brought from specialty quarries in Greece and Asia Minor. The marble trade declined in the seventh century, but the materials of early Constantinople were recycled throughout the Middle Ages.[32]

THE RHYTHMS OF PUBLIC LIFE

Constantinople, as the seat of political and religious authority, had a full calendar of special occasions. Classical pastimes like athletic competi-tions, theatrical performances, and recreational bathing survived into late antiquity but were transformed by economic and social pressures. In their place the church developed its own ceremonies and festivals that were observed here and across the empire.

Imperial Rituals
The emperor was the physical embodiment of the state, and his enactment of prescribed ceremonies was a key part of his job. Byzantine doctrine held that the emperor was chosen by God and ruled as his earthly representative. Imperial cer-emonials were designed to reflect this vision of divine grace, with the splendor of the palace reflecting the imagined glory of a heavenly court. Properly executed, ritual validated the Orthodox sense of order for both citizens and visitors; performance was no frill but a vital part of state-craft. Constantine VII introduces the *Book of Ceremonies* with the hope that imperial power might "reproduce the harmonious movement that the Creator gives to this entire universe, and may appear to our subjects more majestic and, at the same time, more pleasing and admirable."[33]

Stage-managing the elaborate settings, sumptuous costumes, and formal protocols required a team of dedicated professionals. For most of the Middle Ages this was done by high-ranking eunuchs who were brought up within the palace. This permanent staff guided the imperial family at every stage. The future emperor was born in the famed purple chamber of the Great Palace. He was christened and eventually crowned by the patriarch in Hagia Sophia. With his family he attended services in the palace, returning to the cathedral for important festivals and special liturgies. He conducted state affairs in special halls, recognizing officials, bestowing honors, receiving ambassadors, and distributing gifts and rewards. His death was similarly ritualized, from preparations of the body to services in the cathedral and burial in the imperial mausoleum.

State and religious holidays filled the calendar, with as many as 66 major festivals *(panegyreis)* and 27 minor feasts observed in the twelfth century. Constantinople's foundation was celebrated on May 11 with public pageants and dispensations, chariot races in the hippodrome, and church services throughout the city. Traditional observances of the new calendar year and the fall harvest involved the emperor as well. September 1 marked the beginning the liturgical year with its cycle of dominical, Marian, doctrinal, occasional, and sanctoral feasts recorded by the *Typikon of Hagia Sophia* and the *Synaxarion of Constantinople*. Key events included Annunciation (Evangelismos, March 25), Nativity (Christougennos, December 25), Epiphany (January 6), Presentation (Hypapante, February 2), and the mobile feasts of Easter (Pascha) and Pentecost. Festivals associated with the Virgin, such as the annunciation of her birth (September 8) and her ascension into heaven (Koimesis, August 15), were especially important since she was the city's special protector. The Festival of Orthodoxy on the first Sunday of Easter Lent commemorated the ninth-century defeat of iconoclasm. Divinely guided victories over the Arabs, Avars, Rus, and other enemies were regularly observed. The list was rounded out by feast days of local martyrs and saints closely related to the imperial family.

Ritual activities were not confined to the palace but took place throughout town. Together with his bodyguard and other officials, the emperor inspected public works, recognized local functionaries, visited churches and shrines, and venerated relics and icons. At different times he was expected to walk, ride on horseback, or travel in a chariot through the streets, which were hung with garlands, flowers, and silk tapestries and lit by torches. As philanthropist-in-chief the emperor gave food, clothes, and gold coins to the poor. All these occasions involved long processions, colorful banners, noisy musical fanfare, and the participation of many people. Accompanying members of the Blues and Greens led public acclamations in the forums, in front of churches, and especially in the hippodrome.

The happiest moments were when the triumphant emperor returned from battle. After being greeted by civic leaders at the Golden Gate, the *basileus Rhomaion* led his troops down the main street of the capital. Splendidly attired and riding an elaborately caparisoned white horse, he was cheered by the public at scheduled receptions in each forum and plaza. At the Forum of Constantine the emperor was met by the patriarch and from here walked the final stretch of the Mese to the cathedral for a special service of thanksgiving. Afterward he appeared in the imperial box in the hippodrome, presiding over the display of prisoners and booty and distributing the fruits of victory to his people. The exhilarating, day-long sequence of events, which began outside the walls and culminated at the heart of the city, echoed the ritualized triumphs of classical Rome and reinforced Byzantium's sense of tradition and divine sanction.

Spectator sports were the chief entertainment of urban crowds in late antiquity, but by the seventh **Sporting Events** century had withered before rising costs and changing

A triumphal procession through the streets of Constantinople, with the tenth-century emperor John Tzimiskes accompanied by an icon of the Virgin. Detail from the late-twelfth-century edition of the *Skylitzes Chronicle*. Photo courtesy of the Biblioteca Nacional, Madrid (ms. vitr. 26–2).

tastes. Theodosius moved to suppress the Olympic Games around 393, although they continued to be held for a few years in some remote places. Later displays of wrestling, boxing, running, jumping, discus throwing, and archery are known only in the capital. Gladiatorial events were never very popular in the East and in the fourth century were banned altogether. Violent animal combats gradually shifted to staged fights and exhibitions of bears, leopards, lions, and other exotic animals, which could still be seen in the twelfth century. Hunting and falconry were pursued mainly by aristocrats and emperors. The main sport to survive into the late Middle Ages was chariot racing.

The Hippodrome

The hippodrome was one of the most imposing structures in town. This enormous, open-air race track stood next to the imperial palace. The first hippodrome had been built by Septimius Severus as a copy of the Circus Maximus in Rome. Constantine enlarged the structure and later emperors added their own improvements. For a thousand years the hippodrome offered spectators a thrilling stage for action, spectacle, and violence. Certainly the most popular events were chariot races, but at other times the hippodrome was used for displays of wild animals, armed combat, and athletic competitions. Criminals and prisoners were publicly paraded, flogged, burned, or decapitated. Victorious generals displayed their captured prisoners and spoils. Bedecked with special banners and tapestries, the hippodrome offered a place where citizens could see their emperor and express their opinion of his reign.

The hippodrome consisted of an elongated arena measuring some 1,500 feet long and 400 feet wide. The main entrance was to the north and was crowned by a tower supporting four life-size horses of gilded bronze,

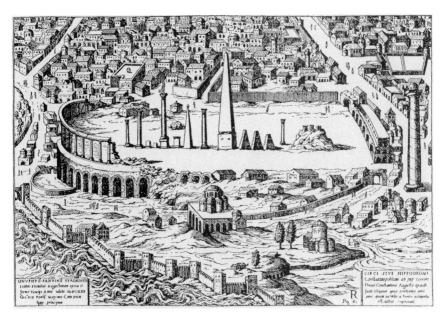

The area of the hippodrome in the sixteenth century. The obelisk of Theodosius was the tallest monument on the central *spina* of the racetrack. Engraving by Onofrio Panvinio, originally published in *De Ludis Circensibus* (Venice, 1600).

originally brought from Chios and taken to Venice after the Fourth Crusade. A high central median *(spina)* ran down the middle of the track, leaving enough room for turning at either end. The racing surface was compacted earth covered with sand. Starting gates *(carceres)* were to the north. The other three sides were surrounded by 30 to 40 stepped rows of seats, with an estimated capacity of 60,000–80,000 spectators. The original seats were made of brick and wood, but gradually were replaced by marble benches that rested on vaulted chambers used by concessionaires. These continued around the south end of the hippodrome in a broad curve known as the *sphendone*. A massive terrace still supports this end of the structure.

The best seats were on the long sides of the track, with the least desirable area in the sphendone. The imperial balcony or box *(kathisma)* on the east side was directly accessible from the palace. Looking across the track the emperor saw the spina with its many monuments, including the famous column of entwined serpents from Delphi, the statue of Herakles Trihesperos by Lysippos, imperial portraits, and other sculptures brought from across the empire. The most impressive surviving monument is the 65-foot-high obelisk of Thutmosis III, which Theodosius I brought from Karnak to commemorate his victories over the Goths and Persians. Figural reliefs carved on the stone base depict the imperial family in the kathisma, surrounded by court officials, soldiers, and defeated enemies. Smaller scenes illustrate the raising of the obelisk, chariot races, public dancing, and other entertainments. These enduring images of imperial power would have been familiar to city residents and visitors throughout the Middle Ages. A second pseudo-obelisk was built of limestone blocks at some later date. Other monuments celebrated the triumphs of particularly successful charioteers.

Races were announced by raising a special banner atop the gate tower. Spectators were admitted free and could see as many as 25 races in a single day. Since seats were hard and uncomfortable, spectators rented chairs or brought cushions or rugs to sit on. There was no shelter and one could expect to endure rain, wind, and sun. None of this dampened public enthusiasm.

Events normally saw four teams of horse-drawn chariots compete in a race of seven laps. Starting lanes were assigned or determined by drawing lots. Horses raced in a counterclockwise direction. In a typical event they might cover two and a half to three miles, more than twice the length of the Kentucky Derby. As in the Roman circus, hippodrome contests were intense and dangerous, which resulted in injuries among spectators as well as participants. Partisan factions known as the Blues, Greens, Reds, and Whites cheered their own teams, sometimes breaking into violent clashes with each other and civil authorities. In their original form these factions were politically motivated. During the sixth century the Blues generally represented conservative, elite interests while the Greens drew from the more radical lower classes. Justinian and Theodora were closely allied with the Blue faction, even though Theodora's father had worked as a bear keeper for the Greens. By the medieval period such political overtones had disappeared and only the Blues and Greens were still active, appearing primarily to lead acclamations of the emperor.

Chariot racing in the hippodrome. Relief from the fourth-century obelisk base of Theodosius, which is depicted standing with other monuments on the spina. Courtesy of the author.

Chariot drivers wore bright tunics in the color of their faction. The most celebrated charioteer of late antiquity was Porphyrius, whose many victories were commemorated by a stone monument on the spina. Intensive rivalries among charioteers and their supporters offered fertile ground for sorcery, and indeed scores of lead curse tablets have been found in provincial cities with inscriptions wishing misfortune on opposing drivers and horses. This was just one more reason for church leaders to denounce the hippodrome and its activities. Charismatic charioteers attracted large crowds of unruly supporters and sometimes were credited as magic workers themselves. Writing in the fourth century, Amphilochus of Iconium characterizes the races as a contest in sorcery as much as athletics.

The hippodrome was fully booked in late antiquity, with races marking public holidays and religious festivals alike. Between events spectators could watch acrobats, dancers, musicians, wild animals, and even fireworks displays. The frequency of competitions gradually succumbed to their high costs and the disapproval of the church, yet racing remained extremely popular with the public. Races were still being held in the twelfth century, mainly on festivals and other special occasions. The races known as *chryson hippodromion,* for example, came the week after Easter. Other equestrian contests included a form of polo *(tzykanion)* brought from Persia in the fifth century. This fast-paced game was played by two mounted teams that pursued an apple-sized leather ball with netted sticks, similar to lacrosse rackets. Twelfth-century mercenaries from western Europe took up the game and introduced a few of their own, with jousting tournaments *(tornemen* and *dzoustra)* taking place in the sphendone. At the same time, the hippodrome remained the capital's main assembly site and place of public spectacles, punishments, and executions.[34]

The theater was the second-most-popular entertainment inherited from classical antiquity. The citizens of Rome had **Theaters** long been in the habit of attending public performances, and by the fifth century at least four open-air theaters were operating in Constantinople. Stage productions were far removed from classical literary drama, and ran from elaborately choreographed pantomime and mime shows to acrobatic and illusionist displays, juggling, and performances by trained animals. One of the most popular events was pantomime, a balletlike reenactment of mythological tales performed by actors wearing large, expressive masks. Mime shows provided more broadly comedic entertainment, with much burlesque and slapstick. The predictable plots were commonly drawn from classical mythology and involved mistaken identities, crime, violence, and sex. Actors wore elaborate costumes over their usual clothes and performed amid stage settings with painted backdrops. Special effects included dramatic lighting, evocative sounds, water displays, and machinery for making flying entrances and exits. Musical accompaniment was provided by voice, flutes, pipes, lyres, and drums.

Unconventional performances and immoderate public response won the theater harsh disapproval by public authorities. Church leaders roundly condemned displays by actors and mimes as licentious, even when they were being invited to play in the palace itself. The stage was known to attract socially marginal individuals, especially foreigners and women, who comprised a cultural demimonde within the city. Fairly or not, women who worked in the theater were widely seen as prostitutes. Public decrees issued in the sixth and seventh centuries banned pantomime and mime performances and left theaters everywhere to decay. The hippodrome, with its reduced schedule of sponsored races, remained the city's main place of entertainment. In the later Middle Ages bands of acrobats, illusionists, jugglers, and storytellers toured towns and villages, while mimelike performers continued to play back streets and tavernas. Acceptable theater moved indoors to become part of religious liturgy, funerary oratory, and palace ceremonials. A surviving example of liturgical drama, "The Three Holy Children in the Fiery Furnace," was still performed in the fifteenth century.[35]

Popular Festivals
The official calendar was dominated by the reassuring cycle of imperial ceremonies and church liturgies, but the people of Constantinople observed other occasions as well. Every family had personal traditions: children's birthdays and name days were joyfully celebrated, and wedding anniversaries were marked with dinners and parties. Departed family members were remembered in graveside rituals continued from early times. Professional or vocational status brought other festive opportunities. Members of the court looked forward to their annual recognition by the emperor, who awarded honorific titles, gifts of land and silk costume, and salaries in the throne room during the week before Palm Sunday. Clerical teachers and students observed the feast of the Holy Notaries on October 25 by donning costumes, staging comic shows, and parading through the streets to the church of their guild patrons, Saints Markianos and Martyrios. Women who were involved in the textile trades celebrated the festival of Agathe on March 12. Wool carders, spinners, and weavers were among those who gathered for a ritualized performance of their crafts and processions with dancing and singing.

Constantinople also had its own distinctive holidays, including some with pre-Christian overtones that lingered well into the Middle Ages. Each new year began with Calends on January 1–4, when residents hung laurel wreaths on doors, held costumed parades, and exchanged gifts. The ancient feast of Bota on January 3 originally involved public prayers and sacrifices, with footraces still being run in the hippodrome in the tenth century. Rome's legendary founding on February 15 was observed by the Lupercalia, a fertility festival mentioned as late as the sixth century. Constantinople's official anniversary on May 11 was a time of grand processions and worship services; the following day was filled with popular celebrations, with dancing in the streets and chariot racing from dawn till dusk. One of the most enduring Byzantine holidays was Brumalia, the feast of Dionysus. This venerable harvest festival ran from November 24 through the winter solstice, and involved the court as well as the citizenry. The high point of Brumalia was unsealing the first vintages of fall. At such times city streets were filled with impromptu processions, boisterous masquerades, displays of exotic animals, races, drinking, and general carousing.

Some church holidays acquired their own extracurricular traditions. Byzantium never developed a pre-Lenten carnival but observed a series of partial fasts *(apokreas* and *tyrophagy)*, which included giving up first meat, then cheese, and finally all animal products during the weeks before Easter. Occasional markets were held in open areas of the medieval city. Commercial fairs *(panegyreis)* grew up around the feast days of local saints near Ephesus, Thessaloniki, Trebizond, Sinope, and other provincial towns. The best-known *panegyreis* coincided with the fall harvest or the sailing seasons, and drew huge crowds that had to gather outside the walls. Such festivals brought together luxury goods, exotic animals, and merchants from Europe, Africa, and Asia. They reproduced, if only for a little while, the worldly society found every day in Constantinople.[36]

NOTES

1. Philip Mansel, *Constantinople: City of the World's Desire, 1453–1924* (New York: St. Martin's Press, 1996); John Freely, *Istanbul: The Imperial City* (New York: Penguin Books, 1998). For general introductions to the Byzantine city see Glanville Downey, *Constantinople in the Age of Justinian* (Norman: University of Oklahoma Press, 1960); John E. N. Hearsey, *City of Constantine, 324–1453* (London: John Murray, 1963); David Talbot Rice, *Constantinople: From Byzantium to Istanbul* (New York: Stein and Day, 1965); M. Maclagan, *The City of Constantinople* (New York: Praeger, 1968); D. Jacobs, *Constantinople: City on the Golden Horn* (New York: Harper and Row, 1969); and Dean A. Miller, *Imperial Constantinople* (New York: Wiley, 1969).

2. For recent conferences on topography and urban history, see Cyril Mango and Gilbert Dagron, eds., *Constantinople and Its Hinterland* (Aldershot, England: Variorum, 1995); "Constantinople: The Fabric of the City," *Dumbarton Oaks Papers* 54 (2000): 157–264; and Nevra Necipoğlu, ed., *Byzantine Constantinople: Monuments, Topography and Everyday Life* (Leiden, the Netherlands: Brill, 2001). A recent survey of buildings is John Freely and Ahmet S. Çakmak, *Byzantine Monuments of Istanbul* (Cambridge: Cambridge University Press, 2004).

3. These forward defenses are surveyed by J. G. Crow, "The Long Walls of Thrace," in Mango and Dagron, *Constantinople and Its Hinterland*, 109–24. For urban fortifications see Freely and Çakmak, *Byzantine Monuments of Istanbul*.

4. For a recent illustrated overview see Stephen Turnbull, *The Walls of Constantinople, A.D. 324–1453* (Oxford: Osprey Publishing, 2004).

5. Cyril Mango, "The Water Supply of Constantinople," in Mango and Dagron, *Constantinople and Its Hinterland*, 9–18. For the classical background see A. Trevor Hodge, *Roman Aqueducts and Water Supply* (London: Duckworth, 1992).

6. Odo of Deuil, *De Profectione Ludovici VII in Orientem: The Journey of Louis VII to the East*, ed. Virginia Gingerick Berry (New York: W. W. Norton, 1948), 53; Johannes Koder, "Fresh Vegetables for the Capital," in Mango and Dagron, *Constantinople and Its Hinterland*, 49–56; Ewald Kislinger, "Christians of the East: Rules and Realities of the Byzantine Diet," in *Food: A Culinary History from Antiquity to the Present*, ed. Jean-Louis Flandrin, Massimo Montanari, and Albert Sonnenfeld, trans. Clarissa Botsford (New York: Columbia University Press, 1999), 194–206.

7. Demetrios J. Constantelos, *Byzantine Philanthropy and Social Welfare* (New Brunswick, N.J.: Rutgers University Press, 1988). For the *orphanotropheion* see Timothy S. Miller, *The Orphans of Byzantium: Child Welfare in the Christian Empire* (Washington, D.C.: Catholic University of America Press, 2003).

8. Odo of Deuil, *Journey of Louis VII to the East*, 65 (clearly a foreigner's perception); building codes are in Deno John Geanakoplos, *Byzantium: Church, Society, and Civilization Seen through Contemporary Eyes* (Chicago: University of Chicago Press, 1984), 261–62; and in general see Marlia Mundell Mango, "The Porticoed Street at Constantinople," in Necipoğlu, *Byzantine Constantinople*, 29–51. Further details of street life are in Virgil S. Crisafulli, trans., *The Miracles of St. Artemios: A Collection of Miracle Stories by an Anonymous Author of Seventh-Century Byzantium* (Leiden, the Netherlands: Brill, 1997).

9. Edmondo de Amicis, *Constantinople*, trans. Caroline Tilton (New York: G. P. Putnam's Sons, 1888), 108–13; Mansel, *Constantinople*, 288–89. Or as recalled by Mark Twain in *Innocents Abroad* (New York: Harper and Bros., 1911), 2:79–83: "sleeping happily, comfortably, serenely, among the hurrying feet, are the famed dogs of Constantinople."

10. Averil Cameron and Judith Herron, eds. and trans., *Constantinople in the Early Eighth Century: The Parastaseis Syntomoi Chronikai* (Leiden, the Netherlands: Brill, 1984), 91; compare other views in Cyril Mango, "Antique Statuary and the Byzantine Beholder," *Dumbarton Oaks Papers* 17 (1963): 55–75; and Helen Sarandi-Mendelovici, "Christian Attitudes toward Pagan Monuments in Late Antiquity and Their Legacy in Later Byzantine Centuries," *Dumbarton Oaks Papers* 44 (1990): 47–61.

11. Procopius, *Buildings*, trans. H. B. Dewing (Cambridge: Harvard University Press, 1940; reprinted 1961), 1.3.6; Michael Psellos, *Chronographia*, trans. E. R. A. Sewter (as *Michael Psellus, Fourteen Byzantine Rulers*) (Harmondsworth, England: Penguin Classics, 1966), 6.186–87; Antony Littlewood, Henry Maguire, and Joachim Wolschke-Bulmahn, eds., *Byzantine Garden Culture* (Washington, D.C.: Dumbarton Oaks, 2002). See Freely and Çakmak, *Byzantine Monuments of Istanbul*, for a recent survey of churches.

12. For Christopher of Mytilene's view see Nicolas Oikonomides, "Life and Society in Eleventh Century Constantinople," *Südost-Forschungen* 49 (1990): 8. The best known of thousands of purported relics are discussed in Liz James, "Bearing Gifts from the East: Imperial Relic Hunters Abroad," in *Eastern Approaches to Byzantium*, ed. Antony Eastmond (Burlington, Vt.: Ashgate, 2001), 119–31. An eleventh-century letter attributed to Alexios I Komnenos lists the most celebrated relics, which were mostly lost or taken to western Europe after the Latin conquest of 1204; see Geanakoplos, *Byzantium*, 199–200. The Virgin's special role is summarized in Ioli Kalavrezou, *Byzantine Women and Their World* (New Haven, Conn.: Yale University Press, 2003), 113–19.

13. Some of Saint Photeine's relics were discovered when an ox was cured of blindness after drinking from a neighborhood well. For local healing cults see Crisafulli, *Miracles of St. Artemios,* 37–39.

14. Hagia Sophia is one of the most discussed monuments in the history of art. An illustrated popular introduction is Lord Kinross, *Hagia Sophia* (New York: Newsweek Books, 1972). Rowland J. Mainstone, *Hagia Sophia: Architecture, Structure, and Liturgy of Justinian's Great Church* (New York: Thames and Hudson, 1988), gives more technical analysis and other sources. For descriptions by Procopius, Paul the Silentiary, and other Byzantine writers see Cyril Mango, *The Art of the Byzantine Empire, 312–1453* (Englewood Cliffs, N.J.: Prentice Hall, 1972; reprint, Toronto: Medieval Academy Reprints for Teaching, 1986), 72–103; Procopius quoted 72–74.

15. Liudprand, *Antapodosis (Tit-for-Tat)* 6.8, in *The Works of Liudprand of Cremona,* trans. F. A. Wright (New York: E. P. Dutton, 1930), 209–10; epigram from the Greek Anthology (1.106) and the *Life* of Basil (83) in Mango, *Art of the Byzantine Empire,* 184, 194, with other accounts.

16. For imperial costume and accoutrements see Maria G. Parani, *Reconstructing the Reality of Images: Byzantine Material Culture and Religious Iconography (11th–15th Centuries)* (Leiden, the Netherlands: Brill, 2003), 11–34.

17. Paul the Silentiary, in *The Greek Anthology,* vol. 3, trans. W. R. Paton (New York: G. P. Putnam's Sons, 1917), 9.651.

18. Among recent introductions to classical dining are John Wilkins, David Harvey, and Mike Dobson, eds., *Food in Antiquity* (Exeter, England: University of Exeter Press, 1995); Andrew Dalby, *Siren Feasts: A History of Food and Gastronomy in Greece* (London: Routledge, 1996); and James N. Davidson, *Courtesans and Fishcakes: The Consuming Passions of Classical Athens* (London: Harper Collins, 1997). Adapted recipes for the adventurous can be found in Ilaria Gozzini Giacosa, *A Taste of Ancient Rome,* trans. Anna Herklotz (Chicago: University of Chicago Press, 1992); and Andrew Dalby and Sally Grainger, *The Classical Cookbook* (Los Angeles: J. Paul Getty Museum, 1996).

19. *Geoponika* 20.46, quoted in Gozzini Giacosa, *A Taste of Ancient Rome,* 29.

20. Food and dining in Byzantium are discussed by Andrew Dalby in "Biscuits from Byzantium," in *Siren Feasts,* 187–211; and idem, *Flavours of Byzantium* (Totnes, England: Prospect Books, 2003). Compare Western traditions at this time in Melitta Weiss Adamson, ed., *Regional Cuisines of Medieval Europe* (New York: Routledge, 2002).

21. Wines are discussed in Dalby, *Flavours of Byzantium,* 85–93. For food, wine, and coffee in Ottoman Istanbul see Suraiya Faroqhi, *Subjects of the Sultan: Culture and Daily Life in the Ottoman Empire* (London: I. B. Tauris and Company, 2000), 204–21.

22. Demetrios J. Constantelos, *Byzantine Philanthropy and Social Welfare* (New Brunswick, N.J.: Rutgers University Press, 1988); Timothy S. Miller, *The Birth of the Hospital in the Byzantine Empire* (Baltimore: Johns Hopkins University Press, 1997).

23. Two English translations are A.E.R. Boak, "The Book of the Prefect," *Journal of Economic and Business History* 1 (1928–29): 597–618; and Edwin Hanson Freshfield, *Roman Law in the Later Roman Empire: Byzantine Guilds, Professional and Commercial* (Cambridge: Cambridge University Press, 1938). This important document occupies a central place in discussion of the city's economy; see in general Gilbert Dagron, "The Urban Economy, Seventh–Twelfth Centuries," in *The Economic History of Byzantium,* ed. Angeliki Laiou (Washington, D.C.: Dumbarton Oaks, 2002), 1:393–461; and

Klaus-Peter Matschke, "The Late Byzantine Urban Economy, Thirteenth–Fifteenth Centuries," in Laiou, *Economic History of Byzantium*, 1:463–95.

24. Adapted from Boak, "The Book of the Prefect."

25. For an introduction see Philip Grierson, *Byzantine Coins* (Berkeley: University of California Press, 1982); and Cécile Morrisson, "Byzantine Money: Its Production and Circulation," in Laiou, *Economic History of Byzantium*, 3:909–66.

26. Nicolas Oikonomides, "Entrepreneurs," in *The Byzantines*, ed. Guglielmo Cavallo (Chicago: University of Chicago Press, 1997), 144–71; Dagron, "The Urban Economy."

27. For the organization of local businesses see Marlia Mundell Mango, "The Commercial Map of Constantinople," *Dumbarton Oaks Papers* 54 (2000): 189–207.

28. Pliny the Elder, *Natural History*, trans. H. Rackham, W.H.S. Jones, and D. E. Eichholz (Cambridge: Harvard University Press, 1938–62), 14.18–19; Dioscorides, *De materia medica* 5.48, in Robert T. Gunther, *The Greek Herbal of Dioscorides* (New York: Hafner Publishing, 1968); Liudprand, *The Embassy to Constantinople* 1.11, in Wright, *Works of Liudprand of Cremona*, 235; Dalby, *Flavours of Byzantium*, 85–93.

29. Dagron, "The Urban Economy," 461.

30. For background see J. Innes Miller, *The Spice Trade of the Roman Empire, 29 B.C. to A.D. 641* (Oxford: Clarendon Press, 1969). In general see Andrew Dalby, *Dangerous Tastes: The Story of Spices* (London: British Museum Press, 2000); and idem, *Food in the Ancient World from A to Z* (New York: Routledge, 2003).

31. Procopius, *Wars*, trans. H. B. Dewing (Cambridge: Harvard University Press, 1914–40; reprinted 1953–62), 8.17.1–8; Robert S. Lopez, "The Silk Industry in the Byzantine Empire," *Speculum* 20 (1945): 1–42.

32. Representative marbles are illustrated in Martin Harrison, *A Temple for Byzantium: The Discovery and Excavation of Anicia Juliana's Palace-Church in Istanbul* (Austin: University of Texas Press, 1989), 76–77. See also Jean-Pierre Sodini, "Marble and Stoneworking in Byzantium," in Laiou, *Economic History of Byzantium*, 1:129–46.

33. *Book of Ceremonies*, quoted in Geanakoplos, *Byzantium*, 21–22. For other perspectives see Miller, *Imperial Constantinople*, 21–41; Michael McCormick, "Emperors," in Cavallo, *The Byzantines*, 230–54; and Albrecht Berger, "Imperial and Ecclesiastical Processions in Constantinople," in Necipoğlu, *Byzantine Constantinople*, 73–87.

34. Racing and polo are discussed by Anthony Bryer, "Byzantine Games," *History Today* 17, no. 7 (July 1967): 453–59; Alan Cameron, *Porphyrius the Charioteer* (Oxford: Oxford University Press, 1973); and Barbara Schrodt, "Sports of the Byzantine Empire," *Journal of Sport History* 8, no. 3 (winter 1981): 40–59.

35. For the stage in late-antique Constantinople see Blake Leyerle, *Theatrical Shows and Ascetic Lives: John Chrysostom's Attack on Spiritual Marriage* (Berkeley: University of California Press, 2001), 13–41. For medieval performance see Walter Puchner, "Acting in the Byzantine Theater: Evidence and Problems," in *Greek and Roman Actors: Aspects of an Ancient Profession*, ed. Pat Easterling and Edith Hall (Cambridge: Cambridge University Press, 2002), 304–24.

36. Speros Vryonis, "The *Panegyris* of the Byzantine Saint: A Study in the Nature of a Medieval Institution, Its Origins and Fate," in his *Byzantine Institutions, Society and Culture*, vol. 1, *The Imperial Institution and Society* (New Rochelle, N.Y.: Aristide D. Caratzas: 1997), 251–91. For medieval festivals see Michael Angold, *Church and Society in Byzantium under the Comneni, 1081–1261* (Cambridge: Cambridge University Press, 1995), 457–60.

5

CITIES AND TOWNS

The Byzantine empire comprised a rich agricultural landscape dotted with settlements of all sizes. The great cities lay along the seacoast, communicating with each other by ship and controlling access to their productive hinterlands. Smaller towns of the interior occupied key positions along rivers and highways. In each case the distinctive patterns of settled life—from town planning to domestic housing, civil governance to family organization—were colored by local terrain and custom. Over the span of a millennium these settlements took on very different forms that reflected changing administrative and economic functions. The founding of Constantinople brought fresh prosperity to hundreds of cities across the Roman East, and in many cases this lasted into the sixth or seventh century. During the following years towns everywhere underwent dramatic changes, often shrinking to a fraction of their earlier extent or vanishing altogether. Medieval writers might still call these places cities, yet most were now only market towns or fortified outposts of minor significance. The revival of the capital, with its urgent demands for food, clothes, and luxuries, stimulated the recovery of cities from the Black Sea to south Italy and as far away as Cyprus. Thessaloniki profited from its strategic location in north Greece. Farther south, Corinth and Thebes grew into important centers of production and exchange. Ephesus, Pergamon, Philadelphia, and Smyrna reclaimed some of their urban significance in western Asia Minor. The Black Sea ports of Cherson, Sinope, and Trebizond blossomed as points for trade with the empire's northern neighbors. Provincial town dwellers shared many of the same experiences as their contemporaries in the capital, but their lives differed in important ways. Of all the cities of Byzantium, only Constantinople was a true *megalopolis*.[1]

PROVINCIAL SOCIETY

The classical city's transformation in late antiquity affected the lives of townspeople across the Mediterranean. For centuries the Greek *polis* (Latin *civitas*) had been considered the hallmark of civilized life and the center of social, economic, and cultural activity. Each city acted as the administrative focus of its own territory. It was ruled by local civic leaders and councilors *(curiales)*, and fashioned a unique identity out of its history and monuments. The mutual dependence of town and countryside created a mosaic of discrete economic units whose surplus production was increasingly absorbed by the imperial palace, first in Rome and then Constantinople, in the form of taxes. Beginning in the late fourth century the upper levels of provincial society were irresistibly drawn by new opportunities in the capital, with its glittering court and expanding bureaucracies. At the same time long-standing patterns of local investment shifted from underwriting honorific monuments and public amenities to setting up churches, monasteries, and charitable foundations. By the seventh century these structural changes had undercut the viability of many provincial centers. The empire's abrupt reorganization into large military districts or *themes (themata)* concentrated power in a handful of strategic centers that served entirely new purposes. Civil, judicial, and security concerns within each theme were managed by a military governor *(strategos)*, who reported directly to the emperor. Appointed subordinates maintained records and oversaw local matters. Viewed from the Great Palace, the main function of settlements was now fiscal: to serve as a base for raising taxes and recruits for the army. With few exceptions Byzantine towns did not develop the distinctive civic institutions found in medieval cities in western Europe. The church hierarchy followed parallel lines, with bishops supervising affairs within their sees and reporting at the diocesan level to a metropolitan. Civil and religious authority often converged as clergy gained considerable say in secular matters. Unsurprisingly, military and religious buildings were among the most conspicuous features of any medieval town.

Along with administrators and church officials, wealthy landowners *(archontes)* played a significant role in urban affairs. The most powerful families derived their wealth from rural holdings that had been built up over generations. Unlike Constantinople's elites, who drew income from court titles and distant estates, local magnates stayed close to their properties and took an active hand in their management. They kept fine houses and joined in the city's social and cultural life throughout the year. They raised their children at home, sent their boys (and sometimes girls) to study with local grammar teachers, visited each other's houses, shopped in local markets, and worshipped in neighborhood churches. Affluent families built villas in the surrounding countryside, where they stayed during the warm summer months. Landowners were well positioned to oversee business affairs. Many chose specialty crops to grow in the country and sell in town. As a result, well-to-do families became involved in all manner of commercial activities, from transporting and processing raw materials to retailing finished goods in regional markets. Some owned or leased space in local shops where they sold commodities from their estates. Others built ships and hired crews to pursue the greater profits of long-distance commerce. The economic success of provincial elites is clear from their imposing townhouses, elegant clothing, self-conscious letters, leisured activities, and especially the churches and monasteries they set up in their home territories.

We know much less about the lives of other townsfolk. Many no doubt coped with urban decline by turning to farming and herding, which left medieval cities much smaller as places of habitation and economic activity. Points of strategic value—administrative centers, harbors, hubs of communication—were heavily fortified and garrisoned by soldiers. Less important sites, often located on high bluffs or hilltops, were reinforced and staffed by a civilian guard drawn from area residents. The empire's economic expansion in the tenth and eleventh centuries helped rural residents find employment in urban workshops. The line between production and retail was extremely fluid. Many families spun flax or wool, wove cloth, or made baskets, pottery, and candles to sell or trade with their neighbors. Even specialized manufacturing was labor-intensive and inefficient, with craftsmen selling their wares out of small shops. In many ways medieval towns were little different from large villages.

THE CITIES OF LATE ANTIQUITY

The early Byzantine centuries saw the last phase of classical urban life. Cities across the Mediterranean had flourished under the patronage of Hellenistic kings and Roman emperors, who had organized labor and resources on a grand scale in building networks of closely knit population centers. By the second century cities of all sizes presented a monumental consistency that showcased the wealth and power of local elites in cooperation with the larger state. Urban planning was based on a framework of paved roads that joined the main buildings and districts. At the heart of any settlement was the civic center with its open-air meeting place, either a traditional Greek agora or a more regularized Roman forum. Around this space were state offices, law courts, records archives, and markets. In larger cities one might find the governor's residence (*praetorium*) together with a theater, stadium, or hippodrome. The most imposing structures were temples and shrines commemorating local religious traditions or the cult of the emperor. Throughout town one saw fountains, baths, and honorific monuments. Neighborhoods were filled with shops, tavernas, tenements, and houses.

Urban Continuity and Change   The shift of government from Rome to Constantinople boosted the fortunes of almost all Eastern cities. Places like Alexandria, Antioch, and Ephesus thrived and may have reached their greatest extent during the fifth and sixth centuries. In most cases the existing urban framework was maintained and Roman public spaces continued serving their intended purposes. City life focused on broad colonnaded streets that ran from the center of town into peripheral quarters. Flanking porticoes and shops formed covered shopping malls that were crowded with residents. The fourth-century orator Libanius praises the porticoes of Antioch as the most attractive and useful feature of his hometown.

Fortifications were one of the chief characteristics of these places. For centuries the Roman Empire's security had rested on legionary armies and a frontier that was secure and far away. Emerging threats during the third and fourth centuries prompted many cities to build defensives. These normally consisted of a tall brick-and-stone barrier reinforced by polygonal towers, less imposing than Constantinople's mighty walls but a formidable presence nonetheless. In the case of large cities, only part of the inhabited area might be enclosed. Builders everywhere seem to have

A gate in the well-preserved fortifications of Nicaea in northwest Asia Minor. First built in the third century, the walls were repaired throughout the Middle Ages. Courtesy of the author.

worked in haste, reclaiming old materials to be included in the walls. Local authorities and provincial governors cooperated in planning for defense.

A second major change was the emergence of the church as a key urban institution. The decline of classical temples over the second and third centuries left an opening for dynamic new religious centers. For most Romans public religion had been a spectator affair marked by occasional festivals that were glimpsed at state-run temples. By contrast, the early Christian liturgy was active and participatory, regularly marshalling noisy crowds for street processions and services in neighborhood churches. The main place of urban worship was the cathedral, normally a large basilica with a bishop and attendant clergy. The bishop's official residence *(episkopeion)* usually stood nearby and served as the center of church administration. Smaller parish churches, shrines, and monasteries sprang up throughout the city and became new landmarks for its inhabitants.

At the same time several familiar urban features were slowly disappearing. Theaters, with their risqué performances and unruly fans, were vigorously denounced by religious leaders, and by the sixth century had fallen into general decline. Chariot races, animal fights, and athletic competitions remained popular spectator sports but eventually succumbed to their immoderate expense. Public bathing in municipal bathhouses similarly suffered from high costs as well as ecclesiastical disapproval. Aging aqueducts could not meet the demand for water for recreation as well as sustenance. Economic and social pressures increasingly diverted local patronage from civic amenities to the activities of the church.

Housing made up the largest part of any city. Residential neighborhoods were defined by broad streets and subdivided by narrow roads and alleys. Fountains, wells, and latrines stood along the way, draining into underground sewers that carried away the city's wastes. Urban blocks were filled with houses that ranged from the fine homes of local elites to the ramshackle dwellings of most townspeople. The better houses were multistoried affairs built of mortared brick, stone, and timber and covered by tiled roofs. Smaller, less durable structures were of rubble and mud brick, and might be roofed with thatch. Rooms usually were arranged about an inner court that brought light and air into the heart of the residence. Separate spaces were designated for working, sleeping, and storage. Particularly large households had special rooms for receiving visitors, conducting business, and even worshipping at private chapels. The owner might use street-side rooms for commercial purposes or rent them out to independent craftsmen.

Excavations at Sardis in western Asia Minor provide a detailed view of life in one early Byzantine city. Located about 60 miles **Sardis** inland from the Mediterranean coast, Sardis was the capital of ancient Lydia and had an illustrious history long before becoming a base of Roman government. The city lay on the edge of a fertile valley near the meeting of two rivers. A high acropolis overlooked nearby highways and gave residents a place of retreat in times of emergency. Roman Sardis had its share of great monuments: an agora, odeon, hillside theater, stadium for races, and temples built in honor of Artemis, Apollo, and the Roman emperors. The main streets were paved with marble and flanked by colonnaded porticoes. Local inhabitants enjoyed bathing in several large complexes that were supplied by long aqueducts. The prominence of the local Jewish community is clear from the presence of a grand, splendidly decorated synagogue. Like other cities, Sardis saw important changes during late antiquity. New fortifications surrounded the central habitation area and rocky acropolis. The theater and stadium were used less often. Temples were abandoned around the same time that churches appeared. Still, at least one magnificent bath was operating well into the sixth century.

Exploration of a long row of street-side shops and apartments has documented the scene of lively commerce. These small, unexceptional spaces formed part of an urban block that included a public bath, gymnasium, and synagogue. Some 30 units stood behind a portico running along one side of the city's main street. This sheltered area was paved with mosaics and covered by a continuous sloping roof. Narrow doorways opened into each shop. Rooms measured about 16 feet square; the most spacious

The urban plain and fortified acropolis of Sardis. Once one of the great cities of western Asia Minor, the site has been sparsely inhabited since the seventh century. Photo © Archaeological Exploration of Sardis/Harvard University.

units were just over 30 feet wide. Floors were packed earth or paved with tiles. Furnishings and artifacts suggest the varied activities that took place here in the late sixth and seventh centuries. Different crafts were practiced side by side: one shop apparently was given over to selling and perhaps making earthenware pots; another dealt in glass goblets, flasks, and lamps; a third sold small pieces of bronze jewelry. One shop specialized in such hardware as iron blades, chisels, weights, and household locks (parts of more than a hundred were identified by the excavators). A few rooms were equipped with stone basins, vats, and mortars, and may have been involved with dyeing fabric or laundering clothes on a domestic if not commercial scale. Several restaurants or tavernas could be identified by heaps of butchered animal bones (mostly sheep, goat, and cattle), storage jars, and portable braziers for cooking. Some proprietors provided a front bench or service window for the convenience of their customers. Steps or a ladder reached from street level to an upper loft that could be used for storage and living quarters. The presence of crosses, menorahs, and sectarian inscriptions reflects the interaction of Christians, Jews, and others in this busy marketplace.[2]

Not far from this shopping district was a residential neighborhood with graceful townhouses. Some of these were built in Roman times and remodeled in late antiquity. One recently excavated *domus* shows how a

Reconstructed interior of a taverna or shop at Sardis in the sixth century. Customers sit on benches next to a serving counter. The proprietor and his family may have lived upstairs. Drawing by Elizabeth Wahle © Archaeological Exploration of Sardis/Harvard University.

well-to-do family lived in the fifth and sixth centuries. The building stood
at the corner of a block with doorways opening onto a colonnaded street
and a narrow alley. A high wall with few windows sheltered the house
from the noise and hazards of city life. Visitors would have arrived at one
of the main entrances and been greeted by the porter or slave assigned to
watch the door. The owner received business associates and clients in a
large room outfitted with a broad apse, paved with marble and mosaics
and surrounded by painted walls. Another part of the house was organized around a paved court with columns. This brightly lit, multipurpose
area was where family members greeted friends, prepared meals, spun
and wove clothes, and worked at household tasks. In one corner was a
large basin filled with fresh water from the city's aqueduct. One of the
most elegant parts of the house was a spacious room with marble floor and
painted walls. A semicircular marble table once set the stage for formal
dinners. Domestic quarters, including bedrooms, indoor latrines flushed

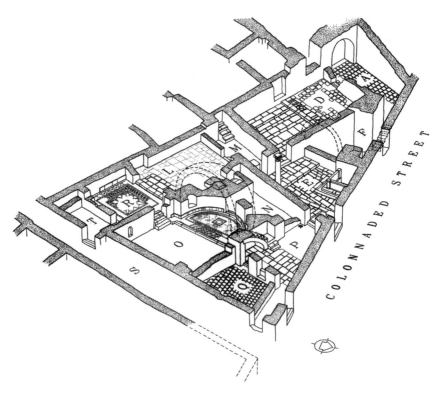

Isometric view of a sixth-century townhouse at Sardis. The building included an
open court with fountain (E), hall for formal receptions (O), and dining room (D).
Bedrooms would have been located on the upper level. Drawing by Philip Stinson
© Archaeological Exploration of Sardis/Harvard University.

with running water, and storage rooms, were located elsewhere on the main floor and on an upper level. The irregular organization of spaces into separate wings reflects the evolution of residential life over generations.

MEDIEVAL CITIES

The seventh- and eighth-century crises forever changed the appearance of Byzantine towns and cities. Military threats coupled with economic decline and recurring outbreaks of plague were met by tightening defenses around much smaller population centers. In many cases a reinforced hilltop complex (*kastro* or *phrourion*) served as both military outpost and short-term refuge for inhabitants in times of attack. Such places went by different names that reflected their functions as administrative stations, gathering points for local tax revenues, and market towns for local exchange. Order was maintained by civilian or paramilitary guards (*phylaxes*) rather than trained soldiers. During less settled times soldiers were garrisoned at strategic kastra, especially those that served as provisioning points for troops on the march. These remote outposts displayed the emperor's power to subjects and foreigners alike.[3]

The status of any medieval settlement was best expressed by its fortifications. Certainly defenses made up the largest **From Public** and most conspicuous part of any town. In most cases **to Private** they were built by state authorities with the help of army engineers and local labor. Major landowners no doubt had considerable influence in bringing kastra to their domains. When finished, these structures gave area residents a sense of security while projecting the presence of the empire at large. Each site posed its own challenges. Ancient cities like Antioch, Nicaea, and Thessaloniki lacked natural defenses and required constant effort to maintain their long walls. At Amorion and Ankara military planners could take advantage of an existing mound or hilltop. Fortifications usually consisted of a reinforced outer circuit and an inner fortress. Builders used whatever materials were available. Both the original circumstances of construction and later military campaigns can be read in the walls that survive.

Other large buildings were uncommon. By the eighth century inhabitants of Corinth, Thebes, Thessaloniki, and Ephesus were occupying a dilapidated physical infrastructure, which they maintained with dwindling success over the years. Changes were apparent everywhere. Instead of walking along wide, paved streets, one meandered through alleyways packed with tiny shops, similar to the crowded *souks* of the later Middle East. Decaying civic structures, theaters, and baths were dismantled for materials. Marble statuary and sculptural decoration were crushed into lime for mortar. The offices of thematic commanders, established at strategically important sites, were among the few public buildings to be consistently maintained.

The strategically important *kastro* of Ankara in Galatia in central Asia Minor. The city's extensive fortifications date from the seventh to ninth centuries. From Georges Perrot, Edmond Guillaume, and Jules Delbet, *Exploration archéologique de la Galatie et de la Bithynie d'une partie de la Mysie de la Phrygie* (Paris: Fermin Didot, 1872).

In most places the only substantial structures were churches and monasteries. These too reflected the medieval town's diminished population and resources. The great basilicas of late antiquity were only partially maintained or abandoned altogether. Small shrines replaced other churches. The most important building was the cathedral, yet this often looked little different from ordinary churches. Such buildings typically were timber-roof structures cobbled together of classical spoils, reused bricks, and stone. Few were vaulted and none was very large. Nearby stood the episcopal residence, whose prominence reflected the bishop's growing role in local affairs, even when he chose to live in Constantinople. The expanding medieval economy prompted some landowners to rebuild derelict churches and set up monasteries. Private wealth combined with tax incentives made new religious complexes the most innovative buildings in many places, with master craftsmen brought from far away to supervise their construction and decoration.

Houses were the scene of economic activity as well as residential life. The tenth- and eleventh-century revival grew out of the close relationship of agricultural production and household industry, with the result that urban houses came to resemble village dwellings in many ways. Elite

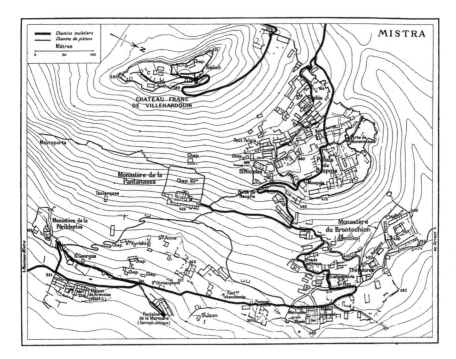

Plan of the late-medieval settlement at Mistra in south Greece. Houses, shops, chapels, churches, and monasteries cling to the steep slopes. The fortified keep at the highest point was likely added by the Latins in the thirteenth century. From Gustave Fougères, *Grèce* (Paris: Hachette, 1911).

residences often combined clusters of workshops and storerooms at street level with comfortable living quarters on an upper floor. A typical house consisted of several rooms facing onto an open court *(aule)* where animals could be stabled and produce stored. In some places the roof or upper floor was supported by low arches spanning the breadth of the room. The line between urban and rural life was increasingly hard to draw.

The site of Mistra in south Greece gives an excellent impression of what one late Byzantine city looked like. The settlement **Mistra** was built on the rocky slopes of Mount Taygetos overlooking the fertile plain of ancient Sparta. Between the thirteen and fifteenth centuries Mistra was home to several thousand residents, including relatives of the reigning Palaiologan family and some of the foremost scholars of the late empire. Their concern for security is clear from the town's hillside location and defensive circuit, which includes the lower settlement, a high kastro, and a fortified keep probably added in the thirteenth century by the Franks. When visiting Mistra today one can see half a dozen well-preserved churches as well as extensive remains of houses.[4]

The grandest residential structures belong to the so-called palace complex. This is a group of multistoried buildings arranged on two sides of a broad plaza, the largest level space in the city. Built over a span of 200 years, these buildings share many features of design and construction. Plans are compact and rectangular, with a portico on one side supporting an upper balcony. At ground level are small, vaulted chambers that were used for storage and other utilitarian purposes. A single large room dominates the main level, often extending the full width of the building. Traces of fireplaces remain in the walls. Broad windows look onto the plaza and across the lower plain. Clearly the owners spent much of their time in these imposing halls, where they received visitors, dined, and enjoyed the view. Curtains hung along the walls warmed the rooms and when drawn created smaller spaces. Bedrooms were nearby or on an upper level, and were similarly equipped with fireplaces, latrines, and windows. Reinforced towers gave added security for household possessions.

Smaller houses opening off narrow, winding roads once crowded the slopes. A typical house was a compact, detached unit set within an irregular yard. The scarcity of flat terrain encouraged builders to adapt to the site, sometimes building into the hillside atop a walkout cellar and utility level for animals and supplies. Residents spent most of their time

A reception room in the palace quarter at Mistra. Large windows looked onto a nearby plaza and across the valley plain. Chimneys, cupboards, and drains were recessed into the walls. Smaller spaces could be enclosed by drawing curtains and hangings. Courtesy of the author.

on the upper floor with its large windows and cooling breezes. Permanent fixtures included cupboards, chimney flues, and drains. If space allowed there might also be a street-side portico or balcony to capitalize on the expansive view so admired in the Middle Ages.

These well-to-do homes belong to the social level most often recorded by contemporary writers, who add further details to our picture of medieval home life. The defensive, inward orientation of houses, with their limited access, thick walls, and small windows, is echoed by frequently voiced concerns for security—from social rivals as well as common thieves. The household's focus was the main room where visitors were received, meals were prepared, and spinning and weaving went on.

A cobbled street lined with houses at Mistra. The walls of the fortified hilltop kastro can be seen throughout the city and across the plain. Courtesy of the author.

Floors were paved with tiles and spread with patterned carpets. Light came through high windows and at night from torches, candles, and oil lamps. Painted plaster and tapestries covered the walls. The fanciful palace described in the twelfth-century epic *Digenis Akritis* had paintings and woven hangings that depicted heroic hunts and battles. Around the same time, Leo Sikountenos decorated his house in Thessaloniki with images of Old Testament figures and more recent heroes. The main room could be subdivided by means of such hangings or wooden partitions. In the winter drafty balconies and windows were closed by heavy curtains as the family retreated to a smaller, fireside enclosure. Bedrooms and storage spaces were found in another wing or upstairs.

Inventories and wills suggest that medieval houses were minimally furnished. Many people owned only a few pieces of movable furniture, perhaps just a table with benches for the main room, locked cabinets or chests for storage, and beds for sleeping. Even in elite homes dining tables were not large but about the size of a modern coffee table, with the result that meals tended to be served one dish at a time. People sat on wooden chairs or benches when gathered at the table. Wood-frame beds with padded mattresses were used for sleeping. Such frequently used pieces of furniture sometimes were replaced by a masonry ledge built against the wall. Often noted by archaeologists, such platforms could have been used for sitting and reclining. Bedding, in the form of linen and wool coverings, woven carpets, and animal hides, was stored during the day and brought out at night. Most families kept a few icons, triptychs, or reliquaries in the bedroom or permanently installed in the main room—a tradition continued by the display of sacred objects in many Orthodox homes. An especially affluent household might have a library as well.[5]

Pergamon A different view of medieval town life comes from Pergamon in western Asia Minor. The onetime capital of the Attalid kings and a key city of late antiquity, Pergamon had been largely abandoned after the seventh century. Recent excavations have uncovered the considerable ruins of a late Byzantine settlement that grew up on the slopes of the ancient acropolis. The city's new administrative status in the mid-twelfth century attracted residents from the countryside to set up houses and shops within its refortified walls.

The remains illustrate the steady expansion of isolated, villagelike clusters of houses into a continuous urban quarter. The earliest buildings may have been shops of local craftsmen and merchants that lined the main road. These soon were joined by houses and workshops that looked onto secondary alleys. By the end of the thirteenth century the lower acropolis slopes were filled with settlers seeking refuge from advancing Turkish armies. Most houses consist of one or two groups of rooms facing an enclosed yard. The smallest combine living, cooking, and storage functions within a single

Reconstructed view of the late-medieval settlement on the acropolis at Pergamon in western Asia Minor. Houses and shops grew up along the main road leading to the summit. Drawing by Ulrike Wulf, in Klaus Rheidt, "Byzantinische Wohnhäuser des 11. bis 14. Jahrhunderts in Pergamon," *Dumbarton Oaks Papers* 44 (1990); reproduced courtesy of Dumbarton Oaks, Washington, D.C.

rectangular space. In larger houses the stables and storage rooms are clearly separated from living quarters, which occupy four or five rooms on two different levels. Stone-lined bins, *pithoi,* and transport jars were used to store grain, oil, preserved vegetables, and other crops. Domestic spaces were more carefully built, paved with stones or tiles, and usually equipped with a small hearth for cooking. Like their counterparts excavated at other sites, the buildings at Pergamon closely resemble traditional Turkish houses in the area.[6]

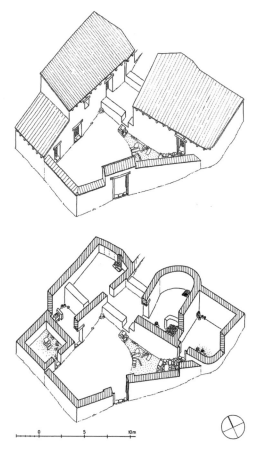

Reconstructed view of a late-medieval house at Pergamon. This residence consists of four or five rooms that open onto an open yard. Drawing by Klaus Rheidt, in Klaus Rheidt, "Byzantinische Wohnhäuser des 11. bis 14. Jahrhunderts in Pergamon," *Dumbarton Oaks Papers* 44 (1990); reproduced courtesy of Dumbarton Oaks, Washington, D.C.

THE URBAN ECONOMY

The economic life of Byzantine towns was based on agriculture, craft, and commerce. These activities had always been closely related but in the medieval period were impossible to separate. Many town dwellers owned fields, vineyards, and orchards that they worked themselves or leased to rural tenants. Households usually prepared their own commodities, hiring employees to mill grain, press grapes and olives, make cheeses, cure hides, and refine metal ores in the countryside before further processing in urban workshops. Some families were involved in distribution as well, from street-corner vending to long-distance trade. Such independence was a fundamental characteristic of Byzantine society. In some places specialized services like money changing, notarizing, and teaching, as well as assigned governmental duties, added to this economic base.[7]

As for families living in nearby villages, the main objectives of each urban household were to provide for its own upkeep and pay recurring taxes. Keeping a kitchen garden was a critical first step in this direction. A small plot with a couple vines and fruit trees was a source of nutrition and might yield a small surplus as well. Family members, especially women and children, wove cloth and made clothes, baskets, candles, and pots for their own use and possible sale. Every town served as a market center for area inhabitants, who exchanged home produce and crafts on the basis of barter if not cash.

Demand for basic commodities and services was directly proportionate to settlement size. A city's location on water or an established land route raised the potential for long-distance trade with other parts of the empire. Large places like Corinth, Thebes, and Thessaloniki supported many of the same business ventures found in Constantinople. Garden crops were purchased in open-air markets near the city gates and the harbor. Bread, meat, and dry goods were available in permanent street-side shops. Most tavernas could offer the customer a quick hot meal and cup of wine, as well as companionship with which to enjoy them. Shops were places of residence as well as business for textile workers, silk weavers, tailors, tanners, carpenters, and smiths. The most often reported occupation in medieval Macedonia was that of shoemaker.

This economic framework clearly rewarded property owners. With time major landowners came to control all stages of the agricultural market, from planting and harvesting raw materials to processing and exchanging finished products. Wealthier families maintained permanent facilities for handling goods from their rural estates. In Corinth and Thessaloniki these could take the form of commercial complexes with workrooms and retail spaces arranged around a central courtyard. Documented examples were one or two stories tall, were built of brick and stone, and had tiled roofs. Covered porticoes looked onto the court or street. A cistern or well added to a property's value. In some cases workshops were limited to the ground floor, with the upper level given over to residential quarters. Owners might supervise employees directly or lease out individual shops to entrepreneurs, who were helped by other family members along with one or two slaves. Finished goods were sold on the premises, hawked in the streets and nearby villages, or shipped in bulk to remote places. The lack of zoning codes meant that commercial operations might be found anywhere in town. Districts for making and selling specific goods appear only in large cities like Thessaloniki and Constantinople.

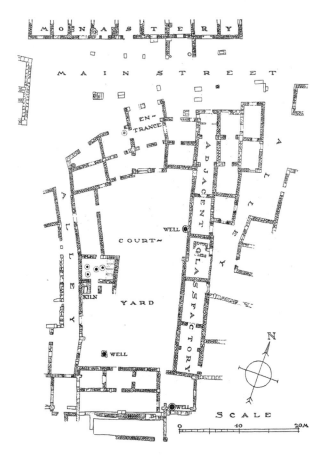

Plan of medieval buildings in central Corinth. Some of
the rooms arranged around the open court were used for
making glass or pottery. From Charles H. Morgan, *Corinth
XI: The Byzantine Pottery* (Cambridge, Mass.: American
School of Classical Studies, 1942); reproduced courtesy of
the Trustees of the American School of Classical Studies
at Athens.

Specialized production allowed different regions to establish a presence in the Mediterranean marketplace. South Greece and the Aegean
islands were highly regarded sources of olive oil and wine. The Corinth
area, known in Italy as Coranto, gave its name to a popular variety of
seedless cooking grapes (called in fourteenth-century England "raysons
of Coraunte," or currants). Inland Asia Minor became a major exporter
of animal products, particularly meat, hides, leather, and parchment.
The upper Balkans produced furs and metals. Wool came especially
from Asia Minor, linen from south Greece, and silk from the south

Aegean coastlands. In the eleventh and twelfth centuries Thebes was a dynamic textile center with large workshops that employed both men and women, whose skill was praised in the faraway capital. Byzantium's northern neighbors supplied amber, furs, and slaves. Traders from the Arab states brought fine ceramics, glass, and ornamental silks. Gems and jewels came from central Asia; ivory, perfumes, and spices from India; ceramics and silks from China. All these goods converged in urban markets, and above all in Constantinople. Recognizing the importance of long-distance commerce, the state regulated the city's merchants and taxed all imports and exports beyond its borders.

The bustle and clamor of construction must have been constant companions in every Byzantine town. Local authorities **Building** were responsible for maintaining the urban infrastructure, which in late antiquity extended to fortifications, aqueducts, streets, civic buildings, and baths. While most of these amenities disappeared after the seventh century, the basic needs for security and water continued throughout the Middle Ages. Churches were kept up by the local bishop while monasteries looked after their own facilities. Houses and apartments were developed and repaired at private expense. Landowners built elaborate residences to shelter their families and businesses, at the same time leasing other properties to artisans and tradesmen. Recurring earthquakes, fires, and warfare took their toll on buildings and created a steady demand for local contractors.

Cities were producers as well as consumers of structural materials. As in Roman times, bricks and roof tiles were among the most important mass-produced materials in Byzantium. Roman bricks had been made on suburban estates, especially those located near coastal ports, and it seems likely that medieval production also took place on the urban fringe. Brick making required abundant supplies of clay, water, and fuel for the kilns. It also needed a substantial labor force, which was drawn from the urban population or nearby villages. Clay was dug from the ground and brought to the kiln site. Here skilled workers mixed it with water, removed coarse impurities, and packed the damp clay by hand into wooden molds. Most bricks were flat, square or rectangular in shape, and of a few standard sizes (up to two inches thick and one-half, one, one-and-a-half, or two feet on a side). Special-purpose shapes were sometimes needed as well. Roof tiles measured up to two or three feet on a side and generally had overlapping edges. When installed on a roof the joints between flat tiles were sealed by a curved cover tile. Individual tiles could weigh as much as 45 or 50 pounds. As a rule, medieval bricks and roof tiles were smaller and less uniform than those made in late antiquity. Bricks and tiles were carefully packed inside a large kiln and then heated over the course of several days to a sustained temperature of 1,000 degrees Celsius. After cooling they were removed, sorted, packed in straw, and carried to the construction site. Finished tiles were heavy and awkward to move by land, and so were used locally or sent by ship. The entire operation made great demands on human and natural resources.

A second source of materials lay inside the city. The long history of Mediterranean urbanism meant that most places had plentiful building debris for reuse in new projects. Constantinople itself was cobbled together of marble blocks, columns, and statues taken from across Greece and western Asia Minor. Byzantine masons routinely mixed fragments of classical buildings with bricks and fieldstones. The prominent display of architectural spoils suggests that some builders consciously acknowledged their cultural heritage. Some especially famous old buildings were remodeled to suit new purposes. By the seventh century three of the most celebrated temples of classical Athens—the Parthenon, Erechtheion, and Hephaisteion—had been pressed into duty as churches, an act of historic preservation that helped ensure their physical survival.

Provincial building ran the gamut from exceptional architecture to rudimentary shelter. Surviving churches attest the high standards of design and craftsmanship that might be summoned for an important commission. The early churches of Antioch, Ephesus, Jerusalem, and Rome rivaled those of the capital in size and splendor. During the medieval period fine churches continued to be built in Nicaea, Thessaloniki, Arta, Mistra, and elsewhere. While few records survive, such buildings would likely have been designed by an *architekton*, a master mason who received the commission and supervised the work. Skilled builders were responsible for the critical tasks of laying foundations, building walls, raising columns, and completing vaults. Other jobs were performed by day laborers. Carpenters assembled scaffolding and formwork. Field

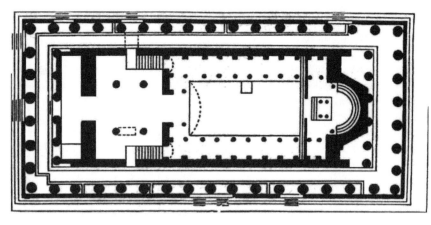

Plan of the Parthenon (fifth century B.C.) in the Byzantine period, when it served as a church. The apse replaced the original entrance at the east end. Adapted from *Archaiologike Ephemeris* 1929.

hands carried bricks and stone and mixed mortar. Plasterers, painters, and mosaic workers might travel some distance to decorate the interior according to the patron's instructions. Fortifications usually were initiated by the regional governor and supervised by army engineers. Other buildings fell to crews of semiskilled laborers engaged for specific projects. Many of these men came to the city from nearby villages, looking for work when not otherwise needed in the fields.[8]

A pottery-making quarter was a fixture of most ancient cities. Usually located along the roads leading **Pottery Making** into town, these workshops turned out thousands of containers every year. The quality and scale of any town's production depended on local demand but also access to wider markets. The Roman tradition of fine red-slipped tablewares was continued by permanent production centers near Carthage in North Africa, around Phocaea in western Asia Minor, and outside Paphos in Cyprus. These industries were made possible by the dynamic commercial environment of late antiquity, and ended with the disruption of major exchange routes in the seventh century. Only after the tenth century was specialized production able to resume on a large scale.

Pots offer insight into the lives of the people who made and used them. Heavy *pithoi* were used for storing grain and oil on the farm, at home, and in the shop. Smaller transport jars were filled at local mills or presses, and then carried to the city and beyond. Kitchenwares reflected local ways of cooking, serving, and dining. Shapes and decoration changed in revealing ways over the years. Amphorae generally reflected regional preferences, with distinct shapes current in south Greece, the Black Sea, and western Asia Minor. Cooking shapes reflect the range of Greek cuisine, with an enduring preference for flat pans and the growing use of deep, lidded stewpots. Vessels were placed directly over the fire, supported by a brazier or suspended by hanging chains. The clearest changes can be seen in fine pottery. Shallow red-slipped wares were replaced by high-footed dishes and deep bowls covered with colorful glazed decoration. Glossy vitreous slips were known in earlier times but were popularized by potters in the ninth and tenth centuries, perhaps first in Constantinople but soon in other areas as well. Apart from differences in shape, the tenth to fourteenth centuries saw decorative techniques using impressed, incised, and polychromatic slipped ornament. The common types used two or three contrasting glazes, usually red and green, though which elaborate patterns were scratched before firing. Glazed pottery was manufactured in Athens, Corinth, Thessaloniki, Pergamon, Serres, and Cyprus in addition to Constantinople itself. Technical innovations by Byzantine potters reflect expanded contact with Arab cities and the Far East, as well as trade with the Latin West.[9]

Medieval glazed dish from Corinth with incised deer, fawn, and rabbit. From Charles H. Morgan, *Corinth* XI: *The Byzantine Pottery* (Cambridge, Mass.: American School of Classical Studies, 1942); reproduced courtesy of the Trustees of the American School of Classical Studies at Athens.

Fairs and Festivals Periodic bazaars and fairs were a popular aspect of medieval city life. Seasonal markets had been held throughout the Roman countryside, bringing together itinerant craftsmen and merchants from across the empire. Byzantine fairs (*panegyreis*) successfully combined this tradition with the observance of religious festivals. The reputations of popular saints attracted crowds of admirers, with celebrations culminating on the day of their festival recorded in the *Synaxarion of Constantinople*. Holidays often coincided with local agrarian or maritime calendars, and might draw thousands of visitors over a span of days or even weeks. During the eighth and ninth centuries the festival of Saint John held near Ephesus, then known as Theologos, generated over a hundred pounds of gold in taxes each year.

Perhaps the best known *panegyris* was the Demetria, which was held outside Thessaloniki in October. Located at the head of the Aegean near the mouth of the Vardar river, the city was the natural focus for Balkan trade. The harbor was the main outlet for a wide agricultural territory, whose fall harvest coincided with the October 26 feast day of the city's patron, Saint Demetrius. A seasonal trade fair is known here as early as the twelfth century, but the Demetria came into its own as Italian merchants expanded their presence in the region. The scene was reenacted through the late Middle Ages. Craftsmen, farmers, merchants, and entertainers traveled great distances to set up long rows of tents on the plain beyond the city walls. The event drew entrepreneurs from across Macedonia as well as customs officials from Constantinople. Jews, Italians, Arabs, and Turks are well attested. At their peak the weeklong festivities were attended by thousands of people. Eyewitnesses describe a commercial and cultural event of wide renown:

There was every kind of material woven or spun by men or women, all those that come from Boeotia and the Peloponnesos, and all that are brought in trading ships from Italy to Greece. Besides this, Phoenicia furnishes numerous articles, and Egypt, and Spain, and the pillars of Hercules, where the finest coverlets are manufactured. These things the merchants bring direct from their respective countries to old Macedonia and Thessaloniki ... I was struck with wonder at the number and variety of the animals, and the extraordinary confusion of their noises which assailed my ears—horses neighing, oxen lowing, sheep bleating, pigs grunting, and dogs barking, for these also accompany their masters as a defense against wolves and thieves.[10]

TRAVEL AND TRANSPORTATION

Byzantine cities needed to maintain close contact with Constantinople and nearby villages and towns. Every provincial capital, coastal city, and market town had its place in the empire's administrative structure, which depended on reliably moving news, people, and materials from one place to another. These connections took many forms. Official business was carried by the state post, a network of staging points in cities and along the roads joining them. Private individuals lacked access to a national mail service and sent letters with messengers or travelers going from one town to another. Estate owners brought their harvest from the countryside in ox-drawn carts, while businessmen commissioned ships to take goods to distant markets. Long-distance transport was usually left to seasoned travelers, with most people choosing to stay close to home.

Personal travel over many miles was a hazardous undertaking. Civil, military, and church officials needed to consult with their supervisors in the provincial capital or Constantinople. Businessmen moved about in order to negotiate contracts, supervise shipments of goods, and arrange markets.

Private individuals might feel compelled to travel for personal reasons, like seeing distant relatives or friends, consulting medical specialists, or visiting a spiritual leader or religious shrine. Recreational tourism for its own sake had little appeal, yet Byzantine travelers were fascinated to see new places on their journeys. Many took time to visit famous landmarks, buy souvenirs, and taste local wares, returning home to describe their adventures for their friends.

**Finding
One's Way**

The empire's size and complexity required maps for many purposes. The foundation for medieval mapmaking had been laid by Hellenistic and Roman geographers, who combined complex mathematical calculations with firsthand observation when preparing schematic diagrams (*descriptios*) of the world and cosmos. Alexandria was the leading center for the study of ancient geography, which culminated in the work of Claudius Ptolemy (ca. 90–175). His *Geography* gives coordinates for a number of places ranging from "Thule" in northern Europe to equatorial Africa, and at one time was accompanied by a set of maps. While Ptolemy's astronomical writings were familiar to Byzantine scholars, his *Geography* may not have been widely available before the late Middle Ages, when several copies were made in Constantinople. Instead, military planners and travelers relied on smaller regional maps. In the early fifth century Theodosius II prepared a monumental map of the empire, apparently displaying it in the capital like an earlier map Augustus had posted in Rome. Provincial maps gave more detailed views of key towns and landscapes. A representation of central Palestine survives in the form of a floor mosaic in a sixth-century church at Madaba in Jordan. Intact sections depict Jerusalem together with nearby cities.

Travelers did not carry maps in the modern sense but relied on local informants, prominent landmarks, and detailed itineraries for the imperial post road. These illustrated guidebooks, known as *itineraria picta*, were schematic lists of towns one passed through on certain routes. Topographic points were indicated along with the location of wayside inns, baths, and staging posts (*mansiones*), as well as with the mileage separating them. The best-preserved example is the Peutinger Table, a late-medieval copy of an original *itinerarium* of the late fourth or fifth century. This unique document takes the form of a roll, measuring 14 inches high by 22 feet long, that covers the land routes from Britain as far as east as India. Landforms were drawn without scale and freely distorted to fit the roll, yet include hundreds of place-names to aid the traveler. Other guides were intended for pilgrims to the Holy Land and belong to a separate category of travel literature. These pay equal attention to points of physical geography and supernatural significance, particularly religious shrines and churches.

Ship crews referred to more practical books known as *periploi*. These descriptive reference works were compiled from classical sources and

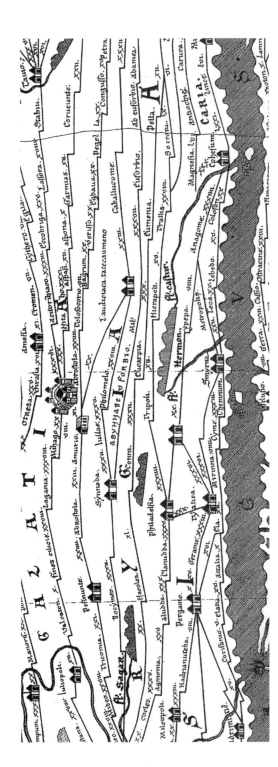

Western Asia Minor as shown on the Peutinger Table. Ankara, near the center, is surrounded by walls. Paired towers indicate cities like Pergamon, Smyrna, Ephesus, and Sardis, which is not labeled. Egypt appears below. From Konrad Miller, *Weltkarte des Castorius genannt die Peutinger'sche Tafel* (Ravensburg, Germany: Otto Maier, 1888).

reflected the accumulated experience of generations of sailors. Surviving examples include valuable information about coastal geography, harbors, sailing currents, and local populations. Narrative in form and rarely illustrated, these guides formed the basis of the late-medieval *portulans.* A unique variant in this tradition was composed by Cosmas Indikopleustes, a sixth-century monk and one of the most celebrated of all Byzantine travelers. Before entering a monastery Cosmas had lived as a merchant in Alexandria and sailed regularly across the Red Sea. His name, meaning "sailor to India," reflects his pride in having traveled as far east as the Malabar coast. Cosmas's illustrated travel book, known from later copies as the *Christian Topography,* combines personal recollections with local legends in support of a distinctive biblical cosmology. For all its eccentric details, his account provides a lively record of traveling on the edge of the Byzantine world.[11]

Pilgrimage   Religious motives prompted many people to undertake devotional pilgrimages. The sacred sites and monuments of biblical lands drew a steady stream of visitors beginning in the early fourth century, when Constantine's mother, Helena, first ventured to Jerusalem and was shown fragments of the True Cross of the Crucifixion. The most important Christian sites in Palestine soon were marked by buildings: the shrine of Abraham at Mamre, the church of the Nativity in Bethlehem, the Eleona church on the Mount of Olives, and in Jerusalem the tomb of Christ and the basilica of the Resurrection (Anastasis). Donations by grateful pilgrims supported the growth of such key pilgrimage centers, together with inns, tavernas, and other conveniences. Even after the arrival of the Arabs in the seventh century, Byzantine and Western pilgrims continued to visit these places, which often were venerated by Jews and Muslims as well.

Other pilgrimage sites were inspired by the lives of holy men and women in different parts of the empire. Many were martyrs of the early church, whose tombs in Antioch, Myra, Rome, and Thessaloniki have always drawn visitors. One of the most popular was the legendary Menas of Egypt (feast day celebrated November 11), whose aid was sought by travelers to his tomb west of Alexandria. The most popular destination after Jerusalem was Constantinople, which rapidly accumulated sacred relics, healing places, and other curiosities that medieval visitors thought worth seeing. When Geoffrey of Villehardouin first saw the capital in the early thirteenth century he found its relics "beyond description, for there were as many at that time in Constantinople as in all the rest of the world."[12] Traditions of pilgrimage grew up around holy men who had distinguished themselves by their ascetic lifestyle or spiritual attainments. The fifth-century monk Symeon Stylites (feast day celebrated September 1) achieved considerable renown by living atop a tall column in the hill country of north Syria. The reputation of the tenth-century monk Luke of Stiris reached far beyond his home in central Greece. In twelfth-century

Cyprus the monk Neophytos the Recluse (feast day January 24) retired to a life of prayer and contemplation in a cave outside Paphos, where he attracted many followers.

The popularity of such figures was enhanced by the steady arrival of pilgrims, who made donations to the caretakers of the tomb or shrine, boosted the local economy with their purchases, and took away stories of their experiences. Some travelers wrote detailed guidebooks urging others to follow their path, which might originate as far away as western Europe. Tangible souvenirs were a key part of the experience. These could take many forms: clay tokens impressed with an image of the saint, ceramic flasks containing soil from the site, or bottles filled with consecrated oil or water. Such mementos were not intrinsically remarkable but embodied the spiritual blessings *(eulogiai)* of the saint, obtained near the holy site. By returning home with such keepsakes, the pilgrim prolonged the spiritual benefits of his or her travels while promoting the reputation of the shrine.[13]

Ceramic ampulla or flask with camels kneeling before Saint Menas. The saint's shrine at Abu Mina in north Egypt was a major pilgrimage destination in late antiquity. Courtesy of the Museum of Art and Archaeology, University of Missouri–Columbia.

Byzantium inherited from Rome an elaborate network
Land Travel   of official roads, the *cursus publicus,* which at its peak
stretched almost 54,000 miles in length. Half of these roads
lay in the East, joining towns throughout Asia Minor and the Balkans.
The most important routes included the Via Egnatia, which ran from
Constantinople through Thessaloniki to the port of Dyrrachium, where
one could catch a ship sailing west to Italy. A more northerly route led
from the capital to Adrianople, Sofia, and the Danube frontier. From the
Asian side of the Bosphorus the main road led to Ankara in Galatia, across
Cappadocia and the Taurus mountains to Tarsus, and through the Cilician
Gates to Antioch. Such public or imperial highways *(demosiakai* or *basilikai
hodoi)* were intended for official and military travel, but also were used by
clergy, merchants, and private travelers. Roads could range from broad,
paved surfaces to a narrow path *(monopation),* with routine maintenance
left to area inhabitants. Military engineers were called in when needed
to build or repair bridges, ramps, and terrace walls. Official milestones
placed at regular intervals marked the distance in miles *(milia)* between
towns. The length of a *milion* seems to have been about seven or seven
and a half classical *stadia* (about 4,300 or 4,600 feet).

Overland journeys forced travelers to make frequent stops along the
way. Food and lodging were available at private and state-run *tavernas,*
inns, and staging points. *Mutationes* maintained a stable of horses for
use by couriers on government business; overnight accommodations as
well as fresh mounts could be had at the larger *mansiones.* These official
changing posts were located about 10 miles apart, a little closer in difficult terrain, with larger stations set at distances of 20 to 30 miles. Private
roadhouses ranged from isolated, single-room *tavernas* to specially
built hostels with small rooms arranged about a central court, similar to
Ottoman *caravansaries.* On some routes monasteries took in pilgrims and
other overnight guests. Secular inns catered to an ever-changing crowd of
couriers, merchants, soldiers, and criminals, and as a result were warily
regarded by members of proper society. Respectable people never traveled alone. Women and pilgrims were admonished about the dangers of
visiting *tavernas* and inns, and churchmen were commonly forbidden
from entering such places. Their lowly standing is clear from the life of
Saint Theodore of Sykeon, who grew up in a roadhouse in Galatia where
his mother served meals and entertained travelers. Written sources and
archaeological remains help us envision the noisy and uncomfortable
conditions with their transient clientele.[14]

Many factors limited the effectiveness of overland travel. Few milestones
were set up after the sixth century. Medieval roads were usually in poor
condition and badly marked. Without regular maintenance major routes
soon reverted to rough country tracks. The paths between most villages
and market towns were probably less clear. Travelers routinely faced rivers,
forests, and high mountain ranges. Weather conditions effectively isolated

many places for at least part of the year. Bridges and mountain roads were vulnerable to floods, earthquakes, and landslides. Streams froze and mountain passes were blocked by snow in winter. Rivers became impassable in springtime. One's greatest worry was not weather, however, but personal safety. Lawlessness and violence were regular features of remote roadways, where travelers made easy prey for brigands and bandits.

Travel times varied a great deal. Under normal circumstances the foot traveler might cover 4 to 5 miles an hour, or about 25 miles in a day. Notwithstanding mountains and snow, this seems to be the pace Odo of Deuil expects for twelfth-century soldiers moving along the shortest land route from Nicaea to Antioch, a distance of about 500 miles; traveling the safer coastal road could take three times as long. Horses offered a quicker and more reliable means of personal transport, especially when they were equipped with iron horseshoes and stirrups. Horses and road surfaces were protected by laws that limited fully loaded saddlebags to 30 pounds. With frequent changes of mount, a quick journey from the capital to Adrianople (about 150 miles) could be managed in three days, while traveling between Nicaea and Antioch took a little over a week. Couriers bearing urgent news might travel as much as 240 miles at a time.[15]

Vehicular transport was intended mainly for short hauls. Donkeys, mules, and oxen were better suited than horses for pulling heavy carts or

The legendary bridge of Arta, in west Greece. Rebuilt in the sixteenth century, the bridge and its medieval predecessors hold a special place in Balkan folklore. Courtesy of the author.

wagons. Fourth-century regulations limited the load of two-wheel carts to 600 pounds and post wagons to half a ton. Byzantine wagons suffered from serious design problems. Like ancient wagons, they lacked ball or roller bearings to reduce axle friction, had no reliable way of braking on steep slopes, and did not have pivoting front axles for turning corners. The wooden yoke and padded neck collar worked well with oxen but were unsuited to the anatomy of donkeys, mules, and horses, who required a lower harness spanning the chest. The silence of Byzantine writers about such matters suggests that these long-standing problems went unresolved for most of the medieval period.

Horses, donkeys, and mules carrying pack-saddles or panniers provided a more dependable way of moving goods overland. Horses were the most versatile but usually were in short supply. A healthy donkey could be expected to carry about 200–225 pounds. Camels were especially useful for long-distance conveyance and routinely carried twice this load. Traditionally used for caravan travel in Egypt and the Near East, camels were the preferred pack animal for making the long haul across Asia. After crossing the Byzantine frontier one still needed six or seven months to reach the westernmost capital of China. Camels appeared on domestic roadways as well and could be seen carrying heavy loads across north Greece into the late Middle Ages. Such caravans were clearly important, and yet camel driving was looked down on as the lowliest of occupations. Continuously on the move and facing countless hazards, these long-distance truckers lived on the fringe of conventional society.[16]

Sea Travel Many towns were located on the water, whose presence was an inescapable factor in the lives of their residents. Key transportation hubs like Alexandria and Thessaloniki saw ships depart regularly for distant ports. Small harbor towns were equally busy with boats sailing to nearby islands and along the coast. The most frequent departures were by local fishermen, who set out each morning and returned with their catch around midday. Much of this activity depended on the weather and reached a peak during the summer sailing season, which lasted from April into October. When not at sea, sailors repaired their ships, mended their sails and nets, and prepared for voyages ahead.

For many people the sea offered a cheaper, faster, and safer way of crossing long distances or moving goods to market. Much of the population lived within a day's walk of the Mediterranean or a navigable river that drained into it. The great coastal cities of the eastern Roman Empire had built spacious harbors to handle commerce and communication. In Constantinople deepwater harbors were created along the Marmara shore and the Golden Horn in the fourth and fifth centuries. The challenge of maintaining such facilities in the medieval period encouraged the use of smaller ships that could dock at seaside wharves and shallow anchorages. Travel by ship was normally more reliable than land travel

Bronze ornament, perhaps from a necklace, proclaiming the loyalty of a camel driver *(kamelaris)* to Saint Sergios. Courtesy of the Museum of Art and Archaeology, University of Missouri–Columbia.

but remained subject to the same seasonal conditions. During the winter months one might wait in port for weeks before setting out. As on land, the sea traveler faced outlaws and pirates. There were no ships that carried only passengers. Most travelers simply inquired at the docks for departing vessels and sailed when they found space, squeezing in among other goods and supplies. One's fellow voyagers came from all levels of society, which frequently discomfited clergy, women, and other respectable sorts. Conversation, storytelling, board games, and gambling helped pass the time. As today, traveling on deck was pleasant during the mild sailing season, especially when protected from the sun by a light canopy.

The geography of the Byzantine empire recommended sending most foodstuffs and trade goods by sea. It was not only quicker but much cheaper to transport goods by water rather than overland. Once placed on board ship, a bag of grain or jar of oil could travel across the empire for less than it cost to carry it only a few miles by cart. Such considerations applied especially to bulky agricultural commodities and mining products, but were also important in the distribution of precious metals, coinage, and luxury goods. The excavation of shipwrecks has shown how fine pottery and glass traveled together with heavy iron tools, amphorae or barrels of oil and wine, and sacks of grain. The discovery of manufactured goods far from their place of origin reflects the reputation of certain products and the interconnectedness of Mediterranean trade. The most economically developed parts of the empire were those areas along the coast with both a productive hinterland and access to a good harbor.[17]

Shipbuilding and Sailing   Merchant ships had always been a factor in the classical economy. In Roman times enormous galleys brought grain each year from Egypt to Italy. Ships sailing between Alexandria and Constantinople may have been smaller but were still of substantial size: most could carry 120–200 tons at a time and the largest had a capacity of over 300 tons. After the seventh century Byzantium's much reduced territory and hazardous sea-lanes meant that sailors faced hostile fleets and pirates, which brought about far-reaching changes in ship design and sailing. The most common ship of the medieval period was a small, agile vessel sometimes called a *dorkon* ("gazelle"). Excavated examples suggest that a typical commercial vessel had a shallow keel and rounded hull, was about 65 feet long, and had a capacity of 60 tons. Most ships had an open deck with a small cabin near the stern for the shipmaster. Such craft were designed to be managed by a small crew, which left more space for provisions and cargo. While large vessels occasionally crossed the open seas to Constantinople, especially during the mild months of summer, Byzantine ships usually peddled their wares to people who lived along the coast. The medieval *Rhodian Sea Law (Nomos nautikos)* suggests that the ship's owner, captain, and merchant often were the same person.

Building methods underwent important developments during the early Byzantine period. For centuries Greek and Roman shipbuilders had based their craft on a sturdy outer hull. They began by laying a heavy keel of oak or elm, to which they attached rising stem- and sternposts. This formed the foundation for a solid shell consisting of narrow, carefully cut planks or strakes laid in overlapping horizontal rows. Each plank was carefully sawed and joined to its neighbor by precisely cut mortise-and-tenon joints. These were spaced every few inches along the hull and fixed in place by wood treenails. The result was a rigid, watertight shell that needed only a light protective sealing of pitch. After completing the hull, shipbuilders added a reinforcing timber framework to carry the superstructure. This traditional approach to construction obviously depended on many skilled carpenters who could shape the boards and cut thousands of mortises in the outer planking. The process was slow and costly, and took place in permanent shipyards that turned out a limited number of large, sturdy craft.

A fundamental shift occurred during the early Middle Ages. Excavated shipwrecks dating from the sixth to tenth centuries document the step-by-step development of an independent skeleton to which the hull was added. An early stage in this transition is preserved by a seventh-century shipwreck discovered near the west coast of Turkey at Yassi Ada ("Flat Island"). The hull was built as a solid mortise-and-tenon shell as high as the water line, but above this level the side timbers or wales were attached by iron nails to an interior timber frame. An eleventh-century shipwreck found at Serçe Limani ("Sparrow Harbor"), off the Lycian coast, had a hull completely supported by an interior frame. Later ships preferred this kind of interior skeleton to support a clinker-built shell of overlapping planks. While the hull needed frequent sealing by caulkers, such frame-first ships could be built rapidly and by relatively unskilled laborers. Their increased popularity reflects the greater importance of small-scale entrepreneurs in medieval commerce and industry.[18]

An equally important change affected sailing techniques with the introduction of the lateen sail. Classical galleys had been propelled by paired banks of rowers, who were assisted by large, square sails mounted on a central mast. The sails were made of heavy linen reinforced with leather patches at the corners and rope along the sides. Anchored by two horizontal beams, such square-rigs were well suited for long-distance summer sailing but could not cope easily with adverse winds. Smaller, triangular sails offered greater flexibility when tacking close to the wind. Lateen sails mounted fore and aft had been known in the Mediterranean as early as the fourth century. They became widely used only around the seventh century, when they gradually replaced square sails on Byzantine ships. Arab sailors were equally quick to recognize the flexibility of these small, triangular sails. Together with the shift toward lightweight skeletal hulls, the lateen sail fundamentally changed the face of Mediterranean sailing.

No ship dared leave port without carrying a supply of anchors, and these often took different forms. Mediterranean sailors had long used

Boat building in Cyprus. The frame-first method of hull construction has changed little since the early Middle Ages. Courtesy of the author.

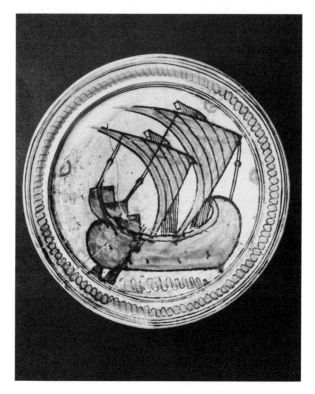

A two-masted ship with lateen sails depicted on a medieval dish from Corinth, perhaps made in south Italy. Photo courtesy of the Corinth Archaeological Museum, reproduced courtesy of the Trustees of the American School of Classical Studies at Athens.

perforated stone disks as ballast and anchors. These could weigh hundreds of pounds and were attached to either a wooden shank or a sturdy rope. Roman sailors used massive anchor stocks made of iron and lead to which a wooden shank and arms were attached. Stock and arms normally projected at perpendicular angles to increase the anchor's overall effectiveness. Solid-cast iron anchors that look very similar to modern examples were used throughout the Byzantine period. Many excavated examples are cruciform in shape and range in length from 3 to nearly 10 feet. The seventh-century merchant ship at Yassi Ada carried at least 11 such anchors with removable wooden stocks. These came in three distinct sizes weighing about 70, 170, and over 300 pounds. Different sizes seem to have been meant for varied seabed and weather conditions; the large number aboard a single ship allowed for damage and loss. By temporarily removing the stocks, one could stack several anchors flat on the deck.

Anchors were cast from both stem and stern, and were raised by simple windlasses and capstans.[19]

Commercial traffic took advantage of prevailing winds and followed familiar paths between major ports. Weather **Life at Sea** forecasting looked to the sailing season, which since the time of Homer had been established by watching the solstice, the equinox, and the constellations. The best time to put to sea was durinyg the summer, when one could count on settled conditions. Across the Aegean this was announced by the shift of winds to the west and above all by the return of swallows from Africa. The grain supply of Constantinople arrived from Egypt at summer's end. The most experienced sailors expected to travel during the winter months as well, especially during the calm "halcyon days" of legend. Reliable forecasting, which not unreasonably was linked with divination, came from long-term familiarity with the seas. Rising cloudbanks, coastal winds, and flocks of seabirds returning to land were signs of unstable conditions and storms.[20]

Attitudes toward the sea were profoundly mixed. Water was the most efficient means of getting around the Mediterranean, and for centuries the Greeks had admired mythical sailors like Odysseus. "Sailing is a noble thing," wrote George Pachymeres around the turn of the fourteenth century, "useful beyond all others to humanity."[21] Dreaming about the sea was considered a sign of future wealth and glory. At the same time everyone knew the sea to be a source of constant hazard. Most people preferred to ignore it altogether, even when living only a few miles from its edge. For inhabitants of the islands and coastal regions, the sea was the source of dangerous winter storms. It offered exposure to brigands, pirates, and foreign invaders. Few seaside families had not lost members to sudden storms, swift currents, or legendary monsters of the deep, like the great whale that haunted the Bosphorus in the sixth century. Travelers on modern steamers can still feel overwhelmed by the immensity of the waters and understand Eustathios of Thessaloniki's suspicion of the "unnatural art of seafaring."[22] Medieval ships carried neither life preservers nor lifeboats and few people were good swimmers. In case of accident one's only hope was to cling to debris from the wrecked ship.

Fishermen, merchants, and others whose lives depended on sailing carried amulets, reliquaries, and icons for protection. They regularly prayed to coastal saints who helped them in many ways: by guiding ships around dangerous reefs, alerting tired crews to sudden storms, and miraculously calming the waters. Saint Nicholas of Sion (later of Myra; feast day observed December 6), a sixth-century monk who lived along the rocky coast of Lycia, was famous for his maritime interventions. The monk Dorotheos, caught at sea by a winter storm, calmed the waves by scattering dust from the Syrian shrine of Saint Symeon the Younger (feast days May 23–24). Saint Phokas of Sinope (feast days September 21–22 and July 22–23) was regularly credited with subduing storms and rescuing ships in the Black Sea. Experienced travelers often invited Saint Phokas to share their meals with them when aboard ship. After arriving safely in port they donated the expense of their hospitality to charity.[23]

NOTES

1. For an introduction to urban issues see Cyril Mango, "The Disappearance and Revival of Cities," in *Byzantium: The Empire of New Rome* (New York: Charles Scribner's Sons, 1980), 60–87; and the recent survey by Clive Foss, "Life in City and Country," in *The Oxford History of Byzantium*, ed. Cyril Mango (Oxford: Oxford University Press, 2002), 71–95.

2. Excavations at Sardis are summarized by George M.A. Hanfmann, *Sardis from Prehistoric to Roman Times* (Cambridge: Harvard University Press, 1982). For later history see Clive Foss, *Byzantine and Turkish Sardis* (Cambridge: Harvard University Press, 1977).

3. Charalambos Bouras, "Aspects of the Byzantine City, Eighth–Fifteenth Centuries," in *The Economic History of Byzantium from the Seventh to the Fifteenth Century*, ed. Angeliki E. Laiou (Washington, D.C.: Dumbarton Oaks, 2002), 2:497–528.

4. Stephen Runciman, *Mistra: Byzantine Capital of the Peloponnese* (London: Thames and Hudson, 1980).

5. Literary sources are discussed by Paul Magdalino, "The Byzantine Aristocratic *Oikos*," in *The Byzantine Aristocracy, IX–XIII Centuries*, ed. Michael Angold (Oxford: British Archaeological Reports, 1984), 92–111; and Nicolas Oikonomides, "The Contents of the Byzantine House from the Eleventh to the Fifteenth Century," *Dumbarton Oaks Papers* 44 (1990): 205–14.

6. Recent work is summarized by Klaus Rheidt, "In the Shadow of Antiquity: Pergamon and the Byzantine Millennium," in *Pergamon: Citadel of the Gods*, ed. Helmut Koester (Harrisburg, Pa.: Trinity Press, 1998), 395–423; and idem, "The Urban Economy of Pergamon," in Laiou, *Economic History of Byzantium*, 2:623–29.

7. For an overview, see Alexander P. Kazhdan and Ann Wharton Epstein, "Urban Economy and Institutions," in *Change in Byzantine Culture in the Eleventh and Twelfth Centuries* (Berkeley: University of California Press, 1985), 45–56. For comprehensive discussion see Gilbert Dagron, "The Urban Economy, Seventh–Twelfth Centuries," in Laiou, *Economic History of Byzantium*, 2:393–461; and Klaus-Peter Matschke, "The Late Byzantine Urban Economy, Thirteenth–Fifteenth Centuries," in Laiou, *Economic History of Byzantium*, 2:463–95.

8. For the building process, see chapter 9.

9. For an introduction, see Ken Dark, *Byzantine Pottery* (Charleston, S.C.: Tempus, 2001).

10. *Timarion*, adapted from H.F. Tozer, "Byzantine Satire," in *Journal of Hellenic Studies* 2 (1881): 230–70; also in Deno John Geanakoplos, *Byzantium: Church, Society, and Civilization Seen through Contemporary Eyes* (Chicago: University of Chicago Press, 1984), 280–81; and Andrew Dalby, *Flavours of Byzantium* (Totnes, England: Prospect Books, 2003), 100–104. Fairs are discussed by Klaus-Peter Matschke, "Commerce, Trade, Markets, and Money: Thirteenth–Fifteenth Centuries," in Laiou, *Economic History of Byzantium*, 2:771–806.

11. For further background see O.A.W. Dilke, *Greek and Roman Maps* (Ithaca, N.Y.: Cornell University Press, 1985); and idem, "Cartography in the Byzantine Empire," in *History of Cartography*, vol. 1, *Cartography in Prehistoric, Ancient, and Medieval Europe and the Mediterranean*, ed. J.B. Harley and David Woodward (Chicago: University of Chicago Press, 1987), 258–75. There are several editions of Cosmas's maps and text, including J.W. McCrindle, trans., *The Christian Topography of Cosmas, an Egyptian Monk* (London: Hakluyt Society, 1897; reprint, New York: Burt Franklin, 1967).

12. Geoffrey of Villehardouin, "The Conquest of Constantinople" 192, in *Chronicles of the Crusades*, trans. Margaret R.B. Shaw (Harmondsworth, England: Penguin Books, 1963), 76.

13. For the early days of Christian pilgrimage see E.D. Hunt, *Holy Land Pilgrimage in the Later Roman Empire, A.D. 312–460* (New York: Oxford University Press, 1982); and the recent symposium "Pilgrimage in the Byzantine Empire, 7th–15th Centuries," *Dumbarton Oaks Papers* 56 (2002): 57–239.

14. For the classical background see Raymond Chevallier, *Roman Roads* (Berkeley: University of California Press, 1976). The *Life* of Theodore of Sykeon is included in Elizabeth Dawes and Norman H. Baynes, trans., *Three Byzantine Saints: Contemporary Biographies of St. Daniel the Stylite, St. Theodore of Sykeon, and St. John the Almsgiver* (Crestwood, N.Y.: St. Vladimir's Seminar Press, 1977), 88–185. Problems of overland transport are reviewed by K.D. White, *Greek and Roman Technology* (Ithaca, N.Y.: Cornell University Press, 1984), 127–40; and Anna Avramea, "Land and Sea Communications, Fourth–Fifteenth Centuries," in Laiou, *Economic History of Byzantium*, 1:57–90. See also Ruth Macrides, ed., *Travel in the Byzantine World* (Burlington, Vt.: Ashgate Publishing, 2002).

15. The breakneck pace still falls short of William "Buffalo Bill" Cody's famous ride for the Pony Express in 1861, when he rode 21 horses over 322 miles in less than 22 hours. For other expectations see Odo of Deuil, *De Profectione Ludovici VII in Orientem: The Journey of Louis VII to the East*, ed. Virginia Gingerick Berry (New York: W.W. Norton, 1948), 89.

16. Much useful information about horses, camels, and related modes of transport is in Jocelyn M.C. Toynbee, *Animals in Roman Life and Art* (London: Thames and Hudson, 1973; reprint, Baltimore: Johns Hopkins University Press, 1996); Richard W. Bulliet, *The Camel and the Wheel* (Cambridge: Harvard University Press, 1975); and Ann Hyland, *Equus: The Horse in the Roman World* (New Haven, Conn.: Yale University Press, 1990).

17. For ships and water travel see Richard W. Unger, *The Ship in the Medieval Economy, 600–1600* (London: Croom Helm, 1980); Lionel Casson, *Ships and Seamanship in the Ancient World*, 2nd ed. (Princeton, N.J.: Princeton University Press, 1986); Michael McCormick, *Origins of the Medieval Economy: Communications and Commerce A.D. 300–900* (Cambridge: Cambridge University Press, 2001); George Makris, "Ships," in Laiou, *Economic History of Byzantium*, 1:91–100; and Seán McGrail, *Boats of the World from the Stone Age to Medieval Times* (Oxford: Oxford University Press, 2001). Recent archaeological work is summarized by Frederick van Doorninck, "Byzantine Shipwrecks," in Laiou, *Economic History of Byzantium*, 2:899–905. Carved chessmen, a backgammon mat, and a small bronze cube with 5 to 14 holes on its six sides were found during excavation of the eleventh-century shipwreck at Serçe Limani.

18. Shipbuilding is a conservative business whose expense and risks do not encourage innovation. For the economic context of technological changes see Unger, *The Ship in the Medieval Economy*, 21–32. Construction methods are discussed in Frederick H. van Doorninck Jr., "Byzantium, Mistress of the Sea: 330–641," in *A History of Seafaring*, ed. George F. Bass (New York: Walker and Company, 1972), 133–58. For a popular account of the excavations see G. F. Bass, *Archaeology beneath the Sea* (New York: Walker and Company, 1975).

19. For the lateen sail see Unger, *The Ship in the Medieval Economy*, 47–50; Casson, *Ships and Seamanship*, 201–23. Anchors and other sailing materials are discussed in George F. Bass and Frederick H. van Doorninck Jr., *Yassi Ada I: A Seventh-Century Byzantine Shipwreck* (College Station: Texas A&M University Press, 1982).

20. The importance of sailing conditions is stressed by Jamie Morton, *The Role of the Physical Environment in Ancient Greek Seafaring* (Leiden, the Netherlands: Brill, 2001).

21. George Pachymeres, quoted in Robert Browning, "The City and the Sea," in *The Greeks and the Sea*, ed. Speros Vryonis (New Rochelle, N.Y.: Aristide D. Caratzas, 1993), 97–110.

22. For medieval anxieties see George T. Dennis, "Perils of the Deep," in *Novum Millennium: Studies on Byzantine History and Culture Dedicated to Paul Speck*, ed. Claudia Sode and Sarolta Takács (Burlington, Vt.: Ashgate, 2001), 81–88. The Bosphorus whale appears in Procopius, *Wars*, trans. H. B. Dewing (Cambridge: Harvard University Press, 1914–40; reprinted 1953–62), 7.29.9.

23. For accounts of Saint Nicholas's miracles see Ihor Ševčenko and Nancy Patterson Ševčenko, *The Life of Saint Nicholas of Sion* (Brookline, Mass.: Hellenic College Press, 1984), 53–57.

6

THE COUNTRYSIDE

Most medieval people lived close to the land, their daily routines shaped in every way by soil and weather. The extent of the landscape that belonged to Byzantium changed considerably with time. In late antiquity this included the Nile valley and coastlands of Syria and Palestine, whose farmers fed Constantinople's growing population. Rural estates in Italy, southern Spain, and North Africa shipped oil and wine to the capital and across the Mediterranean. Most of these productive areas were lost during the seventh and eighth centuries: the Umayyad Arabs swept across the Near East and Africa, while the Goths, Langobards, and Franks established themselves in newly won territories in the West. The countryside of medieval Byzantium was largely confined to the Balkans and Asia Minor, a region of distinct valleys separated by steep mountains but sharing a common sea. Even within these reduced borders there was wide variation in local traditions. The mild Aegean climate supported a wealth of field crops grown by farmers who lived in coastal towns and villages. By contrast, peasants in mountainous areas built hillside terraces and drove their flocks between seasonal pastures. On the Anatolian plateau a rural aristocracy amassed considerable property and raised great herds of livestock. Everywhere spiritual needs were served by churches and monasteries, whose expanding population and properties were key features of the countryside. In each region topography, climate, and culture ensured a fundamental continuity in people's lives.[1]

Information about Byzantine rural life is very uneven. Most writers lived in Constantinople or other cities and paid little attention to the *chora,* or countryside. Those who did write about the hinterland generally viewed it with suspicion and disdain. Saints' lives often take place against a rustic backdrop of colorful incident but uncertain reliability. One of the most interesting documents for understanding village society is the *Farmer's Law (Nomos georgikos),* a compilation of legal codes covering rural affairs in the seventh and eighth centuries. Most of the 85 situations covered by this document deal with mundane disputes, ranging from land transactions and sharecropping arrangements to misbehaving livestock and dog fights. Taken as a whole, the *Farmer's Law* vividly illustrates the common concerns of medieval villagers. Another important source is the *Geoponika,* a popular collection of agricultural writings put together in the tenth century. The 20 books cover basic issues of land use, cultivation of field crops, animal husbandry, and weather forecasting. Drawing on a long tradition of Latin agrarian literature, the *Geoponika* preserves much practical advice on farming ways and hazards.

Selections from the *Farmer's Law*[2]

10. A shareholder's portion is nine bundles, the grantor's one: he who divides outside these limits is accursed.
17. If a farmer enters and works another farmer's woodland, for three years he shall take its profits for himself and then give the land back again to its owner.
18. If a farmer who is too poor to work his own vineyard takes flight and goes abroad, let those from whom claims are made by the public treasury gather in the grapes ...
22. If a farmer at digging-time steals a spade or a hoe, and is afterwards recognized, let him pay its daily hire twelve *folles;* the same rule applies to him who steals a pruning-knife at pruning-time, or a sickle at reaping-time, or an axe at wood-cutting time.
31. If a tree stands on a lot, if the neighboring lot is a garden and is overshadowed by the tree, the owner of the garden may trim its branches; but if there is no garden, the branches are not to be trimmed.
35. If a man is found stealing another's straw, he shall restore it twice over.
52. If a man sets a snare at harvest-time and a dog or a pig falls into it and dies, let its owner go harmless.
56. If a man lights a fire in his own wood or in his field and it happens that the fire spreads and burns houses or cultivated fields, he is not condemned unless he did it in a strong wind.
76. If two dogs are fighting and the master of one gives it to the other dog with a sword or a stick or a stone and by reason of that blow it is blinded or killed or suffers some other detriment, let him make it good to its master and receive twelve lashes.
82. If after the land of the district has been divided, a man finds in his own lot a place which is suitable for the erection of a mill and sets

about it, the farmers of the other lots are not entitled to say anything about the mill.

Topics Covered by the *Geoponika*

1. Astrology and weather
2. Agriculture
3. Calendar
4–8. Vines
9. Olives
10. Fruit trees
11. Ornamental trees
12. Vegetables
13. Pests and vermin
14. Poultry
15. Bees
16. Horses
17. Cattle
18. Sheep, goats, and pigs
19. Dogs and game
20. Fish

Archaeology and ethnography throw further light on this poorly understood subject. Over the last 20 years field surveys have mapped the distribution of towns, villages, and farmsteads of all periods across the Mediterranean. Broadly speaking, rural settlement expanded during the fourth to sixth centuries, withered between the seventh and ninth centuries, and gradually revived in the medieval period. In remote areas traditional lifeways have continued into very recent times. Local ecological systems were affected as new land was brought under cultivation by a growing population and later reverted to scrub and forest. Excavations and surveys are providing detailed information about how rural settlements were built and functioned. Recovered artifacts document the lives and aspirations of their inhabitants.[3]

RURAL SOCIETY AND ECONOMY

The countryside was organized by a network of market towns, villages, and estates located within the territories of major cities. Population densities varied with terrain and climate but tended to be greatest in western Asia Minor. Most land workers or peasants *(georgike)* lived in small villages or hamlets numbering a few hundred people. Over time some larger families were able to increase their holdings to include fields, pastures, and woodlands belonging to several villages. Donations to the church brought some of these estates under the control of monasteries.

Each village's inhabitants made up a community whose members owned property individually and as a group. The community had specific rights as a corporate entity. It held title to nearby pastures, woodlands, streams, lakes, and seashores. It could buy and sell land; build bridges, mills, or public structures; assign the right to use common lands; and initiate legal proceedings. It also was collectively responsible for raising tax revenues on its assigned domains, which were forwarded to provincial administrators and on to Constantinople. Village priests and rural monks followed parallel lines of authority in reporting to local bishops, who in turn were supervised by regional metropolitans. Rural life was strongly influenced by this hierarchical arrangement.

As in other medieval peasant societies, the nuclear family was the primary social and economic unit in the Byzantine village. At any one time such families might number four to six members, including at least two children and a grandparent. The relative stability of household size reflects the carrying capacity of the land worked by traditional methods under normal environmental conditions. Most families owned or controlled an allotment that it farmed for its own benefit. The main concern of each household was to produce enough food to feed itself, and beyond this to pay taxes. A typical family met its own requirements by raising a kitchen garden, tending a few vines and olive trees, and harvesting a large crop of cereals. Basic needs were supplemented through barter or exchange of surplus crops with other villagers. Labor beyond that needed for raising children and farming could be directed to specialized crafts like pottery or textiles. Most of these products were used within the household, but others were swapped with neighbors. Such household industry compensated for a poor harvest in times of drought or war. Surplus production was taken to market in a nearby town, where it was sold for cash to pay taxes, rents, and debts.

Property taxes were assessed at the level of the individual village, with assessments made on all land, both cultivated (field, vineyard, olive grove) and uncultivated (pasture, scrub, woodland), lying within its boundaries. This communal obligation, normally paid once or twice a year, had an important influence on local society. Any shortfall had to be made up by members of the village. Abandoned lands were reassigned to other families, who might end up tending a number of scattered holdings. Contemporary writers often mention the heavy burden of rural taxation. Families used any remaining surplus to buy household necessities. Seed needed to be stored for the next planting season, tools and buildings had to be repaired or replaced, daughters needed dowries to get married. In good times a successful family might save enough to purchase a slave or hire additional help in the field. Archaeological surveys suggest that the fourth through sixth centuries saw the greatest period of settlement dispersion and rural prosperity. The seventh through tenth centuries are hard to identify in the field, and only in the tenth and eleventh century do villages come back into focus. The scarcity of coins and imported luxuries suggests that most peasant production remained in the village.[4]

RURAL SETTLEMENT

Rural inhabitants lived in small, centralized settlements generally known as *komai* in late antiquity and *choria* during the medieval period. Some family members and hired workers might reside for a while in a dependent hamlet *(agridion)* located closer to the fields, or in a temporary shelter at harvest time. The physical layout and legal status of these settlements depended on many factors. During the early empire a growing population established new villages and farmsteads on marginal lands that had not been previously cultivated. By contrast, political instability in the seventh and eighth centuries interrupted long-standing commercial routes. These fundamental changes encouraged many residents to withdraw to defensible hilltops away from the coast and focus on their most pressing needs. Fiscal policies also had a significant impact on rural lives, with agricultural taxation serving at different times as either an economic stimulus or punitive burden. Surviving documents attest a regressive tax structure in which tenant farmers paid more than freeholders, while magnates and monasteries were granted exemptions. The long-term result was to consolidate holdings in the hands of wealthy families and the church.

The nucleated village was the most common form of settlement. Its territory was based on all holdings of its residents **Villages** and included fields, groves, streams, ponds, uncultivated pasture, scrubland, and forest. Property limits were indicated by boundary markers, shallow ditches, and heaped-up mounds of fieldstones. Terraces were built to stabilize sloping hillsides. Family holdings changed over the years as properties were inherited, abandoned, and reassigned. During late antiquity much of the countryside was worked by independent peasants, but between the sixth and eighth centuries a shrinking population combined with rising taxes enabled some landowners, like the future saint Philaretos, to amass sprawling estates that encompassed entire villages. The medieval countryside included small family-run farms as well as such large estates. All of these operations drew on natural resources and contributed to the Byzantine economy.

A village's location depended on its geographic setting, political conditions, and local land-use practices. Basic considerations included security, availability of water, and proximity to suitable fields, vineyards, orchards, and woodlands. Since few villages were fortified, inhabitants relied for safety on distance from the coast or a high point overlooking nearby roads. During the relative calm of late antiquity, settlements were scattered along coastal plains and river valleys. The following centuries saw many exposed locations left behind in favor of less conspicuous hilltop sites. Isolated castles (kastra) offered a place of refuge in times of danger. Brigands and pirates remained a concern even in peacetime.

Like in western Europe, village domains were arranged in three concentric zones. Kitchen gardens, dairy cattle, threshing platforms, and mills were located on the edge of the built settlement. Gardening and dairy farming were labor-intensive and required tending on a daily basis. Outside of this innermost zone were fields for cereals, vineyards, and orchards of olive, fruit, and nut trees. These crops needed attention on a less regular basis, mainly at times of sowing and harvest. Since family holdings commonly were divided among surviving children, villagers often found themselves tilling isolated plots scattered over a wide area. Walking among far-flung holdings obviously took time and reduced productivity. One's commuting range was affected by terrain and vegetation, but rarely exceeded the distance that could be covered in two hours—in most places only three or four miles. Beyond this intermediate zone lay the village's pastures and woodlands. In many places goats and sheep grazed these lands during the winter months, and were herded into cooler uplands for summer.

Farming strategies were conditioned by topography and climate. Villagers drew water from perennial springs and wells, and often built cisterns to conserve resources during the dry summers. Cisterns and wells normally were located in the home or near the household garden. Threshing of cereal crops took place on circular platforms in the fields or around the village periphery, where donkeys or oxen helped trample the scattered sheaves. Milling was done by hand, with animal labor, or in water-driven mills. Olives and grapes could be raised on terraces, yet needed 8 to 10 years of regular care before yielding a marketable crop. Presses for both crops were found across the countryside. Only a few areas saw large-scale irrigation.

The appearance of settlements resulted from gradual growth more than regular planning. One or two paths led from the nearest road to the village center. This was occupied by an open plaza with a substantial public building or church that served as the legal base of the village's territory. Narrow alleys passed between houses that might have only three or four rooms. Where space allowed, a low wall enclosed each home with its kitchen garden and a couple of trees. Some places doubled as workshops for smiths, potters, and weavers. Bakers sold bread but also ran ovens to heat covered dishes for neighborhood families. The density of such settlements likely resembled traditional Near Eastern villages, which have between 50 and 80 inhabitants per acre (120–200 per hectare). Byzantine settlements typically covered an area of less than 10 to 15 acres (4 to 6 hectares).

Most places had one or two churches, usually simple basilicas built of local materials. The centrality of religion in daily life meant that the main church was conspicuously sited. Others might be built in new neighborhoods as a settlement expanded over time. Prosperous families dedicated additional chapels that could attract considerable wealth. In the sixth century the villagers of Kaper Koraon in Syria gave more than 50 pieces of silver plate weighing some 22 pounds to the local church of Saint Sergius.

Schematic plan of the village at Dar Qita in north Syria around the sixth century. From Howard C. Butler, *Publications of the Princeton University Archaeological Expedition to Syria in 1904–1905 and 1909*, division 2, *Ancient Architecture in Syria*, section B, *Northern Syria*, part 4, *The Djebel Barisha* (Leiden, the Netherlands: Brill, 1909).

The prominence of such buildings reflects the clergy's expanding role in rural affairs.

An essential part of any settlement was its cemetery. Priests, monks, and wealthy residents might find tombs within a church, but ordinary people were buried in a communal graveyard on the village outskirts. As in towns, the body of the deceased was washed, dressed, and laid out in the main room of the home. After relatives and friends had gathered, a priest led the procession the short distance to the cemetery. Inhumations were in shallow graves oriented to the east, lined with bricks or fieldstones, and covered with boards or tiles. Family members marked the site with evergreen branches and garlands. They returned on the 3rd, 9th, and 40th days after burial to share funeral cakes *(kollyba)* with the deceased. Wooden crosses and painted panels *(stelai)* might be left at the grave, but permanent markers were unusual. In some places the remains were exhumed after several years, inspected for portents, washed, and deposited in a common ossuary or funerary chapel. The entire graveyard would be moved if a settlement had to relocate. As a ceremonial focus and literal repository of its past, the cemetery was an enduring part of any village's identity.

Private Estates   Landownership was seen as the main form of wealth in Roman and Byzantine times, and major landowners were key players in rural society. Significant private estates existed in late antiquity. These apparently grew in number and size following the crises of the seventh and eighth centuries, as wealthy families increased their holdings at the expense of independent peasants. Medieval emperors struggled unsuccessfully to slow the growth of these private domains. At the lower end of the scale were resident landowners, gentlemen farmers who actively managed their holdings. Such individuals usually kept up a house in their ancestral village as well as a residence in the nearest market town. At the higher end were huge Anatolian estates that were built over generations. These operations were managed by a staff of full-time administrators, accountants, and stewards, who hired laborers to cultivate fields and manage livestock. Grand proprietors normally stayed in the provincial capital if not Constantinople itself, where they lobbied for political favors and further increased their wealth.

The scale of rural estates did not greatly affect the way they functioned or the ideology that lay behind them. Whether actually living in the countryside or not, the Byzantine landowner cultivated the ideal of the self-sustaining farmer and the life of independence or autarky. This notion had been celebrated by Virgil, Pliny, and other Latin writers, and was reinforced by medieval church leaders who were fond of quoting the Psalms and Gospels in its support. It underlies the *Farmer's Law,* the *Geoponika,* and Byzantine fiscal policy. A typical view held that "agriculture is a good thing of great antiquity, a task that brings wealth, a fine occupation that involves no danger, a skill that is natural for man." The eleventh-century landowner Kekaumenos advised the prudent master to meet his own household's needs and approach the marketplace with caution. "Plant all sorts of trees and reeds, which will bring you a yield every year without pain; this way you will be free of worry. Have beasts, draft oxen, pigs, sheep, and everything that grows and multiplies by itself every year: this is how you will secure abundance of your table and pleasure in all things." The emphasis on material and social self-sufficiency was deeply rooted in the Byzantine outlook.[5]

While much is known about how estates were run, their physical organization is not well understood. The location of the administrative center was clearly important. Descriptions of late-antique villas often mention their recreational aspect, with elegant buildings sited near natural springs or a river and surrounded by vineyards and fruit trees. The *Geoponika* recommends that the owner build his residence on a hillside with good views and ready access to water. The house should be set within an enclosed garden for both convenience and the benefits of living close to nature. Crops should be planted near stands of ash, fir, oak, pine, poplar, or willow. Medieval estate residences generally resembled their urban counterparts, offering a sharp contrast to the fortified castles and châteaus of western Europe. Many landowners established chapels, churches, and monasteries on their property to meet the spiritual needs of employees and advertise their own piety. Fortified warehouses and hilltop enclosures reinforced the status of the absentee owner.

The *Life* of Saint Philaretos gives a detailed view of the lifestyle of one provincial landowner. This wealthy eighth-century magnate was credited with 48 sizable estates in Galatia, Paphlagonia, and Pontus. His holdings were clearly marked on the ground and flourished under careful management. Large herds of livestock, including 600 head of cattle, 100 teams of oxen, 800 mares, 80 mules and packhorses, and 12,000 sheep, grazed on family pastures. The ancestral house was old and spacious, with a dining room that could seat 36 people. Estate employees and tenant farmers lived in scattered cottages and support buildings, and paid the owner a share of their annual harvest. Such wealth ranked Philaretos in the highest levels of provincial society.[6]

There were many reasons for founding a rural monastery, but one of the most compelling was to create an **Monasteries** environment for communal religious life far from the distractions of the city. The rural monastery often had significant landed interests. Foundation documents provide much information about how property was donated and the income it generated. Lands in the immediate vicinity of a monastery were cultivated by the monks as part of their daily routine. The area that could be effectively worked depended on the number of able-bodied residents, and not often did this exceed a few dozen. More extensive properties were organized as dependent *metocheia* with a few resident monks, or were leased to local peasants to farm in exchange for agricultural products or cash. Like secular farmsteads, monastic satellites included a residence, chapel, dining room with kitchen, storerooms, and stables, and sometimes a tower for security. Similar farming methods were used in both cases. As a rule monasteries seem to have placed greater emphasis on cultivation than livestock. Monks generally stayed close to the monastery and rarely ate meat.

Outside the compound walls monastic and private estates could be hard to distinguish. Monasteries invariably were surrounded by an enclosure that offered physical security while setting its inhabitants apart from the secular world. Vegetable gardens with vines and fruit trees were

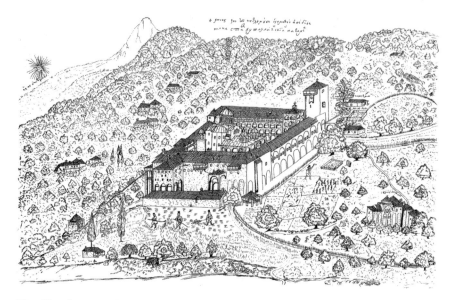

The Koutloumousiou monastery at Mount Athos in the eighteenth century. Drawing by the Russian monk Basil Barsky, in *Vtoroe poseshchenie sviatoi Afonskoi gory Vasilia Grigorovicha-Barskago* (St. Petersburg: Izd. Afonskago russkago Panteleimonova monastyria, 1887).

grown inside the compound or immediately beyond its perimeter. Some late monasteries in Macedonia diverted streams to needy crops. Grain was threshed in the fields or near the monastery walls. Pressing equipment near the compound was used to process grapes and olives. Tools and livestock were kept in stables, while storerooms preserved the harvest through the winter. Some monasteries owned mills and workshops that met internal needs and generated a salable surplus. The operation of a large monastery closely resembled a small, self-supporting village.

At Home in the Country Builders favored materials that were cheap and at hand. Stone, mud brick, timber, and thatch were the most widely used, in some areas together with bricks and roof tiles. In north Syria whole villages were constructed of carefully cut blocks of limestone. Builders in Egypt used sun-dried mud bricks made of river silt mixed with straw. Irregular fieldstones were the primary materials throughout the Balkans and Asia Minor. Villagers living near towns or cities might buy kiln-fired bricks and roof tiles from local producers, but sometimes made their own. Materials were mixed freely: heavy fieldstones and bricks worked best in the foundation and lower wall, while the upper wall and second story was typically mud brick or compressed earth steadied by timber framing. A thick coat of mud or lime was smoothed over uneven surfaces to protect them from weathering. Roofs were sloped with timber beams

A Cypriot village in the nineteenth century. Most traditional houses had an enclosed yard with a cistern, mill, freestanding oven, and trellised vines. Draft animals were stabled in the yard or a facing portico. The flat rooftops made convenient places to work and gather. From the *Illustrated London News*, 26 October 1878.

supporting flat stones or tiles. Steep layers of thatch may have been practical for houses and barns, especially in the mountains. Traditional materials and methods persisted in many regions until recent times. The alternation of strong summer sun with heavy winter rain ensured the need for frequent repairs.

Village houses ranged from single-room hovels to well-built mansions that differed little from fine urban homes. A typical single-family dwelling consisted of three or four rooms facing onto a small yard surrounded by a low wall. Chickens, ducks, and other animals were kept in the enclosure, which included a garden, grapevine, and one or two fruit trees. In one corner stood a small hearth or oven. In another was the latrine or cesspit (*kopron*), regularly emptied for garden fertilizer. A donkey or ox might be penned in the yard or a separate stable. One or two rooms were set aside for storing food, domestic supplies, and household tools. Living and sleeping quarters were kept separate, sometimes on an upper floor. Water came from a stone-lined cistern or well. Plumbing was limited to drains.

Interiors were small, dark, and plainly furnished. Room widths were limited by available timber and rarely exceeded 12 to 15 feet. Walls were

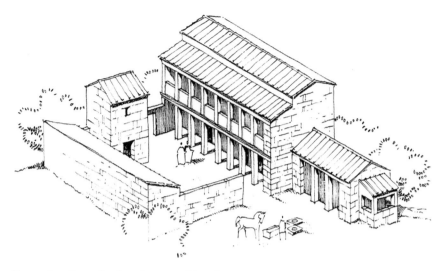

Reconstruction of a farmhouse with oil press at Qirqbize in north Syria around the fifth century. The two-storied main residence and its dependencies opened onto the enclosed yard. The covered oil press stood in front of the gate close to two cisterns. From Olivier Callot, *Huileries antiques de Syrie du nord* (Paris: Institut Français d'archéologie du Proche-Orient, 1984); reproduced courtesy of the Institut Français d'archéologie du Proche-Orient.

plastered with mud or lime. Windows were narrow and lacked glass. Wood shutters and heavy curtains kept out the winter chill and summer heat. Floors were packed earth covered with hides or mats. Some rooms in better houses were paved with stone slabs or tiles. Colorful woven rugs decorated the most important living spaces. People generally sat on benches or on the floor. A small wood table or working surface was used for meals. Many families maintained at least one room for receiving visitors and other special occasions. Religious objects were kept in one corner: terra-cotta lamps or candles, an icon of a local saint, a bronze amulet containing a relic, jewelry decorated with crosses. Many of these things were imbued with supernatural significance or had religious meaning for family members. Another part of this space, if not a separate room, served for sleeping. A typical bed was a narrow wood-frame structure with ropes or boards supporting a straw-filled mattress. Sometimes the only furniture was a bench built against a wall, which served as a sleeping platform at night. Money and other valuables were kept in a locked chest or cabinet.

Domestic routines can be readily imagined within this setting. Daylight hours were spent outdoors. Meals were prepared under the shelter of a porch in the yard. Cooking took place on a portable iron brazier or in a small brick oven. In the winter an indoors hearth served for preparing food as well as warmth. Flat loaves of unleavened bread could be baked directly in the ashes if no oven was available. Firewood and charcoal were always needed, and a generous supply was kept on hand. Fires were started by striking a flint against a metal plate or uncovering previously buried coals.

Grain, oil, and preserved foods were stored in a separate room. Flour was kept dry and free of vermin in large earthenware jars (*pithoi*) with heavy lids. Sealed amphorae were used for storage as well as carrying goods to market. Pickled vegetables and meats were kept in covered jars. Bags and baskets held other commodities. These supplies were vital to the household's survival. They represented the accumulated surplus from the previous harvest and sustained the family from fall through the following spring. While a prosperous family might have some cash set aside, most rural inhabitants kept their savings in land and tangible goods.

Food preparation and eating required special equipment. Stone mortars and pestles were needed to crack wheat and grind pulses. Some families could afford metal implements, but most cooking and serving was done with pottery. Vessels came in all sizes and shapes. Deep pots and baking dishes were made of coarse local clay with added quartz temper. Pitchers, jars, cups, and dishes for the table were more often made of fine clay, carefully shaped and decorated. Carved wood bowls and spoons completed the table setting.

Families lived on what they raised. Grain, garden vegetables, and olives made up the largest part of most meals. Barley and millet were the basis of gruels and porridges. The consumption of meat increased during the medieval period, but more so in towns than the countryside, where it was seen as a relative luxury. Fish, either fresh or dried, was important in coastal areas. Tree fruits were eaten at the table. Grapes were pressed to make wine. Vinegar made from grapes, barley, oats, and other crops was a household staple used for pickling vegetables and meat, cooking and seasoning food, drinking when mixed with water, and as an all-around disinfectant.

WORKING THE LAND

The boundary between cultivated and uncultivated land (the *incultum*) was constantly changing. Dominant forms **The Incultum** of natural vegetation include wild grasses, tough *maquis*-type brush, and forests of coniferous and deciduous trees. Grasses and low shrubs are characteristic of the Balkans and Anatolia. Today dense scrub and aromatic bushes thrive across the Aegean coastlands; in parts of south Greece they cover up to half the countryside. This vegetation is dense, spiny, and persistent, returning quickly to land not under continuous cultivation. The sturdy roots are well adapted to sandy slopes, which they stabilize for other plant forms. With time this scrubland develops into forests of pine and oak. In Byzantine times thick forests were found in the upper Balkans and along the Black Sea coast. Parts of this woodland still survive.

Scrub and forest offered essential resources. Trees provided timber for building, carpentry, and fuel. The branches of smaller trees and bushes were gathered for firewood or burned to make charcoal. Pitch and resin from cedar, juniper, and pine trees were used as wood preservatives, for lining ceramic jars, and for dietary and medicinal purposes. The *Geoponika* notes that such products could be made into soap, skin moisturizers, and insect repellants. They also were the main ingredient in flavoring resinated wine. Dried juniper berries could substitute for imported pepper. The *Book of the Eparch* regulated the sale of dry and liquid pitch in the capital. Certain barks, berries, nuts, leaves, and forest insects were processed into paints and dyes for fabrics and animal hides. Many types of vegetation were suitable for grazing animals. Long grasses, reeds, and supple branches were woven into baskets and ropes. Pigs and domestic fowl browsed in the woods for acorns, nuts, and grubs. Forests were the habitat of wild birds, rabbits, boars, and other game. Families gathered aromatic herbs like oregano, sage, and thyme on hillsides, and in the woods found edible greens, bulbs, mushrooms, tubers, and nuts. Wild herbs and roots like asparagus, mandrake, and poppy were called for by folk remedies and classical pharmacology. Medical writers sometimes specify their harvest in high mountains or out of season.

Shepherds in the countryside, illustrating the hazards of snakes and other venomous creatures. From a tenth-century edition of the Theriaka and Alexipharmaka of Nicander of Colophon. Photo courtesy of the Bibliothèque nationale de France, Paris (ms. suppl. grec 247).

Uncultivated land was assigned to the nearest village and could be used by all its residents. More remote areas belonged to the state and were available for common use, although harvested resources might be taxed or assigned for specific purposes. Most woodland exploitation was done by individual families in order to meet essential needs. Forests near towns or along the coast supported woodcutters, charcoal makers, and hunters. Some estates and monasteries produced timber and other forest commodities on a large scale and shipped them across the empire. At the most basic level, charcoal and firewood were used for cooking and heating in village and palace alike. Timber was in constant demand for building houses and ships. The special needs of the military were met by requisition or corvée.

Environmental and social factors encouraged families to bring new land under cultivation. Working with the permission of neighboring property owners, the enterprising peasant cleared new land with axes and saws. He salvaged timber, burned the accumulated slash, and spread the resulting ash as fertilizer. Loose woodland soils were especially fertile and returned a good crop with little plowing. The *Farmer's Law*, moreover, granted the cultivator the harvest for three years before the land reverted to its rightful owner. The farmer could use this short-term surplus to hire labor and buy additional land. As a property owner he now received sufficient rent from tenant farmers *(paroikoi)* to pay taxes and realize a profit. Favorable circumstances allowed successful families to built up sizable estates over the years. As Kekaumenos and other observers realized, the dependable if modest returns of farming offered the surest way of attaining independence and security.[7]

Rivers, lakes, and the sea were important resources for many villages. Fishing was a vital occupation, and in some **The Sea** places fish, mollusks, and shellfish were mainstays of the local diet. The *Geoponika*, drawing on the second-century treatise by Oppian of Apamea, devotes its final book to different species of marine life and common fishing methods. Fishermen were widely admired out of biblical regard for their profession and for their courage facing the sea throughout the year. Most set out in small boats before dawn. They cast their nets in favorite locations along the coast or at sea, and returned in late morning to sell their catch along the wharf. Torches and lamps were used to attract fish at night. Rural estates often kept ponds for raising fish. Landowners sometimes tried to develop coastal fishing grounds, but this required special legislation. Most commercial fishing was done with hand-knotted nets. Nets that could be cast by hand were relatively small, circular, and carried weights along the edge. Large draw and drift nets were suspended from wooden floats along one long side and weighted along the other. Serviceable weights were made of cast lead, folded lead sheets, perforated terra-cotta disks, and stone. Hook-and-line fishing, with or without a pole, was more commonly pursued for one's personal supply.

Lines were often made of horsehair, with white lines believed not to cast a shadow in the water. Barbed fishhooks were made of bent iron and copper wire, and closely resemble modern equipment. Weights, bobbers, and artificial lures were used as well. Fishing with a pole-mounted spear or trident was best suited to rivers and the coast.

Sea populations depended on currents, climate, and calendar. The most common fish species included bonito, mackerel, and tuna, which migrated annually between the Aegean and the Black Sea. White fish were more highly valued in the market, with the heavier, dark-flesh species sold as a low-cost alternative. Fish that was preserved by drying, salting, or pickling could be kept throughout the year. The economy of most Aegean islands depended largely on the sea, and some villages regularly dispatched large fishing fleets. Processing the tiny murex shell was profitable enough to support small coastal towns that specialized in its purple dye. Harvesting sponges was a particularly risky occupation. The divers, having wrapped one end of a rope above his waist, the diver carried an armload of lead weights to reach the sea bottom, quickly cut a few sponges from the rocks, and trusted his comrades to pull him quickly to the surface. Salt was produced in many coastal areas, with large medieval operations on Corfu and Cyprus and near Thessaloniki.[8]

Cultivation

The largest part of rural production came from gardens, fields, and orchards. Most families farmed on a small scale and continued with little change centuries-old traditions. One's choice of crops was influenced by soils, slope, rainfall, and access to wider markets. Adequate water and proximity to a sizable town might encourage one to concentrate on growing wheat for bread. By contrast, poor soils, an arid climate, or distance from shipping lanes recommended raising fodder for animals, who could transport themselves to market. By planting a variety of crops in different fields the farmer protected himself against the failure of any one. A thirteenth-century estate in north Greece is known to have been planted with 31 units (*modioi*) of wheat, 26 of barley, and 25 of rye, while saving 8 units of summer wheat for seed. Market controls by the state discouraged futures speculation. Except in times of drought, war, or famine, prices remained relatively stable.[9]

Cereals

Cereals had long formed the basis of the Mediterranean diet and were grown across the Byzantine countryside. Wheat (*sitos*) was the most highly regarded grain. While the soft-shelled Roman wheat was widespread through the sixth century, the medieval market came to be dominated by the hard-shelled durum variety (*Triticum turgidum* conv. *durum*), which had a higher nutritional content, was easier to separate from the chaff, and was better suited to transport and storage. Other common grains included the deeply rooted dark summer wheat, barley, rye, and millet. Barley (*krinithos*) and broomcorn millet (*kenchros*) were grown for the low end of the market and especially for animals. They needed little rain and could be successfully raised in poor, rocky soils, and so were favored on small islands and in the mountains. Barley withstood drought and had a short ripening season. Oats *(brome)* were raised for fodder and emergency rations in south Greece. Fifteenth-century records for Macedonia tell us that wheat made up half of all cultivated grains, barley a third, and the remainder comprised millet, oats, and rye.[10]

Cultivation methods depended on the weather. In many places farmers planted a fall crop that would be harvested by midsummer. Writing in the late eleventh century, Michael Psellos recommends planting wheat by mid-November in order to avoid working during the rainy winter months. If the winter crop failed, it could be plowed under and another crop sown in February or March. The soil was broken up by plowing and hoed by hand. Seed grain was distributed by broadcast sowing. Frequent weeding conserved ground moisture and encouraged the crop.

Cereals were harvested in summer or early fall with the hand sickle *(drepanon)*. Cut sheaves were brought to threshing platforms *(alonia)*. In major wheat-producing areas these were privately owned and located in the fields. Elsewhere communal threshing areas were set up on the village margin. Platforms were circular in plan and had a hard-packed surface that was swept to minimize dirt and dust. Sheaves were spread across the platform and flailed by hand or trampled by hoofed animals to shake the grain loose of chaff and straw. In some areas a flat threshing sled *(doukane)* with embedded flints or iron teeth was dragged over the sheaves by donkeys or oxen. After threshing and drying, grain had to be separated from chaff by winnowing. A multipronged pitchfork was used to toss the harvest into

Threshing in south Greece in the 1930s. Courtesy of the author.

the wind, which carried off the lighter chaff while allowing the grain to fall. A special winnowing basket or coarsely woven sieve helped complete the process. Sorting by hand removed small stones and insects before milling.

Each grain had its own reputation. Finely sorted white flour fetched the highest price. Blended flours combining white wheat with darker winter grains were less costly. Barley, rye, and millet were eaten mainly by livestock and by people who otherwise faced starvation. Small pebbles were routinely milled with poorly sorted grains, increasing their weight but naturally accelerating wear on the teeth. Consumption levels of bread are hard to determine. Some scholars have suggested that the average Byzantine ate three to six pounds of bread in late antiquity. This amount apparently dropped after the seventh century as the taste for meat became more widespread. During the late Middle Ages annual cereal consumption may have been around 440 to 530 pounds per person, depending on what other nutritional sources were available.

Grapes   Grape vines *(ampelos, Vitis vinifera)* have long flourished across the Mediterranean, especially in hillside areas near the coast.

The elder Pliny, writing in the first century A.D., stressed the importance of good soil and mild climate for their successful cultivation. The value of vines to the Byzantine economy is reflected in the *Geoponika*, which devotes 5 of its 20 books to the subject. Wine *(oinos)* from Palestine was among the most widely praised products of late antiquity. Medieval writers distinguished by name domestic wines coming from Attica, Thrace, Cappadocia, and the islands of Crete, Euboea, Thasos, Lesbos, Chios, Samos, Rhodes, and Cyprus. Sweet Cretan and Cypriot wines shipped through the Peloponnesian port at Monemvasia were known in the West as *malvosia,* or malmsey in England. Much of this production came from large estates. The tax-exempt status of monasteries brought considerable profit to operations on Mount Athos and Patmos. Tending a few vines was also a good way for peasant families to produce a small, salable surplus. While most grapes went into making wine, raisins were easily dried, stored, and shipped over long distances. By the late Middle Ages Greek raisins were being sold in the markets of western Europe.

Vineyards were taxed at a higher rate than other cultivated fields and required work throughout the year. Dark, well-drained soils are best for vines, especially in sheltered coastal areas. Careful plowing and harrowing was necessary to keep weeds down during the spring and summer. A flourishing vine needed regular trimming and shaping, and did best when tied to a trellis for support. Vines could also be trained up olive and fruit trees. In the fall grapes were harvested and carried in baskets to a stone press, which usually was located in the village and shared by several families. Branches were pruned and grafted during late winter and early spring.[11]

Olives   Pliny describes the soils and temperate climate that olives *(elaia, Olea europaea)* need to flourish, and these conditions can be found across much of the Mediterranean. Carefully planted and nurtured when young, olive trees can do well in poor, sandy soils without a great deal of rainfall. Under normal conditions a tree does not yield much fruit for the first few seasons, but when older reliably produces a good crop every other year. An established orchard requires little maintenance apart from careful plowing in the summer, manuring in the fall, and occasional pruning. Harvesting methods have changed little since antiquity, and usually involve spreading blankets on the ground and flailing the branches with sticks. A well-situated and skillfully pruned tree was an excellent long-term investment that could bear fruit for generations. Within a few years a single tree might provide a family with 10 to 18 pounds of olives, and up to three times as much when it reached maturity. This harvest could be pressed to yield nearly a gallon (two to three liters) of oil per tree. Much of this was consumed by the household, but any surplus was readily sold to others. Large groves are known to have been cultivated by the owners of secular and monastic estates. For this reason olive trees, like vineyards, were heavily taxed.[12]

Olive oil *(elaion)* was an indispensable part of Byzantine life. It was widely used for cooking and was an essential nutritional source for most people. Recent estimates of medieval consumption have ranged from 5 to 13 gallons (20 to 50 liters) per year. By this reckoning a village of 1,000 may have needed between 5,000 and 15,000 gallons (20,000 to 60,000 liters) each year for food. Oil was burned as fuel in candles and lamps. Assuming that a quart (liter) of oil lasted about 134 hours and that everyone needed an hour of lamplight each evening, a settlement of 500 might have required 350 gallons (1,350 liters) per year just for lighting. Oil also went into soap, skin moisturizer, garden fertilizer, insect repellent, and food preservatives. The greatest part of this supply would have come from the orchards that surrounded every village, town, and monastery.

Each family kept its own kitchen garden. Small plots were located next to the house, within the enclosure of a separate **Gardens** farmstead, or near the edge of settlement. Larger gardens lay within easy walking distance on the village outskirts. It has been estimated that an area of about 50 square yards was needed to supply an individual with vegetables under preindustrial conditions in central Europe. By this measure an average Byzantine family had to raise a garden of over half an acre (about a quarter hectare) just to support itself.

Family members watched their garden closely and visited it daily through the growing season. Frequent weeding saved ground moisture. Manure was needed to maintain the productivity of intensively worked plots. Household wastes from latrines and cesspits were carried to the garden and spread as fertilizer. Manure from domestic fowl and livestock was composted, ideally in a shallow pit or ditch, before being spread on the fields. The manure of donkeys, goats, and sheep was especially valued, while cattle and horse manure was less highly regarded. Growing leguminous plants was another way of restoring nitrogen to the soil.

A typical garden was planted with vegetables, herbs, and some trellised vines, with a tree or two for shade. The most common crops were broad beans, lentils, chickpeas, and vetches. Nearly a hundred different vegetable species were known in Byzantine territories, including dill, carrot, cucumber, white cabbage, kohlrabi, cress, leeks, mangold, radish, beetroot, turnip, onion, Swedish turnip, mangold root, rape, orach, parsnip, hedge mustard, common rue, savory, Jewish mallow, eggplant, and artichokes. Gourds, pumpkins, and melons were widely grown but not highly valued. Not all of these vegetables would be immediately recognized by a modern shopper. Carrots, for example, were yellow in antiquity and only gained their distinctive reddish color through medieval experiments with central Asian varieties. Most produce did not travel well and was consumed within the home, often after drying or pickling for winter storage.[13]

Herbs were raised for seasoning as well as medical applications. The *Geoponika* lists basil, marjoram, rosemary, savory, coriander, saffron, dill, rue, fenugreek, cress, mallow, fennel, mint, borage, costmary, squill, and mustard as common household herbs. Cumin, parsley, and tarragon are known from other sources. One would expect to find a few flowers in even the smallest garden.

Orchards   Almost all families raised at least one or two fruit trees, and many tended small orchards that included several species. Tree crops depended on soil and climate. Apples, cherries, figs, pears, and pomegranates were widely grown. Traveling in north Greece in the late Middle Ages, one could see orchards of apples, pears, peaches, plums, cherries, pomegranates, figs, and quince. The most common nuts were almond, chestnut, and walnut. Like vegetables, most of these perishable crops were eaten by family members or exchanged in the local market. Nuts, figs, and quince could be dried and stored without difficulty. Mulberry trees were grown less for their fruit than for the silkworms that fed on their leaves. Major mulberry areas were in coastal Syria, western Asia Minor, south Greece, and south Italy. Corinth, Thebes, Thessaloniki, Nicaea, and Constantinople were known for their silk industries in the medieval period.

AGRICULTURAL METHODS AND TECHNOLOGY

Farming methods were influenced by physical and social factors that changed little over time. Environmental conditions made demands on Byzantine farmers that differed from their Western counterparts. Soils were generally thin, rocky, and located on a slope. Most regions experienced sharply accentuated rainfall cycles with cool, rainy winters followed by long, dry summers. Well-maintained boundary walls and terraces minimized runoff and slowed soil erosion. Catch-basins and cisterns stored water during the winter months and supplemented the supply drawn from nearby streams and wells. Traditional cultivation methods allowed farmers to make the most of available resources. Shallow tilling and hand weeding reduced moisture loss from evaporation and weeds. Household waste was used to fertilize gardens, and animals were allowed to graze in fields between plantings. Crops were selectively intercultivated to their mutual benefit: kitchen gardens included vegetables, pulses, and herbs, while wheat was grown among olive trees. Regions with harsher conditions were planted with sturdy grains like barley, oats, and millet.

The pursuits of spring: herding live-stock, pruning vines, catching birds, fishing, and tending bees as shown in an eleventh-century edition of the *Homilies of Gregory Nazienzos.* Photo courtesy of the Bibliothèque natio-nale de France, Paris (ms. grec 533).

Allowing fields to lie fallow in alternate years conserved water and restored nutrients. A regime of orderly crop rotation was never devised.

Agricultural technology saw few advances during the Byzantine period. Many of the practices described by Cato, Verro, and Columella reappear in the tenth-century *Geoponika*. Traditional Roman-style tools continued to be made by medieval blacksmiths and were illustrated by contemporary artists. The fragmented pattern of land holdings discouraged the development of efficient farming methods, but at the same time reduced one's vulnerability to flood, landslide, and infestation. During the late Middle Ages some large estates developed water systems for irrigating gardens, orchards, and animals. Documents for north Greece regularly mention disputes over water rights and the diversion of streams to fields and power mills.

Plowing Fields were tilled using a sole ard or scratch plow *(gyes)* outfitted with a vertical plowshare made of wood or iron. This simple device was an essential tool that had been used since Roman times. The farmer controlled the plowshare by foot as one or two yoked oxen pulled it across the field, cutting a narrow furrow to a depth of a few inches. Unlike the heavy moldboard plow that was developed in western Europe, the sole ard did not turn the earth but required a separate pass with hoe and maddock. This seemingly inefficient approach has been blamed for Byzantium's slow agricultural development, and yet the persistence of the sole ard reflects the fact that it was well suited to local conditions. It was relatively inexpensive for a single family to make and repair without visiting a smith or toolmaker. It could be drawn by a single team of animals. Most importantly, the sole ard worked well with light soils, and shallow plowing conserved ground moisture. The heavy Western plow was not appropriate for Byzantine fields and was employed on only a few large estates in the late Middle Ages. The sole ard continued to be used effectively in parts of Greece and Turkey until recent times.[14]

Hand Tools Most of the tools mentioned in the *Farmer's Law* were known in Roman times. Land was initially cleared with a hand axe, bow saw, and fire. After plowing, the most versatile tool for working fields and gardens was the forked spade *(lisgarion)*, an implement with two sharp iron prongs mounted on a long wooden handle. The forked spade could be used for tilling fields and turning garden soil, and was essential for controlling weeds. Equally useful was the mattock *(makele)*, a hoe with a single broad blade that could be made of wood if not iron. Rakes and pitchforks were made not of iron but appropriately shaped tree branches. Vines and olive trees were pruned using a special knife with a hooked iron blade *(kladeuterion)*.[15]

Cereals were harvested with a *drepanon*, a curved handheld sickle with a smooth or serrated iron blade. Historians have long wondered why the more efficient scythe, which was widely known in western Europe, did not become popular in the East. The tall handle lets one use the scythe without

Shearing sheep, sailing, and plowing with a sole ard, as shown in the *Homilies of Gregory Nazienzos.* Photo courtesy of the Bibliothèque nationale de France, Paris (ms. grec 533).

stooping, after all, and its long blade cuts a broad swath in slow, rhythmic sweeps. The apparent reason for the Byzantine preference is that the hand sickle left longer stubble in the field for grazing livestock. This was a convenient way of providing fodder in a climate where animals could graze outdoors throughout the year. By contrast, livestock in northern Europe needed to be fed through a long winter confinement. Grazing was also the main way of manuring fields and pastures in the east Mediterranean. Using the hand sickle and grazing livestock in cut fields met the needs of humans, animals, and the land.

Most farming tools were made of iron blades mounted on wooden handles. A great deal of iron came from state-controlled mines and went directly into military equipment. Saints' lives, court documents, and archaeological discoveries make clear that iron also was widely used in farming. Most equipment was fabricated by local smiths or bought from traveling merchants or in nearby towns. Not every village had a skilled craftsman who could make tools from scratch, but there was always someone who could repair broken blades or improvise spare parts. Such implements were essential for all rural households.

Presses
Stone basins, vats, and weights were needed to process grapes and olives. Different sizes and configurations of pressing equipment have been identified in the field, which reflects the importance of working near the point of harvest. The same basic equipment served for both grapes and olives: a broad crushing basin and a collecting tank. Processing olives required in addition a heavy crushing stone or press weight attached to a timber beam. Large estates had their own operations, with multiple presses worked by skilled employees. While some families may have owned their equipment, most brought their grapes

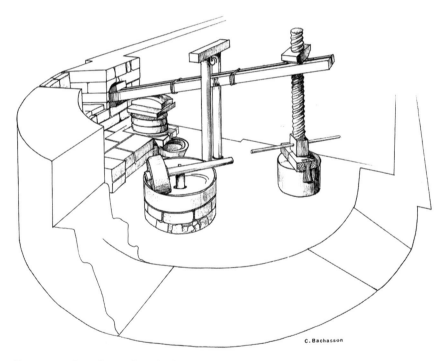

C. Bachasson

Reconstruction of a medieval oil press at Salamis-Constantia in Cyprus. The screw-threaded lever, anchored by a massive press weight, could apply tremendous force to each batch of olives in the crushing basin, with the oil draining off into a collecting tank. The rotary mill with stone roller may have been used for grain as well. Drawing by C. Bachasson, in *Salamine de Chypre IV: Anthologie Salaminienne* (Paris: Mission archéologique Salamine de Chypre, 1973); reproduced courtesy of the Mission archéologique Salamine de Chypre.

and olives to a communal press located close to their home village. Massive stone components weighing hundreds of pounds represented a significant investment of resources. Their sheer durability may have slowed the drive for technological innovation. Indeed, traditional pressing methods changed very little between antiquity and recent times.

Wine making involved several distinct steps. In the first stage grapes were washed, placed in a shallow vat, and tread by foot, with the juice draining off into large jars. The *Geoponika* describes the importance of this process: "The men that tread must get into the press, having scrupulously cleaned their feet, and none of them must eat or drink while in the press, nor must they climb in and out frequently. If they have to leave the press, they must not go with bare feet. The men that tread must also be fully clad and have their girdles on, on account of the violent sweating." The residue was strained and mechanically pressed a second time. The juice from treading and pressing was reduced by boiling and blended with water or other vintages. Finally the juice was seasoned with minerals and spices before being sealed in amphorae to ferment. In some regions amphorae were lined with mastic or pitch, the tarry residue left after heating the wood of certain coniferous trees. This interior coating prevented the contents from evaporating through the ceramic wall and at the same time gave the wine a distinctive resinated flavor. Carefully stored wine might last for several months before turning to vinegar, which had its own uses. Adding an apple—with or without a written biblical text—could extend the life of a fresh vintage. Under ideal conditions two and a half acres (about a hectare) planted in vines might yield 26 gallons (100 liters) of wine.[16]

Unlike grapes, olives had to be mechanically processed. Several methods known to Roman authors continued to be used in Byzantine times. The simplest was to place loose olives in a broad stone basin *(mola olearia)* and crush them under a heavy roller turned by hand or animals. Pressing allowed greater control of the process. Bags of olives were placed above a collecting basin and gradually squeezed by a long timber beam or lever. A carved wooden screw, anchored by a huge weight, was needed to raise and lower the beam. The highest-quality oil came from the first pressing. Great care was taken at this stage not to crush the pits, for this would spoil the flavor. The second pressing or crushing gave an inferior oil that was destined for making soap, skin moisturizers, candles, lamp fuel, and similar products. In both cases settling tanks were used to separate the oil from water and other impurities. The remaining oil was strained, sorted by grade, and poured into jars for storage or transport. About two to three pounds of olives yielded a liter of oil. The pits and pulpy residue were saved for fertilizer, cattle feed, and fuel.

After threshing in the field, grain was brought to mills for grinding or pounding into flour. Roman and Byzantine farmers **Mills** used pairs of specially shaped stone blocks for crushing grain.

In the simplest kind of mill a heavy stone roller was turned within a flat circular basin. Grain was poured into the basin and the flour swept up by hand. The stone hopper mill employed a conical millstone set into a deep bowl-shaped base, through which the fine flour sifted into waiting bags or jars. Hard, coarse-grained stone was preferred for these purposes, with volcanic basalt from south Asia Minor and Syria especially good for milling. Most mills were operated by hand or with the help of a donkey, mule, or ox.

Water-driven mills offered a better way to process large quantities of grain. The basic technology had been known since the first century B.C., and by late antiquity water mills *(hydromylones)* were a familiar sight across the Mediterranean. Water mills are regularly mentioned in the *Farmer's Law,* which is particularly concerned with the rights of water use. Two basic arrangements were possible. As in the hand mill, a horizontal paddlewheel mounted on a vertical axle turned a horizontal grinding stone. This type of mill worked best when built next to a sizable river or stream. A more effective alternative was to mount the waterwheel vertically and use cogged wooden gears to turn the millstone. Different sizes of gears permitted efficient grinding with a minimal supply of water. The

Reconstruction of a fifth-century water mill in Athens. A stone-lined channel directed water to the overshot wheel, with simple gearing used to turn the horizontal millstone. From Homer A. Thompson and R. E. Wycherley, *The Athenian Agora* XIV. *The Agora of Athens* (Princeton, N.J.: American School of Classical Studies, 1972); reproduced courtesy of the Trustees of the American School of Classical Studies at Athens.

force of a fast-moving stream was needed to turn an undershot wheel. The overshot approach, in which falling water was directed to the top of the wheel, worked even when the flow was limited. Such an arrangement required diverting a stream or building a stone-lined water course. An undershot mill is depicted in a floor mosaic in Constantinople. A small overshot mill has been excavated in Athens.

Despite the advantages of the vertical wheel, it was the horizontal wheel that was more widely used in the east Mediterranean, even as late as the twentieth century. Again, regional factors may have discouraged the move to more efficient technology, as happened in western Europe. It is important to remember that most Byzantine farming involved subsistence-level cultivation of small fields by single families. The limited production of most villages was easily handled by a small mill driven by an animal. The growth of large estates prompted investment in water mills, especially in areas like Macedonia where there was plentiful fast-flowing water and interest in irrigation. As a rule the horizontal wheel worked well under a variety of circumstances. It was easy to build and did not need complex gearing. The preference for the horizontal wheel reflects both the nature of local waterways and the small scale of most producers, who did not see milling as a separate source of income.[17]

Windmills *(anemomylones)* are thought to have originated in Persia around the seventh century, spreading east to **Windmills** Afghanistan by the ninth century and west to Normandy and England by the twelfth century. The gusty Aegean islands would have offered a logical path for the diffusion of wind technology. An early fourteenth-century document mentions a windmill near Thessaloniki. Identified remains in the islands include solidly built circular foundations 12 to 16 feet in diameter. Like threshing floors, windmills normally were located near rural settlements, rather than close to fields, and were owned by individuals or communities. Later windmills were a picturesque feature of the Cycladic and Dodecanese islands.[18]

Rural travel was always challenging. Long-distance communication was limited to state-supported post **Transportation** roads and the sea. Roads were intended mainly for official travelers and only occasionally passed through villages. Few anchorages or harbors could handle the ships that sailed between port cities. Most villagers rarely traveled outside their home territory. Essential needs were met by exchange with neighbors or by purchase from traveling merchants, who brought their wares on the back of a donkey, mule, or camel. Once or twice a year each family took its surplus harvest to the nearest town to sell. Produce was loaded on wooden carts and wagons that had changed little since Roman times. The inefficient neck collar, which limited the load an animal could draw, was still being used in the tenth century. Donkeys, mules, and sometimes oxen pulled carts along winding paths and beaten tracks that passed between fields and along rivers, following topographic contours wherever possible. Travel along these poorly developed routes was often hindered by bad weather, flood, or landslide. The inevitable isolation experienced by many villages underscored the benefits of self-sufficiency.

ANIMALS AND LIVESTOCK

Almost everyone kept at least a few animals. The most common live-stock were sheep, goats, pigs, cattle, and domestic fowl. These versatile creatures supplemented garden crops by providing milk, cheese, and meat for the table as well as manure for the fields. Animals normally were kept close to home rather than in separate barns. Chickens, ducks, and pigs stayed in the yard and fed on domestic refuse. Oxen and other working animals usually were stabled in the lower level of the house. Donkeys and mules hauled goods, since horses were an expensive luxury. Sheep and goats needed more space for grazing and were herded in flocks outside the village. Bees were kept in wood and ceramic hives on the edge of fields and woodlands. While costly and time-consuming to maintain, a diverse population of species distributed the family's exposure to economic and infectious risk. The number of dependent animals directly reflected the status of their owners.

Dogs
For thousands of years dogs have been valued companions of farmers and pastoralists across the Near East. They were frequently mentioned by Greek and Roman authors and were revered in Persian society. The Roman agriculturalist Columella reminds us that everyone knows of the unsurpassed loyalty of dogs. Oppian of Apamea, followed by the *Geoponika*, describes the main breeds and characteristics of hunting canines. Dogs for the chase were bred for speed and agility. They should not bark and needed special training to pursue their quarry quietly, "for silence is the rule for hunters and above all for trackers." Shepherd dogs, the "friendly force" (*amica vis pastoribus*) of the poet Horace, should be light in color, alert, loud of bark, and quick. They worked in teams when herding sheep, goats, and cattle and warding off predators. Large, dark dogs were best for patrolling vineyards and orchards and guarding the house. Puppies should be given short names and trained to follow briskly spoken commands. Dogs accompanied family members on routine errands and expeditions away from home.

Such useful animals would have been well taken care of by their owners. Besides scavenging from the table, they likely were fed a mixture of whey and barley flour or bread boiled with bean liquid, similar to Columella's recommended canine diet. Like sheep and goats, dogs could be treated for fleas and ticks by applying natural pesticides made from cedar, cumin, or cyperus. Rubbing the ears with crushed bitter almonds kept away biting flies. Both the *Farmer's Law* and *Geoponika* indicate how essential dogs were for rural life.[19]

Most families could afford to keep a few sheep and
goats. The two species were raised everywhere and　**Sheep and Goats**
formed the economic mainstay of some small islands.
Both are extensive grazers. Goats in particular can survive on scrubland
unsuited to other animals. Sheep and goats get along well and were often
herded together. Leather collars and bronze bells were worn to indicate
who owned which animals. In many regions mixed herds belonging to
several families or an entire village were driven seasonally between pastures, spending summers in cooler elevations and returning to graze near
the village in winter. While away from home shepherds slept under tents
or in temporary shelters. They also built sheepfolds out of brushwood
and fieldstones. Only in Asia Minor was there enough pasturage to support large herds and permanent pastoral buildings.

Even a small number of sheep and goats could provide a family with
milk, cheese, meat, and skins. Cheese making was a good way to extend
the nutritional value of milk. After curdling, the fresh cheese *(tyros)* was
smoked or stored in brine. The best kinds of cheese were said to be made
from the milk of goats who grazed in high mountains. Sheep wool was
especially valued on the wider market, with the finest grades known to
come from Anatolia. Then no less than now, shepherds were concerned
with lice and ticks. The *Geoponika* describes how to fight parasites by heating cedar oil, cyperus, mandrake, or maple roots in water and applying
the warm mixture to the parted wool along the animal's back.[20]

In well-watered areas pigs offered an environmentally efficient
source of protein. Unlike cattle, swine reproduce in large litters—as　**Pigs**
many as two a year—and grow quickly to maturity. They require
little space, can be kept in a small yard, and are content eating household scraps and other waste. Some estates raised them in large numbers.
Uncultivated woodlands offered pigs the opportunity to forage for acorns,
chestnuts, leaves, roots, and grubs. Their docile temperament and slow gait
made small herds of swine suitable for children to tend. An eight-month-
old pig might yield over a hundred pounds of meat and by-products, four
to five times more than a sheep or goat. Hams were preserved by drying
in salt or soaking in brine before curing in a smokehouse. Smaller pieces of
meat and fat were made into sausage. Pork may have been widely available
in the medieval countryside but was not highly regarded by city dwellers.
Pork fat and lard were used in cooking and making candles. Pigskin was
good for boots and other leather goods.[21]

Apart from land and buildings, a couple of cows or oxen represented the biggest investment of most families. Both species　**Cattle**
reproduce and mature slowly, need extensive summer pasturage
and lots of winter fodder, and have to be sheltered in bad weather. Cattle
in particular consumed huge quantities of grain. For this reason the largest
herds seem to have been raised in drier regions that favored the hardier species of dark wheat and millet. Despite their considerable expense, oxen were

needed for plowing fields and pulling heavy loads. The growing demand for meat, leather, and hides was met by large herds raised in Anatolia.

Domestic Fowl   Chickens, ducks, geese, or pigeons were raised by most rural families. Chickens are the easiest to manage. They can be kept in a small enclosure or allowed to roam, constantly forage, and thrive on coarse grains and kitchen scraps. Of all poultry they are the most easily cared for by children and give a steady supply of eggs and meat. Exotic fowl like guinea hens and peacocks were raised near medieval cities and sold to elite households, where various poultry dishes were served. Feathers were gathered for stuffing mattresses. Goose down was highly prized for pillows and bedding.

Bees and Silkworms   Beekeeping spanned several agricultural categories. In addition to producing honey and wax, bees *(Apis mellifera)* were essential for pollinating crops. Their recognized importance in Greek and Roman farming continued throughout Byzantine times, and an entire book of the *Geoponika* discusses how care for them. Bees produce the most honey in areas with plentiful pasture and pine woodlands. Many families maintained a few beehives made of wood or ceramic. Large quantities of honey were produced in Cyprus and along the Black Sea coast. In the eighth century Philaretos tended 250 hives on his estates in Paphlagonia. Mount Hymettos in Attica has been a famous source of honey from antiquity to the present day. The flavor of any honey varies with local flora and harvesting methods. The practice of using smoke to clear beehives, for example, imparts a dark, smoky flavor. Honey *(meli)* was the only sweetener available in Byzantium before the fourteenth century, when the cultivation of sugarcane was introduced to the Mediterranean by the Arabs. Beeswax was important for making candles, the main source of lighting in the later Middle Ages.[22]

Silkworms were brought to the Mediterranean from China in the sixth century. White and purple mulberry trees were native to coastal regions and proved to be an ideal host for silk caterpillars and moths (especially *Bombyx mori*). Cocoons were harvested seasonally in south Greece and western Asia Minor.

VILLAGE CRAFTS

The basic equipment of rural life—tools, containers, and furnishings—was made mainly in the village. Families looked to their gardens and animals for their own food and clothing. Other domestic goods, from baskets to candles and pottery, might equally be made within the home. Even a small surplus could be sold or swapped for other needed items. All but the smallest settlements supported individuals who specialized in essential crafts like carpentry, smithing, pottery making, weaving, and leatherworking.

All agricultural equipment, from field tools to wagons and permanent shelters, was at least partly made of **Woodworking** wood. Carved handles served for digging and cutting implements. Greater skill was needed when assembling a plow or an ox yoke, or building a cart or wagon. Most of these projects involved precision joinery, in which parts were carefully cut, drilled, and fit together. Common woodworking tools have changed little over the years, and one can easily recognize single-edge axes, adzes, bow saws, chisels, knives, and rasps. Planes and files were needed for trimming and smoothing boards. Saws, drills, augers, lathes, squares, and clamps were used when making mortise-and-tenon and dovetail joints in furniture and carts. Craftsmen employed similar expertise when making barrels of closely fitted wooden staves, reinforced by iron bands, to store and move goods to market. The same skills were needed in coastal areas for building boats and ships. Household furnishings like tables, benches, chairs, and beds might be made by carpenters or enterprising family members. Carved spoons, spindles, and toys could be exchanged locally.

Most villages supported one or more smiths to make and repair the tools that everyone needed. Agricultural **Metalworking** implements generally had iron blades and were used for specific purposes. Pruning knives were small and hooked, while sickles had long curving blades. Spades and mattocks needed iron heads to withstand daily use through much of the year. Iron protected the wooden share of the sole ard plow as it tilled stony fields. Special bits and trappings were needed to harness oxen, donkeys, and horses. Iron horseshoes were necessary when working rocky ground or traveling paved surfaces. Sheep and goats were known to wear small bronze bells. Metal also figured prominently in village homes. Iron nails in all sizes were used in roofs, doors, windows, tables, and chairs. Doors turned on iron hinges and were closed by lock and key. Smaller hinges and locks were used to secure boxes and chests. Routine household tools included iron hammers, knives, scrapers, and pincers. The best knives, like swords, were made of carburized iron or steel, mainly in urban workshops. Excavations have recovered bronze and iron kettles and pots for cooking as well as bowls and pitchers for the table. The well-dressed villager wore a belt with a bronze or iron buckle over his tunic, and closed his outer cloak with a pin or brooch. Many of these items were made in towns and sold by traveling peddlers.

The *Farmer's Law* confirms the value of metal tools. Iron ore was mined at a number of places in the Balkans and Asia Minor. Unlike large Roman operations, medieval mines were run on a small scale by private operators who employed local inhabitants on a seasonal basis. The ore was roasted near its source before being carried in bags or baskets to nearby villages and towns. Here the iron was smelted in a special furnace. Several assistants helped the smith stoke the furnace and operate the hand bellows over the span of several hours. Larger workshops, including state-run armaments

factories, could cut costs by working over longer periods. Repeated heating, hammering, and immersion in water improved the quality of the
iron, which could be further strengthened (primarily for weapons) by
adding carbon. The entire process involved a great deal of time, effort, and
resources. It has been estimated that the 160 pounds of iron belts worn
by the seventh-century saint Theodore of Sykeon represents 3.6 tons
of charcoal and 2.2 tons of iron ore, which were smelted over 12 days and
nights. The discovery of iron tools on many sites tangibly documents their
importance.[23]

Pottery Making
The making of pottery *(keramia)* was an essential
part of village life. Its contribution is recognized by the
Geoponika, which numbers pot makers among the key
artisans of the countryside. Neighborhood potters supplied most of the
tablewares and storage vessels that were used—and broken—on a daily
basis. Greater specialization, which involved searching for finer clays and
consistently shaping and firing pots, was more typical of larger operations. In later times pottery making helped support exchange among
neighboring villages at periodic markets and festivals. In small settlements basic needs were met within the household itself.[24]

Pithoi were large jars for storing grain, oil, and other commodities.
Cheeses were soaked in brine-filled vessels; fish and meat were dried
between layers of salt. Pithoi were made in a few basic shapes following
local tradition. Many were ovoid with a flat base, broad shoulder, narrow
mouth, and reinforced rim. A typical pithos was about as tall as it was
wide. Examples ranged from two to more than five feet high, and were
designed to hold hundreds of pounds. The thick wall and sturdy shape
were good for stationary storage; many pithoi were simply built into a
counter or recessed into the floor. The mouth could be covered with a
piece of cloth, roof tile, or wood lid. The reinforced rim protected the jar
when pouring or dipping out its contents.

Most pithoi were made in small workshops, either in the village or
a settlement closer to suitable clay, fuel, and water. Methods of manufacture have changed little over the years, and in Cyprus some potters
still make *pitharia* in traditional ways. Raw clay was dug out of hillside
beds or river banks. Large lumps were broken up by a wood mallet into
a coarse powder. Pebbles and coarse impurities were removed by dry
sieving, while fine sand, quartz, or other temper was added to strengthen
the body. After adding water the malleable clay was thoroughly mixed in
vats or tubs before being left to dry to a leather-hard consistency suitable
for shaping. Most pithoi were built by hand. Long clay strips were coiled
atop a flat disk base and smoothed into a solid wall. A slow turntable may
have helped in making small vessels, but larger pithoi were built directly
on the ground. Strips of cloth or rope might be tied around the pot while
it dried. A heavy triangular rim and small, sturdy handles were sometimes attached to the upper wall. At this point the potter added pinched,

Large storage jars (pitharia) made in Cyprus. Such unwieldy vessels were made by hand and rarely traveled any distance. Most rural families stored their household supply of grain and oil in such vessels. Courtesy of the author.

incised, or stamped details and smoothed the surface with a clay slip. Such features could have been intended to indicate a specific potter or simply enliven the vessel's appearance. Groups of dried pithoi would be carefully stacked and covered with heaps of firewood. Firing took place over several days and had to be constantly tended, with wood added regularly to the flames. After cooling, the kiln was carefully unpacked and intact vessels cleaned. The large size and awkward shape of most pithoi suggest that they were used close to where they were made.

Amphorae were smaller and more easily moved storage jars. Their main purpose was to carry foodstuffs over long distances, and for this reason they were made near the point of harvest. These jars were designed for liquids like oil and wine, but could also be used for grain, olives, fish sauces, and other commodities. Most amphorae were cylindrical or ovoid vessels with thin walls and a reinforced base. A tall neck and narrow mouth facilitated pouring and sealing. Two handles (as the term *amphora* implies) were attached to the upper wall for carrying. The base was rounded or pointed since vessels usually were stored leaning against each other instead of freestanding. When full, a typical amphora weighed 50 to 100 pounds.

As in earlier times, Byzantine amphorae advertised their intended contents and place of origin, which encouraged their manufacture in enormous quantities in a few basic shapes and sizes. Amphorae made in south Greece or western Asia Minor, for example, looked very different

An amphora workshop in western Turkey. After shaping on a fast-moving wheel, the pots are allowed to dry for several weeks before firing in the kiln. The slender shape and paired handles are well suited for commercial transport. Courtesy of the author.

from those made in Syria and Palestine or along the Black Sea. Such standardization suggests that they were made by organized teams on a regular basis. Large-scale production required abundant clay and plenty of fuel and water. The thin-walled vessels were built in sections on a wheel and fired in large batches. Kilns were built of brick and tile in order to control the firing conditions. Amphora making was an integral part of the agrarian cycle, with thousands of vessels made each year to receive the fall harvest.

Kitchen and table pottery includes vessels for cooking, serving, and eating. Cooking- and tablewares can be distinguished by the coarse temper that was added to protect pots repeatedly exposed to the fire. Typical shapes were shallow dishes and pans for baking and frying, broad casseroles with fitted lids, and deep rounded stewpots. Variations suggest dietary and ethnic preferences in different regions. Baking dishes had a thick floor and low curved rim. Other pots were thin-walled with a rounded bottom and two or three small handles for suspending over the fire. Outer walls were often lightly ridged. Some narrow-mouth jars were used for heating liquids.

Different shapes and sizes of vessels were available for meals. Shallow bowls and dishes were common in late antiquity, when the main course often was served on a shared platter. Medieval custom showed a preference

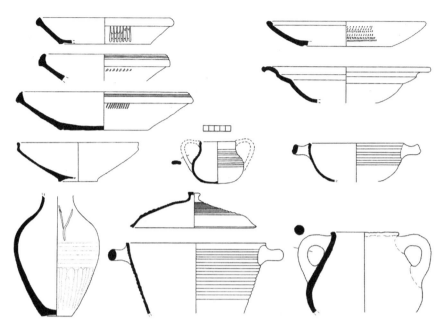

Representative table and cooking wares used in an early seventh-century village excavated near Kalavasos in Cyprus. Broad, open vessels were preferred for serving and eating, while food was heated over the fire in deep, lidded pans and pots. Courtesy of the author.

for smaller, deeper dishes and bowls, sometimes mounted on a high base and covered by a thick vitreous glaze. Wine and water were poured from tall flagons and rounded pitchers. For drinking people used heavy mugs, handleless cups, and delicate beakers and goblets made of glass.

Most kitchen- and tablewares were made in quantity by skilled craftsmen to be sold on a regional scale. Clays were carefully chosen and prepared. Standard shapes made it easier to stack pots in the kiln. Finished vessels were often covered with a thin protective slip or colored glaze that copied urban fashions. When demand warranted, village potters hired other men who were not busy in the fields or mines. Less elegant but serviceable pottery was made at home and fired at low temperatures in the hearth or neighborhood oven. As in other agricultural societies, many of these utilitarian vessels were made by village women helped by their children.

Other ceramic products were made by village potters. Ceramic beehives were large cylinders with a deeply scored inner surface for bees to attach their honeycomb. Narrow tubular pipes were used for carrying fresh water and drainage. Terra-cotta building materials were made wherever local resources allowed. Flat bricks sometimes were built into walls, but fieldstones were a cheap alternative. Since bricks weighed less than stones they were preferred for the vaults of churches and cisterns; for this reason they might be brought some distance. Roof tiles were a higher priority in rainy areas that lacked a natural source of flat stone. Most bricks and tiles made in rural workshops were intended for specific projects and fired in open kilns. In many places they remain the most enduring sign of medieval occupation.

Spinning and Weaving Village clothes were functional by design and manufactured in traditional ways. The main materials were flax, cotton, and wool. Flax *(linos, linarion)* was widely grown in late antiquity, particularly in Italy, north Greece, and Asia Minor, and during the medieval period was supplemented by increasing amounts of cotton *(bambax)* from Crete, Cyprus, and the Near East. Both crops were harvested in the fall. The slender stalks of the flax plant were soaked and beaten to free its fine fibers for spinning linen thread. Cotton bolls were painstakingly opened and combed by hand. Sheep were shorn with the return of warm weather in the spring. Burrs were manually removed from the clipped wool before washing and carding. The clean flax or wool was mounted on a tall distaff and twisted into thread or yard using a hand-spun spindle. Felt was made by stretching the fleece on the ground, soaking it with warm detergents, and pressing it under flat stones or by foot.

Spun thread or yarn was woven into cloth on an upright loom. The traditional Near Eastern loom had a wood frame with side posts supporting horizontal crossbars. The warp of the fabric was formed by long strands of wool that were attached to the top bar and held tight by small weights. Alternate warp threads were separated by hand or with a movable crossbar to interweave the horizontal weft threads. The woven fabric was rolled up on the anchoring crossbar until reaching the end of the warp, which was finished by braiding or knotting. When weaving one stood in front of the loom and passed the weft shuttle back and forth. The process was considerably improved in late antiquity when a foot treadle was developed for mechanically separating the warp threads—an innovation that appeared mainly in urban workshops. The basic equipment for weaving was easily made at home. Archaeologists regularly find small pierced disks of clay and stone that could have served as spindle whorls and loom weights, confirming that these vital activities were practiced everywhere. Wool yarn was also knit by hand into stockings and cloth.

Different techniques produced finished linen, cotton, and wool cloth. The fabric was washed with detergents like fuller's earth *(creta fullonica)* in order to remove dirt and grease. Linen was normally bleached or left in its natural state, while cotton and wool readily took colorful dyes. Different colors came from plants, minerals, and animal products. Since the Bronze Age saffron had been harvested from the purple crocus *(Crocus sativa)* to make yellow and red dyes. The wood of the sumac *(Rhus coriara)* was known to produce yellow, while sumac berries and madder *(Rubia*

Making textiles was an important activity in both town and country. The women shown here are weaving cloth on a pedal loom and embroidering details by hand. The figure style and costume reflect Western influence in the late Middle Ages. From a fourteenth-century edition of the *Book of Job with Commentaries*. Photo courtesy of the Bibliothèque Nationale de France, Paris (ms. grec 135).

tinctoria) gave dark shades of red. Violet was commonly produced from the kermes worm *(Kermis elices)*, and deep purple came from sea snails *(Murex brandaris* and *purpura)*. Tunics were made of linen and cotton, and might be decorated with embroidered patterns or hems. The heavier wool cloth was warmer, more durable, and naturally repelled water, and so was preferred for outer cloaks.

Other hand-woven village products included baskets, rope, and floor coverings. Baskets were made by interweaving long grasses, reeds, or branches. Rope consisted of twined or braided plant fibers like hemp sometimes reinforced with wool. Floor mats were made of coiled rope, while rugs were woven on the same looms used for cloth. Baskets and rope had countless uses, while mats and rugs added to the comfort of any home.

Working with animal hides was a messy process that involved several steps. Fresh skins were stretched on **Leatherworking** a frame for salting or drying in the sun. Cured hides could be stored at home until there were enough to warrant processing, which for many families may have been only once a year. Tanning usually took place on the village outskirts. One began by soaking, boiling, and coating the hides with powdered lime or caustic lye in order to loosen the hair and fat. Hides were spread on a table and scrapped with a two-handled drawknife. Rubbing the hide with sandstone blocks produced a finer surface texture. The actual tanning consisted of soaking hides in a toxic solution of alum, salt, and tree bark. After drying, the hides were stained and brushed to the desired color and texture. Furriers soaked and degreased the hair while scraping only the inner surface of the animal skin. Finished hides might be worked in the village or sent to towns to be finished in large workshops.

Leather goods were everywhere in constant demand. Straps, belts, cloaks, sandals, and boots were basic items of personal apparel as well as necessary equipment for rural life. Cobblers are the most frequently mentioned craftsmen in medieval village records from Macedonia, reflecting the importance of sturdy footwear among working people. The army always required a great deal of leather for saddles and other cavalry fittings; leather also was needed for armor, shields, and tents. Cowhides, sheepskins, and furs were valued as warm winter clothing and bedding. Fine parchment made from calf and sheep skins was in short supply in Constantinople and even scarcer in other cities. Anatolian livestock herds supplied the growing market for leather goods in the medieval period.

THE CHALLENGE OF RURAL LIFE

Life in the countryside—which is to say the experience of most Byzantine people—was difficult and hazardous. Housing was modest and comforts few. Meals were adequate at best, consisting of bread, cheese, olives, beans, vegetables, a little meat, and mediocre wine. Farming was the dangerous occupation it has always been. Even in modern, industrialized countries agricultural workers risk injury from equipment, large animals, and falls. These dangers were significantly greater in the Middle Ages, when minor wounds could easily become infected and lead to permanent disability or death. Lacking access to the modest benefits of Byzantine medicine, one's options for treatment were limited to folk remedies and prayer.

Under optimal conditions, hard year-round labor returned enough harvest to feed one's family and pay debts, yet effort did not guarantee success. Natural hazards were unavoidable. Extreme weather could destroy a crop with hail, an unexpected frost, or prolonged cold. Periodic climatic fluctuations led to periods of flood and drought. Earthquakes damaged buildings and terraces, brought about landslides, and accelerated erosion. Insects ravaged crops in the field while vermin and mold attacked the storerooms. Wildfires depleted local supplies of timber, fuel, and game. Domestic fires spread easily among closely built wood-roofed houses and churches. Social hazards were equally varied. Warfare was a concern for many villages, particularly those near the frontier or the long Mediterranean coast. Taxes were regularly and at times harshly collected by officials who could seem as rapacious as the brigands and thieves who preyed on rural travelers. In times of emergency the state would readily conscript supplies as well as labor. The main guarantor of social order was the solidarity of the village community.

Various strategies were employed in facing such occupational hazards. Crops and farming methods were well established by late antiquity. Diversification offered one's best insurance against agricultural failure, and for this reason many farmers raised different crops on small, scattered fields. Keeping a few animals provided help in the fields while supplementing the household diet and wardrobe. Baskets, pottery, clothing, and other crafts made at home meant a margin of domestic comfort as well as a hedge against disaster. In all events the family improved its odds by scrupulously observing folk customs and asking the protection of local saints. Two of the most common themes of Byzantine saints' lives are the perils of the countryside and the miraculous powers of holy men in overcoming them. The popularity of such legends reflects both the reality of rural hardships and the hope people placed in supernatural forces surrounding them.[25]

NOTES

1. For the setting see Bernard Geyer, "Physical Factors in the Evolution of the Landscape and Land Use," in *The Economic History of Byzantium from the Seventh to the Fifteenth Century*, ed. Angeliki E. Laiou (Washington, D.C.: Dumbarton Oaks, 2002), 31–45. A good introduction to rural life is Alexander Kazhdan, "The Peasantry," in *The Byzantines*, ed. Guglielmo Cavallo (Chicago: University of Chicago Press, 1997), 43–73.

2. Adapted from Walter Ashburner, "The Farmer's Law," *Journal of Hellenic Studies* 32 (1912): 68–95.

3. An English translation is Ashburner, "The Farmer's Law," reprinted along with other relevant sources in Charles M. Brand, ed., *Icon and Minaret: Sources of Byzantine and Islamic Civilization* (Englewood Cliffs, N.J.: Prentice Hall, 1969), 70–78; and Deno John Geanakoplos, *Byzantium: Church, Society, and Civilization Seen through Contemporary Eyes* (Chicago: University of Chicago Press, 1984), 231–34. A new edition of the *Geoponika* is needed; for an outdated English translation see Thomas Owen, trans., *Geoponika: Agricultural Pursuits* (London: privately printed, 1805–6), available online at http://www.ancientlibrary.com/geoponika/. Important classical sources with much fascinating detail include Columella, *On Agriculture*, trans. Harrison Boyd Ash, E. S. Forster, and Edward H. Heffner, 3 vols. (Cambridge: Harvard University Press, 1941–55); and Pliny the Elder, *Natural History*, trans. H. Rackham, W.H.S. Jones, and D. E. Eichholz, 10 vols. (Cambridge: Harvard University Press, 1938–62). For other classical authors see K.D. White, *Roman Farming* (Ithaca, N.Y.: Cornell University Press, 1970), 14–41.

4. The extensive bibliography on the economics of the Byzantine countryside includes J. L. Teall, "The Byzantine Agricultural Tradition," *Dumbarton Oaks Papers* 25 (1971): 34–59; Paul Lemerle, *The Agrarian History of Byzantium from the Origins to the Twelfth Century* (Galway, Ireland: Galway University Press, 1979); Alan Harvey, *Economic Expansion in the Byzantine Empire, 900–1200* (Cambridge: Cambridge

University Press, 1989); Jean Lefort, "The Rural Economy, Seventh–Twelfth Centuries," in Laiou, *Economic History of Byzantium,* 1:231–310; and Angeliki E. Laiou, "The Agrarian Economy, Thirteenth–Fifteenth Centuries," in Laiou, *Economic History of Byzantium,* 1:311–75.

    5. Philotheos the Opsikian, quoted in A. R. Littlewood, "Gardens of Byzantium," *Journal of Garden History* 12 (1992): 129. Kekaumenos is quoted in Lefort, "The Rural Economy," in Laiou, *Economic History of Byzantium,* 1:298.

    6. John W. Nesbitt, "The Life of St. Philaretos (702–792) and Its Significance for Byzantine Agriculture," *Greek Orthodox Theological Review* 14 (1969): 150–58.

    7. For uses of uncultivated land see Archibald Dunn, "The Exploitation and Control of Woodland and Scrubland in the Byzantine World," *Byzantine and Modern Greek Studies* 16 (1992): 235–98.

    8. For the *Halieutica* ("On Fishing") by Oppian of Apamea see A. W. Mair, trans., *Oppian, Colluthus, Tryphiodorus* (Cambridge: Harvard University Press, 1963). For an engaging introduction see William Radcliffe, *Fishing from Earliest Times,* 2nd ed. (New York: E. P. Dutton, 1921).

    9. The classical background is summarized by K. D. White, "Farming and Animal Husbandry," in *Civilization of the Ancient Mediterranean: Greece and Rome,* ed. Michael Grant and Rachel Kitzinger (New York: Charles Scribner's Sons, 1988), 1:211–45; and idem, *Roman Farming.* For crop yields see Harvey, *Economic Expansion in the Byzantine Empire,* 126.

    10. Lin Foxhall and Hamish A. Forbes, "*Sitometreia:* The Role of Grain as a Staple Food in Classical Antiquity," *Chiron* 12 (1982): 41–90; and Andrew Dalby, *Food in the Ancient World from A to Z* (New York: Routledge, 2003).

    11. Columella, *On Agriculture* 3.2; Pliny the Elder, *Natural History* 14.8–29; White, *Roman Farming,* 229–46; Dalby, *Food in the Ancient World,* 163–66.

    12. Columella, *On Agriculture* 5.8–9; Pliny the Elder, *Natural History* 15.2–6; White, *Roman Farming,* 225–27; Dalby, *Food in the Ancient World,* 237–40.

    13. See in general Andrew Dalby, *Flavours of Byzantium* (Totnes, England: Prospect Books, 2003).

    14. Typical plow types are discussed by K. D. White, *Agricultural Implements of the Roman World* (Cambridge: Cambridge University Press, 1967), 125–29. For social implications of the heavy plow see Lynn White, *Medieval Technology and Social Change* (Oxford: Oxford University Press, 1962), 41–57.

    15. Anthony Bryer, "The Means of Agricultural Production: Muscle and Tools," in Laiou, *Economic History of Byzantium,* 1:101–13.

    16. *Geoponika* 6.11, quoted in White, *Roman Farming,* 46; Dalby, *Food in the Ancient World,* 352–53.

    17. K. D. White, *Greek and Roman Technology* (Ithaca, N.Y.: Cornell University Press, 1984); Frances Gies and Joseph Gies, *Cathedral, Forge, and Waterwheel: Technology and Invention in the Middle Ages* (New York: Harper Collins, 1994). For the Athens mill see Homer A. Thompson and R. E. Wycherley, *The Athenian Agora* XIV. *The Agora of Athens* (Princeton, N.J.: American School of Classical Studies, 1972), 214.

    18. Early windmills are discussed by White, *Medieval Technology and Social Change,* 85–86; and Gies and Gies, *Cathedral, Forge, and Waterwheel,* 117.

    19. For Roman dogs see Columella, *On Agriculture* 7.12–13; Oppian, *Cynegetica* ("On Hunting") 1.368–538 (trans. Mair, 39–53); and Jocelyn M. C. Toynbee, *Animals*

in Roman Life and Art (London: Thames and Hudson, 1973; reprint, Baltimore: Johns Hopkins University Press, 1996), 102–24, quoting Horace's 6th Epode at 106.

20. *Geoponika* 17.16, quoted in John Scarborough, "Herbs of the Field and Herbs of the Garden in Byzantine Medicinal Pharmacy," in *Byzantine Garden Culture,* ed. Antony Littlewood, Henry Maguire, and Joachim Wolschke-Bulmahn (Washington, D.C.: Dumbarton Oaks, 2002), 177–88, at 186.

21. Frank Frost, "Sausage and Meat Processing in Antiquity," *Greek, Roman, and Byzantine Studies* 40 (1999): 241–52; Dalby, *Food in the Ancient World,* 268–69.

22. Eva Crane, *The World History of Beekeeping and Honey Hunting* (New York: Routledge, 1999).

23. Maria K. Papathanassiou, "Metallurgy and Metalworking Techniques," in Laiou, *Economic History of Byzantium,* 1:121–27. For these estimates and other information about medieval rural life see Anthony Bryer, "The Estates of the Empire of Trebizond: Evidence for Their Resources, Products, Agriculture, Ownership, and Location," *Archeion Pontou* 35 (1979): 370–477, especially 395 n. 1.

24. For an overview of styles and manufacturing methods see Ken Dark, *Byzantine Pottery* (Charleston, S.C.: Tempus, 2001).

25. The perilous countryside appears clearly in saints' lives in Elizabeth Dawes and Norman H. Baynes, trans., *Three Byzantine Saints: Contemporary Biographies of St. Daniel the Stylite, St. Theodore of Sykeon, and St. John the Almsgiver* (Crestwood, N.Y.: St. Vladimir's Seminar Press, 1977); and Alice-Mary Talbot, ed., *Holy Women of Byzantium: Ten Saints' Lives in English Translation* (Washington, D.C.: Dumbarton Oaks, 1996).

7

MILITARY LIFE

Byzantium owed its long survival to a combination of military power and diplomatic efforts to avoid using it. The far-flung territories of the fourth-century state spanned much of Europe and the Near East, including almost all lands bordering the Mediterranean Sea. The difficulty of defending this extended border in the face of ever-increasing threats ensured that Byzantine military strategy would be reactive in nature. By the mid-seventh century the empire had lost about half of its territory: large parts of the western empire now were controlled by Germanic groups, Avars and Slavs had crossed the Danube, and Arab rule stretched across western Asia and North Africa. Constantinople's medieval authority was effectively limited to the lower Balkans and Anatolia, a Byzantine heartland that the emperor defended against constant pressure from its neighbors.

This defensive geographic outlook, maintained with dwindling success over the next 800 years, naturally colored attitudes to warfare. Security was the state's largest expense and a constant drain on its resources. Ambitious officers pursued successful army careers, gaining wealth and prestige through triumphs in the field, but for most soldiers military life was hard and brought few rewards. A sixth-century military treatise, composed against the background of constant campaigns in East and West, calls war "a great evil and the worst of all evils." The tenth-century tactical handbook compiled by the emperor Leo VI emphasizes that peace is to be preferred to all else in military planning. Writing in Constantinople in the twelfth century, Anna Komnene succinctly praises her father Alexios's military policies: "He cultivated peace to an unusual degree; its presence was always and by every means cherished and its absence worried him, so that he often spent sleepless nights wondering how it might return."[1]

Such attitudes contrasted sharply with the expansionist policies of Byzantium's neighbors, and in particular with the concept of holy *jihad* or crusade waged by Arab and Latin states. Byzantine writers generally condemned the religious justification of wars of (re)conquest as an excuse for personal enrichment and strategic advantage, even while praising the valor of their own troops. There was little sustained interest in demonizing the infidel, monks and priests were not encouraged to take up arms, and fallen soldiers were not normally proclaimed martyrs. Apart from the early seventh-century campaign led by Heraclius to recapture Jerusalem from the Persians, the Byzantine understanding of "holy war" centered more on the internal struggle of the soul against evil. When priests blessed troops before battle, they stressed support for the emperor in his defense of national borders and his people.[2]

The reluctance to take up arms encouraged leaders to explore other means of achieving political ends. Negotiation, bribery, and tribute were seen as equally valid—and usually preferable—ways of maintaining peace and stability. Commanding officers collected books of history and strategy, and sought to avoid decisive engagements with the enemy. One of the most effective strategies was to recruit mercenaries from neighboring peoples. Germanic warriors made up a significant part of the army in late antiquity, with Arabs, Turks, Norsemen, and west Europeans serving in later times. Subtle diplomatic maneuvering and strategic prevarication departed sharply from the combative ideal of the Latin Crusaders, who scorned the Byzantines as devious and weak.

SOURCES

The military, as one of the state's essential institutions, is well documented by written sources. Contemporary chronicles, saints' lives, letters, and treatises provide much information about how the army was organized and supported, how troops were trained, and how battles should be conducted. The various branches of the military were run by career officers under the emperor's direct supervision. Over the years these professional soldiers wrote specialized books covering all aspects of military life. Latin remained the language of the Byzantine army well into the Middle Ages, and many technical terms preserve their Latin roots. Clashes with foreign troops introduced different fighting methods that needed their own descriptive vocabulary as well. Some of the most important manuals include the late-sixth-century *Handbook on Strategy (Strategikon)* written by (or for) the emperor Maurice, the *Tactics (Taktika)* of Leo VI, and the *Tactical Constitutions (Sylloge Tacticorum)* of the mid-tenth century. An anonymous *Treatise on Strategy* surviving from the sixth century gives practical information about field engineering and building, while the *Naval Warfare (Naumachika)* of Leo VI deals with maritime expeditions. Many of these books were compiled from classical military treatises and include scholarly commentaries on famous historical expeditions. Other manuals, especially those prepared during the successful campaigns of the tenth century, are informed by practical experience gained along the eastern frontier. Authors regularly stress the need to maintain supply lines, build siege machinery, and effectively wage war at sea. Written in straightforward language and copied in compact editions, such handbooks clearly were intended to be read by officers in their home barracks and while on campaign.[3]

Two kinds of material evidence enlarge this picture: the physical geography of the east Mediterranean, and the remains of fortified towns, castles, and towers that still survive there. Steep mountains, narrow valleys, and a long, rugged coastline were permanent landscape features with inescapable strategic implications. Remote parts of the empire, especially in eastern Anatolia, remain sparsely populated and preserve extensive traces of medieval fortifications. Even in south Italy, Greece, and western Turkey one can explore hilltop ruins and get a good sense of their setting and design.[4]

Other physical evidence is surprisingly scarce. Roman-style armor and weapons were made in state-run factories as late as the sixth century, but

The well-preserved hilltop fortifications of Byzantine Kotyaion, today Kütahya, in west central Asia Minor. From Gustave Schlumberger, *L'Epopée byzantine a la fin du dixième siècle* (Paris: Hachette, 1896).

very little equipment of the later period has been identified. Medieval soldiers generally brought their own supplies, which were made by independent smiths, tailors, and tanners in towns and villages across the empire. The lack of industrial-scale manufacturing standards meant that equipment and uniforms must have varied widely among different units. Armor and weaponry were increasingly influenced by neighboring armies. By the eleventh century Western ideas had become influential in Constantinople, and a mixture of Italian, Norman, and Turkish elements can be detected in the written and visual sources. Illuminated manuscripts regularly depict Byzantine soldiers. The best known of these is the twelfth-century copy of the chronicle of John Skylitzes, now in Madrid, which contains detailed illustrations of recent campaigns. Images of soldier saints survive in the decorative arts and frescoes of medieval churches as well. In all cases it is difficult to know whether dress and weaponry accurately attest current practices or continue long-standing artistic conventions. Old Testament warriors like Joshua and David, for example, were usually presented wearing a combination of Roman and medieval costume. Cautiously viewed, such sources at least give an impression of Byzantine equipment and its possible variations.[5]

MILITARY ORGANIZATION

Byzantine military operations represent the final chapters in the history of ancient warfare. The organization of land and sea forces was based on Roman tradition but was modified in the face of new opponents and different objectives. The steady territorial expansion won by Roman legions during the late republic and early empire gave way in late antiquity to the defense of seriously overextended borders. The arrival of mounted warriors from central Asia in the third and fourth centuries increased the strategic value of rapid mobility and field archery among frontier troops. The considerable power of the Roman navy could not counter emerging threats in the upper Balkans and the Near East. Serious reverses suffered during the seventh century led to the military's sweeping reorganization. The loss of distant provinces left Byzantium with more manageable borders but far fewer human and natural resources with which to defend them. Long-standing pressures along the eastern and northern frontiers were complicated by the crusading expeditions mounted by the Latin states, which led to the capture of Constantinople in 1204. For the last 250 years of its life the much-reduced Byzantine state struggled with new challenges posed by gunpowder and the Ottoman empire.[6]

Land Forces
The late Roman army was reorganized by Diocletian and Constantine into two main parts: the frontier troops (*limitanei*), which were stationed along the borders, and the mobile cavalry (*comitatenses*). Most soldiers were recruited from the provinces and received grants of land in exchange for service. They were joined by

foreign allies *(foederati)* enlisted from the Goths and other neighboring peoples. The crises of the sixth and seventh centuries brought about the dramatic reorganization of provincial government into 7 large geographic units or *themes,* a number that later grew to more than 20. Each theme was assigned a general *(strategos),* who recruited and maintained soldiers *(stratiotai)* from the local population. All landowners owed military obligations that they filled in person or by proxy. Recruits were expected to be between 18 and 40 years of age, in good health, and to stand at least five and a half feet tall. Monks and priests were disqualified from service, as were convicted criminals and other social undesirables. Each soldier brought his own equipment and horse, if he had one, and was paid for his term of service. Except in times of crisis, these provincial armies *(themata)* were posted in their home territories.

Constantinople and its environs were defended by five elite regiments or *tagmata,* each commanded by a high-ranking palace official *(domestikos).* In the tenth century the tagmata were known as the Scholai, Exkoubitoi, Vigla ("Guards"), Hikanatoi ("Worthies"), and Athanatoi ("Immortals"). Each regiment had its own traditions and included at least 1,500 men organized in 30 or more operation units *(banda).* Unlike the short-term conscripts who made up the thematic armies, soldiers of the imperial tagmata were recruited and maintained by the state. These were seen as the empire's finest men, career warriors drawn from foreign units as well as native ranks, and were posted near the capital when not accompanying the emperor on campaign. The cohort of the palace guard was drawn from these troops and often described by foreign visitors to Constantinople. Several divisions were distinguished by name, ethnicity, and weapons. The best known were the Varangian Guard, which was established in the late tenth century. Guard members were recruited from north Europe and apparently were named after the Old Norse for "oath" *(var),* since they were sworn to protect the imperial family. Anna Komnene relates that the Varangians "regard loyalty to the emperors and the protection of their persons as a family tradition, a kind of sacred trust and inheritance handed down from generation to generation." Originally drawn from Scandinavia and Russia, late-medieval Varangians comprised mostly Anglo-Saxon warriors who functioned mainly in ceremonial roles and may even have acclaimed the emperor in English. They normally carried heavy swords and on ceremonial occasions wielded their distinctive double-edged axe *(pelekys).*[7]

The command structure of the Byzantine military resembled the palace hierarchy. The emperor acted as commander-in-chief through his domestics and generals. When not personally leading troops in the field, he was represented by the grand domestic *(megas domestikos).* Most commanders came from the aristocracy and held court dignities in addition to military appointments. Among the most important were the *protovestiarios* (an officer, usually a eunuch, who oversaw the imperial wardrobe and private treasury), the *protospatharios* ("first sword bearer"), the *protostrator,* and lesser *spatharioi* and *stratores.* Titles and responsibilities changed constantly and by the late Middle Ages had become independent of actual commands. Magistrates were responsible for settling disputes and handling cases of desertion. Thematic commanders were rotated through different assignments as a precaution against building too much support among local troops. Lower-level officers are less well known but came from those soldiers who had received grants of land *(pronoia)* in the provinces. The importance of personal loyalty while on campaign recommended that officers be drawn from the same geographic region or ethnic group as the men they commanded.

Successful service presented career officers with opportunities for personal advancement and profit. Some soldiers of modest background, like Justin I, Justinian I, and Basil I, achieved great power through a combination of hard work and good fortune. Rewards for most of the rank and file were less obvious. Local authorities kept records and were responsible for notifying landowners and holders of pronoia of their service obligations. Depending on the nature of his grant, one might have to appear himself, together with personal retainers and servants, or send a specified number of men. Most *pronoiars* provided their own armor, weapons, and horse, as well as supplies for their attendants. A horse was a precious asset equally for farmer and soldier, and its presence was the chief difference between cavalry officers and foot soldiers *(pezoi).* Higher-ranking pronoia soldiers might bring along two or three horses for different occasions. The infantry, by contrast, was drawn from the peasantry and urban poor, and often lacked weapons of their own.

The number of troops could change significantly during an expedition. Poor morale, logistical support, bad weather, and high casualties encouraged desertion, while a successful campaign attracted new recruits along the way. Compensation varied a great deal. Soldiers could expect to receive rations, a cash stipend, and occasional gifts while in the field; in addition, fodder was provided for accompanying animals. Pay took the form of gold coins, land, or other grants. Provisions were purchased or requisitioned by the state and stockpiled in fortified warehouses or towns *(kastra)* along the campaign path. Opportunities for plunder were an important supplement to military pay. Scavenging a battlefield or abandoned campsite could yield clothing, armor, weapons, animals, slaves, and food, while the enemy countryside offered even greater prospects for profiteering. Roman tradition stipulated that both the emperor and commanding officer should receive one-fifth of the spoils, with the remainder divided among the enlisted men. Such opportunities were powerful incentive for military service.

Infantry   Foot soldiers always made up the largest part of the field army, yet despite their numbers are little discussed by contemporary writers. Infantry troops were recruited mainly from the lower levels of society. They often were poorly equipped and served relatively short tours of duty. Medieval infantry troops were organized in *taxiarchia* of 1,000 soldiers, which were commanded by *taxiarches*. Men were broadly distinguished as heavily or lightly armed on the basis of their primary weapons. One tenth-century source describes the composition of a taxiarchia as consisting of 400 heavily armed foot soldiers *(hoplitai)*, 300 archers *(toxotai)*, 200 light infantry with javelins and slings, and 100 spear bearers *(menaulatoi)*. Other treatises detail training exercises assigned each class of soldier.[8]

Personal equipment varied with availability and need. Infantrymen generally wore a knee-length tunic made of lightly padded or quilted material, with wide, slit sleeves that allowed easy movement of the arms. A corselet or cuirass *(thorax)* made of felt, wool, boiled leather, or horn lamellar (sometimes called *klibanion*) covered the chest. During the winter a short wool cloak *(kabadion)* was worn as well. The head was protected from sun and glancing blows by a cap made of quilted felt. Late-medieval examples included a wide brim with a cloth back to shade the neck. Some soldiers owned padded iron helmets *(kranea)*. The most common form of helmet was tall, conical or even onion-shaped, and was crowned by a short iron spike. Some helmets had a narrow brim with rigid metal or mail attachments along the back and sides. Nose guards of the sort seen on west European helmets are not known. High leather boots and mail stockings protected the feet and legs. On some occasions ground troops wore reinforced arm guards and knee-high greaves. In general, the mountainous terrain and warm climate limited the effectiveness of heavy infantry armor, which easily could weigh 30 pounds or more. Such equipment was carried by animals when not needed.[9]

Soldiers normally carried a wood shield covered with linen or hardened leather, sometimes reinforced by iron. The basic shield *(thureos)* was a small round disk with a diameter of 12 to 30 inches. The inner surface had a handgrip as well as a long leather strap for carrying over the shoulder. The heavy infantry shield *(skoutarion)* consisted of a large oval or rectangle measuring about three or four feet across. Iron was too costly and heavy to cover the entire surface. Instead an embossed iron circlet with a projecting central spike was used "to unnerve the enemy when they see it from a distance and to inflict serious injury when used at close range."[10] Later medieval sources mention tall triangular shields, similar to those used in western Europe. This kind of shield bowed outward along its width and was worn strapped to the shoulder or carried on the back. Manuscript illustrations show these sometimes painted with crosses, birds, and animals.

Common weapons included swords, hand axes, clubs, maces, slings, and spears. The basic sidearm of late antiquity was the *spathion*, a double-edged sword that was worn on a belt or baldric slung over the shoulder. In contrast to the short Roman *gladius*, Byzantine swords measured about

Medieval glazed bowl with a foot soldier. The mail armor, helmet, shield, and lance may reflect Western influence. Louvre Museum, Paris. Réunion des Musées Nationaux/Art Resource, New York.

three feet long. Iron axes, clubs, and maces were used in close-quarter combat. The hand axe had a single curved or straight blade and sometimes a thick spike on the opposite side. This seems to have been the weapon of choice among northern mercenaries like the Rus and the Varangians. For most troops a long thrusting spear was essential. Infantry spears *(kontaria)* were about 12 feet long and carried a sharp iron point. The *menaulion* was an especially sturdy pike, 9 to 12 feet long and with a 20-inch-long blade, that was effective against armored cavalry. Javelin bearers carried two or three throwing spears *(akontia)* about 10 feet in length. Bamboo and cane were well suited to these lightweight weapons. Many foot soldiers also carried a leather sling *(sphendone)*, sometimes mounted on a four-foot-long shaft *(sphendobolon)*. Few soldiers would have gone without such basic tools as a knife, awl, and file for repairing the equipment on which their lives depended. Despite the low technology, such simple weapons could be very effective in battle, especially when used in formation.

Archers were an essential part of the late Roman army that grew in importance through the medieval period. Military authors praise bowmen for their accuracy, power, and rapidity of fire. Several types of bows seem to have been common. The standard longbow *(toxon)* was cut from a single piece of flexible wood about six feet tall, which was strung into a gently curved D-shaped profile. This basic weapon could be made quickly and was extremely versatile in the field. Knowledge of the more specialized composite bow was picked up after clashes with the Huns in the fourth century. This kind of bow was made of multiple thin layers of wood reinforced with animal horn glued along the belly, and with sinew and tendon along the back. In both cases the bow was strung against the wood's natural flex, which gave an experienced bowman a range of about 1,000 feet; experiments with recent Turkish bows have achieved even greater distances. Smaller cavalry bows, which stood about four feet tall, were designed for greater accuracy at close range. Bowstrings were made of animal gut. Sturdy wood arrows measured about 30 inches long and carried sharp copper or iron tips with two or three blades. Three short fletchings were attached to the tail end of the shaft. Some authorities recommend cutting furrows along the shaft so it would shatter on impact and not be reused by the enemy. Arrows were carried in a leather pouch hung from the belt or worn over the shoulder. Byzantine authors distinguish different methods of drawing and sighting arrows. Archers in the Mediterranean tradition pulled the bowstring with two or three fingers and sighted to the left of the bow. In the faster Hunnic (Asiatic or Mongolian) draw, the archer sighted to the right and wore a broad stone or bronze ring (thumblock) on the drawing hand to ensure a sharp release. A leather or metal brace laced onto the bow hand protected it from the snapped bowstring. A skilled bowman might be able to shoot up to 10 arrows a minute. Tenth-century manuals recommend that each archer carry two bows, four bowstrings, and two quivers with up to a hundred arrows. During the later Middle Ages the slower but more powerful crossbow *(solenarion)* was assigned to some infantry units. The well-equipped archer might also carry a sword, axe, spear, and small shield.[11]

Less numerous than the infantry, cavalry units were an essential part of the Byzantine army. As early as the fourth century B.C. **Cavalry** the Hellenistic general Xenophon noted the advantages of fielding soldiers on horseback. Contact with Persians, Huns, and other mounted warriors from central Asia forced late Roman commanders to develop a comparable fighting force. Sophisticated breeding programs in Asia Minor and Syria produced large, strong horses that could carry great loads across difficult terrain. By the fifth century heavily armored horses and riders were being deployed along the Persian frontier. Clashes with the Avars in the late sixth and early seventh centuries taught Byzantine horsemen the advantages of using stirrups for mounting and riding. This major technological development greatly increased the cavalry's effectiveness. Procopius, Theophanes, and other historians characterize the cavalry as one of the empire's most strategic assets.[12]

Mounted troops were drawn mainly from small landholders, whose assignment depended on bringing one or more horses on campaign. Loss of his horse meant a soldier had to fight on foot until he found a replacement. Most horsemen were responsible for their other equipment as well. Basic horse trappings included an iron bridle with reins, blanket, padded saddle, and iron stirrups. Extra ropes, straps, grooming equipment, and fodder were carried in saddlebags. Calvary soldiers wore a waist-length corselet of lamellar or scale armor *(klibanion)* and iron helmets, had small shields of different shapes, and used a variety of weapons. The long, double-edged spathion was widely used in late antiquity. During the medieval period many mounted soldiers carried a curved saberlike weapon *(paramerion)* of similar length, presumably adopted after contact with armies in the East. Some of the personal weapons of officers were elaborately decorated, at least for ceremonial occasions. The asymmetrical hand guards used in later times presumably reflect Turkish custom. The main weapon of mounted troops was the 12-foot-long kontarion with its thick wood shaft and long iron blade. A leather thong attached at midshaft helped the rider support his lance during combat. Bamboo and cane might be used for throwing spears, but battlefield use of the European-style couched lance, held high under the arm, needed harder wood. Other horsemen were trained in archery.

The heavily armed cavalry *(kataphraktoi)* was one of the most distinctive parts of the Byzantine army. Large-scale deployment of armored horsemen was revived around the middle of the tenth century as part of the state-organized tagmata. Banda of 200–400 men were grouped into larger formations *(moiras)* numbering several thousand. The most striking feature of these special mounted troops was the elaborate armor worn by horse and soldier alike (the term *kataphraktos* means "enclosed"). Horses were covered by a layer of quilted felt or boiled leather with armor covering the head, neck, and chest. Heavy iron plates protected the hooves. Mounted soldiers wore long felt cloaks covered by horn, lamellar, or mail armor. This weighty combination could not have been comfortable and no doubt was adjusted according to the season. Heavy iron helmets covered the head and face, leaving only narrow openings for the eyes. Tall almond-shaped or triangular shields protected the left leg and upper body. The main weapons were long lances and iron maces with a sharply angled head *(siderorabdia)*. So equipped, these troops charged in wedge formations with the goal of smashing through infantry lines and fighting at close range. Tenth-century Arab sources describe the awesome sight of kataphraktoi on the battlefield, "advancing on horses which seemed to

Mounted troops with military standard and pennants. The future emperor Basil I pursues and returns an escaped horse to Michael III. Detail from the late-twelfth-century edition of the *Skylitzes Chronicle*. Photo courtesy of the Biblioteca Nacional, Madrid (ms. vitr. 26–2).

have no legs" and protected by "helmets and garments [that] were of iron like their swords."[13]

The Roman Empire's security had rested in large part on its navy, and Byzantium's maritime situation made the need for naval power even more acute. No other power **Naval Power** could challenge imperial domination of the sea in late antiquity, but by the mid-seventh century Arab ships were attacking much of the east Mediterranean coast and the major islands of Cyprus and Rhodes. The Arabs' rapid advance across North Africa and besieging of Constantinople in 717 reflected the fundamental weakness of the Byzantine navy around this time. By the eighth century the Slavs had established a significant presence in the Black Sea. These obvious threats brought about the navy's reorganization along similar lines to its land forces. An elite core unit was based in the Sea of Marmara to defend the capital, and separate fleets were organized by the coastal provinces. Naval themes were assigned to the coastal regions of Kibyrrhaiotai (the south coast of Asia Minor), Samos, and the Aegean islands. Each of these units was commanded by the thematic strategos and consisted of multiple squadrons and flotillas.

Such measures helped stabilize Byzantine power and led to the recovery of Crete and Cyprus in the tenth century. Strategists recognized the importance of the navy to the empire's security, yet it always lagged behind the land armies in support. Naval commanders were paid less than generals of the Anatolian themes, and their usual duties involved shuttling ground forces and provisions from home bases to the frontier. Common assignments included harrying foreign shipping and troop movements, blockading cities, and supporting ground attacks. On several occasions great fleets of fighting ships were marshaled to counter specific dangers.[14]

The Byzantine navy included different kinds of ships. The standard vessel was a fast-sailing, oared galley known as a *dromon* ("runner"). This shallow, sleek warship was the successor of the Greek trireme and Roman quinquereme, and like them came in different sizes. A typical dromon measured about 130 feet long by 18 feet wide, and held 100–200 sailors. Smaller ships (variously referred to as *ousiakoi* or *pamphyloi*) had about 100 rowers; larger, slower vessels could carry 300 or more men. The dromon was powered by rowers below deck arranged in one or two tiers on both sides. Two or three masts supported large canvas sails that were used in good weather on the open seas. By the seventh century the triangular lateen sail had been widely adopted by Byzantine sailors. This major advance over traditional square-rigged sails permitted greater speed and maneuverability in adverse winds. For combat the typical dromon was equipped with a reinforced battering ram at the prow, and a wood tower *(xylokastro)* for archers and catapults at the stern. Designated warships also carried supplies of incendiary materials and a metal siphon for spraying the much-feared "Greek Fire" on enemy ships. Some writers distinguish a smaller galley, the *chelandion,* for hauling soldiers and supplies. Swift and nimble in shallow water, this light ship was especially good for gathering intelligence, carrying messages, and raiding the coast for provisions. Late-medieval sources also mention a smaller ship known as a *galea* (the source for "galley"), which seems to have been an easily maneuvered vessel for reconnaissance and communication. Like classical galleys, Byzantine warships were designed for power and speed rather than structural strength. They usually fared poorly under difficult sailing conditions.[15]

Naval expeditions had to be carefully organized. Large operations were planned for the balmy months of summer, although communications and emergencies often required sailing in winter as well. Before embarking hulls needed to be caulked and sealed, sails patched, nets mended, and ropes replaced. Several days' supply of food and water had to be stowed below deck. Crews were recruited and included carpenters, sail makers, sailors, and armed marines. Especially valued were experienced seamen who could predict the weather by studying winds, clouds, and flights of gulls, herons, and other seabirds. The appearance of Zephyros, the westerly wind of antiquity, announced the arrival of the sailing season after late-winter storms had passed. Most crewmembers tended the sails

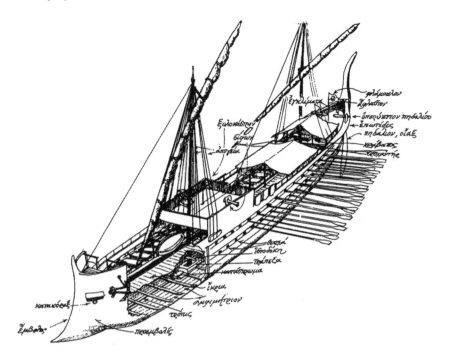

A ninth-century dromon powered by two paired rows of 25 oars. Troops stayed above deck and fought from the reinforced tower *(xylokastro)*. From Richard W. Unger, *The Ship in the Medieval Economy, 600–1600* (London: Croom Helm, 1980); reproduced by permission of Taylor & Francis Ltd.

or manned the oars. Synchronized rowing was hard work and much training was needed to coordinate large teams, especially in the confusion of battle. Before they set out the ships were blessed with holy water by priests and imperial standards were hoisted from the main mast. The fleet commander flew a special banner, which at one point included the cross and flamethrowers. Each captain kept on board tactical handbooks, weather treatises, and *portulans* for his projected route. Like most commercial traffic, naval expeditions tended to keep within sight of the shore, which offered landmarks for navigation as well as sources of fresh food and water. Toward nightfall ships looked for safe anchorage along the coast, a task made more dangerous when large fleets were operating in poor weather.[16]

For most sailors life at sea was an arduous experience. The ship's captain and officers stayed in reinforced cabins above deck. Specialized sailors, armed troops, and animals also remained in the open, leaving rowers to work in hot, crowded quarters below deck. Oarsmen were assigned to rotating shifts, their efforts coordinated by the drone of a unifying beat. Most rowers kneeled or sat on a low bench with a pail of drinking water close by. Recent sailing reenactments have shown just how vital water is for Mediterranean sailors, with oarsmen needing to drink about a quart of water every hour. Given the importance of water, ships had little space for carrying other provisions. Food was often limited to bread and biscuits, which often needed soaking in wine or oil before eating. This frugal diet kept the crew going between scheduled stops in port. At other times supplies were replenished by foraging expeditions along the coast. Fishing was an important supplement to the naval diet.

The high cost of building and outfitting a ship recommended special care when preparing for engagements at sea. Most maritime and land campaigns took place during the late spring and summer months. Strategists preferred to avoid direct confrontations except when they held a clear advantage in situation or numbers of ships. Night, fog, and poor weather were good reasons to postpone fighting. Fast scouting ships were dispatched to determine the opposing fleet's size and composition as well as the prospects of staging a surprise attack. Tactics generally resembled land campaigns. The preferred formation was a broad crescent with the flagship located near the center. Messages were relayed by colored flags, trumpet calls, and smoke signals; lamps and flares were used at night. Tactical writers recommend staging naval engagements close to the enemy's coastline. Such a setting would tempt opposing sailors to abandon ship and swim for shore, while encouraging Byzantine seamen to fight harder to avoid capture. The chief objective was to ram opposing ships below the water line and then board the disabled vessel. Greek Fire and other projectiles were used with great effectiveness against opposing fleets.

ON THE MARCH

Military manuals give detailed instructions for land maneuvers as well as combat, reflecting the importance of maintaining order at all times. Mounted scouts and advance parties were sent out to survey unfamiliar terrain and assess enemy forces. They chose the safest routes and identified sources of water and potential campsites. Infantrymen made up the largest part of any ground force and traveled on foot with their personal weapons. Mules and donkeys carried armor and other supplies. The imperial baggage train alone required the service of hundreds of mules and horses with their handlers. In good weather a field army might move 15 miles across level terrain in an eight-hour day, roughly comparable to the pace of other medieval and early modern armies. Foot soldiers arranged in regular columns could maintain an average speed of three miles an hour over open ground, slower when crossing rivers or hilly terrain. Small mounted units moved more quickly, covering as much as 40 to 50 miles under optimal conditions. Several additional hours were required to break camp, organize units for movement, and establish a new site at the end of each day's march. By any measure this was a hard and tiring process that often continued for weeks at a time. Shortages of water, food, supplies, and physical comforts naturally took their toll on morale. Such conditions help explain why unruly troops occasionally turned to pillaging rural settlements in their own lands. Maintaining order was an ongoing concern of field commanders. Matters of discipline were referred to special magistrates, who settled disputes and presided at trials for brigandage and desertion.

Animals were a vital part of the Byzantine army, and military writers often discuss their requisition and care. Horses played the most important supporting role. A supply of fresh horses had to be kept available at all

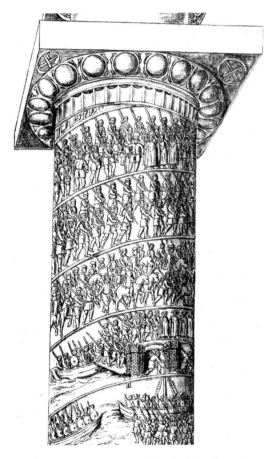

The late Roman army crossing the Danube and on the march. Spiral relief on the Column of Arcadius, Constantinople, as recorded in the sixteenth century before its destruction. From *Archaeologia* 72 (1922).

times for use by commanding officers. Trained equines were needed for the cavalry, especially the armored kataphraktoi. Others brought by individual soldiers made possible rapid communication among units, scouting expeditions, and foraging parties. When security was not an issue, horses were hobbled and allowed to graze under watchful eyes. Closer to enemy lines it was necessary to provide them with fodder and water in camp. Their strategic value is clear from veterinary treatises on equine physiology and treatment of injuries. Mules and donkeys were the main pack animals, carrying supplies and weapons on their backs and drawing heavily laden carts. Camels were useful for transporting supplies over long distances, especially in the more arid eastern provinces. Some medieval officers may have remembered classical accounts of horses that were spooked by the sight and smell of these large strange animals, and so kept their own horses familiar with them. Dogs had always played a role in ancient warfare: they are regularly mentioned by classical authors and often appear in Near Eastern, Greek, and Roman art. A constant if little-remarked presence in town and countryside, dogs no doubt gathered around barracks and accompanied armies on campaign. Their keen senses, speed, agility, and loyalty made them clear assets as hunters, sentries, and particularly as companions for men stationed far from home.[17]

A reliable food supply was essential for maintaining the health and numbers of troops. Over the years soldiers became increasingly responsible for bringing several days of their own rations when they began their service. Provisions were picked up from state-run granaries located at fortified staging posts, and were carried by pack animals and wagons. The cornerstone of the military diet was *boukellaton*, a ring-shaped loaf of dense millet bread. While on campaign soldiers relied on a barley hardtack known as *paximadion*. Both kinds of bread were baked twice or dried in the sun to extend their shelf life and lighten their weight, and had to be soaked in water or oil. Other common rations were cheese, dried meat, and salted fish. This basic fare was supplemented in the field by livestock, wild game, and seasonal produce. Organized hunting expeditions could involve hundreds of men, closely spaced and arranged in a broad arc, who gradually encircled their quarry. The everyday military beverage was *phouska*, a diluted mixture of beer, wine or vinegar, which made a dubious water supply more palatable as well as providing medicinal benefits. Troops stationed along the northern frontier may also have consumed beer made of barley and millet, which had a long local history. The *Strategy* of Maurice recommends having captives sample any water, wine, or grain acquired in hostile territories before distributing it to soldiers and horses.[18]

Byzantine treatises frequently mention the importance of keeping up morale. Troops in the thematic armies normally were stationed in the region where they were raised and were rarely far from home. Campaigns typically were mounted in the spring and concluded by late fall, so avoiding the difficulties of travel and shelter during the cold winter months. Except for times of crisis, service was for a fixed term that disrupted the agrarian schedule as little as possible. Timely payment of stipends and provision of food and supplies were high priorities for all military planners. Gifts, honors, and opportunities for rest and recreation were provided regularly to keep spirits high.

Military writers stress the importance of making camp in an orderly way. The site should be located in **Setting up Camp** the open and away from forests or overlooking hills; ideally a river, lake, or bluff offered protection on one or more sides. It was important to situate troops near a dependable source of water, preferably on both sides of a small stream. A trained surveyor (*mensurator*) laid out the camp according to firm Roman rules, using a rectilinear plan wherever terrain permitted. This was supposed to be surrounded by a ditch five to eight feet wide and equally deep, with a low embankment heaped up on the interior. Shields and bundled spears were set atop this barrier to provide added protection. Whenever possible the camp plan was organized by two or four roads that intersected near the center. Secondary roads within each quadrant allowed for inspection of troops and ready communication among units. Quarters for the emperor and commanding officers were set up on a high point near the center, beyond the reach of enemy archers. Cavalrymen with their horses were stationed nearby, as were quartermasters with their supplies and animals. Infantry troops were arranged along the outer margin. Foot soldiers were organized into small units of 8 to 16 men who slept in one or two large tents. Supplies were stowed at the center of each tent, animals were kept nearby, and meals were taken together. Shields were leaned against spears stuck in the ground, where they could be quickly gathered. Each unit posted its own sentry at night. Such close-knit living arrangements reinforced the sense of camaraderie needed on the battlefield.[19]

Security was the main concern of military planners. Access to camp was limited to a small number of reinforced gates. Guards used passwords to identify spies and watched for signs of attack. A rotating watch drawn from the infantry units regularly patrolled the perimeter. When provisions ran short, small detachments were sent out to gather supplies from the surrounding countryside. Hunting expeditions offered opportunities for recreation and honing archery skills. Soldiers generally stayed with their units and were not permitted to leave camp after dark. Sentries might be accompanied by dogs, who provided company through their lonely nighttime watch.

Soldiers used a variety of banners and flags to identify themselves during training, in processions, and while on campaigns. **Banners** The Roman practice of carrying legionary standards was maintained into late antiquity. Since the early empire these had consisted of a tall pole bearing a carved image of an eagle, to which was attached a tall square-shaped cloth known as a *vexillum*. Painted or embroidered legends on the vexillum identified the legion and battle unit, and sometimes bore an image of the emperor as well. The most notable change from earlier tradition was the inclusion of expressly Christian symbols and images. At the battle of the Milvian bridge Constantine had used a special standard later known as the *labarum*. This was described by the emperor's biographer, Eusebius of Caesarea, as cross-shaped; coins and sculptural reliefs depict this as a monogram combining the initials of Christ, the Greek letters *chi* and *rho*, within a circle. Christograms and similar protective invocations were regularly featured on standards and shields.

Specialized insignia appeared during the medieval period. Sixth-century sources describe the common battle standard *(bandon* or *signum)* as a rectangular cloth ornamented with circles, squares, or crosses. Colorful flamelike streamers *(phlamoula)* were sometimes attached to the supporting pole. Cross-decorated standards were favored by the iconoclastic emperors in the eighth and early ninth centuries. By the tenth century the vertical standard had been largely replaced by a horizontal flag. Several treatises mention the *drakontion*, a special pole-mounted dragon mask of wood or metal. A pennant or streamer was attached to this mask and carried by archery units, who looked to it as a kind of wind sock. Lance-wielding soldiers sometimes attached small triangular or swallow-tailed pennants near the tip of their weapons while in camp or marching. These were removed before battle began, Maurice's *Strategy* explains, "for they are as useless in combat as they are valuable for presenting a fine appearance at inspections, sieges, or parades."[20] Red and scarlet were preferred colors for banners, apparently because of their symbolic and religious meanings. Banners often carried pictures of the Virgin that were based on contemporary icons. One of the best-known images of the late Middle Ages is the standing two-headed eagle. This striking image had a long history in Near Eastern art and became particularly popular during the Komnene and Palaiologan periods, even though it never became an official symbol of state. Different insignia are depicted in medieval manuscripts. Few actual banners have survived.[21]

Banners and flags marked the location of units when they set up camp. These banners were the main way of signaling rallying points and coordinating attacks. Each unit's bandon was carried by a heavily armored soldier *(bandophoros)*, who stood next to the commander near the middle of his formation. A special cohort was assigned to protect the banner. The loss of official insignia was not only disgraceful but dangerous, since they could be used deceptively by the enemy. The highest priority was put on negotiating the return of captured standards as soon as hostilities were over.

Communication

Fast and reliable communications are essential for the success of any military undertaking. Routine contact among army units was maintained by couriers who traveled by horseback along the highways of the state post. Riders normally covered about 25 miles each day, stopping at public inns and state-owned stations to rest. With more frequent changes of horses, urgent news could be sent up to 240 miles in a day. The importance of the eastern frontier prompted the construction of a special system for rapid long-distance communication. Leo the Mathematician, a leading court scholar and inventor of the ninth century, established a chain of hilltop signal towers stretching from the palace in Constantinople to the Taurus mountains in southeast Asia Minor. Nine beacons spaced at intervals of 30 to 65 miles relayed messages over a total distance of some 450 miles in only an hour's time. While signal fires had been employed in antiquity, Leo's system marked a major advance by using timekeeping devices to coordinate its operation. The same flammable materials used for incendiary weapons could successfully ignite individual fires on short notice.[22] Battlefield communications were less readily managed. Heralds shouted voice messages between officers and their troops before engagement. Once fighting was underway, trumpets, bells, and signal flags were the primary means of relaying orders. Most contact was confined to individual cohorts, who reported casualties to their commanding officers after fighting had stopped.

Soldiers took their faith with them into the field. Military treatises from the sixth through tenth centuries, especially **Religion** the *Strategy* of Maurice and the *Tactics* of Leo VI, emphasize the importance of maintaining religious traditions and group morale by holding regular services and prayers. Chaplains accompanied troops on training expeditions and to the battlefield. Soldiers often consulted local hermits and other holy men they met in the course of their campaigns.[23]

While in the field each detachment of soldiers was supposed to sing the Trisagion, "Holy God, holy mighty one, holy immortal one, have mercy on us," at dawn and twilight. On Sundays and key feast days chaplains set up portable altars under tents and in the open air to celebrate the Eucharist among the troops. Such services were intended to comfort soldiers while away from home and steady their resolve in combat. Formal liturgies were held on the eve of battle: sins were absolved, prayers of supplication said, and standards and banners blessed. Unlike Latin monks, who sometimes took up arms during the Crusades, Byzantine clergymen were strictly noncombatants. After fighting had ceased, prayers of thanks were offered and fallen comrades given proper burial. Special commemorations were held in the cathedral of Hagia Sophia and other churches upon returning to Constantinople.

Potent symbols like the cross and labarum were always good for building confidence. Priests took along liturgical objects and sacred relics when they accompanied troops on campaign. Many soldiers wore magical charms or amulets (*phylakteria*) for personal protection. In the late sixth century the emperor Maurice took into the field a fragment of the True Cross mounted atop a golden spear. In the tenth century Constantine VII sent relics to encourage men stationed along the eastern frontier. Troops carried icons of all sorts, from traditional panels to specially painted banners. More than once soldiers were ordered to paint images of protective saints on their shields before heading into battle. Michael Psellos tells how Basil II faced the insurgent Phokas with a sword in one hand and an icon of the Virgin in the other. Of the many soldier saints listed in the *Synaxarion of Constantinople,* the most famous are George (feast day observed April 23), Demetrius of Thessaloniki (October 26), Prokopios (July 8), and Theodore Teron (February 17). The Syrian pair Sergius and Bacchus (October 7) are remembered as officers in the Roman army who were martyred under Maximian. The legend of the Forty Martyrs of Sebasteia (March 9) celebrates the steadfast faith of early soldiers along the Pontic coast.[24]

Specialized Weaponry

Like its Roman predecessor, the early Byzantine empire produced weapons, armor, and uniforms in state-run factories *(fabricae)* located in strategic cities. During the later Middle Ages some military supplies came from specialized workshops near Constantinople, but most were obtained by individual soldiers from smiths working in scattered villages. Recruits were expected to bring their own equipment and as a result carried a wide variety of armor and hand weapons. At least a few weapons are known to have been imported from Italy and the Arab states as well. Warships were made in imperial shipyards, and engineers *(technitai)* built siege equipment in the field.

One of the most feared weapons of the medieval period was the portable crossbow *(solenarion* or *tzangra).* This was a T-shaped device with a central wooden stock attached to a short transverse bow. The bow was strung by steadying the weapon on the ground and using both arms to pull the string to a catch-plate. A recessed hollow along the length of the stock held a number of short, iron-tipped arrows, commonly known as "mice," which could be launched all at once. While the Byzantines may have experimented earlier with a similar weapon, the medieval crossbow was apparently brought to the east Mediterranean by the Latins in the eleventh century. Anna Komnene called it "a weapon of the barbarians, absolutely unknown to the Greeks ... The unfortunate man who is struck by it dies without feeling the blow; however strong the impact he knows nothing of it." The larger, stationary crossbow *(cheiroballistron)* was used to launch arrows, bolts, and small stones. Such mechanical weapons were considered so horrific in western Europe that in 1139 the Pope banned their use against other Christians; the Arabs were equally reluctant to use them against fellow Muslims. Despite their range and power, crossbows were heavy and awkward to use, and were deployed mainly in sieges and naval battles.[25]

Siege operations needed large weapons. The most important piece of artillery was the trebuchet-type catapult *(petrobola).* Torsion catapults powered by ropes of twisted hair and sinew had been widely used in antiquity. The traction-powered trebuchet, which had originated in central

Fragmentary bronze plaque with a military saint who originally stood next to Saint Demetrius. The figure appears to wear a long-sleeved tunic, lamellar corselet (klibanion), and outer cloak. He holds his drawn sword (spathion) and scabbard. Courtesy of the Museum of Art and Archaeology, University of Missouri–Columbia.

Asia before the fourth century B.C., was a less complicated but equally effective device for throwing stones. This consisted of a long beam mounted asymmetrically on a crossbar. When pulled by attached ropes, the beam hurled stones or other large projectiles loaded in a sling. By classical times the weapon was known throughout the Mediterranean and the Near East. Around the eighth century Arab engineers developed a modified trebuchet combining traction cables with a suspended weight. This hybrid anticipated the counterweight trebuchet, a much more powerful weapon that was driven entirely by gravity. Byzantine artillery specialists apparently played a key role in developing these new "rock-throwing engines" *(petrobola mechanemata)* during the eleventh and twelfth centuries. Anna Komnene writes about her father's experimental designs for siege equipment. Niketas Choniates uses different terms to describe how the beam with attached sling *(sphendone)* was mounted on a triangular trestle built of wood and mounted on wheels. In some cases a windlass or block-and-tackle helped draw the throwing arm into place. Such equipment enabled Byzantine soldiers to fling much larger stones over considerable distances with unprecedented accuracy. Modern trebuchets built with a 50-foot beam and 10-ton counterweight have been able to throw 300-pound stones up to 300 yards. The *Tactics* of Leo also recommends other payloads, including baskets or pots filled with live scorpions and venomous snakes. Containers of finely powdered quicklime produced on impact a dust cloud that could suffocate and blind the enemy. Such schemes were notoriously double-edged, of course, and with a shift of wind or turn of battle could equally afflict the perpetrators. The nearly continuous state of warfare in the twelfth century ensured that Latin and Arab armies adopted similar artillery, which led to sweeping changes in defensive architecture on all sides. As the first significant mechanical application of gravity, the counterweight trebuchet represents one of the major technological achievements of the Middle Ages.[26]

Firearms appeared in the east Mediterranean toward the end of the medieval period but were never widely adopted by the Byzantine army.

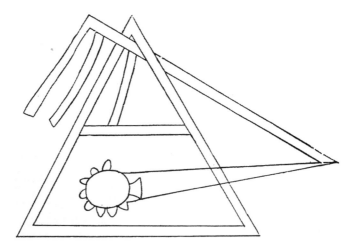

Medieval trebuchet for hurling a vessel with flammable materials, as illustrated in an Arab manuscript in the Bibliothèque nationale de France, Paris. From Gustave Schlumberger, *Un empereur byzantin aux dixième siècle, Nicéphore Phocas* (Paris: Firmin Didot, 1890).

It was well known that gunpowder was made from crushed sulfur, saltpeter (potassium nitrate), and charcoal. By the later fourteenth century large cannons known as bombards were being used by the Adriatic cities of Dubrovnik and Kotor in defense against the Venetians and Ottomans, who also were using firearms. These early cannons ranged from three to five feet in length and were solid cast in large furnaces over the course of several days. The first bombards were made of iron, but bronze was quickly recognized as being stronger and capable of propelling stones weighing as much as a hundred pounds. Byzantine strategists were aware of these developments but lacked money to invest in a technology whose potential they may not have fully grasped. The late empire's approach to military planning basically continued classical methods of warfare and had no place for firearms. Medieval Constantinople's main defense remained its fifth-century walls, which had been designed to neither withstand assault by cannons nor support their defensive emplacement. The artillery assembled by Mehmet II for his siege of the capital in 1453 was the most formidable in Europe. It included one or more colossal cannons supposedly made by a Hungarian engineer, Urban, who first had offered his services to the Byzantine emperor. The largest of these guns were said to been over 26 feet long and capable of hurling 1,000-pound stones a distance of one to two miles. Against such awesome weaponry the Byzantines had no response.[27]

The most notorious Byzantine weapon was the incendiary mixture known to the Latin Crusaders as "Greek Fire" **Greek Fire** (*le feu grégeois*). The first recorded account of this "liquid flame" (*hygron pyr*) dates to 678. Later traditions tell us that the Syrian military engineer Kallinikos introduced the secrets of pyrotechnology to the Byzantine navy, who used it to repel the Arab fleet then besieging the capital. Such fortuitous circumstances may be less likely than alchemists or chemists working in Constantinople discovering its recipe while studying classical treatises on chemistry and physics. Either way, the formula was quickly perfected and the weapon was used with equal success in sea battles with the Arabs in 717 and again against the Hungarians in 936. The weapon was crucial in deflecting the assault on the capital by the Kievan Rus in 941, when a large fleet of besieging ships was defeated by 15 Byzantine warships that sprayed liquid fire from the prow, stern, and sides. Similar weapons were used with land-based siege machinery. Writing in the twelfth century, Anna Komnene describes the fearsome use of Greek Fire at sea:

On the prow of each ship Alexios Komnenos mounted the heads of lions and other land animals, made of bronze or iron and with the mouths open; the thin layer of gold with which they were covered made the very sight of them terrifying. The fire was hurled at the enemy through tubes that passed through the mouths of the beasts, so that it seemed as if they were belching out fire.[28]

Greek Fire deployed in naval combat near Constantinople. A bronze siphon or firing tube is used to direct the deadly weapon. Detail from the late-twelfth-century edition of the *Skylitzes Chronicle*. Photo courtesy of the Biblioteca Nacional, Madrid (ms. vitr. 26–2).

Flammable substances were known in ancient warfare. Late Hellenistic and Roman writers mention incendiary arrows and missiles launched by machines. Such weapons included a mixture of combustible materials that were packed into an envelope surrounding the shaft to keep from being extinguished during flight. Cauldrons or terra-cotta pots filled with bitumen, sulfur, and similar flammable materials were being launched by catapults by the fourth century B.C. The development of Greek Fire represents a major advance in this tradition. Byzantine writers considered this spectacular weapon to be a carefully guarded secret, and its precise formula still stirs debate. Most authorities believe that it involved a mixture of crude oil, bitumen, naphtha, resin, and sulfur. These were cautiously heated and sprayed by bellows through a firing tube (*strepton*) before being ignited. Apart from practical difficulties in acquiring the materials, the main Byzantine contribution seems to have been in devising new ways of deploying the weapon. Obviously caution and technical skill were needed. Equipment and ships were fireproofed with vinegar, alum, and talc, and crewmen wore specially treated leather garments for their personal safety. Measures were taken to protect fortifications and buildings against fire-throwing equipment during land campaigns. Clothing and wood that has been soaked in vinegar tends to dry more slowly than if only water is used, and this would have prevented mixtures containing burning sulfur or oils from sticking to the surface. The Arabs also were fielding incendiary weapons by the early eighth century. By contrast, Bulgarian soldiers were said to be unable to use supplies they captured in the field. Tenth-century sources mention the incidental use of hand grenades that were packed with pitch and quicklime and exploded on impact. Excavations across the Near East have recovered distinctive ceramic containers, small and spherical in shape, that may have been used in this way. The search for further applications contributed to the development of gunpowder and heavy artillery by Byzantium's neighbors in the fourteenth century.[29]

Field manuals often review how to choose a defensible site for a fort or city. The location should be strategically situated, **Building** preferably on a promontory with steep slopes and a view of approaching routes. There should be a supply of stone and timber for building. In some cases it may be necessary to manufacture bricks as well. A low forward wall with broad ditch provides the first of several lines of defense. Walls should be at least 10 feet thick and 40 feet high, with large stones in the lower 10 to 12 feet in order to resist battering, mining, and scaling assaults. Towers should be hexagonal in plan. Reliable supplies of water and food are vital to support the defenders and inhabitants.

Fortified hilltops, castles, and towers were key elements in Byzantine military planning. Terms like *kastron, kastellion,* and *phrourion* designated a variety of defensible places, which ranged from small cities to remote outposts. Many early cities are named as kastra during their later phases of occupation. These were small defensive enclosures that usually stood atop a hill or ridge overlooking roads or other strategic paths. In a kastro one typically found administrative offices, barracks, stables for horses and other animals, and sometimes even a prison. Such outposts were supported by fortified towers *(pyrgoi)* built in villages, monasteries, and on hilltops, which served mainly as observation points for watchmen drawn from the local population. In the later Middle Ages nearby inhabitants were compelled to built and maintain kastra as part of the defense of the eastern frontier. Construction could undertake the form of a special tax *(kastroktisia)* or corvée. Upon its completion, the kastro was staffed by a garrison under a local commander *(kastrophylax)*. The remains of many such castles can still be seen across the east Mediterranean.

Byzantine authors focused much of their attention on waging offensive campaigns, but an equally important **Siege Warfare** part of military planning was directed to the defense of **and Defense** fortified places. As had been the case throughout antiquity, medieval siege strategies were mainly concerned with cutting off

Tower and fortifications at Nicaea, showing masonry of
different periods. Large blocks of limestone and marble
were preferred for the foundations and lower levels, with
the vaulted superstructure made of lighter-weight bricks.
Courtesy of the author.

supplies of food and water, hurling objects over the walls, and assaulting
the walls directly. Byzantine, Islamic, and Crusader armies employed
similar means of attack and defense.

Encirclement was the most effective way of isolating a fortress from
communication and resupply. In the case of coastal towns, a besieging
force needed to mount a naval blockade as well as a landward barrier. In
both cases strategists emphasize the importance of positioning the best
troops as close to the walls as possible in order to intimidate defenders
and gain early surrender. A raised aqueduct outside the walls could be
easily cut or diverted, so cisterns and wells were essential to any defense.

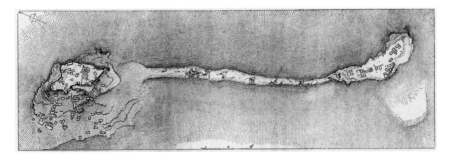

Plan of the hilltop fortifications at Geraki in south Greece. Most of the walls and houses date to the eleventh and twelfth centuries. The keep was added by the Latins in the thirteenth century. From *Annual of the British School at Athens* 13 (1906–7).

Several times the great cisterns of Constantinople helped the capital survive prolonged siege.

Long-distance projectiles offered an effective means of weakening a defensive force. Fire arrows shot at random over the walls carried the potential for starting fires, distracting defenders and consuming needed water and other resources. Catapults could throw bundles of flaming pitch and similar incendiary materials. Other destructive payloads were bee-hives and baskets of scorpions or snakes. Disease-bearing rats or plague corpses may have been delivered during extended campaigns.

If these measures did not bring about the surrender of a fortress, the attacker turned to the walls themselves. A well-equipped army would build special machinery in order to carry out a two-pronged assault on the walls, both above and below ground. The most important device was a tall siege tower variously known as a "tortoise" or "city taker" *(helepolis)*. This consisted of a timber-reinforced shell mounted on a wheeled cart, some-times together with sturdy battering rams. Thick hides and rope netting offered further protection to the soldiers using it. One of the main pur-poses of the armored "tortoise" was to provide cover for teams of miners as they dug a path toward the walls. Tunneling at an oblique angle so as not to give away their point of attack, these miners replaced the foundation blocks of the defensive wall with timber shoring. After removing a large enough part of the foundation, the attackers coordinated their assault: fires were set in the tunnel to bring down the upper masonry, while siege towers and battering rams were directed at surviving sections.

Faced with such challenges, the Byzantines put a high priority on the design and protection of their fortifications. Large cities were surrounded by multiple defensive walls, with a low advance barrier *(proteichismon)* standing forward of the main curtain. Perpendicular ditches offered protection against tunneling efforts and could be flooded if necessary.

Byzantine forces besieging the Bulgarian city of Preslav. Detail from the late-twelfth-century edition of the *Skylitzes Chronicle*. Photo courtesy of the Biblioteca Nacional, Madrid (ms. vitr. 26–2).

Human intelligence and remote sensing guided the digging of counter-tunnels: one medieval source recommends suspending a series of thin-walled metal vessels and listening closely for the echoes of nearby miners. Once intercepted the enemy tunnel was flushed with water, smoke, or swarms of bees. Battlements above ground sheltered defending archers while projecting towers served as reinforced battle stations. On some occasions the defenders hung reinforced nets of linen or wool rope a foot or two before the wall to cushion the impact of projectiles and battering rams. Other defensive measures centered on dropping objects onto the besieging forces. Bundles of dry grass, reeds, and wood might be laced with sulfur for greater combustibility. Beehives and nests of hornets and wasps carried powerful adversaries. Venomous snakes and scorpions distracted the most determined attackers. Other animals had defensive potential as well. The sixth-century Persian siege of Edessa collapsed when the elephant-mounted cavalry of Chosroes was repelled by the sight of a squealing pig.[30]

The Aftermath of Battle

Injury and death, whether incurred by accident or during combat, are inescapable parts of military life. Surgeons and their assistants followed Byzantine troops on campaigns. After any hostile action it was necessary to identify casualties, treat the wounded, and bury the dead. Small bands of medical corpsmen were recruited to bring the injured to field hospitals. The main qualifications for the task were to be alert and quick. The *Strategy* of Maurice recommends using less skilled soldiers to retrieve the wounded as well as scavenge usable weapons and supplies from the

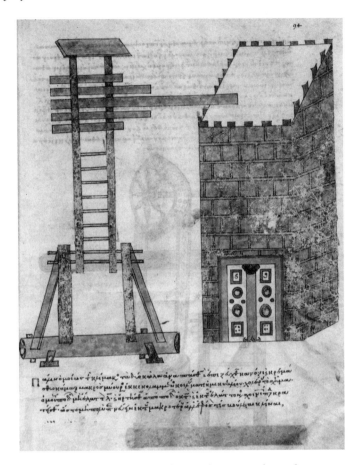

Siege tower before a walled city. From an eleventh-century treatise on military tactics and siegecraft. Photo courtesy of the Bibliothèque Nationale de France, Paris (ms. grec 2442).

battlefield. Officers and cavalrymen were cared for by members of their personal entourage. Of the other soldiers, the mortally wounded were set aside for priests to attend while doctors went about removing arrowheads, setting broken limbs, and bandaging wounds. Medical handbooks describe the grim consequences of medieval warfare and offer practical guidance in treating injuries. As their condition stabilized, wounded soldiers were carried by pack animals back to permanent bases. Despite such efforts, more men succumbed to infection and secondary complications than to combat itself. The bodies of high-ranking officers might be taken back to their families for private commemoration. In most cases fallen soldiers were simply interred in mass burials near the battlefield or along the road home.

Prisoners
Acquiring captives was a main objective of warfare. The *Tactics* of Leo VI recommends keeping enemy prisoners for their negotiating potential, at least until a truce was declared. The fate of foreign captives varied with the situation. If it proved impractical to guard, transport, or liberate captive soldiers and civilians, large numbers might be executed or otherwise neutralized. Basil II, for example, is reported to have blinded 14,000 Bulgarian soldiers following his victory at Belasica in 1014. On other occasions captured soldiers were brought back to the capital to be displayed in triumphal processions before being imprisoned or sold; public execution at this point was uncommon. Depending on the circumstances, captured soldiers might be enrolled in the imperial tagmata or recruited to serve in the palace household.

The usual point of taking captives was for exchange or ransom. Soldiers commanded the highest priority for these purposes, and officers generally were treated well during their captivity. Prisoners intended for exchange might be transported great distances and held for years. Captive Bulgarian troops, for example, are known to have been moved from Macedonia to southeast Asia Minor in the tenth century, where they were garrisoned for 10 years while awaiting exchange for Byzantine soldiers. Frequent clashes with the Arabs in the medieval period led on several occasions to the mass exchange of men. Officers and holders of high titles were ransomed by the state. The ransom for individual soldiers was usually raised by relatives, who might sell off land and other personal possessions. Donations to a church or monastery were sometimes reclaimed for this purpose; the only legal grounds for selling ecclesiastical silver plate was to ransom prisoners of war. Like other war spoils, about a fifth of all captives were retained by the state, with the rest distributed among the troops. Nonransomed soldiers and civilians were kept as slaves or sold on the market.

Veterans
The span of military careers varied widely. Career officers, primarily members of powerful aristocratic families, might continue to hold positions and draw pay for service well into middle age. Professional soldiers of the tagmata served full-time between the ages of about 20 and 40, and then retired to their homes in Byzantium or abroad. Able-bodied conscripts in the provincial or thematic armies generally served on a seasonal basis for specific terms, shorter in peacetime and less definite during war, before returning to work in their native town or village.

For most soldiers the main benefit that came with retirement was the chance to resume their nonmilitary lives. Officers might receive grants of land or remission of tax obligations, but the traditional pensions granted Roman soldiers came to an end in the seventh or eighth century. Soldiers who met their obligations without sustaining serious injury generally returned home with the intention of cultivating ancestral lands or rejoining the family business. Close relatives played an important role in helping these men adjust to their new lives, yet long years spent on a distant frontier certainly strained the social networks of many, who might come back to find their closest relatives dead and households transformed. Under such circumstances it is hardly surprising that many soldiers took monastic vows after leaving active duty. For them the monastery held the promise of a stable spiritual family that could provide religious comfort as well as material support. However much the Byzantines celebrated military success, the act of killing—even in warfare—was regarded as at best a necessary evil, for which Basil of Caesarea had prescribed three years of penance. The round of monastic services offered an effective way to atone for sins committed in battle, while one's fellow monks tended the sick and buried the dead. After years of hardship, drudgery, and violence, these men were content to end their days in rural monasteries, surrounded by images of saintly soldiers and hermits.

NOTES

1. George T. Dennis, ed. and trans., *Three Byzantine Military Treatises* (Washington, D.C.: Dumbarton Oaks, 1985), 21; Anna Komnene, *Alexiad*, trans. E.R.A. Sewter (as *The Alexiad of Anna Comnena*) (Harmondsworth, England: Penguin Classics, 1969), 12.5.

2. For Heraclius's campaign see Geoffrey Regan, *First Crusader: Byzantium's Holy Wars* (London: Palgrave Macmillan, 2003).

3. Among the sources available in translation: George T. Dennis ed. and trans., *Maurice's Strategikon: Handbook of Byzantine Military Strategy* (Philadelphia: University of Pennsylvania Press, 1984); and Eric McGeer, *Sowing the Dragon's Teeth: Byzantine Warfare in the Tenth Century* (Washington, D.C.: Dumbarton Oaks, 1995). Recent, well-illustrated introductions to late-antique and medieval armies are Michael Whitby, *Rome at War, A.D. 293–696* (New York: Routledge, 2003); and John F. Haldon, *Byzantium at War, A.D. 600–1453* (New York: Routledge, 2003). Other studies of the medieval army include Arnold Toynbee, *Constantine Porphyrogenitus and His World* (London: Oxford University Press, 1973) 282–322; Mark C. Bartusis, *The Late Byzantine Army: Arms and Society, 1204–1453* (Philadelphia: University of Pennsylvania Press, 1992); and Warren Treadgold, *Byzantium and Its Army, 284–1081* (Stanford, Calif.: Stanford University Press, 1995).

4. Medieval fortifications saw hard use and constant repairs that are difficult to date. For examples see A. W. Lawrence, "A Skeletal Guide to Byzantine Fortifications," *Annual of the British School at Athens* 78 (1983): 171–227; and Clive Foss and David Winfield, *An Introduction to Byzantine Fortifications* (Pretoria: University of South Africa Press, 1986). For neighboring states see Robert W. Edwards, *The Fortifications of Armenian Cilicia* (Washington, D.C.: Dumbarton Oaks, 1987); Hugh Kennedy, *Crusader Castles* (Cambridge: Cambridge University Press, 1994); and Kristian Molin, *Unknown Crusader Castles* (New York: Hambledon and London, 2001).

5. The difficulty of separating contemporary practice from artistic convention is illustrated by David Nicolle, *Arms and Armour of the Crusading Era, 1050–1350: Islam,*

Eastern Europe, and Asia (Mechanicsburg, Pa.: Stackpole Books, 1999), 19–51; and discussed by Maria G. Parani, *Reconstructing the Reality of Images: Byzantine Material Culture and Religious Iconography (11th–15th Centuries)* (Leiden, the Netherlands: Brill, 2003), 101–58. For an introduction to west European equipment see David Nicolle, *The Crusades and the Crusader States* (London: Osprey Publishing, 1988).

6. For an overview see John F. Haldon, *The Byzantine Wars: Battles and Campaigns of the Byzantine Era* (Charleston, S.C.: Tempus, 2000).

7. Anna Komnene, trans., Sewter, *Alexiad* 2.9; S. Blöndal, *The Varangians of Byzantium* (Cambridge: Cambridge University Press, 1978).

8. The main study of Byzantine weapons is Taxiarchis G. Kolias, *Byzantinische Waffen: Ein Beitrag zur byzantinischen Waffenkunde von den Anfängen bis zur lateinischen Eroberung* (Vienna: Austrian Academy of Sciences, 1988). For medieval infantry and weaponry see McGeer, *Sowing the Dragon's Teeth*, 202–214; and Bartusis, *The Late Byzantine Army*, 322–30.

9. Reconstructions of medieval armor and weaponry can be found in illustrated guides by Ian Heath: *Byzantine Armies, 886–1118* (London: Osprey Publishing, 1979) and *Byzantine Armies, 1118–1462* (London: Osprey Publishing, 1995). See also John F. Haldon, "Some Aspects of Byzantine Military Technology from the Sixth to the Tenth Centuries," *Byzantine and Modern Greek Studies* 1 (1975): 11–47; and Timothy Dawson, "*Kremasmata, Kabadion, Klibanion:* Some Aspects of Middle Byzantine Military Equipment Reconsidered," *Byzantine and Modern Greek Studies* 22 (1998): 38–50, who reports on experimental manufacturing techniques.

10. Dennis, *Three Byzantine Military Treatises*, 53.

11. Ibid., 129; and idem, *Maurice's Strategikon* 1.1–2.

12. A good introduction to medieval horses and their strategic contribution is Ann Hyland, *The Medieval Warhorse from Byzantium to the Crusades* (Dover, N.H.: Alan Sutton Publishing, 1994), 18–53. The European adoption of the stirrup had far-reaching social implications, sometimes overemphasized by historians; see Lynn White, *Medieval Technology and Social Change* (Oxford: Oxford University Press, 1962), 14–28.

13. Al-Mutanabbi's impression of the Byzantine cavalry is quoted in McGeer, *Sowing the Dragon's Teeth*, 214.

14. For the Byzantine navy see Helénè Ahrweiler, *Byzance et la mer* (Paris: University Presses of France, 1966); Toynbee, *Constantine Porphyrogenitus and His World*, 323–45.

15. For warships see Robert Gardiner, ed., *The Age of the Galley: Mediterranean Oared Vessels since Pre-Classical Times* (Annapolis, Md.: Naval Institute Press, 1995), especially F. Hocker, "Late Roman, Byzantine, and Islamic Galleys and Fleets," 86–100; and John H. Pryor, "From Dromon to Galea: Mediterranean Bireme Galleys, A.D. 500–1300," 101–16.

16. For practical lessons learned from recent reenactments see Lionel Casson, *Ships and Seafaring in Ancient Times* (Austin: University of Texas Press, 1994); and John S. Morrison, John F. Coates, and N. B. Rankov, *The Athenian Trireme: The History and Reconstruction of an Ancient Greek Warship*, 2nd ed. (Cambridge: Cambridge University Press, 2000). Underwater archaeology has documented the many hazards faced by ships at anchor; see George F. Bass, ed., *A History of Seafaring Based on Underwater Archaeology* (New York: Thames and Hudson, 1972).

17. Caesar took fighting mastiffs on his campaigns in northern Europe, and the legendary war dogs of Asia Minor were known to Roman military authors like Polyaenus; see Adrienne Mayor, *Greek Fire, Poison Arrows, and Scorpion Bombs: Biological and Chemical Warfare in the Ancient World* (Woodstock: Overlook Press, 2003), 190–93. Dogs were especially useful for hunting. For these and other animals see Jocelyn M. C. Toynbee, *Animals in Roman Life and Art* (London: Thames and Hudson, 1973; reprint, Baltimore: Johns Hopkins University Press, 1996); and Douglas Brewer, Terence Clark, and Adrian Phillips, *Dogs in Antiquity: Anubis to Cerberus; The Origins of the Domestic Dog* (Warminster, England: Aris and Phillips, 2001).

18. Dennis, *Maurice's Strategikon* 9.3, 12.D. For army fare see Procopius, *Wars*, trans. H. B. Dewing (Cambridge: Harvard University Press, 1914–40; reprinted 1953–62), 3.13–15; and Andrew Dalby, *Flavours of Byzantium* (Totnes, England: Prospect Books, 2003), 99–100.

19. Encampments are discussed in Dennis, *Three Military Treatises*, 246–61; McGeer, *Sowing the Dragon's Teeth*, 348–54; and Haldon, *Byzantium at War*, 65–67.

20. "For whether throwing or stabbing with the lance, the pennon reduces both accuracy and range, and when the shooting begins, it interferes with the fire of the archers in the rear ranks." Dennis, *Maurice's Strategikon* 2.10.

21. For military banners and a few illustrations see George T. Dennis, "Byzantine Battle Flags," *Byzantinische Forschungen* 8 (1982): 51–60; and A. Babuin, "Standards and Insignia of Byzantium," *Byzantion* 71 (2001): 5–59.

22. The workings of the relay system are discussed in Philip Pattenden, "The Early Byzantine Warning System," *Byzantion* 53 (1983): 258–99.

23. Peter Schreiner, "Soldiers," in *The Byzantines*, ed. Guglielmo Cavallo (Chicago: University of Chicago Press, 1997), 87–90; George T. Dennis, "Religious Services in the Byzantine Army," in *Eulogema: Studies in Honor of Robert Taft, S.J.*, ed. E. Carr et al. (Rome: Studia Anselmiana, 1993), 107–17.

24. Michael Psellos, *Chronographia*, trans. E.R.A. Sewter (as *Michael Psellus, Fourteen Byzantine Rulers*) (Harmondsworth, England: Penguin Classics, 1966), 1.16. For military saints see Schreiner, "Soldiers," 91–92.

25. Anna Komnene, trans., Sewter, *Alexiad* 10.8; George T. Dennis, "Flies, Mice, and the Byzantine Crossbow," *Byzantine and Modern Greek Studies* 7 (1981): 1–5.

26. Anna Komnene, *Alexiad* 11.2; White, *Medieval Technology and Social Change*, 101–3; J.R. Partington, *A History of Greek Fire and Gunpowder* (Cambridge: Cambridge University Press, 1960), 18. A recent assessment of the Byzantine contribution is Paul E. Chevedden, "The Invention of the Counterweight Trebuchet: A Study in Cultural Diffusion," *Dumbarton Oaks Papers* 54 (2000): 71–111.

27. See Partington, *A History of Greek Fire and Gunpowder*, 124–29; and D. Petrovic, "Fire-arms in the Balkans on the Eve of and after the Ottoman Conquest of the Fourteenth and Fifteenth Centuries," in *War, Technology and Society in the Middle East*, ed. V.J. Parry and M.E. Yapp (London: Oxford University Press, 1975), 164–94. There are several eyewitnesses to the final siege: John R. Melville Jones, *The Siege of Constantinople 1453: Seven Contemporary Accounts* (Amsterdam: Adolf M. Hakkert, 1972); Harry Magoulias, trans., *Doukas, Decline and Fall of Byzantium to the Ottoman Turks* (Detroit: Wayne State University Press, 1975); and Margaret Carroll, *A Contemporary Greek Source for the Siege of Constantinople: The Sphrantzes Chronicle* (Amsterdam: Adolf M. Hakkert, 1985). For the use of firearms see Mark Bartusis, *The Late Byzantine Army*, 334–41.

28. Adapted from Anna Komnene, trans., Sewter, *Alexiad* 11.10.

29. Early incendiary weapons have fired the scholarly imagination. For further discussion of this "liquid flame" see Partington, *A History of Greek Fire and Gunpowder*, 10–21; and H. R. Ellis-Davidson, "The Secret Weapon of Byzantium," *Byzantinische Zeitschrift* 66 (1973): 61–74, quoting eyewitness accounts.

30. Procopius, *Wars* 8.14.35–38; Mayor, *Greek Fire, Poison Arrows, and Scorpion Bombs*, 202. Much practical information can be found in Denis F. Sullivan, "A Byzantine Instructional Manual on Siege Defense: The *De Obsidione Toleranda*," in *Byzantine Authors: Literary Activities and Preoccupations*, ed. John W. Nesbitt (Leiden, the Netherlands: Brill, 2003), 139–266.

8

THE MONASTERY

Monasticism was one of the most characteristic features of the medieval world, in Byzantium as well as in western Europe. Whether located in crowded cities or remote mountains, convents and monasteries were an inescapable part of the Eastern landscape. As a religious movement, monasticism originated in the turning away from worldly concerns in order to focus on spiritual concerns, yet as institutions Byzantine monasteries were never far removed from society at large. Monks and nuns clad in distinctive black garb were a familiar sight in town and village, and often were sought out for advice and help. Many families had members who had taken monastic vows, whether as young adults, when their grown children left home, upon the death of a spouse, or in old age. People regularly attended services at local monasteries, and supported monks and nuns with the harvest of their gardens, cash, religious objects, and land. Mundane monastic affairs appear regularly in saints' lives, sermons, letters, and legal documents. The relative autonomy of monasteries ensured close, mutually supportive relations with local residents, for whom they were spiritual outposts amid the hazards and uncertainties of daily life.[1]

ORIGINS AND DEVELOPMENT

The individualistic nature of Byzantine society led to the development of several forms of monastic life, and it may be more accurate to speak of a variety of spiritual paths rather than a single approach. The idea of withdrawing from workaday society is of great antiquity in the Near East, and in its Christian form derives from the example of Jesus going into the wilderness (Matthew 4:1–11). Among the first known monks were Christian hermits who found refuge from urban pressures in the desert of Roman Egypt. The best known of these early solitaries was Antony (ca. 251–356), whose reputation soon attracted a number of followers. Many of his disciples pursued a physically demanding routine as part of a *lavra,* a group of individuals who lived separately but assembled for weekly worship. Others banded together in more actively supportive cenobitic communities that were supervised by a senior monk or abbot. Around the middle of the fourth century the Egyptian monk Pachomius (ca. 290–346) drew up guidelines to help local communities organize themselves. The ideals of poverty, chastity, and obedience formed the basis for later monastics in eastern and western Europe.

Byzantine monasticism assumed its distinctive character under the influence of Basil of Caesarea (ca. 329–79). Writing in Cappadocia in central Asia Minor, Basil developed a set of general guidelines, known as the 55 *Long Rules* and the 313 *Lesser Rules,* governing spiritual life. Rather than prescribe a clear monastic order of the kind that would develop later in the West, Basil sketched a contemplative lifestyle that gradually spread throughout the Orthodox world. He recommends that monks live in individual cells for privacy but gather at regular intervals for services, meals, and labor. All monks share responsibility for supporting each other with work and prayer. The abbot provides spiritual guidance for the community, supervises internal affairs, and negotiates relations with the outside world. Most significantly, Basil saw that monks should actively contribute to society as a whole by exemplifying the Christian virtues of piety, devotion, and charity. Piety and devotion are best cultivated within the monastery by participating in a regular program of worship. Charitable activities could take many forms, including the sponsorship of soup kitchens, orphanages, hospitals, hospices, and similar programs. Cities no less than villages benefited from the presence of monasteries, which grew rapidly in size and numbers.[2]

Monasteries varied a great deal with place and time, and provided conditions ranging from spartan to relatively luxurious. The sacred sites of Egypt, Palestine, and Syria attracted many men and women to follow the example of early martyrs in popular folklore, leaving behind their old identities in favor of new spiritual lifeways. Some of these monastic centers offered hospitality to pilgrims traveling through the Christian Holy Land; the gifts and bequests they received in return fueled their growing number and facilities. Others were established by disciples of renown holy men who had led rigorously ascetic lives. One of the most famous of these "spiritual athletes," Symeon Stylites (ca. 389–459), followed his solitary path by living in the Syrian wilderness atop a towering column. After his death a major pilgrimage center was established to commemorate the site and his life.

Monasteries appeared in Constantinople in the fourth and fifth centuries, first in outlying neighborhoods and soon spreading throughout the city. One early foundation, the monastery of Saint John Stoudios, was set up on a private suburban estate and quickly became one of the empire's most powerful institutions—a wealthy church, intellectual enclave, and training center for church leaders and scholars. By the sixth century local families had organized more than 70 separate convents and monasteries. Many of these disappeared during the medieval period, but others were renovated or established anew. One of the largest was the monastery of Christ Pantokrator, founded in the early twelfth century by the emperor John II Komnenos with his wife, Irene. This enormous religious center included soup kitchens, a hospice, and a famous hospital staffed by trained physicians. The main church buildings still stand atop the fourth hill in central Istanbul.

Monasteries were a common feature of the Byzantine countryside. The ideals of detachment and self-sufficiency were central to Basil's view of the spiritual life, and these goals were best achieved through agricultural production. Rural monasteries often began with a gift of property by local landowners to a group of monks, who supported themselves by raising subsistence crops. Unlike village families, which were constantly changing in age and size, a rural monastery constituted a large, stable household of willing adult laborers. As independent and untaxed agricultural units that were voluntarily worked by their residents, most monasteries could support themselves even under adverse conditions. They also were well positioned to receive bequests of additional parcels of land, both nearby and far away. Over the span of generations or centuries some monasteries amassed considerable territory that included arable fields, shops, villages, and dependent monastic outposts known as *metocheia*. Daily routines focused on raising crops and livestock, and might differ little from life on secular estates. The accumulation of diverse properties—coastal plains, inland terraces, pastures, and woodlands—broadened a foundation's productive base. Some of these lands could be rented out to tenant farmers, whose rents allowed the monks to focus on other activities. In short, the same circumstances that underlay the expansion of secular estates during the tenth to twelfth centuries supported monastic growth in all parts of the empire. Surviving documents in the archives of Mount Athos are filled with the complicated details of property transactions and estate management. Eustathios, metropolitan of Thessaloniki in the twelfth century, complained about how much time and energy administrators had to spend supervising agricultural affairs.

Certain regions were especially attractive to spiritual seekers, who over the years gathered in loosely organized enclaves under the direction of a senior abbot *(protos)*. In addition to the sacred sites of Syria and Palestine, these special areas included the craggy mountains of Ganos in Thrace, Auxentios and Olympos in Bithynia, and Gelasios and Latros in western Asia Minor. In central Greece the remarkable setting of Meteora ("in the air"), where tall, rocky cliffs tower above the fertile plain of Thessaly, attracted a number of monks during the late Middle Ages.

The largest and best known of these monastic federations is Mount Athos. Located in Chalkidiki in north Greece, the "Holy Mountain" (Hagion Oron) of Athos consists of a narrow, rocky peninsula that juts about 28 miles into the Aegean, with a sharp mountainous ridge rising over 6,600 feet above the surrounding sea. A number of hermits had settled here before

The late-medieval monastery of Saint Barlaam at Meteora, in central Greece. The craggy, isolated location protected the resident monks from robbery and secular distraction. From *Annales archéologiques* 1 (1844).

the ninth century, but the first cenobitic monastery seems to have been the Great Lavra, which was founded by the future saint Athanasios (feast day observed July 5) in the mid 900s. Other monks soon were drawn by this leader's spiritual reputation and the area's dramatic, isolated setting. Over the following centuries dozens of other monasteries and smaller metocheia were established by leading Byzantine families and the rulers of neighboring states to which monks had brought Christianity. The Vatopedi monastery, which dates to the late tenth century, is one of the largest centers on Athos, with more than 15 chapels on its grounds. The slightly later monastery of Iviron was associated with monks from Georgia during its early years. The Chilandar monastery was founded by the ruler of Serbia in the early fourteenth century and remains affiliated with the Serbian Orthodox church. The dramatically situated monastery of Dionysiou was set up with imperial support in the later fourteenth century. Over time these foundations accumulated extensive properties in Macedonia, the Aegean islands, and western Asia Minor, which supplemented the production of their own gardens, vineyards, and orchards. Together these two dozen monasteries constituted a powerful force that influenced political as well as religious affairs in the capital. Even after the fall of Constantinople the spiritual integrity of Mount Athos was respected by Ottoman rulers, with older foundations flourishing again at Simopetra, Stavronikita, and elsewhere on the Athonite slopes. Virtually surrounded by water and walled off from the mainland, famously excluding females of all species, Mount Athos remains to this day a unique outpost of Orthodox monastic life.[3]

MONASTIC ORGANIZATION

Byzantine monasteries varied widely in their organization, size, and facilities. Eastern monasticism's individualistic nature derived from the circumstances under which each foundation was established. A renowned hermit or holy man might draw followers, a landowner could set up a group of monks on his estate, or a wealthy couple might decide to take vows themselves. Unlike the Benedictine, Cluniac, or Cistercian orders in the West, Byzantine monasteries were largely autonomous institutions that looked to Basil's rules for general guidance. Most were organized as independent lavras or on a cenobitic basis. Anchorites and hermits preferred to live by themselves in remote shelters, depending for their survival on the charity of local residents.

Each monastery was established by a written charter of foundation, known as a *typikon*. The main purpose of this document was to spell out the spiritual intentions of the founders and indicate how inhabitants of the new monastery were supposed to achieve them. Commonly expressed goals were to provide spiritual retreat for its residents, sponsor cultural or philanthropic activities, and perpetually commemorate the founders with special prayers. The rest of the document outlined the

The Dionysiou monastery on Mount Athos, balanced between mountains and the sea. From Eugène-Melchior de Vogüé, *Syrie, Palestine, Mont Athos* (Paris: E. Plon and Company, 1876).

intended size of the monastery, who should live there, how it should be governed, what the residents should do with their time, and which worship services should be observed. Most critically, the donor recorded the land or income-producing properties that were given to support the new foundation. The 61 known medieval typika provide unique insight into commonly expressed spiritual hopes as well as the most prosaic routines of monastic life.[4] Many founders remained closely involved with the details of organization and management throughout their lives. Some supervised the construction of the main church and supporting buildings, appointed the first abbot, and recruited the first cohort of monks or nuns to live there. Others were content to leave these responsibilities in the hands of professional administrators.

The canonical minimum for a monastery was originally set at 3 monks and later raised to 8 to 10, but the goal of productive self-sufficiency usually demanded larger numbers. Most medieval foundations averaged 20 to 50 inhabitants, with some famous monasteries attracting 100 or more monks or nuns. Up to 700 monks are said to have lived at the Athonite Great Lavra in the eleventh century. The typikon and nature of endowment were the most important factors affecting size. Few records survive for the small foundations that were common everywhere.

Most monasteries were populated by mature men, yet children, young adults, and women might be attracted to monasticism as well. The ideal of celibacy was enforced by strictly separating inhabitants by age and sex. Novices and beardless youths who had not yet taken vows lived under close supervision in separate quarters. Eunuchs were viewed with suspicion by church leaders and were assigned to special facilities. As in society as a whole, women were regarded as a special temptation and were expressly excluded from monasteries, often including the main church *(katholikon)*. Most convents were completely separate foundations, usually located in cities and administered by a senior nun. Male visitors were limited to immediate family members and officiating priests at services. In a few cases jointly managed "double monasteries" were set up as separate residences for men and women from the same family.

A monastery's viability depended on the clear assignment of responsibilities. Each community was supervised by a resident abbot *(hegoumenos* or *archimandrite)*, who was appointed for life. The first abbot might be named by the founder, but his successors were elected by resident monks and installed by the local bishop. The abbot acted in different capacities: as spiritual guide, personal counselor, liturgical leader, and facilities superintendent. The physical possessions of a monastery, essential for supporting its residents, were overseen by the abbot, assisted when necessary by a special business manager *(oikonomos)*. Other roles were more or less clearly defined, depending on the size of the community. Responsibility for conducting daily liturgies was assigned to monks or nuns who could read and sing *(ekklesiastikoi)*. The size of the choir varied with the total population and the number of services that were observed. Larger monasteries might include special offices like precentor *(kanonarches)* or lector *(anagnostes)*. The *aphypnistes* or *horologos* was responsible for summoning monks to morning prayers. The *taxiarches* maintained order and awakened monks who dozed during the liturgy. During the day residents performed manual tasks in fields or workrooms, tended domestic chores, and occupied themselves in prayer.

While most monks lived in well-defined groups, the solitary temperament that underlies the monastic impulse led some to move from one monastery to another or even strike out on their own. A change of residence could be understood as a normal part of a monk's spiritual development, and over time one might feel it necessary to seek a more suitable environment or liturgical regimen. Some monks adopted a wandering or peripatetic lifestyle for a period of time, seeing their deliberate homelessness as a form of ascetic exercise. Others found their ultimate goal in retiring from cenobitic life to a small hermitage apart from the monastery itself. Such changes were not lightly made and theoretically required the approval of one's abbot as well as the local bishop. Yet the relative frequency with which Eastern monks changed their residence is very different from the tradition of Western monasticism, and the continuity of place *(stabilitas loci)* that Benedict of Nursia emphasized in his sixth-century rules.

ENTERING MONASTIC LIFE

Monks and nuns came from all social levels and took vows for different reasons: out of a sense of personal devotion, for lack of a dowry, as an escape from an impending marriage, military service, or other obligations, as a thank-offering for a miraculous cure or deliverance, or in hope of shelter and care in retirement or toward the end of life. Like priests, monks were excused from military service, and monasteries were not supposed to accept soldiers on active duty. In most cases personal belongings were handed over to the community one was joining. Some monasteries permitted residents to keep a few personal items like a prayer book or icon; others banned all possessions and even redistributed clothing on a weekly basis. Entering monastic life did not require cutting all family ties and personal friendships. Many monks and nuns remained in touch with their children or parents throughout their lives. Most nuns lived in convents located in cities, but monks lived in monasteries both urban and rural. They were a familiar sight in cities and villages, and were widely respected models for spiritual life. Many monks became church leaders and advised the emperor and members of his family.

Entering a monastery was a serious undertaking for both the individual and the community. While this kind of institutionalized spiritual retreat had obvious attractions, not everyone was suited to its rigor and lifelong commitment. The nominal age for taking vows was about 16 years, although in special cases a monastery might end up caring for much younger children. Prospective members normally underwent an extended novitiate or probationary period when their motives and stamina, both physical and spiritual, were tested. This trial period was supposed to last as long as three years, but could be shortened for individuals who were known to have lived an especially holy life outside the monastery or were seriously ill. Compulsory entrants to the monastery, including members of deposed ruling families, disgraced officials, prostitutes, and certain criminals, may have continued for a longer period at this level. Monks neither shaved their beards nor cut their hair. The postulant continued to wear lay clothing and eventually was given a tunic *(rason)* to mark

Council of monastic elders at Mount Athos in the nineteenth century. From Eugène-Melchior de Vogüé, *Syrie, Palestine, Mont Athos* (Paris: E. Plon and Company, 1876).

his emerging status as a monk at the beginning *rasophore* level. During one's novitiate it was necessary to put personal affairs in order, including making arrangements for the care of any dependent children or parents. Monastic life was not intended to serve as a refuge from an existing marriage, and a spouse could be left behind only by mutual consent. Personal possessions became the common property of the house one was joining.

The successful novice was formally received into the monastery in a frocking ceremony known as the Euchologion. At this time the monk or nun took formal vows of poverty, chastity, obedience before the abbot and the rest of the community. The postulant was tonsured according to local custom: the hair might be cut in a circle, in the form of a cross, or completely shaved. A monastic name was bestowed, often beginning with the same initial as the initiate's given name, to mark a new spiritual identity: Alexios might become Athanasios, or Theodora now Theodoule. Certain names, like Gabriel, Iakovos (Jacob), Isaiah, and Makarios, were rare outside the monastery. Finally, the new member received a set of black robes that were known as the lesser habit *(mikron schema)*. For women this included a tunic *(himation)*, long outer cloak *(mandyas)*, and head covering *(skepe)*. In some monasteries the monk also received a pendant wooden cross *(stavros)*, and became known as a *stavrophore* ("cross bearer"). Further spiritual development over a period of several years was recognized by wearing of the greater habit *(angelikon schema)*. This distinctive, multilayered costume included the inner tunic, an ankle-length outer tunic with long sleeves, the veiled cowl *(koukoulion)*, and the *analabos*, a distinguishing smock that depicted the cross on Golgotha. Sandals or slippers and a long hooded cloak that was worn to services completed the garb of the *megaloschemos* monk. Individuals at this highest level of dedication were expected to remain within the monastery, observe strict fasts, and devote much of their time to prayer as an example to other monks. Upon death the body of the megaloschemos was laid out, wrapped in his mandyas, and buried in full monastic habit.

PARTS OF THE MONASTERY

A monastery's physical organization depended on many factors, including its location, intentions of the founders, and resources at hand. The layout of the complex reflected its situation in town or countryside, and was influenced by the availability of land and need for security. A mild climate, fertile soils, and perennial streams were important assets. Essential buildings included living quarters and a place for worship. The choice of materials, mainly brick, stone, earth, and timber, reflected local sources and practices. Where circumstances permitted, a perimeter wall was built around an open court in front of or surrounding the church. Such arrangements were common in all parts of the empire throughout the Byzantine millennium. They embody practical and spiritual concerns by clearly setting the physical limits and devotional focus of monastic life.

The outer wall formed a defensive buffer between the secular wilderness and the spiritual world within. In remote settings this took the form of a thick, fortresslike barrier to discourage casual raids by brigands and pirates. Urban monasteries, like aristocratic houses, were screened from the street by a high wall. In both cases the perimeter wall was closed or had only small windows at ground level. The main entrance was through a wide portal, often marked by a special gateway and watched by a porter, which was used by visitors and for making deliveries. This gate might be left open during the day but was locked at night. In rural monasteries small service doors opened from stables or storerooms to the surrounding fields. The severe, defensive appearance of many monasteries was completed by a sturdy tower or keep, which offered a lookout, signal point, and final line of defense. Some rural monasteries, like St. Catherine's in the Sinai desert, actually occupied a military kastro that was garrisoned for strategic purposes. Most were not intended to resist sustained attack but stood as spiritual fortresses to encourage neighboring communities.

Monks and nuns lived in dormitory-like cells *(kellia)* that were arranged in long rows along the compound walls looking onto the central court. In most places these rooms were at ground level, but in larger communities

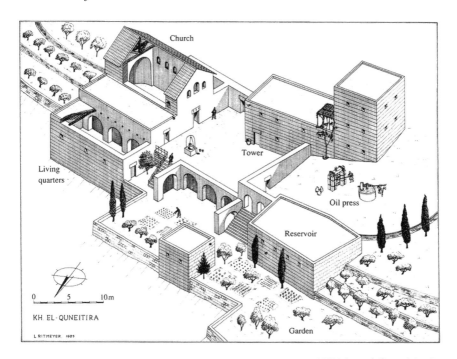

Reconstruction of the fifth- or sixth-century monastery of Khirbet el-Quneitira in the Judean desert. Most rural monasteries tried to raise enough crops to support themselves. Drawing by L. Ritmeyer, in Yizhar Hirschfeld, *The Judean Desert Monasteries in the Byzantine Period* (New Haven, Conn.: Yale University Press, © 1992); reproduced by permission of Yale University Press.

they might be arranged in two, three, or four stories of nearly identical spaces joined by a continuous portico on columns. Individual cells were typically small, about 10 feet square, with enough space for a bed, table, and chair. A hearth in one corner gave heat during the winter. Furnishings were minimal and might be limited to a devotional icon, prayer book, and one's clothes. The abbot's room was located near the main gate and was a bit larger. An attached office served for pastoral consultations and receiving visitors.

The arrangement of the interior court varied widely. In larger monasteries the outer wall was lined by multistoried porticoes that gave sheltered access to the rows of cells. Benches often lined the portico walls. The courtyard itself often was planted with shade or fruit trees. Tall cypress trees represented the individual's spiritual quest, proclaiming "the way in which they are to walk and strive upward, laying aside gradually as they go up the excess of their material part and growing thinner as they rise."[5] One invariable feature of the interior was a communal well

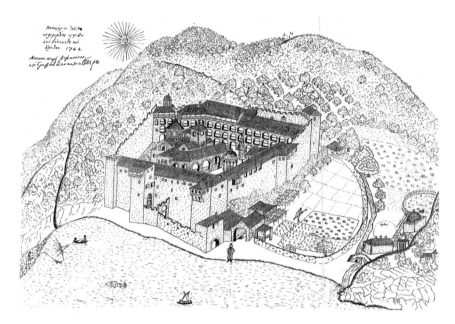

Esphigmenou monastery on Mount Athos in the eighteenth century. The katholikon stands in the center of the monastic yard and is surrounded by multistoried porticoes with cells. The *phiale* stands in front of the katholikon. Drawing by the Russian monk Basil Barsky, in *Vtoroe poseshchenie sviatoi Afonskoi gory Vasilia Grigorovicha-Barskago* (St. Petersburg: Izd. Afonskago russkago Panteleimonova monastyria, 1887).

or cistern fed by runoff from the court paving and surrounding roofs. Cisterns could take the form of a simple underground tank or an elaborate vaulted chamber. In some places it was marked by a special wellhead and freestanding baldachino, and was known as the *phiale* or sacred well (*hagiasma*). The monastery's dependence on water clearly paralleled the monk's dependence on Christ.

The most important part of any monastery was the main church or *katholikon*. This was the liturgical heart of the complex and the place where all monks or nuns gathered for services. The importance of the katholikon is reflected in its central location within the compound, either detached from other buildings or opening off the central yard. This was the largest and most splendidly decorated part of any monastery, and normally the only building open to visitors. Katholika were not fundamentally different from regular, nonmonastic churches. Most were longitudinal basilicas covered by a pitched timber roof. Many churches of the medieval period were based on a more compact plan and had a central dome supported on four columns or piers. This distinctive centralized design was ideal for the

The covered fountain or phiale before the katholikon of the Great Lavra on Mount Athos. From Gustave Schlumberger, *Un empereur byzantin aux dixième siècle, Nicéphore Phocas* (Paris: Firmin Didot, 1890).

needs of small monastic communities, which helped spread its popularity. A variation combining the central dome with three curved walls often appeared on Mount Athos. Every church had a main sanctuary with an altar; many had one or more additional altars as well. The katholikon was never an especially large building, even in populous monasteries where its liturgical operations were supplemented by multiple chapels *(parekklesia)*. Funerals were held in special chapels set aside for this purpose.

Church interiors were dimly lit by small, high windows, with narrative scenes and biblical figures painted on the surrounding walls and vaults. Images of monastic saints and patriarchs were especially popular. By the twelfth century the most important portable icons were being displayed on the *iconostasis*, a high screen separating the sanctuary from the rest

The katholikon of the small monastery at Kaisariani, located on the slopes of Mount Hymettos outside Athens. From *Archaiologike Ephemeris* 1902.

of the church. A door at the center of the iconostasis accommodated the ritualized entrances of the medieval liturgy. Other painted panels were supported on stands along the walls. Various lighting devices were used. Small glass lamps were kept lit throughout the day and especially during nighttime services and vigils. Multiple lamps were placed in a suspended metal holder *(polykandelon)* and filled with oil, which supplied a floating wick. Other lamps and candleholders were made of bronze and silver. Large candles *(kandelai)* were carried in processions and together with incense marked the opening of the liturgy. Votive candles were lit by visitors to the katholikon as tokens of personal devotion. The sanctified atmosphere was completed by incense sprinkled on glowing coals held in decorated censers *(thymiateria)*, either suspended by chains or carried on a long handle.[6]

The refectory or dining hall *(trapeza)* was another place where residents routinely gathered. In larger monasteries this building stood within the court apart from its neighbors, but more often it was built along one side of the enclosure. The refectory entrance usually faced the main door of the church and sometimes was joined to it by a covered portico. The building itself was a long open room with one or more tables and benches for communal dining. In some examples there was a lectern for readings or singing psalms during meals, which might otherwise be held in silence. All able-bodied monks were supposed to dine together, although in larger monasteries this might be done in shifts. Residents also assembled in the refectory for meetings and discussions. The number and resources of the group determined the room's size and furnishings. Since the liturgical ideal included communal meals, the walls were often painted with images of monastic saints. The kitchen and bake-house stood next door. The main feature of the kitchen was an open hearth, often located at the center of the room with a high chimney set well away from other buildings. The most important part of the bake-house was a brick oven with a domed roof. The prominence of bread in the monastic diet meant that these rooms were used day and night. Nearby storerooms held sacks and jars filled with grain, vegetables, wine, and other commodities.

Other parts of the monastery included the library, archives, and treasury. These were located in a tower or separate wing, well away from the hazardous fireplaces and ovens of domestic quarters. Library holdings ranged from a few liturgical volumes to vast collections built up over centuries. In larger monasteries these were supervised by a special librarian (*bibliophylax*). A clerk (*chartophylax*) kept records of monastic finances, properties, and privileges in a similarly safe location. Since new books were made by laboriously copying older editions, scriptoria were located nearby. Older and more sumptuously decorated manuscripts were kept in a treasury (*skeuophylakeion*) along with gold and silver plate, icons, and reliquaries. Such precious objects formed an important part of the monastery's identity and were used in the katholikon on special occasions.

Most monasteries maintained both a bathhouse and infirmary. Bathing was viewed as a luxury that should be kept to a hygienic minimum, with the result that monks bathed on average about once a month. The few known examples of medieval bathhouses were small, vaulted structures with separate rooms for washing in hot and cold water. Pipes, storage tanks, a heating chamber, and a reliable water supply were needed to function properly. In many cases the baths formed part of the health-care facilities for residents and guests. The lifelong commitment of its residents meant that illness and the afflictions of old age were constant companions in medieval monasteries. Younger monks and nuns cared for their less able-bodied colleagues and often were sought out by the wider public as well. Options for treatment centered on diet, hygiene, palliative care, and prayer. A few large foundations, like the Pantokrator in Constantinople, provided specialized medical care as part of their charitable work.

Death was a necessary part of monastic life, which was widely seen as one's spiritual preparation for facing it. The typikon usually named members of the founding family who hoped to be remembered in the course of daily services. Residents were given funerals, often in the narthex of the katholikon or a separate chapel, before being interred. Burial customs ranged from simple subterranean graves to communal ossuaries at

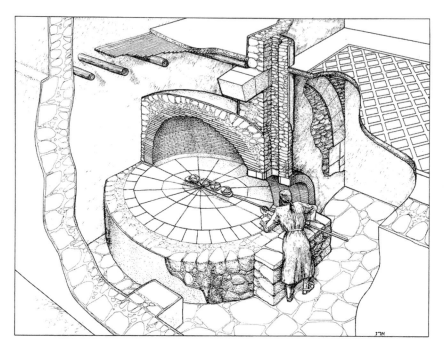

Reconstruction of the monastic oven at Khirbet ed-Deir. The domed oven was heated by burning fuel directly on the tiled surface, with coals swept to the side when baking. From Yizhar Hirschfeld, *The Judean Desert Monasteries in the Byzantine Period* (New Haven, Conn.: Yale University Press, © 1992); reproduced by permission of Yale University Press.

St. Catherine's and on Mount Athos. These were crypts, often underlying the main church, where the bodies of deceased monks were allowed gradually to decompose. After a few years the skulls and other bones were washed and reorganized for more compact, permanent storage.[7]

Most monasteries were supported by monetary gifts and donated real estate. Commercial buildings in towns provided regular income, but agricultural land was the best way for an institution to support itself. Properties were supervised by the hegoumenos or, if they were especially extensive, by an oikonomos. Larger estates might be organized into small metocheia that were worked by their own residents. Like dependent farmsteads, these monastic satellites typically included a residence with one or more cells, a chapel, dining room, kitchen, storerooms, and stables. The inhabitants of each metocheion went about their daily lives more or less independently, returning to the main monastery on important festivals or other special occasions.

THE MONASTIC DAY

Each individual's spiritual struggle was an ongoing process, and all parts of the day contributed to one's quest for personal sanctity. The daily succession of worship services, shared meals, productive labor, and private prayers was carefully arranged to minimize distractions and cultivate spiritual virtue. One late Byzantine church leader, Theoleptos of Philadelphia in western Asia Minor, drew up a list of 10 goals for followers of the monastic life: "Freedom from possessions, flight from people, abstinence from willed pleasures, patient endurance of unwilled afflictions, regular psalmody, reading with concentration, attentive prayer, moderated denial of sleep, genuflections performed with compunction, and eloquent silence."[8]

Life was organized around a sequence of activities that were set out in the foundation charter. A typical day began before sunrise with an hour of prayer, either in individual cells or in the main church. A designated monk was responsible for awakening residents by striking a bell, gong, or suspended wood post (*semantron*) with a mallet. Early prayers were followed by matins (*orthros*), held at dawn in the katholikon. After this early service the residents processed to the refectory for the morning meal (*ariston*), which might be accompanied by readings. Daylight hours were devoted to agricultural labor, copying manuscripts, or performing charitable services, which alternated with private or communal prayers held at regular intervals. The main services were held at the first, third, sixth, and ninth hours of the day, which corresponds to prime, terce, sext, and none in the Latin schedule. All residents again gathered in the katholikon for vespers at sunset. The evening meal (*deipnon*) was followed by the final canonical service of compline (*apodeipnon*). Some larger monasteries also held nighttime services (*mesonyktikon*). Nocturnal vigils were observed at special times of year including Nativity (Christougennos), Epiphany, and Easter (Pascha).

The order of monastic worship evolved over time but generally resembled the liturgy found in other churches. The essential parts include the preparation of the bread and wine (*prothesis*), the introductory litanies and prayers (*enarxis*), the liturgy of the word, and the sharing of the Eucharist. Ritual processions punctuated the service, with the "Lesser Entrance" heralding the Gospels and the "Great Entrance" of the Eucharist. To this basic structure were added special prayers on behalf of the founders and their descendants, deceased monks, and other church officials, which often were held at secondary chapels.

One of the most recognizable aspects of monastic worship was the nearly continuous chanting or singing of the daily offices, processions, and other commemorations. The Psalter stood at the heart of monastic life, and the importance of singing is clear from many medieval typika. As one eleventh-century monastic patron put it: "The whole daily divine

A wooden gong or sounding board *(semantron)* at
Mount Athos. The board was struck with a mal-
let to announce the hours of services. From Robert
Curzon, *Visits to Monasteries in the Levant,* 6th ed.
(London: John Murray, 1881).

office expressed in the singing of psalms could reasonably be thought of as
the soul of the monastery, whereas the monastery itself and all the things
that benefit our bodies could be considered its body."[9] The therapeutic
benefits of psalmody, or "singing with the angels," were widely recognized as a way to gather divine aid in resisting worldly temptations and
transcending one's limitations. Psalms often were sung antiphonally by
two separate choirs located in the left or right part of church. Singing
long liturgies and nighttime offices was physically demanding as well
as spiritually beneficial. Particularly large foundations, like the Stoudios
monastery, held perpetual services chanted by their "sleepless" monks
(akoimetai). Chanted or sung, the Psalms were an expression of spiritual
solidarity both in shared services and in the solitude of one's cell.[10]
    Attendance at services was the primary responsibility of monks and
nuns, whose inevitable shortcomings are discussed by monastic writers.
Rising for nighttime vigils or early morning prayers was not an easy
task. Continuous oversleeping or missing services was seen as a serious
offense. It was important to pay attention and conduct oneself properly
during worship as well as at meals. Designated monitors enforced strict
regulations against sitting or wandering about the katholikon, leaning
against the wall, smiling, laughing, talking, or doing handiwork during
services. Refectories had their own rules governing conversation and

sharing meals. Punishments for such infractions ranged from lying face down on the floor to being confined to one's cell with only bread and water to eat.

Monastic life was pursued apart from the everyday world, yet remained connected to it in important ways. Days were long and filled with familiar, repetitive tasks. The perpetual cycle of services provided a supportive framework for spiritual living, but most domestic duties, production of household crafts, and agricultural labor were indistinguishable from life outside the monastery. One's clothing naturally varied with different activities, and while working in the fields the traditional habit might be replaced by a belted sleeveless tunic and hooded goatskin cloak. Many monks and nuns recognized existing family ties, sometimes traveling to visit parents and siblings on birthdays and other occasions. As spiritual exemplars, Byzantine monastics were an invaluable source of advice and consolation in times of crisis.[11]

DIET

Food was an essential part of any monastery. Typika comment regularly on food as either an aid or distraction from leading the religious life, and recommend special diets for certain occasions. The available supply varied with the season, location, and economic status of a monastery, but everywhere was seen as contributing in a direct way to cultivating spiritual virtues and controlling physical passions. Like other material concerns, food was limited to what was thought necessary to survive and for this reason was kept simple and monotonous. The monastic diet typically consisted of grain and vegetables, with little if any meat. This compulsory low-fat diet, like the cloistered life in general, brought monks and nuns many incidental health benefits. Such circumstances help account for the long lives attributed to famous hermetic saints.

Most monasteries were involved in some way in producing their own food. Agricultural labor was seen as a basic kind of contemplative activity, and rural monks spent their days tending field crops or herding livestock. Larger monasteries leased out arable land or employed farm laborers to help cultivate them. During the medieval period some monasteries acquired additional holdings and sold a considerable surplus in neighboring towns. Even in the city most foundations tried to support themselves by raising kitchen gardens with vegetables, herbs, and at least a few fruit trees.[12]

Bread was the cornerstone of the monastic diet. Many places raised and milled their own cereal crops with the help of animals or water mills. Finely ground wheat flour was preferred for daily consumption, with coarse, dark grains considered a sign of penance, especially during times of fasting. All but the smallest monasteries had their own bakeries. Bread usually was baked in round, flattened loaves. Wood and bronze stamps

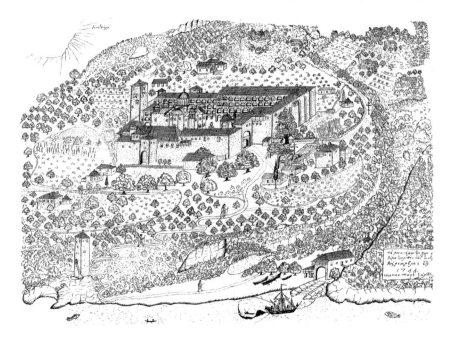

The Xeropotamou monastery at Mount Athos in the eighteenth century. Most rural monasteries were surrounded by lands that the monks cultivated for their own support. Drawing by the Russian monk Basil Barsky, in *Vtoroe poseshchenie sviatoi Afonskoi gory Vasilia Grigorovicha-Barskago* (St. Petersburg: Izd. Afonskago russkago Panteleimonova monastyria, 1887).

were used to impress sacred texts or images on loaves intended for the Eucharist or charitable distribution.

The number of meals varied between one and three, and normally included some sort of food taken at midday. On most days a typical menu included a range of vegetables, legumes, and salad greens prepared with olive oil. These were served with cheese, eggs, and perhaps fish, usually salted or dried, and were accompanied by seasonal fruit. Limited quantities of wine were available at the refectory table. Monks were well aware of differences in cuisine among different monasteries, and some thought that administrators ate better than they did. The typikon of the well-funded Pantokrator monastery in Constantinople, for instance, recommends that monks be given a substantial allotment of bread, meat, cheese, seasonal legumes and fruit, and wine. Fish was featured twice a week, and on other days eggs and cheese were served. During the Lenten season this menu was reduced to bread, rehydrated legumes, dried figs, and nuts. At the nearby monastery of Mamas twelfth-century monks regularly enjoyed cooked meat, fish, cheese, legumes, cabbage, and fruit.

A recurring concern with food appears in the Ptochoprodromos poems, a series of medieval verses presenting a satiric view of how monks ate. The hungry monk tells how in his monastery he has to make do with beans and dried tuna cooked with onions, marjoram, and a little oil. At the same time the abbot and other officials regularly enjoy extravagant feasts with fish cooked in rich sauces, egg soup cooked with chicken, and three kinds of cheese. All of this is prepared in rich olive oil, seasoned with garlic, onions, and pepper, and served with fine wine brought from Chios. While the contrast in lifestyles was no doubt exaggerated, the poems reflect the considerable, at times obsessive attention that food could command within the monastic environment.[13]

One's awareness of food is never so acute as when it is withheld during times of fasting. Byzantine monastic life entailed a rigorous schedule of lents or fasts that took place throughout the liturgical year. The lent of Saints Peter and Paul took place in late spring following Pentecost. Two weeks of fasting normally preceded the festival of the Assumption of the Virgin (Koimesis) on August 15. The Christmas fast began on November 15 and lasted until the eve of Nativity. The most widely observed fast was the Great Lent, which took place over the seven weeks leading up to Easter. Individual monasteries might additionally prescribe a weekly regime of fasting on Mondays, Wednesdays, and Fridays, during the three days before receiving communion, in observance of minor festivals, and for disciplinary reasons. Such occasions did not necessarily entail total abstinence but were intended to focus pious reflection on penance and as a guide to spiritual growth. Typical lenten fare was based on bread, legumes, and beans served with water in a single daily meal. Fish, meat, oil, butter, cheese, and eggs were commonly withheld. Longer fasts often concluded in a great banquet that was held as part of the liturgical festival. On Mount Athos such celebrations continue to be held on the name day of each monastery's patron saint, with monks from neighboring foundations joining in the festivities.[14]

CULTURAL LIFE

As centers of learning and worship, many monasteries became important cultural institutions in their own right. The best known of these were located near Constantinople and were supported by the highest levels of imperial, aristocratic, and clerical society. The Stoudios monastery always enjoyed close ties with the patriarch and for centuries was a major intellectual center. The Pantokrator complex received an annual stipend from the Komnenos family to sustain commemorative prayers and philanthropic activities. Other foundations in town accumulated sizable collections of books and become significant places of scholarship. Such cultural and intellectual opportunities were largely limited to male monasteries, however, with fewer activities encouraged within nunneries.

Libraries

Reading was essential for worship and no less important for private devotion. In the guidelines he drew up for the Stoudios monastery, the ninth-century abbot Theodore recommends that monks be allowed to choose a book from the library and spend the day reading privately when not working outdoors. Foundation documents, inventories, and wills clearly indicate the prestige of libraries. It is unsurprising that many of the largest collections of books were in the capital. The Constantinopolitan monastery of Christ Panoiktirmon, founded in the eleventh century by Michael Attaleiates, held nearly 70 volumes, including 29 that had been donated by benefactors. Some provincial monasteries had comparable collections. The monastery of the Theotokos at Skoteine in western Asia Minor had about 70 books in the thirteenth century. By the fifteenth century the monastery of the Theotokos Eleousa in Stroumitza in the upper Balkans had acquired over 60 volumes.[15]

Scriptoria

Most monasteries that collected books also made new ones. The presence of a reading library meant that facilities for repairing older books and preparing replacement copies were equally necessary. The close relationship of library and scriptorium is clearly expressed in the twelfth-century typikon for the monastery of Christ Savior in Messina in south Greece: "We introduced others who could perform necessary and useful service for the physical well-being of the monks and also many trained in diverse crafts; then, scribes and calligraphers, and teachers of our sacred books who were sufficiently trained in profane literature. We collected many beautiful books pertaining to our own sacred writings, totally familiar to us, as well as [other books] not pertaining to our sacred writings." Convents had much smaller collections and lacked specialized scriptoria—a situation that did not encourage literary activities among women. When Theodora Raoulaina entered a convent in the fourteenth century, for example, she copied her own books since there was no scriptorium.[16]

Schools

The education of children and young adults was an ongoing concern in many monasteries, yet monastic schools never gained the state-supported status they enjoyed elsewhere in the medieval world. Basil of Caesarea, writing in the mid-fourth century, devoted part of his *Long Rules* to the role of education. For him schools should provide training for girls as well as boys, and should accept orphans as well as children with parents. Children were housed in one part of the monastery, apart from the monks, and were separated by sex and age. Instruction took place in small groups under the guidance of a specially trained monk. As students grew older and became more responsible they could be asked to help teach younger children. Grammar was based on close study of essential biblical texts. The book of Proverbs was especially instructive as a guide to ethical conduct. Basil's personal study of pre-Christian literature shaped his tolerant attitude to classical texts and encouraged their preservation by copying in new editions. The

Iliad and *Odyssey* were essential parts of the educational curriculum. With proper supervision advanced students might be permitted to study other works of classical history and literature as well. Contests and games were recommended as a way of reinforcing their lessons. While some church leaders promoted a broader role for such schools, most monasteries focused their pedagogical efforts on postulants and others intending to take monastic vows.

NOTES

1. Good introductions to Eastern monasticism include Cyril Mango, "Monasticism," in *Byzantium: The Empire of New Rome* (New York: Charles Scribner's Sons, 1980), 105–24; and Alice-Mary Talbot, "An Introduction to Byzantine Monasticism," *Illinois Classical Studies* 12 (1987): 229–41. For discussion of present-day monastic life see Philip Sherrard, *Athos: The Mountain of Silence* (London: Oxford University Press, 1960); idem, *Athos: The Holy Mountain* (Woodstock, N.Y.: Overlook Press, 1982); and Chris Hellier, *Monasteries of Greece* (London: Tauris Parke Books, 1997). For the monastery of St. Catherine and its desert setting see Beno Rothenberg, *God's Wilderness: Discoveries in Sinai* (London: Thames and Hudson, 1961); and Morsi Saad El-Din et al., *Sinai: The Site and the History* (New York: New York University Press, 1998).

2. The contributions of Pachomius, Basil, and other eastern traditions are succinctly summarized in John Thomas and Angela Constantinides Hero, eds., *Byzantine Monastic Foundation Documents* (Washington, D.C.: Dumbarton Oaks, 2000), 1:21–41. For Basil's *Long Rules* see Monica Wagner, trans., *Saint Basil: Ascetical Works* (New York: Fathers of the Church, 1950), 223–337.

3. For an illustrated survey see Hellier, *Monasteries of Greece*. The history of these two main centers of Greek monasticism are covered by Donald M. Nicol, *Meteora: The Rock Monasteries of Thessaly* (London: Chapman and Hall, 1963); and Graham Speake, *Mount Athos: Renewal in Paradise* (New Haven, Conn.: Yale University Press, 2002).

4. These invaluable sources are readily available in Thomas and Constantinides, *Byzantine Monastic Foundation Documents*.

5. Theodore Metochites, *The Nicene Oration* 11, quoted in Clive Foss, *Nicaea: A Byzantine Capital and Its Praises* (Brookline, Mass.: Hellenic College Press, 1996), 181.

6. The fifteenth-century typikon of the Theotokos Eleousa monastery at Stroumitza lists nine candelabra or candleholders as well as various sizes of suspension lamps. In his typikon Michael Attaleiates gives an annual sum of 12 nomismata for wax candles, 1 nomisma for small glass lamps *(hyelia)*, and 2 nomismata for incense. See Thomas and Constantinides, *Byzantine Monastic Foundation Documents*, 1:350, 4:1674.

7. Monastic funerary practices are discussed by Dorothy Abrahamse, "Rituals of Death in the Middle Byzantine Period," *Greek Orthodox Theological Review* 29 (1984): 125–34.

8. Robert E. Sinkewicz, ed. and trans., *Theoleptos of Philadelphia: The Monastic Discourses* (Toronto: Pontifical Institute of Mediaeval Studies, 1992), 3.12.

9. For the typikon of the monastery of the Theotokos Evergetis, see Thomas and Constantinides, *Byzantine Monastic Foundation Documents*, 2:454–506, quotation at 478.

10. The role of music is discussed by Rosemary Dubowchik, "Singing with the Angels: Foundation Documents as Evidence for Musical Life in Monasteries of the Byzantine Empire," *Dumbarton Oaks Papers* 56 (2002): 277–96. For singing in contemporary Orthodox service see Timothy Ware, *The Orthodox Church* (London: Penguin, 1993), 268. For a general survey see Egon Wellesz, "Byzantine Music and Liturgy," in *The Cambridge Medieval History*, vol. 4, *The Byzantine Empire*, pt. 2, *Government, Church and Civilization*, ed. Joan M. Hussey (Cambridge: Cambridge University Press, 1966–67), 135–60.

11. For the interconnections of secular and monastic society see Rosemary Morris, *Monks and Laymen in Byzantium, 843–1118* (Cambridge: Cambridge University Press, 1995).

12. Saints' lives and typika provide information about both monastic and secular gardening; see Alice-Mary Talbot, "Byzantine Monastic Horticulture: The Textual Evidence," in *Byzantine Garden Culture*, ed. Antony Littlewood, Henry Maguire, and Joachim Wolschke-Bulmahn (Washington, D.C.: Dumbarton Oaks, 2002), 37–67.

13. Hans Eideneier, "Ptochoprodromos' Tafelfreud und Tafelleid," in *Fest und Alltag in Byzanz*, ed. Gunter Prinzing and Dieter Simon (Munich: C. H. Beck, 1990), 77–90. Typika offer much dietary information. For more on Byzantine food in the monastery (and in general) see Andrew Dalby, *Flavours of Byzantium* (Totnes, England: Prospect Books, 2003), 93–97.

14. For observances see Sherrard, *Athos: The Mountain of Silence.*

15. For Michael Attaleiates' typikon see Thomas and Constantinides, *Byzantine Monastic Foundation Documents*, 1:326–76; for books held at Skoteine near Philadelphia in western Asia Minor see 3:1185; for the north Balkan monastery at Stroumitza see 4:1672–73.

16. Typikon of the monastery of Christ in Messina in ibid., 2:637–48.

9

ARTISTIC LIFE

Today Byzantium may be best known by its artistic legacy. Across the east Mediterranean scores of painted churches still serve as places of worship and admiration, echoing with the liturgical music of the Orthodox rite. Museums in Europe and North America routinely display striking objects, intricately worked in enamel, ivory, silver, gold, and other precious materials. Colorful illuminations in manuscripts remain familiar and necessary companions of their densely lettered Greek texts. Most distinctive of all are the icons, painted wood panels that represent holy figures and narrative scenes according to long-established pictorial conventions. Such objects claimed a central place in medieval lives, whether shaping space, defining personal identity, or putting theological abstractions into tangible form.

While the arts of Byzantium were esteemed throughout the Middle Ages, the people who produced them are almost entirely unknown. Visitors to Constantinople regularly commented on the exquisite detail and transcendent beauty of its churches with their wall paintings and mosaics. They walked the streets looking for shops to buy fine clothing and jewelry, silver plate and glassware, often made by skilled craftsmen who worked on the premises. Such sumptuous goods could be readily acquired and were highly prized by their owners, yet an "art market" in the term's modern sense did not exist. Objects were made with a specific purpose in mind and were not normally valued as speculative commodities or collected for their own sake. Domestic crafts, coins, and pilgrimage tokens might be manufactured in quantity, but in every case met a pressing need. Most works of luxury, by contrast, were commissioned by a patron of a craftsman. The main point was the object's intended purpose, whether for public worship, personal adornment, or enjoyment within the home. All aspects of the commission were discussed in advance, from the materials to be used and the size of the finished work to its decorative setting, figural ornament, and accompanying inscription. The most desirable materials were undeniably expensive: traffic in silk, precious metals, and gems was regulated by the state, ivory was brought from distant Africa and Asia, and parchment was costly to make and often unavailable. Medieval writers seem to value these intrinsic qualities even more than the craftsmanship that went into their working. Surviving objects preserve this delicate negotiation of function and material combined with the ability of the artist.

Like other aspects of Byzantine culture, most luxury goods were manufactured in the capital for residents of the palace and elite households. Particular skill was needed to carve ivory or work enamel, and such artistry could flourish only where there was steady demand. Certain kinds of objects, like gold and silver plate, jewelry, silks, and books, were made by specialized craftsmen employed by imperial workshops. Others were purchased by wealthy families and churchmen who lived in the provinces. It is hard to determine exactly where small, portable objects were made. This uncertainty has led to the frequent assumption that works from the provinces must have been qualitatively inferior to those made in the capital. In fact, different levels of artistic skill and style are known to have existed throughout the empire, in Constantinople as well as in lesser towns. Surviving churches, for example, show that architectural excellence was neither an invariable feature nor a monopoly of the capital. Two particularly important kinds of objects—books and icons—are known to have been made by craftsmen who worked in city centers and rural monasteries alike.[1]

REPRESENTATIONAL ARTS

One of Byzantium's most distinctive features is the relatively consistent approach that artists took to subject matter and presentation. Such stability does not mean that the visual arts did not change over time. Certainly the long interlude of iconoclasm in the eighth and early ninth centuries affected everyone involved in their production. The history of Byzantine art is often presented today as a series of overlapping chronological phases that varied with place and circumstance. Yet from late antiquity through the fifteenth century—and continuing in many places to the present—the major artistic traditions reflected the religious views articulated by the church and promoted by the capital. The visual expression of this ideal, including the cosmological centrality of Christ, the cycle of liturgical festivals, and the enduring community of Orthodox believers, underlies most religious art.[2]

The earliest Christian groups preferred art that was symbolic in content, usually consisting of familiar images like a fish, lamb, or shepherd that could carry doctrinal overtones. One of the most basic symbols, the cross, was represented in several distinct ways. Only the most schematic form was used by Christians before Constantine placed the cross or a cruciform monogram on his banner at the Milvian bridge. This triumphal *labarum*, as it became known, was taken up by later generations to stand for Christian victory in both worldly and cosmic terms. During the years of iconoclasm the cross remained one of the few acceptable forms of religious art. Several kinds of crosses emerged during the Middle Ages. The most familiar is the elongated Latin cross. One or two short crossbars were sometimes added to strengthen its connection with the crucifixion: an upper plaque identifying "Jesus of Nazareth, king of the Jews," and a lower bar or footrest. The resulting double or patriarchal cross continues to be used throughout the Orthodox world. Other crosses were shown mounted on an orb or low stepped base, or encrusted with gems and pearls. Such variants may have been inspired by one of the monumental crosses that had been set up on the mound of Golgotha in Jerusalem. When surrounded by decorative foliage and flowers, the cross became known as the Tree of Life. The Greek cross with equal arms and decorative terminals was widely used in the medieval period. These different versions appeared in processional and liturgical objects, invocations on shields and walls, and jewelry for personal adornment. Their protective powers were invoked everywhere.

Despite the symbolic importance of the cross, most Byzantine artists were fundamentally concerned with representing the human figure. The importance of the body in classical culture formed a philosophical basis for the Christian emphasis on the human incarnation of Christ. Disagreements about what Jesus actually looked like presented early artists with a distinct problem, and as a result several competing image types circulated in late antiquity. Belief in God's unique intervention in human affairs encouraged artists to develop detailed pictorial narratives drawn from the Hebrew Bible and the Gospels. The most frequently illustrated accounts in the early period were based on stories of the Miracles and Passion. During the later Middle Ages scenes of the Infancy and Passion were most often represented. Growing popular devotion to the Virgin led to new visual cycles illustrating her life as well. These pictorial episodes, commemorated by special services throughout the year, became integral parts of the decorated church interior, affirming in successive generations a consistent, Orthodox view of the world. They were accompanied by rows of apostles, martyrs, saints, monks, bishops, and soldiers. Looking out at the viewer from church walls and manuscript pages, these halo-wearing figures represent the timeless spiritual community of which the viewer formed a part.

ICONS

From their origins through the present day, painted icons of religious figures have always held a central place in Byzantine culture. The oldest known examples, dating from the fifth and sixth centuries, continue Roman traditions of portrait, funerary, and votive painting. Flat panels were assembled of cedar, cypress, or pine and covered with a smooth layer of gesso, a mixture of gypsum plaster and glue. Most early painting was done in the encaustic technique. Mineral and vegetal pigments were ground into powder and mixed into a bowl of molten wax. The warm mixture was applied with bristle brushes in thin layers on the gesso surface. During the medieval period artists preferred tempera compounds suspended in an egg-yolk medium.[3]

Over the centuries icons were produced by painters who had different backgrounds and abilities but shared a deep respect for visual precedent. Medieval legend credits the first icon to the apostle Luke, who was said to have painted the portrait of the Virgin and Child from life. Other traditions speak of *acheiropoietoi* (not made by human hands), images that were produced miraculously. Such shadowy archtypes established models that were passed down from generation to generation. By the eleventh and twelfth centuries several distinct ways of representing Christ, the Virgin, and major saints were known. Such familiar images might be made to order or bought secondhand in the marketplace. Their cost, normally modest, meant that most households could afford to own one or two.

Technical and stylistic similarities between panel icons and monumental frescoes suggest that many craftsmen worked in both media. Apart from the artist's training and skill, panel painting required little equipment beside pigments and brushes, and could be done almost anywhere. Some painters, particularly monks, specialized in producing small, portable icons, which would not have required traveling from place to place to work on frescoes. While some craftsmen gained modest renown, particularly as muralists, icon painting seems to have brought little financial reward. A devotional panel was appreciated more for its spiritual powers, and these depended on its relation to a spiritual prototype, a miraculous connection largely independent of the work's material qualities. In the same way, devotion or prayers directed to the image were relayed to the person represented. The Virgin Hodegetria ("Pointer of the Way"), supposedly brought to the capital from Palestine in the fifth century, was copied innumerable times. The icon of the Virgin Blachernitissa was believed to have saved the besieged capital on several occasions. The Virgin of Vladimir, a famous example of the "Virgin of Tenderness" (Eleousa) type, was credited with defending Moscow from the Mongols in the fourteenth century. Over time the reputation of such icons was attested, and reinforced, by the accumulation of sumptuous gold and silver ornament on the surface and frame.[4]

Sixteenth-century icon of the Virgin. This late example, probably painted in south Greece, continues the essential elements of earlier devotional art. Courtesy of the Museum of Art and Archaeology, University of Missouri–Columbia.

ARTS OF LUXURY

Metalworking was highly regarded in antiquity and the Middle Ages. Byzantine artists continued Hellenistic and Roman techniques of casting, hammering, and incising, and passed them on to neighboring cultures to the east and west.

Gold and Silver Plate

Everyday implements were made of iron and bronze by specialized craftsmen and casual smiths, from Constantinople to rural villages and estates. Gold and silver, by contrast, were scarce materials whose availability was controlled by the state and concentrated in the capital. Their intrinsic value made them fluid in form, and over time most decorative metal was melted down to make coins, bullion, and other objects. The thinner walls and lower purity of objects made after the seventh and eighth centuries reflect the dwindling supply of these materials in the empire's later years. The tenth-century *Book of the Eparch* forbade the working of gold and silver outside the permanent shops *(ergasteria)* of sanctioned jewelers *(argyropratai)*. Much of the gold and silver used in the medieval West arrived in the form of Byzantine coins and plate. The output of Byzantine workshops has been found as far away as Britain and China.

Pure gold does not occur in nature but has to be separated from other metals. Important technical sources for working gold and silver are the writings of Pliny the Elder and the German craftsman Theophilus, who lived in the early twelfth century and knew of contemporary Byzantine work.[5] The ore was brought to the surface, crushed, and heated to remove base metals. Salt was used to separate silver from the refined gold. Silver also was obtained by refining galena or other lead ores, with which it naturally occurs. The state regulated the purity of gold and silver for coinage and plate. The gold solidus was kept at about 98 percent purity in late antiquity, slipping to 85 percent in the eleventh century. Gold normally was alloyed with silver to produce the more durable electrum for plate and jewelry. Silver coinage averaged 80 percent purity and was alloyed with copper to increase its strength. Most plate was hammered into shape with ornament added by repoussé, chasing, and incising. Silver plate was gilded by applying gold mixed with mercury and then heated—a toxic process that must have taken place out of doors. Dark black niello, or silver sulfide, was added to emphasize inscriptions and decorative details.

Precious metals were widely used in Byzantium. State salaries *(rogai)* were distributed mainly in coins. Foreign policy depended on paying bribes and tribute in gold coins to neighboring states. Plate constituted another kind of currency. Liudprand of Cremona describes the splendid all-gold dinner service that was used in the Great Palace in the tenth century, while lesser households had to make do with silver or ceramic. Table vessels included flat dishes, bowls, flasks, and goblets. Large platters with raised and incised decoration were used for serving and displayed on the walls; biblical, military, and mythological subjects are known as well as generic dining scenes. Knives and spoons were the main eating implements, with forks appearing in aristocratic circles during the late Middle Ages.

A great deal of silver plate was given to churches or monasteries, customarily in the form of liturgical objects. The most common donations were deep, stemmed chalices and broad circular patens that were hammered, incised, and gilded for eucharistic use. Such expensive gifts were not limited to the capital but were found across the empire. In the sixth century more than 50 silver objects, including chalices, patens, spoons, candleholders, fans, and revetment plaques, were given to the village church of Saint Sergius at Kaper Koraon in north Syria. Other donations ranged from caskets and furniture appliques to large doors cast in bronze

Small sixth-century silver dish with niello monogram of an owner (perhaps named Palladiou). Similar vessels often were donated to churches or monasteries. Courtesy of the Museum of Art and Archaeology, University of Missouri–Columbia.

and decorated with silver inlay and niello ornament. Large doors, reveted with bronze and inlaid with copper and silver, were installed in Hagia Sophia in the capital in the ninth and tenth centuries.[6]

Gold, silver, and bronze formed the basis of a nearly limitless variety of personal adornment. The most popular forms of jewelry **Jewelry** were fibulae, brooches, buckles, pins, rings, earrings, and pendants. All these articles served to advertise the wearer's rank or office. The hierarchy of materials generally reflected social status, with the glittering fashions of court elites echoed by bronze imitations in the provinces. Still, the widespread currency of precious metals in Byzantine society meant that even families of modest means might own a couple pieces of gold or silver jewelry as personal savings or a daughter's dowry. The future saint Theodore of Sykeon, for example, at the age of six received a gold belt and accessories from his mother. Medieval jewelry makers liked to combine gold, sometimes in the form of coins, with precious and semiprecious gems, classical cameos, and decorative enamel plaques. The same materials were regularly used for amulets and reliquaries ranging from plain boxes to elaborate crosses. The purpose of these small containers was to preserve an object of religious significance like a relic, holy water, or soil from a pilgrimage site. In a similar spirit, worked sheets of gold and silver were applied to the face of painted icons to protect and honor the holy figure it represented.[7]

Enamel   Earlier Mediterranean craftsmen had made jewelry with glass paste and inlaid stones, but the taste for polychrome ornament grew after the Goths and Huns entered southeast Europe in the fourth and fifth centuries. These people brought with them their own metalworking traditions, which involved attaching small gems to a heavy gold setting for pins and buckles. Byzantine jewelers soon were creating similar works using cut gems and later colored glass packed into tiny compartments shaped by metal wires *(cloisons)*. The finest examples of the medieval period used gold wires to build complex patterns on a gold base, which reflected light through the translucent enamel. When polished with fine abrasive sand, the smooth *cloisonné* surface created patterns of intense colors arranged in great complexity. The technique was first used for objects of personal adornment, but by the tenth century cloisonné ornament was being used in circular medallions with bust-length portraits. Later works depict slender standing figures wrapped in swirling drapery, sometimes arranged in narrative scenes. As did jewelry, enamel working required excellent vision, great patience and skill, and expensive materials, and for these reasons was sponsored mainly by the court. Preserved examples include crowns, reliquaries, and decorative plaques that often had some connection with the imperial family.[8]

Ivory Carving   The production of miniature sculptures in ivory was an ancient craft with roots in prehistoric times. Ivory, obtained from the tusks of African and Indian elephants, was a durable, fine-grained material that could be carved with little difficulty. Animal bone might be used as an economical alternative as well as for practice. The Roman Empire's vast trading networks had long ensured a reliable supply of ivory, but this was disrupted by the Arab conquests of the seventh and eighth centuries. The relative scarcity of ivory in later centuries is clear from the smaller size and limited number of medieval carvings that survive.

Late-antique ivories were used for a variety of purposes, from official diptychs and commemorative plaques to jewelry boxes, reliquaries, hairpins, and cosmetic implements. The gradual disappearance of monumental stone sculpture may have stimulated imperial interest in carving ivory, which flourished especially in the tenth and eleventh centuries. Craftsmen apparently worked in small, independent shops, using traditional carving tools and methods. Given the difficulty of obtaining ivory, many of these artists also carved small-scale works out of materials like bone, jasper, and steatite. Among the best-known medieval ivories are objects marking the coronation or betrothal of the emperor and a series of elegant boxes covered with scenes from classical mythology. More numerous are ivory

Tenth-century reliquary of the True Cross richly decorated with enamels and gems, now in the treasury of Limburg Cathedral in Germany. From Gustave Schlumberger, *Un empereur byzantin aux dixième siècle, Nicéphore Phocas* (Paris: Firmin Didot, 1890).

and stone plaques representing saints and other holy figures, who were arranged singly, paired, and in larger groups on triptychs with hinged wings. These functioned as devotional pieces in the same way as painted icons, and may have been favored by private families. The generally fine quality of surviving examples suggests that most craftsmen worked for the elites of the capital.[9]

Roman traditions of glassmaking were continued by Byzantine craftsmen. The long Mediterranean coastline offered plentiful supplies of sand and other materials necessary for large-scale glass production, which first took place near the cities of Palestine and

Glass

Tenth- or eleventh-century carved ivory *pyxis* or box. Such containers may have been used by elite families for storing cosmetics or jewelry. From Gustave Schlumberger, *L'Epopée byzantine a la fin du dixième siècle* (Paris: Hachette, 1896).

Syria. Silica was heated in hot furnaces to produce a molten flux that could be shaped into vessels with a metal blowing tube. Color and transparency were readily adjusted by mixing minerals into the flux. Handles and other decoration were added after the body was formed. During the medieval period, when access to raw materials was limited, Byzantine glassmakers relied increasingly on glass scrap or cullet gathered for recycling. The main cargo of the eleventh-century ship found at Serçe Limani off the Lycian coast was an enormous amount of cullet.

Byzantine glassware took many forms, with bottles, goblets, flasks, and bracelets being the most common. Small cup-shaped vessels, filled with oil and equipped with a floating wick, were widely used as lamps during the medieval period. Written sources and archaeological excavations indicate that these objects of modest luxury were widely made and used in towns and villages alike. Specialized vessels of elaborate shape, color, and decoration supplied the imperial palace and aristocratic households.

Glass rolled into flat sheets was used for windowpanes in well-to-do houses and public buildings. Excavations have established that colored glass panels were known in at least a few medieval churches in Constantinople, echoing the great stained-glass windows of Gothic Europe. A wide variety of colored glass was needed as well to make *tesserae* for wall and vault mosaics. Slabs of carefully tinted glass were cut into millions of tiny cubes, typically about a quarter inch on a side, whose luminosity was heightened by applying a thin layer of gold foil to the back. Manufacturing, sorting, and distributing such large quantities of materials clearly required the organization of specialized workshops. The recycling of glass tesserae and the increased reliance on stone and brick in later medieval mosaics suggest that glass was costly and not always available. On some occasions tesserae may even have been used for currency.[10]

Cotton, flax, linen, and wool were woven in almost every home, but luxury textiles were limited to per- **Luxury Textiles** manent urban workshops. The production of silk and specialty cloth expanded in the medieval period when large operations flourished in Athens, Thebes, Thessaloniki, and Constantinople. The sumptuous costumes worn by court officials and urban elites came mostly from state-sponsored workshops, probably located near the capital. The dazzling Ravenna mosaics depicting Justinian, Theodora, and their attendants illustrate the splendor of courtly costume in the sixth century.

Byzantine fashions employed a wide range of colors. Most dyes were obtained from vegetal and mineral sources. Popular colors include shades of red, blue, green, ocher, and yellow, and came from familiar natural materials. Yellow was obtained from weld. Indigo and madder were used to make red, blue, and a common form of purple. Indigo mixed with weld produced shades of green. Certain colors were supposedly restricted to courtly patrons. The highest quality of purple was painstakingly extracted from the tiny murex shell. Specialty dyes were imported from Abbasid states to the east. Many colors were charged with religious symbolism.[11]

Books were at the heart of Byzantine culture, fundamental to its religious outlook and intellectual self-image. The realization **Books** of the book as a *codex,* or bound volume of uniform pages, took place in late antiquity. Almost all classical literary works, from letters and legal documents to drama, poetry, and history, had first been recorded on sheets of papyrus glued together into rolls as long as 20 feet. Texts were written in short, parallel columns and read by simultaneously unfurling and winding up the roll. By contrast, codices were made up of sheets of standard size stitched together along one side. Pages could carry text on both sides, and were easily turned and kept in place. Early Christian groups of the second century popularized the codex as a way of providing ready access to biblical texts and apostolic letters.[12]

Many early books were made of papyrus, a material for writing that went back to early Egypt. Rolls made of pressed, interwoven stalks of the papyrus plant *(Cyperus papyrus)* are known as early as the third millennium B.C. Production remained a big business in Egypt in classical times and late antiquity. Papyrus was made in rectangular sheets and long rolls of varying qualities, and was commonly used for public and private documents. Excavations at Oxyrhynchus in Egypt have recovered hundreds of rolls dating from Ptolemaic times through the seventh-century Arab conquest. Documents range from personal letters and family wills to official accounts, contracts, and tax rolls. Even though papyrus was used for letters well into the medieval period, by the twelfth century it had been mostly replaced by paper.

Parchment's greater flexibility and durability were clear advantages over papyrus. The word (from the Latin *pergamena*) reflects its supposed invention for the royal libraries of Hellenistic Pergamon. Parchment came from animal skins, most commonly of sheep, goats, and calves. Hides were soaked in a mixture of water and lime, scraped clean, and stretched on a frame for drying. Additional scrapping and cutting of the hide reduced it to a uniform thickness. The dried surface was rubbed with fine sand, pumice, or chalk until smooth enough for writing or painting. Commercial production tended to be seasonal, with shortages occurring mainly in fall and winter. Michael Choniates complained about the loss of parchment to the Italian market in the twelfth century. The thirteenth-century monk Maximos Planoudes wrote to one of his friends asking him to send fresh parchment since it was unavailable in Constantinople. Chronic shortages led some provincial scribes to erase earlier texts and reuse parchment as palimpsests—a practice that in the case of biblical texts was expressly forbidden.

Large parchment sheets (*folia*) were folded in quarters before being cut to a standard size with knives or scissors. The hide of an average-size calf or lamb produced four leaves (eight pages); six leaves were possible for Psalters and other small books. At this point individual pages were laid out: margins were established, guidelines were ruled using a pointed stylus and dividers, and the text was carefully copied. While Byzantine art frequently represents the evangelists writing in a bound codex, pages normally were copied before being bound. Gathered folia were sewn into quires along one side with awl and thread, trimmed, and flattened between boards before being bound. Bindings were covered with durable cloth or leather, which might with time be replaced by more elaborate covers.

Parchment's scarcity and high cost encouraged people to turn to paper for routine record keeping, letters, and even books in the later Middle Ages. The main source for Byzantium was the Arabs, who learned Chinese papermaking techniques in the eighth century. Oriental paper consisted of shredded rag and vegetable fibers that were fixed in thin sheets with a starch glue; the final product was light brown in color and had a smooth surface well suited to writing. By the twelfth century paper was being used for imperial documents as well as books. Coarse, light-colored Italian papers, made with gelatin glue and carrying the manufacturer's watermark, dominated the Eastern market after the Fourth Crusade.

Most books were made by copying directly from a model, page by page, for weeks on end. Standard pigments for writing were carbon or lampblack, gum arabic or cherry gum, and cuttlefish ink, which tends to be sepia in color. Ink was kept in glass bottles and poured into glass, metal, or terra-cotta inkwells when needed. A hollow reed with a slit, sharpened tip (*kalamos*) was the most common writing implement. Bone and metal pens are also known, but it is unclear whether goose quills, always popular in the medieval West, were widely adopted. Calligraphy (from *kalli graphia,* or "good writing") was regarded as a special skill. Among emperors, Constantine VII was said to be an especially adept calligrapher. Late-antique scribes generally wrote in boxy, evenly spaced capital letters *(majuscle),* which over the eighth and ninth centuries gave way to a standardized cursive *(minuscule)* script. Errors were corrected by rubbing with a sponge, gentle scraping with a knife, or sanding with pumice. All this equipment—inkwells, pens, and knives—might be stored together in a special box *(kalamarion).*

While some classical rolls included small drawings between text columns, the codex format was far better suited to illustration. The rectangular page offered a flat, bounded surface for the painting of miniature pictures. The earliest preserved codices with illustrations were made in Rome around 400. The famous Vatican edition of Virgil, which includes the *Georgics, Eclogues,* and the *Aeneid,* was accompanied by scores of framed pictures. The most commonly decorated books of the medieval period were the Gospels, Psalter, Bible, lectionaries, and *menologia* listing feast days of the saints. Scientific treatises often included diagrams and pictures, but histories and chronicles were rarely illustrated; the Madrid Skylitzes manuscript is a rare exception. In most cases the text was copied first with spaces set aside for illustrating significant passages. The most elaborate decoration consisted of full-page paintings with figures, buildings, and landscapes, and often were bound at the front of a book or between chapters. Text pages presented opportunities to insert abstract and floral decoration in the margins.[13]

Scribes worked in private studios, state libraries, and monasteries. Some owned their own street-side shops, where they earned a regular income by drawing up betrothal papers, wills, and similar legal documents. One such scribe named Theodore is known to have kept a studio in a place called John-and-Phocas in Constantinople. The high cost of materials and labor meant that most books were specifically commissioned. Large monasteries, like the Stoudios in the capital, had workshops for making paper and copying books, yet there were few large-scale monastic scriptoria as in western Europe. Medieval colophons suggest that in the ninth through eleventh centuries two out of three manuscripts were copied by clergy or monks, with lay scribes more active during the late empire. Some worked in teams and a few are known by name. Theodore Hagiopetrites, a lower-level cleric in Thessaloniki ca. 1300, worked as both a copyist and decorator of books. His daughter Eirene followed his example and also made manuscripts on her own. After entering a convent the noblewoman Theodora Raoulaina copied books for her personal use.

Such highly skilled, labor-intensive production ensured that books were always expensive and hard to come by. Individual volumes are known to have cost as much as half a court official's annual salary in the tenth century. Sizable personal libraries were the prized possessions of upper-class intellectuals like Michael Attaleiates, Eustathios Boilas, and Theodore Metochites. Even undecorated books fetched high prices. Unlike classical Rome or Ottoman Istanbul, a market for books with specialized booksellers never developed in Constantinople. Older volumes circulated among friends and through pawn shops, before eventually finding their way into monastic libraries.[14]

ARCHITECTURE

The Byzantines met their needs for shelter in various ways. Villagers and farmers built simple structures ranging from houses and chapels to cisterns and sheepfolds. Utilitarian boathouses, mills, sheds, and workshops were cobbled together to handle the products of rural estates. Military engineers designed harbors, roads, bridges, and fortifications, calling on local inhabitants to contribute materials and labor. Architecture of a more ambitious sort, including baths and public buildings but after the sixth century mainly elite houses and domed churches, was left to experienced masons. The training of professional architects (*mechanikoi*) did not survive late antiquity. As a result, most medieval buildings were the work of more or less loosely organized teams of workers (*oikodomoi* or *technitai*) directed by a master (*protomaistor*). In larger cities skilled artisans banded together in permanent workshops that operated under their own charters and local ordinances. More often a master builder and his assistants traveled to small towns and estates to undertake specific commissions, such as a wealthy landowner's suburban villa or a new monastery.[15]

Building Materials and Methods High transportation costs encouraged the use of locally available materials. Foundations and rising walls were mainly of brick and stone. Bricks and roof tiles were made in suburban brickyards and seasonal workshops close to their intended destination. Fieldstones were pulled from nearby fields while limestone blocks were roughly shaped in local quarries. Bricks and fieldstones were bedded in thick mortar layers, sometimes forming herringbone, zigzags, meanders, and other decorative patterns. Important projects might call for fine white stone brought from Prokonnesos or Attica, distinctive green marble from Thessaly or south Greece, or dark purple porphyry from Egypt. Many builders looked to classical ruins for columns and capitals to reuse. Other spoils were crushed and burned to make lime mortar. Earth, mud brick, and clay figured prominently in village houses and farm buildings. Timber was needed for scaffolding while building was underway as well as to support upper stories and roofs.

Any structure's design reflected its location, intended purpose, and patronage. Measuring systems and building methods usually following regional custom. By the sixth century state authorities and military

Workmen excavating foundations and building a palace for the emperor Romanos I. Detail from the late-twelfth-century edition of the Skylitzes Chronicle. Photo courtesy of the Biblioteca Nacional, Madrid (ms. vitr. 26–2).

engineers had settled on an official foot *(pous)* of about 12 1/4 inches, somewhat longer than the Roman foot. Standard-length rods were issued to encourage consistency, but surveyors and building crews generally used knotted cords for measuring distances, which inevitably led to minor errors. While the design of Justinian's Hagia Sophia and other complex buildings embodies formal geometric principles, most buildings took shape without such premeditation. The relative consistency of Byzantine churches meant that schematic drawings were rarely needed. The normal procedure was to determine the overall size of a project and let details emerge during construction. A building's overall length typically determined its secondary dimensions. Most of these were based on simple proportional relationships among spatial units and were fixed using wood stakes and rope. A master builder *(architekton)* may have been called to town to advise on some matters, but work was largely carried out by local laborers.

Builders applied familiar Roman methods to local materials and circumstances. Rising walls and piers had to rest on sturdy footings of well-mortared rubble and stone. Walls needed to be plumb and in most places consisted of a rubble core sandwiched between inner and outer faces of fieldstones. Pains were taken to regularize the appearance of the outer surface by including horizontal bands of bricks, large marble blocks, sculptural spoils, and decorative details. By contrast, inner surfaces were plastered and decorated with fresco or mosaic. Reused marble columns shaped the interior and supported the roof, which might be pitched in

timber or vaulted in brick. The main forms were the familiar barrel or
tunnel vault, intersecting cross or groin vault, and domical or sail vault.
Hemispherical domes were often raised on drums and reinforced with
brick ribs or internally scalloped. Supporting elements included sets of
spherical triangles known as pendentives or transitional squinches, all
built of lightweight brick.

**Interior
Decoration**   Public buildings, elite residences, and churches were outfitted as generously as money allowed. Marble was the most
highly prized material and held a key place in decoration.

Marble and other ornamental stones were cut into flat slabs
for floor paving and wall revetment. Columns, bases, capitals, entablatures,
moldings, and window supports were recycled from earlier buildings
or carved anew. Marble also appeared in household tables, benches, and
chests. Liturgical furniture in churches included altar and table surfaces,
ambos or pulpits, templons and icon barriers, and chancel screens.

While marble sculpture and revetment embodied material wealth, the
real decorative interest was the frescoes and mosaics that covered the
walls. Both techniques had deep Mediterranean roots and became widespread during the Byzantine millennium. The expense and splendor of
these monumental media were well suited to palaces and churches, and
by the time of Justinian the vocabulary of interior decoration had moved
far beyond its Roman origins. In churches of the medieval period frescoes
and mosaics constituted a unique decorative program that both expressed
and reinforced the building's spiritual use. The mosaics of Hagia Sophia,
whose colossal holy figures stood against an endless gold field, were
among the city's most dazzling sights. Speaking for his contemporaries,

Cloisonné masonry with brick meander and decorative details, from the
church of the Panagia at Merbaka in south Greece. From Gabriel Millet,
La École grecque dans l'architecture byzantins (Paris: Ernst Leroux, 1916).

the ninth-century patriarch Photios makes clear their unique visual impact: "With such exactitude has the art of painting, which is a reflection of inspiration from above, set up a lifelike imitation ... To such an extent have the lips been made flesh by the colors." Like portable icons, these images were valued more for their authenticity than originality. Their consistency in churches across the empire was an essential part of the Byzantine tradition.[16]

Fresco was used everywhere. This very old technique involved pigments suspended in water and spread onto a smooth plaster surface. Several layers of fine plaster made of powdered sand, shell, bone, lime, or marble were applied to the wall over a series of days or even weeks. Pigments for painting walls, as for dyeing fabrics, came from different sources. Minerals like cinnabar and lead were used for making vermilion and other reddish tones; azurite and copper for blues; malachite, glanconite, and verdigris for shades of greens; and ochres for various earth tones. Common vegetable dyes came from indigo, woad, and madder. Charcoal and other carbonized materials were used for black. These were pulverized in stone mortars and mixed with water. Particles of pigment bonded best when applied to a damp plaster ground, which produces a true fresco (from the Italian "fresh") that preserves bright colors. When working with dry surfaces the painter mixed pigments with egg, honey, or animal glue. Small teams working with these methods could cover several square yards of surface in a day, depending on local conditions and the amount of pictorial detail. Even though they did not generally sign their works, several late-medieval painters are known by name. Documents suggest that the pay scale for muralists was comparable to the other building crafts. Experienced painters likely made portable icons and mosaics as well.[17]

Roman artists had popularized the use of mosaics in ornamental floors, but left it to the artists of late antiquity to apply them to aboveground surfaces. The technique involved forming shapes with tesserae set in a mortar or plaster bed. Tesserae generally were cut in different sizes and shapes out of brick, colored stone, marble, and tinted glass. Translucent cubes capped with gold or silver foil were particularly popular in backgrounds and for emphasizing key passages. Mosaic working on a large scale posed obvious challenges. Walls and vaults required two or three layers of increasingly fine plaster anchored by metal pins, which obscured any preliminary drawings on the masonry. Small teams of mosaicists worked in limited areas while the plaster dried. Complex details may have composed in advance and moved into place using glue and fabric, but most mosaics were made by experienced craftsmen while on timber scaffolds. The tall proportions and irregular, curving surfaces of palace halls and churches presented artists with unprecedented difficulties. Maintaining the correct perspective and visual coherence of large figures was a constant challenge.

Churches

Churches make up the most distinctive and best-preserved examples of Byzantine architecture, and might even be called the most complex works of Byzantine art. From diminutive country chapels to great urban cathedrals, religious buildings dotted the landscape and shaped local lives. Most of these are known only by fragmentary foundations uncovered by excavation; others survive in varying states of repair and are still in use.

Churches varied considerably with date, location, and function. Christianity's rapid spread in the fourth to sixth centuries prompted a spate of church building across the empire. Large assembly halls were set up to serve the crowds of large cities, establishing models for smaller churches in nearby towns and villages. The pace of construction slowed with the empire's military troubles in the seventh and eighth centuries, but its medieval revival saw many new churches built between the tenth and fifteenth centuries. Standing buildings preserve a number of regional traditions, such as brick-faced walls in north Italy, limestone masonry in north Syria, and mud brick in Egypt. Even within the late empire's reduced borders one can differentiate the mortared rubble work of Asia Minor from the carefully built cloisonné masonry found in central Greece. Equally broad distinctions can be drawn among the intended functions of Byzantine churches, between the urban cathedrals and pilgrimage centers that handled huge crowds in late antiquity, and much smaller churches built after the ninth century. Most later examples were founded by private patrons in their ancestral villages and belonged to small monasteries.

The basic Christian basilica took shape during the fourth and fifth centuries. Like its Roman predecessor, the basilica church consisted of a long hall or nave subdivided into parallel aisles by two, sometimes four, rows of columns. There were windows in the side walls and in the clerestory above the colonnades; a pitched tile roof on a timber frame covered the interior. At the front of the hall was a vestibule or narthex, sometimes accompanied by an open court that acted as a gathering place for worshippers. Processions led down the length of the nave to the altar, which was placed in a semicircular apse usually oriented to the east. Interior walls often had paintings or mosaics depicting stories from the Old and New Testaments. The tall semidome above the altar soon received its own distinctive treatment, echoing and reinforcing the liturgy celebrated below.

Builders generally approached their task in a pragmatic way that allowed plenty of flexibility. The timber-roofed basilica could be readily adapted to suit local needs and resources. In some cases builders turned to more complex architectural forms, such as the immense, vaulted superstructure of Justinian's Hagia Sophia. With a total area of nearly 58,000 square feet, this was the largest interior space of antiquity. The plan consisted of a broad central nave with flanking aisles and upper galleries. The enormous dome was supported by monumental pendentives at a height of over a hundred feet. Windows in the base of the dome,

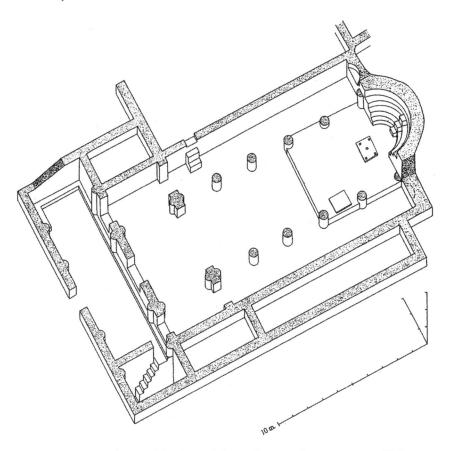

Perspective view of a rural basilica of the early seventh century near Kalavasos in Cyprus. One passed through a wide narthex before reaching the three-aisled nave. The raised floor of the sanctuary originally was surrounded by a low barrier. The base for the altar was mortared into the floor. The clergy sat on three tiers of benches in the apse. Courtesy of the author.

semidomes, and nave walls flooded the interior with light. Its audacious design and unprecedented scale set a lasting precedent for later Byzantine and Islamic builders.[18]

The most characteristic churches of the tenth to fifteenth centuries translated the soaring dome of Hagia Sophia into the familiar setting of the monastery. The typical monastic katholikon was a compact structure that stood within a walled precinct. One entered the building by a low narthex extending the full width of the church. From here one moved into the main hall or *naos*, whose vaults were supported by walls, piers, and columns, and usually included a tall central dome. The sanctuary had three distinct parts: the central *bema* with the altar standing before the main apse; on the north side the *prothesis,* where the elements of the Eucharist were prepared; and the *diakonikon,* or supporting sacristy, to the south. Larger churches included subsidiary chapels at the ends of the flanking aisles. Small, isolated windows preserved the subdued, meditative lighting of the interior.

The broad consistency of Byzantine church decoration ensured that wherever they went, medieval travelers never felt far from their spiritual base. Regardless of size or plan, one entered an intimate liturgical environment filled with images arranged according to hierarchy and function. Standing saints—martyrs, soldiers, monks, bishops—lined the lower walls, surrounding the worshipper with the historical community of believers. Portable icons of Christ, the Virgin, John the Baptist, and other saints hung on the sanctuary barrier or *iconostasis.* On the upper walls and vaults one saw biblical narratives, especially the major liturgical feasts running from the Annunciation and Nativity through the Passion and Pentecost. The solitary image of the Virgin rose in the semidome behind the altar, justifying the Incarnation and providing a focus for the liturgy. The highest and most central part of church, the dome, was occupied by a bust-length image of Christ. Here the commanding, reassuring Pantokrator offered a summation of the Byzantine worldview, enfolding the worshipper within an unchanging artistic environment.

MUSIC

The unique setting of the Byzantine church was fully realized only when services were underway. Vocal music was an inseparable part of the liturgy and took the form of nearly continuous chanting that underscored the rhythm of spoken words. The most distinct feature of late Byzantine chant, still heard in Eastern churches, was the drone *(ison)* that accompanied hymns *(stichera),* psalms *(prokeimena),* and liturgical responses. In larger churches separate choirs contributed different parts of the liturgical ceremony. No instruments were used apart from the human voice.

Outside the church Byzantine music was performed at the palace, in the streets and taverns, and at home. The tenth-century *Book of Ceremonies* describes how the emperor was hailed with chanted acclamations and accompanying fanfare. The most prominent instrument used for such occasions was the pneumatic organ, a late-antique adaptation of the Roman hydraulis. The organ's low, sustained notes were sounded at receptions, banquets, and appearances in the hippodrome, and must have resembled liturgical chant. Other wind instruments included horns and trumpets *(boukina* and *salpinx),* pipes *(syrinx),* and flutes or reeds *(aulos).* Bells *(semantra),* cymbals *(kymbala, anakara),* drums *(tympana),* and rattles *(seistra)* provided rhythmic accompaniment. All these had their place in imperial processions and street parades. Horns, bells, and drums accompanied the army in the field, with trumpets used for battlefield communication. Strings

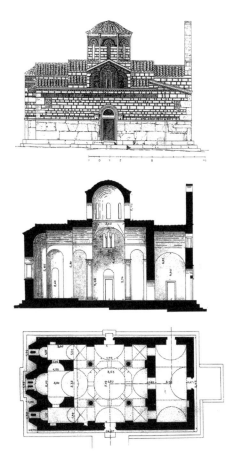

Elevation, section, and plan of the church of the Panagia at Merbaka. Byzantine churches of the medieval period were generally small and compact, with light coming through a few windows in the upper walls and central dome. From *Athenische Mitteilungen* 34 (1909).

included the lute *(pandoura)*, harp or lyre *(kithara, psalterion,* and *tamboura)*, and similar instruments that were played with a bow, strummed with the fingers, or plucked with a *plektron*. Pipes, reeds, and stringed instruments accompanied staged mime shows and impromptu street performances, not to mention dancing and singing in the taverna and at home; for this reason musicians were held in low esteem by the church. Elite families staged elaborate banquets with musical entertainment *(symposia)* into the late

Middle Ages. Lyrical *akritika,* based on the epic of Digenis Akritis, and other vernacular folksongs sung to a solitary pipe or syrinx remained a regular feature of pastoral life.[19]

NOTES

1. The classical background is surveyed in Donald Strong and David Brown, eds., *Roman Crafts* (New York: New York University Press, 1976). The economic processes behind the luxury arts and monumental decoration are well discussed by Anthony Cutler, "The Industries of Art," in *The Economic History of Byzantium from the Seventh to the Fifteenth Century,* ed. Angeliki E. Laiou (Washington, D.C.: Dumbarton Oaks, 2002), 555–87. More critical views of the arts expressed by Michael Psellos stand out by exception.

2. See bibliography for recent surveys of Byzantine art, all centering on works expressly religious in content.

3. The connection between ancient mummy paintings and early icons is explored by Thomas F. Mathews, *Byzantium: From Antiquity to the Renaissance* (New York: Harry N. Abrams, 1998). There are many books on medieval icons, including Kurt Weitzmann and R. E. Wolf, *Icons from South Eastern Europe and Sinai* (London: Thames and Hudson, 1968); Kurt Weitzmann, *The Icon: Holy Images— Sixth to Fourteenth Century* (New York: George Braziller, 1978); John Baggley, *Doors of Perception: Icons and Their Spiritual Significance* (London: Mowbray, 1987); and Richard Temple, *Icons: Divine Beauty* (London: Saqi Books, 2004).

4. Nicholas Oikonomides, "The Holy Icon as Asset," *Dumbarton Oaks Papers* 45 (1991): 35–44; Maria Vassilaki, ed., *Mother of God: Representations of the Virgin in Byzantine Art* (New York: Abbeville, 2000).

5. Pliny the Elder, *Natural History,* trans. H. Rackham, W.H.S. Jones, and D. E. Eichholz (Cambridge: Harvard University Press, 1938–62), bk. 33; John G. Hawthorne and Cyril Stanley Smith, trans., *On Divers Arts: The Treatise of Theophilus* (Chicago: University of Chicago Press, 1963).

6. Liudprand of Cremona, *Antapodosis (Tit-for-Tat)* 6.8, in F. A. Wright, trans., *Works of Liudprand of Cremona,* (New York: E. P. Dutton, 1930), 209–10. Metalworking methods are covered by several articles in Strong and Brown, *Roman Crafts;* and for the medieval period by Maria K. Papathanassiou, "Metallurgy and Metalworking Techniques," in Laiou, *Economic History of Byzantium,* 1:121–27. The story of the discovery and dispersal of the Syrian collection is told by Marlia Mundell Mango, *Silver from Early Byzantium: The Kaper Koraon and Related Treasures* (Baltimore: Walters Art Gallery, 1986).

7. *Life* of Theodore of Sykeon, in Elizabeth Dawes and Norman H. Baynes, trans., *Three Byzantine Saints: Contemporary Biographies of St. Daniel the Stylite, St. Theodore of Sykeon, and St. John the Almsgiver* (Crestwood, N.Y.: St. Vladimir's Seminar Press, 1977), 89. For an overview of techniques see Reynold Higgins, "Jewellery," in Strong and Brown, *Roman Crafts,* 53–61.

8. Sarnia A. Butcher, "Enamelling," in Strong and Brown, *Roman Crafts,* 43–51; Klaus Wessel, *Byzantine Enamels* (Greenwich, N.Y.: New York Graphic Society, 1969).

9. Ivory working is comprehensively treated by Anthony Cutler, *The Hand of the Master: Craftsmanship, Ivory, and Society in Byzantium (9th–11th Centuries)* (Princeton, N.J.: Princeton University Press, 1994).

10. E. Marianne Stern, *Roman, Byzantine, and Early Medieval Glass, 10 B.C.E.–700 C.E.* (Ostfildern-Ruit, Germany: Hatje Cantz Publishers, 2001); Véronique François and Jean-Michel Spieser, "Pottery and Glass in Byzantium," in Laiou, *Economic History of Byzantium,* 2:593–609.

11. Liz James, *Light and Colour in Byzantine Art* (Oxford: Clarendon Press, 1996).

12. A good introduction is Nigel Wilson, "Books and Readers in Byzantium," in *Byzantine Books and Bookmen* (Washington, D.C.: Dumbarton Oaks, 1975), 1–16. For the material background see Susan A. Stephens, "Book Production," in *Civilization of the Ancient Mediterranean: Greece and Rome,* ed. Michael Grant and Rachel Kitzinger (New York: Charles Scribner's Sons, 1988), 1:421–36; and Nicolas Oikonomides, "Writing Materials, Documents, and Books," in Laiou, *Economic History of Byzantium,* 2:589–92.

13. Kurt Weitzmann, *Late Antique and Early Christian Book Illumination* (New York: George Braziller, 1977). John Lowden, *Early Christian and Byzantine Art* (London: Phaidon Press, 1997), offers a good introduction to later manuscripts.

14. *Byzantine Books and Bookmen;* Oikonomides, "Writing Materials, Documents, and Books."

15. Architectural surveys include Richard Krautheimer, *Early Christian and Byzantine Architecture,* 4th ed. (Harmondsworth, England: Penguin Books, 1986); and Cyril Mango, *Byzantine Architecture* (New York: Harry N. Abrams, 1976; reprint, New York: Rizzoli, 1991). For recent summaries of the building process see Robert G. Ousterhout, *Master Builders of Byzantium* (Princeton, N.J.: Princeton University Press, 1999); and Charalambos Bouras, "Master Craftsmen, Craftsmen, and Building Activities in Byzantium," in Laiou, *Economic History of Byzantium,* 2:539–54.

16. Photios, 17th homily, translated in Cyril Mango, *The Art of the Byzantine Empire, 312–1453* (Englewood Cliffs, N.J.: Prentice Hall, 1972; reprint, Toronto: Medieval Academy Reprints for Teaching, 1986), 187. The classic study remains Otto Demus, *Byzantine Mosaic Decoration: Aspects of Monumental Art in Byzantium* (New Rochelle, N.Y.: Caratzas, 1976). An early eighteenth-century view of the muralist's task survives in P. Hetherington, trans., *The "Painter's Manual" of Dionysios of Fourna* (London: Sagittarius Press, 1974).

17. Pliny the Elder (*Natural History,* bks. 33–35), Vitruvius (Morris Hicky Morgan, trans., *Vitruvius. The Ten Books on Architecture* [Cambridge: Harvard University Press, 1914; reprint, New York: Dover Publications, 1960], bks. 2, 7), and other classical authors provide a great deal of information about the materials and methods of wall painting. See Roger Ling, *Roman Painting* (New York: Cambridge University Press, 1991); and for Byzantium David C. Winfield, "Middle and Later Byzantine Wall Painting Methods: A Comparative Study," *Dumbarton Oaks Papers* 22 (1968): 63–139.

18. For a recent illustrated survey of the modern architectural legacy see J. B. Bullen, *Byzantium Rediscovered* (New York: Phaidon, 2003).

19. See Egon Wellesz, "Byzantine Music and Liturgy," in *The Cambridge Medieval History,* vol. 4, *The Byzantine Empire,* pt. 2, *Government, Church and Civilization,* ed. Joan M. Hussey (Cambridge: Cambridge University Press, 1966–67), 135–60; and Diane Touliatos, "The Evolution of Ancient Greek Music in Byzantium: Instruments, Women Musicians, Dance, and Other Sundry Matters," http://www.geocities.com/hellenicmind/byzantium.html.

10

LIFE OF THE MIND

Byzantium's intellectual life was shaped by its material environment, social structure, religious outlook, and historical self-consciousness. Many Byzantines thought of themselves as heirs to classical culture in the same way that they saw their language going back to fifth-century B.C. Athens and their state as the direct continuation of Rome. Internal tensions with Christianity and external pressures from beyond the frontier shaped new traditions in art, literature, philosophy, and science that brought the legacy of antiquity to the threshold of the modern world.

LITERACY AND CULTURE

Education

The Byzantine education system grew out of the curriculum of classical antiquity tempered by teachings of the church. General education, as developed by Roman school masters, was founded on study of the seven liberal arts: the *trivium,* comprising grammar, rhetoric, and dialectic, and the *quadrivium* of mathematical arts, namely arithmetic, geometry, astronomy, and music. This rich pedagogical tradition was conveyed to students through a three-stage system that continued through late antiquity. At the primary level small groups of children were supervised by a teacher *(didaskalos),* who taught them the essentials of literacy. Studies at the second stage were supervised by a grammarian *(grammatikos),* who concentrated on key works of classical poetry, first of all the Homeric epics, which Basil of Caesarea thought comprised "an *enkomion* of virtue." Advanced students took on classical rhetoric, literature, and other subjects under the guidance of special tutors. Unlike the early medieval West, where education took place mainly in monasteries, rudimentary literacy was widespread in Byzantine society as a whole.[1]

This general curriculum *(enkyklios paideia)* was sharply reduced amid the crises of the seventh and eighth centuries. Education for most medieval people was limited to what could be learned at home and from private didaskaloi in towns and larger villages. Teachers conducted lessons with few if any books, and these soon became even more scarce than before. Limited access to papyrus and paper meant that writing exercises were done on slate and wax tablets. The first task was to learn the 24 letters of the Greek alphabet, which were drilled forward and backward. After mastering individual letters, students moved on to forming syllables, spelling the names of mythological or biblical figures, and writing out pithy sayings and stories associated with them. Memorizing psalms and key biblical texts was a favored technique. A common written exercise was paraphrasing or explaining certain Gospel miracles. Teachers were advised to use games and contests as a way of motivating pupils.

There were few opportunities for advanced study outside of Constantinople, whose bureaucracies required a steady supply of young men trained in reading and writing. Secondary schooling was normally guided by a private grammatikos in exchange for negotiated fees. Children of prominent families were sent to teachers with the best reputations. Some of these received imperial grants in addition to student fees, perhaps for taking on state-sponsored pupils. The program of studies was not fixed and in some respects resembled the curriculum of a modern American secondary school, with courses in grammar, rhetoric, and poetry. A common objective was to learn by heart the classics of Greek poetry, primarily long passages of Hesiod and Homer, at an average pace of 30 lines a day. The *Iliad* and *Odyssey* were the most frequently read ancient texts. Advanced students in the capital formed school teams that competed in rhetorical contests, which were closely followed by local elites and sometimes took place before the emperor. Beyond this point one's education was overseen by a teacher of rhetoric *(rhetor)*, either individually or in small groups. After completing their studies such students normally entered the civil service.

Byzantium did not have universities in the sense of organized institutions of higher education with set curricula and permanent faculty. In late antiquity groups of independent teachers could be found in Alexandria, Antioch, Athens, and Beirut, where students flocked to study law, religion, philosophy, and religion. Students paid fees directly to their tutors, who sometimes were subsidized by the city. The famous Academy in Athens thrived as a Neoplatonic study group with a private endowment that permitted it to accept students without charging tuition. Some teachers were attracted to opportunities in the new capital. In the early fifth century Theodosius II founded a privileged secondary school to prepare young men for state service. Such a career path was followed by John the

ca.330	ca.400	ca.506	s.VII	650/60	675

The 24-character Greek alphabet had been in use for over a thousand years before Constantinople was founded, but its letter forms continued to evolve throughout the Middle Ages. After the eighth and ninth centuries, the traditional capital letters (uncials) were increasingly supplemented by lowercase minuscule letters, accents, and breathing marks. From V. Gardthausen, *Griechische Palaeographie* (Leipzig: B.G. Teubner, 1879).

Lydian, who came to Constantinople at the age of 21, studied rhetoric and philosophy for a few years, and entered the civil administration. During his 40-year career he wrote several treatises and held his own teaching post, where he presumably trained other future officials. Many teachers struggled to gain state sponsorship or otherwise make ends meet. The scholar-teacher's undeserved poverty is a familiar theme in medieval sources, both Eastern and Western. All were concerned with holding on to paying students, and many even made house calls. Some scholars economized by transcribing their own work for students instead of hiring a copyist. Theodore Hyrtakenos, an aspiring intellectual who took on

α	= 1	ι	= 10	ρ	= 100
β	= 2	κ	= 20	ϲ	= 200
γ	= 3	λ	= 30	τ	= 300
δ	= 4	μ	= 40	υ	= 400
ε	= 5	ν	= 50	φ	= 500
ϛ	= 6	ξ	= 60	χ	= 600
ζ	= 7	ο	= 70	ψ	= 700
η	= 8	π	= 80	ω	= 800
θ	= 9	ϙ	= 90	ϡ	= 900.

The Greek alphabet was also used for dates and mathematical notation, with a superimposed dash indicating a numeral. Specific letters, plus three archaic characters—*sti, koppa,* and *sampi*—were used in the place of ones, tens, and hundreds; larger numbers were given an additional accent mark. The concept of zero was never widely accepted in Byzantium. From V. Gardthausen, *Griechische Palaeographie* (Leipzig: B.G. Teubner, 1879).

private pupils in early fourteenth-century Constantinople, constantly complained of his limited means in his letters. Despite their circumstances such men developed a strong sense of superiority to the lower social classes, for whom they showed surprisingly little regard.[2]

Both emperors and patriarchs helped revive higher education in medieval Constantinople. In the mid-ninth century the Caesar Bardas appointed the polymath Leo the Mathematician to reorganize the teaching of advanced students. Under his direction a school in the Magnaura palace quarter taught parts of the quadrivium and offered instruction in mathematics, astronomy, and philosophy as well as grammar. By the eleventh century these palace schools were training notaries, lawyers, and other civil functionaries, and could be considered a kind of secular university. At the same time the patriarchate supported its own school to instruct clergymen and monks. This "patriarchal academy" stood close to Hagia Sophia and had its own faculty, a conservative theological curriculum, and large library of religious books. Together these two very different institutions maintained Constantinople's status as a major center of learning through the late Middle Ages.[3]

Writing   The change from roll to codex in late antiquity had enormous implications for writing and literacy. The roll's linear format imposed obvious limits on length, requiring long works to be broken into chapters written on multiple rolls. The codex, with its many pages of uniform size, did not have the same limitations. Copyists assumed greater control by grouping multiple chapters of a text, or even including entirely different works in the same volume. The shift to codex resulted in a number of fresh compilations of classical works, including literary and dramatic writings but also legal, medical, philosophical, and scientific treatises. The wider margins of the codex additionally offered scribes the chance to add their own interpretations of venerable texts. These commentaries *(scholia)* preserve a running dialogue across the generations that helped shape Byzantine intellectual life.

Another technical change with far-reaching implications was the development of cursive script in the eighth and ninth centuries. Classical manuscripts had traditionally been written in capital letters known as *uncials*. These normally were recorded as a continuous line of text without spaces between words and with little punctuation. Each letter had to be carefully formed by multiple pen strokes, which was a slow and exacting task. The finished text may have been beautiful but was not easy to read. The flowing cursive or *minuscule* script was more rapidly penned and took up about a third of the blocky *majuscle* version. Texts could be quickly copied in more compact form, which encouraged scholars to write paraphrases in the margins of older works, produce new editions, and compose up-to-date commentaries on their contents. At the same time scribes punctuated sentences, added clarifying accents and breathing marks, and eventually separated words. Uncial letters were used sparingly to give old-fashioned authority to title blocks, chapter headings, and captions of key illustrations. Clearly the new script was easier to write and read. It apparently originated in monastic scriptoria in the capital, and was soon adopted for record keeping by the civil and military bureaucracies. Most books produced after the tenth century used the new script.

Letter writing was a habit of cultured Romans that was transformed in Byzantine times. Hundreds of known letters **Letters** preserve an extensive correspondence linking members of the intellectual and political elites. The fourth and fifth centuries brought a new level of stylistic formality to these exchanges, in which writers passed on information along with their personal reactions. The self-conscious, studied composition of such letters showed off the author's educated background, with flowery language evoking fourth-century B.C. Athens and frequent references to classical and biblical literature. Texts were written on papyrus or paper and were intended to be read aloud to one's friends, rather like a literary salon. Some authors thought so highly of their writing that they bundled copies of their correspondence into collections to be savored by later generations. Compilations of fourth-century letters written by Libanius, Gregory of Nazianzos, and John Chrysostomos were still being cited by Byzantine scholars in the fourteenth century, even while they prepared new editions of their own.

Minuscule script in a tenth-century gospel book. From
Gustave Schlumberger, *Un empereur byzantin aux dixième
siècle, Nicéphore Phocas* (Paris: Firmin Didot, 1890).

Letters tell us a great deal about the writer while at the same time
containing much information about his surroundings. In many of his
93 preserved letters Theodore Hyrtakenos explains how poverty drives
his effort to secure a position in the imperial palace. Letters sometimes
accompanied gifts of books or perishable delicacies like fruit or fish, such
as those Eustathios of Thessaloniki sent to his friends. Beyond sharing
news and feelings, the larger purpose of letters was to reaffirm the social
status of both parties in what Demetrios Kydones calls the "communion
of words." Learned allusions, citations, and mannerisms reflect long
hours spent studying earlier literature and could be deciphered only by
those with similarly refined values. Writing in the fourteenth century,
Nikephoros Gregoras differentiates his letter-writing friends from the

street crowds, peasants, and common laborers, who spoke an entirely different sort of Greek and wrote little, if at all. This rarified gift exchange among intellectual equals reveals the correspondents' attitudes as much as the world in which they lived.[4]

Particularly important letters, especially official and diplomatic documents, were folded and secured with a small sealing or *bulla* of wax or lead. Wax seals preserve the impression of a signet ring or other personal marker that was pressed directly onto a document, sometimes attaching ribbons or strings to the page. Lead seals locked a piece of ribbon or cord tied around a document with a small perforated disk. Clamped between the hammerlike jaws of a special iron pincers *(boulloterion)*, the seal fixed the cord and imprinted the writer's monogram or title. Most correspondence seals were broken and discarded when one opened the letter. Lead bullae were known in Roman times but became widespread around the seventh century. In the late Middle Ages the emperor's personal seal was stamped in gold and attached to a purple silk string, which gave his documents the status of imperial *chrysobulls*. As in western Europe, seals were widely used by civil and church bureaucracies to validate and preserve the confidentiality of special texts. Surviving wax seals come mainly from medieval documents preserved in the archives of Mount Athos. The 50,000 surviving examples in lead give a detailed picture of the reach of Byzantine officialdom, at home and abroad. The largest number have come to light near the palace quarter of the capital.[5]

In the same way that literacy was basic to Byzantium, books were an essential part of intellectual life. Bureaucrats, doctors, lawyers, military officers, schoolmasters, and clergy regularly consulted books for professional reasons. Independent reading was seen as a worthy pastime. Theodore of Stoudios recommended that monks

**Books and
Intellectual
Life**

be allowed to read until twilight on days that they were free of other duties. Leo the Mathematician was said to have pursued his advanced studies by himself in monastic libraries. The retired Kekaumenos recommended reading whenever one was alone: "Read a lot, and you will

Official seals. The cruciform type of monogram was widely used in the sixth and seventh centuries. From Gustave Schlumberger, *Sigillographie de l'empire byzantin* (Paris: Ernest Leroux, 1884).

learn a lot. And, if you don't understand, take heart; when you have gone through the book frequently, knowledge will be given to you by God, and you will understand it."[6]

Classical learning was widespread in the great cities of late antiquity, but with the loss of the eastern provinces intellectual activity increasingly centered on Constantinople. By the tenth century it was only here that one could aspire to advanced rhetorical skills and joining the ranks of literati. Most of what survives of classical literature comes to us through manuscripts copied by scribes in the capital. A passing acquaintance, if not intimate familiarity, with the major works of Greek and Latin distinguished the educated person from provincial bumpkins and foreigners. This open-mindedness dates to the time of Basil of Caesarea, who favored the study of early authors for their literary value: "Since it is through virtue that we must enter this life of ours, and since much has been uttered in praise of virtue by poets, much by historians, and much more still by philosophers, we ought especially to apply ourselves to such literature." Classical texts were copied in monasteries and private studios, and circulated among small reading groups in Constantinople. Homer was fundamental. Aristotle also was copied often, appearing in more than a thousand manuscripts between the ninth and sixteenth centuries. The ninth-century *Bibliotheka* of Patriarch Photios consists of an annotated record of personal readings in the classics, both classical and Christian. "These 279 works are those I remember to have read myself in the course of my literary studies from the time I began having some critical understanding of literature until now." Best sellers regularly appeared in new editions, sometimes in translation. The first-century *Materials of Medicine (De materia medica)* of Dioscorides survives in a number of richly illustrated manuscripts. Over 50 copies of the tenth-century *Geoponika* are known in different languages.[7]

Despite their elevated reputation, books as a practical matter were scarce and expensive. High prices discouraged antiquarian book dealing. An illustrated secondhand Gospel book might easily cost as much as a horse or mule, while commissioning a large volume could take half the annual salary of a midlevel civil servant. At a time when day laborers earned 6 to 10 nomismata a year, new books ran 15 to 30. Certain titles could be hard to find. The patriarchate in Constantinople often resorted to commissioning copies of books held in monastic collections. Theodore Hyrtakenos unsuccessfully searched the fourteenth-century city for a copy of the *Odyssey* to send a former pupil in Trebizond.

Constantinople, unlike Hellenistic Alexandria or classical Rome, never built a central state library. The patriarchal residence kept the empire's largest collection of religious works, but even its holdings had significant gaps. A few prominent monasteries built up sizable collections over the centuries; the Stoudios monastery, the Great Lavra on Mount Athos, and the monastery of Saint John on Patmos owned hundreds of volumes. One of the medieval empire's great bibliophiles, Michael Attaleiates, gave his collection of 54 books, including Gospels, Psalters, homilies, catechisms, and other religious works, to the Constantinopolitan monastery of Christ Panoiktirmon. When Eustathios Boilas drew up his will in 1059 he listed 78 volumes, mostly religious works and saints' lives but also law books, chronicles, the stray novel, and a copy of Aesop's fables. Writing in the early fourteenth century, Theodore Metochites cites over 80 classical authors whose works were presumably in his personal collection. Still, such large holdings are unusual, and a typical aristocratic family of the medieval period owned perhaps 10 to 20 volumes on various subjects. Inscribed lending notes indicate that books rarely circulated outside churches, monasteries, and elite families. Most Byzantine people never handled or read them.[8]

While Byzantium is usually seen as a serious, high-minded culture, humor no doubt played a significant role in the daily **Humor** lives of many people. As is the case with other cultures, humor reflects the sense the Byzantines made of their world. It helped them negotiate relationships in varied situations, whether expressing intimacy, reinforcing friendships, venting anger or anxiety, or showing contempt. By flaunting social conventions and juxtaposing incongruities, humor defined by exception prevailing social views and revealed deeply held attitudes and prejudices. The strict hierarchies of society made humor a vital way of controlling interpersonal tensions.

Church leaders consistently warned against laughter for its cruelties and subverting of pious thoughts. Performances of comedy, burlesque, and slapstick were routinely condemned as a distraction from sober comportment. Such repeated warnings, of course, indicate just how little effect they had on ordinary lives. Mime, parody, and satirical displays continued to be popular in tavernas, street theater, religious festivals, and periodic fairs. Practical jokes and public humiliations were known at court, and satire remained an effective form of social and political commentary. Writing in the twelfth century, the Komnene court poet Theodore Prodromos records a broad range of contemporary humor, from sophisticated cosmopolitan wit to the earthy sexual and scatological ribaldry of the lower classes. Verse fables and epic poems with animal characters, like the fourteenth-century *Tale of the Quadrupeds* or the *Book of Birds*, can be read as satirical commentaries on late-medieval society.[9]

Byzantine literature preserves a variety of humorous works. The *Philogelos* ("laughter lover") is a collection of witticisms assembled in the late fourth century. Selected entries run the gamut of tired jokes and lame puns long popular in Rome. Typical examples include "Don't go near the water without first learning how to swim" and "May all your weddings be happy ones." Popular sayings reflect the timeless traditionalism of medieval society. "Seek other more profitable houses, you robbers, for poverty constantly keeps guard over this" corresponds to the modern "Stereo broken" sign displayed in parked cars. The nonchoice between poor alternatives implied by "I departed matins and found the liturgy waiting for me" echoes with irony, as does the biblically inspired "We kept her unmarried and she turned out to be pregnant."[10]

Anecdotes of this sort explore the gap separating the Byzantines from their less civilized neighbors. Ethnic stereotyping was familiar from Greek and Roman historians, who used satire to shape their own identities. Typical examples in late antiquity mention blood-drinking Arabs and treacherous Goths—perhaps significantly at the very time that both were being recruited as mercenaries. During the later Middle Ages the Latins were characterized as impetuous, undisciplined, drunken, and verbose, even while they were winning notable victories in the East. Similarly broad caricature distinguished the elites of the capital from their provincial inferiors. Armenians were said to be lazy and irresponsible, Cappadocians dim-witted, Paphlagonians ignorant. Recalling his time in Cyprus, the twelfth-century writer Constantine Manasses characterizes the islanders as slovenly, drunken, and reeking of garlic, even when attending church services.[11]

The conventions of humor also defined the boundaries of the family, the cornerstone of Byzantine society. One often-quoted medieval joke is especially revealing in this respect: A man runs up to a neighbor in the street and says to him, "Hey, your house is on fire!" "Don't worry," is the reply, "I've got the key." Set against the protective, inward orientation of the medieval household epitomized by Kekaumenos, the nonsensical retort becomes a warning to look to one's own concerns and stay out of others' affairs.[12]

TECHNOLOGY

As late as the twelfth century Byzantium was the most technologically sophisticated state in Europe, despite harboring attitudes to innovation that were conflicted and hesitant. Scholars knew the discoveries of Hellenistic and Roman scientists from scholarly treatises as well as surviving instruments and models. The principal works of authorities like Archimedes, Pliny, Ptolemy, and Vitruvius were studied by scientists and engineers, who often applied them in creative ways. Craftsmen made scientific equipment ranging from precision tools and surgical implements to astrolabes and sundials with complex gearing. Military leaders quickly grasped the possibilities of new weapons and adapted them for their purposes. Artisans, builders, and farmers refined their methods through observation and experimenting with materials at hand. It may seem surprising that this theoretical background did not lead to more dramatic practical breakthroughs. Orthodox Christianity generally discouraged cosmological speculation, but the structure of Byzantine society posed more significant constraints. Most farming and commerce was done on a family scale and not by profit-making corporations. Large and small households pursued the universal goal of self-sufficiency instead of developing specialized production. Unresolved difficulties of transportation limited the scale of local markets, which offered little incentive to boost yield through mechanization. In general, Byzantium's cautious approach to technological innovation reflects practical economic decisions and environmental factors as well as a deeply traditional social outlook.[13]

The routines of rural life saw few technological changes over the Byzantine millennium, with most farming prac-   **Agriculture** tices continued from Roman and earlier times. Tools were made locally of iron and wood, and were suitable for small-scale production. Farm operations were conditioned by the physical and social environment, which differed in several important respects from western Europe. Cultivators preferred the ox-drawn sole ard plow for tilling the soil rather than the deep mortarboard plow used in the West. Agricultural efficiency was slowed by the persistence of the traditional padded neck collar, which handicapped donkeys and horses pulling heavy loads. Only after the tenth century was a modified harness drawn around the breast rather than choking the neck. Grain was harvested with the hand sickle and not the long scythe. Cereals were threshed on small platforms and processed in mills powered by animals and water. The scale and efficiency of water-driven mills were limited by topography, since perennial rivers were found mainly in mountainous areas better suited to noncereal crops. Windmills were not adopted until the end of the Middle Ages.[14]

Byzantine military planners continued to employ time-tested Roman field technology while quickly adjusting   **Military** to the tactics and weaponry of their adversaries. By the   **Technology** seventh century the army had adopted the stirrup after the example of the Avars, a discovery with profound implications for western Europe as well. Alchemists in Constantinople were likely responsible for discovering the formula for incendiary weapons like Greek Fire, which made its debut in the seventh century. The medieval attribution of its discovery to a refugee engineer from Syria reflects the assumption, common to many cultures, that only nonspecialists equipped with outside knowledge can offer significant conceptual breakthroughs.[15] In the ninth century Leo the Mathematician built a chain of signal towers to relay quick messages between the capital and the Cilician frontier. Clashes with heavily armed Turkic armies prompted the development of armored cavalry in the tenth century. The crossbow and similar mechanical weapons were adopted after contact with the Latin Crusaders in the eleventh and twelfth centuries. Byzantium's failure to take up gunpowder and advanced artillery was the result of financial as well as ideological constraints.[16]

Transport by ship, especially over great distance, was a cheap and safe alternative to land travel. Large   **Transportation** sailing craft carried the bulk of commercial goods in late antiquity. Around the seventh century navigation changed significantly with the widespread introduction of the lateen sail, which gave sailors more flexibility when tacking into prevailing winds. Between the seventh and eleventh centuries ship builders moved from constructing mortise-jointed solid-hull vessels to using a skeletal frame to support a shell of overlapping planks. The result was a significant increase in the rate of production.[17]

Earlier technologies were left behind when they were no longer needed. Centuries-old methods of quarrying and moving huge stone blocks were essential to Constantinople's early development. In the late fourth century the eparch Proculus took 32 days to erect the 64-foot-tall obelisk of Thutmosis III in the hippodrome. Enormous freestanding columns stood along the Mese and in key public plazas. The eight colossal nave columns of Hagia Sophia were brought from Greece, while other large elements came from Egypt. Later architects concentrated on repairing earlier structures and reusing materials from abandoned buildings. No less than the classical countryside, medieval Constantinople offered a plentiful supply of marble spoils for new projects. Even the reception halls and throne rooms of the Great Palace were remodeled with recut marbles from the environs of the capital.

Engineering   Some of Byzantium's greatest technological triumphs survive in the monumental construction projects of late antiquity. Constantinople's early years saw the laying out of a vast urban infrastructure, with the longest aqueduct of the classical world, huge cisterns, and extensive harbors. The capital's water supply represents one of the most ambitious feats of surveying and engineering of preindustrial times. The fifth-century land walls included a forward moat, advance fortification, and main wall with over 90 towers and six gates spread over a length of three and a half miles. The building of Hagia Sophia remains a singular achievement. Designed by Anthemius of Tralles and Isidorus of Miletus, the structure employs vaults, pendentives, and domes on a grand scale to enclose an unprecedented interior space. Justinian's simultaneous construction of fortifications, roads, bridges, warehouses, and churches across the empire reflects considerable organizational effort in support of state programs.

Most technological innovation took place in Constantinople under imperial sponsorship. Practical and scientific instrumentation included the dioptra for land surveying and the astrolabe for celestial observation, both inventions of the Hellenistic period. The heliostat, as described by Anthemius of Tralles, was a device that could focus the rays of the sun throughout the day. Huge public sundials (*horologia*) could be seen in the capital and other large cities. Medieval visitors to the palace marveled at mechanical roaring lions and trees with twittering birds. Driven by hydraulic or pneumatic pressure, these elaborate automata continued a Hellenistic tradition pioneered by Hero of Alexandria.

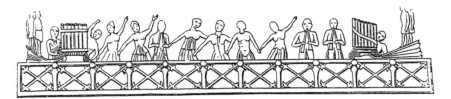

Dancing to the accompaniment of pipes and two pneumatic organs in the hippo-drome. Detail from the obelisk base of Theodosius. From *Annales archéologiques* 3 (1845).

Byzantine musical instruments, from the *aulos* and *syrinx* to the *kymbala* and *tympana*, were derived from classical Greek forms and are known mainly from drawings in medieval manuscripts. The most technologically sophisticated instrument was the pipe organ, which held a prominent place in court pageantry. It needed a set of tuned reeds or pipes, a steady supply of wind, and a way of directing this to individual pipes. These requirements had changed little since Ctesibios of Alexandria invented the *hydraulis* or water organ in the third century B.C. Hero of Alexandria recorded and refined the idea, adding an air pump to supply wind that was controlled by sliding bars to sound specific notes. Roman improvements included a set of hinged keys to operate the valves and multiple hand-worked bellows to maintain air pressure. Larger models produced plenty of sound, and the organ became a regular feature of public events, from banquets to street processions and chariot races in the hippodrome. Examples of such organs, with bellows worked by two attendants, are depicted on the base of the Egyptian obelisk that stood on the spina.

Musical Instruments

The pneumatic organ was a fixture of palace ceremony. One ninth-century author describes an organ that had 60 gilded pipes and was powered by three levers. In the mid-tenth century three separate organs served one large hall: a gold organ hailed the empress, and two silver ones played antiphonally when acclaiming the emperor. These were operated by pulling sliding bars instead of pressing keys, which clearly worked best when playing long, sustained notes. Two organs were sent as diplomatic gifts to the Frankish court in the eighth and ninth centuries. These stimulated Carolingian craftsmen to make their own versions, which are shown in contemporary manuscripts like the Utrecht Psalter. Here the organ is played by two men assisted by two more working the bellows, implying that the instrument was double-voiced.

SCIENCE

Greek science had flourished under the Ptolemaic kings, who supported intellectual centers across the east Mediterranean. During the first through fourth centuries Alexandria, with its famous library, was home to Hero, Ptolemy, Diophantos, Theon, Hypaetia, and other scholars; it remained the leading center for Byzantine medicine until the seventh century. Antioch and Beirut supported famous schools of philosophy. The Neoplatonic school of Plotinus in Athens was continued by Syrianus, Proclus, and others until the Academy was closed by Justinian in 529. Scholars from across the region were drawn to teach in Constantinople, where their studies were inevitably affected by church authorities. Some felt alienated by the growing religious conflicts of late antiquity, and decided that Persian Ctesiphon and Nisibis, and later Arab Baghdad, offered more hospitable places to work. Scholarship in the Byzantine capital flourished under imperial and patriarchal patronage during the ninth and tenth centuries. Almost the entire body of Greek science known today comes to us through new editions that were prepared around this time.

Science held an equivocal place in the minds of many people. Medieval scholars broadly respected the authority of Greek mathematics, geography, astronomy, and medicine, even while they struggled to interpret them within the intellectual outlook of Orthodox Christianity. Most scientific studies were based on a close reading of Plato and Aristotle, whose texts were seen as guides to fundamental natural laws. Scholars in a number of fields concentrated their efforts on producing thematic compilations of classical writing, drawn mainly from ancient sources but often with corrections and fresh observations. Byzantine science operated largely within this framework, respecting the teachings of antiquity while tinkering with the details. Interest in science was not limited to specialists. The well-read Michael Psellos wrote across the cultural spectrum, turning out studies of acoustics, medicinal foods, physics, and zoology as well as rhetoric and theology. Theodore Metochites, while serving as prime minister, authored treatises on astronomy and mathematics as well as volumes of poetry. George Pachymeres, a teacher of mathematics in the fourteenth-century capital, justified science as a subject of obvious interest to educated men.[18]

Mathematics and Geometry Advanced study of the mathematical sciences was based on classical Greek authorities like Archimedes and Diophantos. Mathematics may have been regarded not so much as a specialized field as one essential branch of scientific inquiry. A number of intellectuals wrote books about and taught mathematics in Constantinople. The builders of Hagia Sophia were well grounded in theoretical mathematics: Anthemius wrote treatises on geometry and conic sections, and Isidorus taught courses in stereometry and physics. One of the most accomplished figures of the ninth century was Leo the Mathematician. A physician, poet, and scholar, Leo directed the university reestablished by Bardas in the mid-ninth century. He assembled an impressive collection of mathematical, astronomical, and medical texts and wrote treatises on related topics. His chain of signal beacons spanned the width of Asia Minor, while within the palace he created trees with mechanical birds, roaring lions, and the emperor's fabled levitating throne. Today we can see in Leo's accomplishments the talents of a true renaissance man.[19] Centuries later George Pachymeres wrote textbooks on the four sciences of arithmetic, music, geometry, and astronomy. His late-medieval colleague Maximos Planoudes lectured on Euclid and put together a new edition of Diophantos's *Arithmetica*. In the empire's fading years Byzantine mathematicians took up the new Indian numerical system with its innovative use of zero, a revolutionary discovery that was not widely appreciated outside the academy.

Byzantine thinking about geography operated on two planes. On the practical level people knew how to get from **Geography** place to place, and routinely sent messages, goods, and troops by land and sea. Such travel was linear and purposeful, and was recorded by narrative itineraries. On the theoretical level most people viewed the visible world as the material embodiment of Orthodox theology, which placed Jerusalem squarely at the world's center. As with other scientific fields, the main challenge was to harmonize firsthand observation with biblical authority and Christian doctrine. Since the two views served different purposes, they usually coexisted in relative peace. In both cases the overriding interest in landscapes and the sea was literary, not spatial. Maps are rarely mentioned by Byzantine writers and may not have been widely used.

Systematic study of physical geography dates back to ancient Mesopotamia, where centuries of close observation of land and sky were recorded in diagrams and tables. Greek geographers built on this foundation and produced a series of maps sketching the relationship of major landmasses within a grid of latitude and longitude. It was widely acknowledged that the sun rises along the equator at the time of equinox, so anyone could determine latitude by subtracting the observed height of the sun above the horizon from 90 degrees. Problems with establishing longitude, by contrast, persisted into the early modern period. In the third century B.C. Eratosthenes was able to calculate the circumference of the earth with surprising accuracy. Hellenistic scholars generally conceived of the world as a spherical globe about which orbited the sun, planets, and constellations. Working in Alexandria in the second century, Claudius Ptolemy (ca. 90–175) summarized prevailing views of the world in the eight volumes of his monumental *Geography*.

The daily demands of running an empire led the Romans to develop great practical skill in surveying and mapping land. Army engineers used precision equipment to plan cities and divide the countryside among retired soldiers. The spatial relationship of settlements along roads became the foundation of descriptive travel guides, or *itineraria picta*. The most fully preserved example, the fifth-century Peutinger Table, locates about 4,000 places along the network of major highways. Narrative travel guides were especially helpful for pilgrims who wanted to visit the holy sites of the Near East, and these naturally emphasized key destinations like Jerusalem and Bethlehem. One of the only surviving maps of the period takes the form of a large mosaic floor in the mid-sixth-century church at Madaba in Palestine. The preserved mosaic depicts a number of regional cities, with Jerusalem appearing large and at the center.

A similar view is presented in the *Christian Topography,* a compilation of geography, travel stories, and fantastic folklore assembled by the sixth-century merchant from Antioch who wrote under the name of Cosmas Indikopleustes. Accompanying drawings present the earth as a vaulted chest, with the visible world occupying the lower levels and the heavens the canopy. Cosmas's basic scheme dates back to the so-called T-O map of the first century B.C., which located the Mediterranean at its center surrounded by Europe, Asia, and Africa. An outer ocean separated these three known continents from more distant, legendary places, like Britain to the west and India, China, and Paradise to the east.

For most of the Middle Ages the study of geography was based on the descriptive works of Strabo and Pausanias, and consisted mainly of lists of place-names, sometimes combined with local legends, miracles, and oracles. Ptolemy's *Geography* remained largely unread by Byzantine scholars, who were more interested in his astronomical writings. Theoretical geography was actively pursued by Arab geographers, who knew of Ptolemy as well as Strabo. Arab writings may have encouraged Maximos Planoudes to reconstruct Ptolemy's Greek text in the late thirteenth century. At least three illustrated copies of the *Geography* were made around this time, and the text was translated into Latin in 1406. Several surviving fifteenth-century maps probably drew upon lost Byzantine originals.[20]

Astronomy and Astrology
Since earliest times humans have looked to the skies for help in understanding the universe and themselves. By the second millennium B.C. Babylonian observers were tracking the moon and stars on their regular paths along the horizon. Early astronomers were practical people who were mainly interested in marking seasons and predicting the weather. From this it was not a big step to arranging important events to take place amid optimal celestial conditions, or discovering that the planets and stars might somehow influence the course of future events. Such views became widespread during the Hellenistic period and profoundly affected classical religion and science. The belief in *apotelesmatics,* or the influence of the stars on human lives, prompted Augustus and other Roman emperors to consult astrologers when they made policies and planned campaigns. The best-known practitioner of the art was Ptolemy, whose fundamental treatises on astronomy and astrology were familiar to Byzantine scholars. Of course Christian leaders strongly defended the concepts of personal morality and free will against astrological claims. Their rise to power in the fourth century effectively ended public support for astrology and serious astronomy

as well, which was thought to have few practical benefits. Interest in the stars survived mainly in the shadows of popular belief.

The scientific study of astronomy languished through much of the medieval period. Knowledge was based almost entirely on Ptolemy's *Amalgest*, which was republished in Constantinople in a number of illustrated editions. Apart from the sun and moon, the most prominent celestial features were the five known planets: Mercury, Venus, Mars, Jupiter, and Saturn. The 48 constellations listed by Ptolemy include the 12 clusters of the zodiac, 21 northern constellations, and 15 southern constellations. Byzantine astronomers combined close observation of the movement of the stars with advanced geometric calculations. Several sources describe the operation of the astrolabe, an instrument devised by Ptolemy for measuring the altitude of the stars and telling time; at least one example in bronze has survived from the eleventh century. Serious work in astronomy likely was limited to scholars working in Constantinople, where it enjoyed surging interest in the fourteenth and fifteenth centuries. Persian and Arab astronomical tables began to reach the capital around this time and soon were recognized as significant improvements over classical authorities. Better instruments were made for observation. Fresh scholarly treatises were produced, including a new introduction to astronomy written by Theodore Metochites. Other works were translated from Latin and Hebrew editions.

Popular knowledge of astronomy appears above all in the sequence of the seasons and the 12 constellations. The zodiac was a familiar concept in Roman times and often appeared in mosaic floors, calendars, and books. Church leaders discouraged study of classical mythology, astrology, and other forms of divination, which left little room for the zodiac in visual culture. The constellations appear in an eighth-century manuscript edition of Ptolemy, and another version was built into the marble-paved floor of the Pantokrator monastery around 1130. Memorable in its own way was a cake into which were baked the 12 symbols of the zodiac along with 18 eggs representing other celestial features. These three unusual examples only underscore the zodiac's general absence from the arts.[21]

Astrology, or the divination of future events by studying the planets and stars, was of equal antiquity and more persistent interest in Byzantium. Horoscopes based on careful astronomical observation were prepared in Babylon as early as the fifth century B.C. Greek astronomers, especially Aristarchos of Samos and Ptolemy, extended this work by producing a series of predictive tables. The heliocentric system that formed the basis of these tables allowed Theon and others to predict solar and lunar eclipses, terrestrial weather, and other phenomena. Such seeming prescience readily expanded to include powers of divination that explored the effects of planets and constellations on individual lives. One of the last astrologers of late antiquity, John the Lydian (ca. 490–565) came from Philadelphia in western Asia Minor. State and church sought to counter popular credulity, yet it persisted throughout Roman and Byzantine times. Medieval astrologers cast elaborate horoscopes based on the aspects of ruling planets and the positions of constellations on the horizon. Michael Psellos was familiar with eleventh-century astrology but expressed reservations about its validity. Anna Komnene, having once dabbled in the practice, criticizes astrologers for diverting "most of the more simple-minded from their faith in God to a blind belief in the influence of the stars."[22]

MEDICINE AND HEALTH CARE

Medical knowledge and practices reflect both classical Greek scientific theories and prevailing popular views, which encompassed elements of astrology, demonology, folklore, and magic. Most classical treatises and handbooks are known only by compilations assembled during the Middle Ages and ultimately translated into Arabic and Latin. Historical chronicles document the availability of specialized medical care among the upper classes as well as the respect generally given Byzantine doctors. Saints' lives, guidebooks, and vernacular sources provide glimpses of the more limited medical resources and alternative therapies available to most sufferers. Medical saints were frequently depicted holding a box or satchel full of medicines and surgical instruments. Many sources record a basic tension between the roles of medical practice and religious belief in the healing process. Other writers express suspicions that doctors were greedy promoters of ineffective cures who took advantage of the misery of others.

Medical knowledge rested on the essential works of Hippocrates, who lived in the fifth to fourth centuries B.C., and Galen of Pergamon (129–ca. 210), a Greek doctor who wrote a series of theoretical treatises and practical manuals. Both authors were summarized in the great medical encyclopedia *(Synagogai)* drawn up by Oribasius of Pergamon (ca. 325–400). Later authorities built on this foundation by supplementing classical sources with fresh observations and commentary on the effectiveness of specific remedies. Medical texts often present keen insights and discoveries. The military importance of mounted troops encouraged the development of veterinary medicine, with specific treatises written on the treatment of dogs and especially horses.[23]

Awareness of beneficial and toxic properties of natural materials was an important part of classical culture with which Byzantine doctors were quite familiar. The medicinal uses of plants were known from the writings of Theophrastos (late fourth century B.C.), Dioscorides Pedanios of Anazarbos (flourished ca. 40–80), and other early authors. The *Materials of Medicine (De materia medica)* of Dioscorides is the best known of these pharmacological treatises. This is a detailed guide to the medicinal uses of plants, animals, and minerals commonly found around the Mediterranean.

In five systematic chapters the author carefully describes hundreds of individual specimens and explains how to use them in treating various ailments. The root of the common violet *(Viola odorata)*, for example, is said to have cooling properties for treating a burning stomach or inflammations of the eye. The myosotis or "mouse-ear" plant (*Lithospermum purpureo-coeruleum*, related to the forget-me-not) was recommended for more serious eye wounds. The tiny seeds of the cultivated poppy *(Papaver somniferum)* can substitute for sesame when baking breads and pastries; the extract (latex) of wild poppies, crushed and mixed with honey and water, eases pain and induces sleep, yet is lethal if too much is consumed. The narcotic properties of the mandrake root (six species, including *Mandragora officinarum*) were famous: this reliable anesthetic can also be used as a purgative or emetic agent, and appears in countless folk remedies treating allergies, asthma, and headaches. The huge impact Dioscorides had on medieval medicine is clear from the many editions copied by Byzantine, Arab, and Latin hands. Many of these, like the luxury editions today in New York, Paris, and Vienna, include startlingly beautiful botanical illustrations. Such reference works clearly were intended for an aristocratic clientele, but they reflect a broad current of plant lore that ran throughout medieval society.[24]

Professional schooling entailed a period of apprenticeship combined with attending lectures of medical professors *(iatroso-phistes)*. Alexandria was the most prestigious center for training **Medical Training** doctors and attracted students from across the Mediterranean, from Ptolemaic times down to the seventh century. The standard curriculum lasted about four years and covered the basic works of Hippocrates and Galen. This gave aspiring doctors a broad grounding in anatomy, physiology, etiology, diagnostics, and therapeutics. Significantly lacking was specialty training in obstetrics and pediatrics, which were left to midwives and laywomen. Nor was dentistry considered a separate discipline, despite discussion of afflictions and treatment of gums and teeth by medical writers. Later students relied heavily on the works of Oribasius, Aetius of Amida (sixth century), and Alexander of Tralles (ca. 525–605), who composed his *Twelve Books on Medicine* in the mid-sixth century. Aetius follows earlier writers in stressing the importance of hygiene and sanitation. Drawing on a lifetime of practical experience, Alexander critically reviews classical medical theory and outlines the treatments found most effective in his practice. He stresses that as a general rule the therapeutic benefits of diet and hygiene are preferable to treatment with drugs. Always central to his approach was the importance of maintaining the patient's comfort, and Alexander concedes the usefulness of amulets, charms, and folk remedies if they are believed to work.

The most important institution in Byzantine health care was the hospital, which developed from its origins as a late-antique **Hospitals** charitable foundation to become a key feature of urban life. The earliest *xenones* were guesthouses located amid fresh air and water near

The "mouse-ear" plant for treating afflictions of the eye, illustrated in an eighth-century edition of Dioscorides' *De materia medica*. Photo courtesy of the Bibliothèque nationale de France, Paris (ms. grec 2179).

thermal springs, places long associated with healing cults. Under church sponsorship such facilities came to play a valued role in the care of the poor, sick, and elderly. In the early fifth century several cities are known to have had a treatment center *(nosokomeion)* with priests, doctors, cooks, and other support staff. By the seventh century several xenones had been built in Constantinople and were recognized as the main sites of medical care. All of these places were administered by clergymen but were staffed by physicians with various specialties. Doctors normally divided their time between providing subsidized health services for hospital residents and caring for private patients. Physicians at the Christodotes hospital followed a monthly rotation of shifts. The clearest picture of an urban hospital's operation is the

Physician treating a dislocated shoulder, in a tenth-century edition of the *Articulations* by Apollonius of Kition. Photo courtesy of the Biblioteca Laurenziana, Florence (cod. Plut. 74.7).

xenon attached to the Pantokrator monastery in Constantinople. Founded by the emperor John II Komnenos and his wife, Irene, the complex featured a walk-in clinic for treating minor injuries and ailments. More serious cases led to admission by attending physicians, who prescribed a course of treatment. Nurses and medical assistants helped doctors carry out minor procedures and handed out medicines. Women were cared for by a female physician *(iatraina)*, who was supervised by two (better-paid) male doctors. Female nurses, midwives, and other assistants were assigned to the women's ward. A further responsibility of the medical staff was to train their children to follow them into the field of medicine.[25]

Several Byzantine sources document the practice of surgery. One commonly used handbook was the *Epitome of Medicine*, written by Paul of Aegina in the mid-seventh century. Drawing

Surgery

heavily on classical treatises, Paul surveys over a hundred surgical procedures as well as the instruments needed to perform them. Common operations include hernia repair, removal of bladder stones, and amputations. Like accidental wounds, incisions were cauterized by applying either heated instruments or pharmacological mixtures. Later written sources were less detailed, implying that surgery may have become less routine with time, at least outside Constantinople. Autopsies and dissections continued to be widely performed. Excavations in Greece, Egypt, and elsewhere have recovered forceps, probes, scalpels, chisels, bifurcated tools, and other surgical implements. Most were made of bronze and finely finished. Written sources suggest that basic instrument shapes remained essentially unchanged through the end of the Middle Ages.

Public Health   Health concerns in large cities focused on maintaining sanitation and a safe water supply, especially during the warm summer months. Among the most serious challenges were recurring outbreaks of epidemic disease. The great plague *(loimos)* of the mid-sixth century may have originated in east Africa and in 541 arrived in Egypt, from which it spread rapidly across the empire. Cities were depopulated and entire villages wiped out in its wake. Contemporary observers like Procopius and John of Ephesus describe how corpses were left in streets and plazas before being dumped in plague pits or at sea. Constantinople's population may have been reduced by half around this time. The plague subsided by 545 but recurred throughout the Near East through the mid-eighth century. Centuries later the Black Death swept out of Asia, devastating the capital in 1348–49 before continuing on to western Europe. Mortality estimates are uncertain, but both of these great pandemics clearly reduced the empire's human resources and left it seriously weakened.[26]

More pervasive health problems were apparent everywhere, especially among the lower social levels, and often were addressed by miraculous means. The average life expectancy of 35 to 40 years for men (somewhat less for women) stems in part from shortcomings of the prevailing diet. From the beginning Greek writers had differentiated foods with positive or negative effects on vitality and health. Medieval dietary guidelines drawn up by Michael Psellos and Symeon Seth *(Lexikon on the Properties of Food)* recommend the salubrious foods, seasonings, and cooking methods for different times of year. In more basic terms of quantity, food production suffered from recurring drought, floods, hail, insect pests, and political instability. Difficulties of transport and storage led to shortages and famine, especially when grain supplies dwindled toward spring. Saints' lives regularly mention the aid of supernatural intercessors during such critical times.

Spiritual Healing   Spiritual means offered an important course of treatment throughout the Middle Ages. Physicians could treat some injuries and wounds, but other afflictions—particularly those caused by incorrect belief—could only be dealt with by

Fifth- or sixth-century bronze amulet with the Crucifixion. On the reverse is the "holy rider," a pre-Christian image associated with healing and guarding against evil. Photo courtesy of the Museum of Art and Archaeology, University of Missouri–Columbia.

miraculous methods. Many people trusted in the effectiveness of medical amulets *(phylakteria)*. These small tokens, usually made of bronze or terra-cotta, were carried in one's pocket or worn around the neck. Each amulet included an image or written invocation of proven effectiveness in treating certain ailments. Different types of amulets calmed digestive disorders, stopped persistent hemorrhages, healed broken limbs, and ensured restful sleep. Women often wore amulets throughout their pregnancy to protect their child and ease delivery.

A number of well-known saints dealt with the same essential concerns. Residents of medieval Constantinople visited the shrine of Saint Therapon seeking aid for various afflictions. Saint Artemios specialized in treating hernias and genital disorders. The fourth-century saint Panteleimon (feast day celebrated July 27) used the name of Christ to treat those possessed by demons. Healing saints like Cosmas and Damian (feast day October 17) were known as *anargyroi* ("silverless ones") since they had worked cures without charge. Remedies often involved incubation, during which a patient slept near a sacred site or tomb; after purification and prayers, the patient was visited by the saint in a dream. Medieval writers sometimes referred to these treatments as visiting the "free hospital." Saints' lives routinely stress the superiority of saintly doctors to medical workers. The eighth-century *Miracles of Saint Artemios* criticizes physicians for their moral and medical failings. That saints also had recourse to magical means is underscored by the story of Theodore, a seventh-century Cypriot doctor who was paralyzed by sorcery. The healing saints Cyrus and John appeared to Theodore in a dream, prescribed a course of treatment (an ointment made of roasted pig lungs mixed with wine), and revealed that the cause of his affliction was a charm buried by a malefactor beneath the threshold of his room.[27]

MAGIC AND THE SUPERNATURAL

Beneath the level of orthodox thought ran a current of popular belief that continued traditional views of the world and how to deal with it. Research in social anthropology has shown that the need for magicians, miracle workers, and witches reflects deep-seated tensions as people seek to make sense of their existence, particularly when confronting inexplicable loss, misfortune, and death. Byzantine saints' lives attest a deep stratum of magic that pervaded everyday experiences, with charms, curses, spells, and potions regularly employed for both good and bad purposes. The supernatural power of words could be invoked by summing the numerical value of their letters: 535 invoked the lord *(Kyrie)*, while 99 offered *amen*. An apple with a Bible verse written on it could extend the life of a cask of wine or restore a spoiled barrel. Like conventional prayers, many of these invocations accompanied protective amulets, relics, and other material tokens that were credited with special powers.[28]

Byzantine writers, like Romans before them, distinguished several levels of magic. At the high end was exotic sorcery, a learned craft practiced by a male elite steeped in books of great antiquity. The notoriety of such mystical powers was widespread. In the first century Pliny the Elder wrote that "there is no one who is not afraid of becoming the object of lethal spells."[29] The most frequent accusations of medieval sorcery occurred among the educated, affluent urban classes, primarily against men and especially during the upheavals of the eighth and ninth centuries. The less esoteric female counterpart to sorcery was witchcraft. Unlike the more abstract and scholarly magical arts, witchcraft reflected the covert knowledge of women who were able to advise and intervene in matters of health, similarly for good or ill. There also existed a broad current of folk belief in oral traditions, agrarian cycles, and common superstitions.

Official attitudes to magic were ambiguous and inconsistent. Church teaching viewed the powers of sorcerers as illusory; after all, had not Christ vanquished the demonic forces by his resurrection? In this view the magical arts were only a delusion that was perpetuated by the devil. All the same, frequent attacks on the validity of supernatural powers reflected lingering worries about their effectiveness. Church leaders did not so much contest the existence of such shadowy powers as condemn their use for evil purposes.[30]

The boundary between conventional and heterodox appeals for supernatural aid could be hard to draw, especially for a sufferer desperate for relief from injury or disease. Protective and healing spells were among the most frequent magical appeals and were combined with charms and potions. Ritual spell books include folk remedies and incantations for treating afflictions ranging from headaches and eye diseases to colic and gout. Other common spells relieved fever, induced sleep, provided protection from snakebite, and eased the pain of childbirth. Miracle-working icons and relics were seen as more powerful means of supernatural healing, and were preferred to medicine by many people.

Hundreds of surviving phylakteria, invocations, votives, and written sources attest the intimate involvement of magic in daily life. Apotropaic symbols could reinforce a city's walls or defend one's home against the evil eye, the gaze of envious neighbors. Charmed images—lunar crescents, concentric circles, geometric shapes, pentalpha stars, knotted cords, serpents—were incorporated in belt buckles, pins, clothing patterns, and personal talismans. Such hopeful, protective objects were usually modest and personal.[31]

Most magical texts originally took the form of inscribed lead tablets or small rolls of papyrus. Often fragmentary, these documents preserve the urgency of intimate, furtively expressed concerns. Worried men and women ask for supernatural help in recovering a lost vessel, ensuring a successful fishing expedition, or developing a better singing voice. Protection is sought against threats both diabolic and domestic, from evil spirits and headless powers to reptiles and household vermin. The abundance of curses attests the cutthroat competition of business and politics: "O lord, master of the earth, avenge me on the one who opposes me and on the one who has driven me from my place, and pay him back at once, lord, so that he may fall into hands harsher than his own." Other spells reflect the timeless tensions found in any community: to afflict an enemy with multiple diseases, or to alienate the affections of a son's newfound female companion. A prayer to silence a watchdog may reflect advance planning for a domestic burglary.

Magical spells often deal with sex. Erotic binding charms were intended to attract the devotion of a love interest: "I adjure [you by] your names and your powers and your amulets" so that by eating this food "you may give her desire for me, and she may desire me with endless desire and come to me in the place where I am, and I may lay my breast upon her and satisfy all my desire with her, and she may satisfy all my desire, right now, right now, at once, at once!" Conversely, women cast graphic curses to render certain men impotent and protect themselves from unwanted advances. Ritual compilations or "cookbooks" give recipes for making potions of mixed oils, ground minerals, herbs, spices, and animal parts.

Curses and spells might require making a clay or wax figurine, which would be bound or pierced and then buried or destroyed. Other sources direct the supplicant to copy a formula in menstrual blood on a tile or potsherd and then sleep near it, cast it into a fire, or bury it at a crossroad.[32]

Naturally many women looked to magic in negotiating life transitions like marriage, childbirth, and death. Charms and potions could help in choosing a mate or ensuring his fidelity. Reproductive health was understandably the focus of most female lives, whether conceiving a child, determining the sex of one's offspring, surviving delivery, or avoiding another pregnancy. Magic was one of the few ways one could address these concerns. One of the most feared of all medieval demons was Gylou, that half-female, half-serpent monster who caused miscarriages and strangled newborn infants. Women assumed a central role when there was a death in the family, washing and preparing the body for burial, leading the mourning, and reorganizing the family structure. Many of these practices still survive in traditional Balkan and Mediterranean societies. In western Europe such folk customs frequently led to accusations of witchcraft, which can be understood as a way of relieving social pressures. The comparative rarity of such charges in Byzantium suggests that beliefs in folk magic and ritual had their own, tacitly accepted place in the Eastern worldview.[33]

Divination and Dreams Foretelling the future was a useful skill of great antiquity. All ancient cultures knew some form of divination, whether by watching the skies, tracking flights of birds, reading tea leaves or barley grains, casting dice, or drawing lots. Augury, which involved studying the entrails of ritually killed animals, was condemned by early Christian authors as blood sacrifice and contrary to teachings of free will, and yet imperial tradition led Constantine to consult augurs or *haruspices* when founding his new capital. In the medieval city one could turn to foreign soothsayers, clairvoyant animals, or even ancient statues for advice about the future. A trained midwife might be asked to glimpse the future of a newborn in the placenta. Reading a *brontologion* helped one understand such portents as thunder, lightning, and comets. Diviners of every generation claimed to be able to consult dead spirits or arouse demons for mischievous ends. Churchmen and other educated people looked down on practitioners of the dark arts, whom they grouped with actors, musicians, wrestlers, public performers, and members of the lower social levels.

For many people books offered a promising way of foretelling the future. A favorite source of advice in late antiquity was a form of bibliomancy known as the "Virgilian oracle." One took a bound copy of the *Aeneid*, opened it at random, and arbitrarily choose a verse to read. The Bible served as a similar object of divine interrogation throughout the medieval period. Augustine (354–430) recounts that his own conversion to Christianity came about as the result such a consultation. Following the example of Antony before him, he joined a friend, where "I had put down the book of the apostle when I got up. I seized it, opened it, and in silence read the first passage on which my eyes lit: 'Not in riots and drunken parties, not in eroticism and indecencies, not in strife and rivalry, but put on the Lord Jesus Christ and make no provision for the flesh in its lusts' (Romans 13:13–14)."[34] Oracular lots, known in western Europe as the "lots of the saints" *(sortes sanctorum)*, were drawn for advice. As was the case when dealing with classical oracles, the response involved thoughtful interpretation: "This will not happen now; rather, it will happen in a little while." "The lord will lessen the ordeal that has come upon you. Only believe and you will be delivered from [it]." And the ever-helpful caveat: "Reject [those who] advise you. Their counsel is empty and very bad."[35]

The uneasy relationship of magic and religion is clear in attitudes to dreams. Byzantine intellectuals knew that classical writers held conflicting views about the shadowy dream world. Commentators since the time of Herodotus had criticized as irrational and unreliable the practice of interpreting dreams, usually dismissing it as a form of divination. By contrast, Plato, the Stoics, and philosophers of later antiquity were less skeptical of the possibility that one could glimpse higher realities through extra-sensory, dream-time perception. As with astrology and medicine, official attitudes to the practice of dream interpretation *(oneiromancy)* ranged from vehement suppression to guarded interest. In the sixth century Justinian issued a ban on professional dream interpreters, but 400 years later emperors were carrying dream books with them while on campaign. In fact, the practice of dream interpretation was never expressly forbidden by the church. Biblical prophets like Joseph and Daniel were good precedents for understanding dreams as divinely inspired visions, and this was the way Constantine had received his message of Christian triumph. Dreams and personal visions were recorded regularly in saints' lives. Ailing patients were visited by healing saints while sleeping at their shrines.

While most ancient authorities believed dreams depended on the individual, Byzantine dream books present some images as universally valid. Gardens and fruit are associated with fertility, walls with strength and security, wild animals with threatening enemies, broken vessels with impending disaster. Fine clothes indicate future happiness or the birth of a male heir; a frayed cloak or *chlamys*, by contrast, means trouble ahead. Sexuality, strictly regulated by social norms, is likely to surface in the course of dreams. The general consensus is that dreams originate in the innermost soul, and depending on one's spiritual state reflect either the voice of God or the influence of demons. In this light it is unsurprising to find people commonly resorting to amulets and charms to protect themselves while sleeping and safeguard their dreams. Like all aspects of Byzantine culture, the fluid boundary between waking and dreaming, the material and the spiritual, the visible and the hoped for, reflects the immanence of the divine in the world of everyday.[36]

NOTES

1. For the classical background see H.I. Marrou, *A History of Education in Antiquity* (Madison: University of Wisconsin Press, 1982); and compare Roy Joseph Deferrai and Martin R.P. McGuire, trans., *Saint Basil: The Letters* (Cambridge: Harvard University Press, 1934), 4:395.

2. See late Roman attitudes in Barry Baldwin, *The Philogelos or Laughter-Lover* (Amsterdam: Adolf M. Hakkert, 1983); brought up to date in the twelfth-century poems attributed to Theodore Prodromos, for example "Cursed be Learning," in *The Penguin Book of Greek Verse*, ed. Constantine A. Trypanis (Harmondsworth, England: Penguin Books, 1971), 442–44; and Margaret Alexiou, "The Poverty of Écriture and the Craft of Writing," *Byzantine and Modern Greek Studies* 10 (1986): 1–40.

3. For higher education see N.G. Wilson, *Scholars of Byzantium* (Baltimore: Johns Hopkins University Press, 1983).

4. Margaret E. Mullett, "Byzantium: A Friendly Society?" *Past and Present* 118 (1988): 3–24; George T. Dennis, "The Byzantines as Revealed in Their Letters," in *Gonimos: Neoplatonic and Byzantine Studies Presented to Leendert G. Westerink at 75*, ed. John Duffy and John Peradotto (Buffalo: State University of New York, Department of Classics, 1988), 155–65, for Kydones see 160.

5. Two well-illustrated guides to the subject are Gary Vikan and John Nesbitt, *Security in Byzantium* (Washington, D.C.: Dumbarton Oaks, 1980); and Nicolas Oikonomides, *Byzantine Lead Seals* (Washington, D.C.: Dumbarton Oaks, 1985).

6. Kekaumenos is quoted in Charlotte Rouché, "Byzantine Writers and Readers: Storytelling in the Eleventh Century," in *The Greek Novel, AD 1–1985*, ed. Roderick Beaton (London: Croom Helm, 1988), 123–33, at 125. See in general Nigel G. Wilson, "Books and Readers in Byzantium," in *Byzantine Books and Bookmen* (Washington, D.C.: Dumbarton Oaks, 1975), 1–15.

7. Deferrai and McGuire, *Saint Basil: The Letters*, 4:393; and Deno John Geanakoplos, *Byzantium: Church, Society, and Civilization Seen through Contemporary Eyes* (Chicago: University of Chicago Press, 1984), 393–94. Photios's postscript to his *Bibliotheka* is quoted by Cyril Mango, "The Availability of Books in the Byzantine Empire, A.D. 750–850," in *Byzantine Books and Bookmen*, 29–45, at 39.

8. Mango, "The Availability of Books"; Speros Vryonis, "The Will of a Provincial Magnate, Eustathius Boilas (1059)," *Dumbarton Oaks Papers* 11 (1957): 263–77. For the collection of Attaleiates see his typikon in John Thomas and Angela Constantinides Hero, eds., *Byzantine Monastic Foundation Documents* (Washington, D.C.: Dumbarton Oaks, 2000), 1:326–76.

9. Alexiou, "The Poverty of Écriture." Nick Nicholas and George Baloglou, trans., *An Entertaining Tale of Quadrupeds* (New York: Columbia University Press, 2003), offers a lively translation and much information about Greek life, beliefs, and expressions at the end of the Middle Ages.

10. These and more of similar quality are in Baldwin, *The Philogelos*; Julian, a fifth-century prefect in Egypt, in *The Greek Anthology*, vol. 3, trans. W.R. Paton (New York: G.P. Putnam's Sons, 1917), 9.654. For the cultural context of medieval sayings see Michael Angold, *Church and Society in Byzantium under the Comneni, 1081–1261* (Cambridge: Cambridge University Press, 1995), 460–64.

11. For stereotyping see Anna Komnene, *Alexiad*, trans. E.R.A. Sewter (as *The Alexiad of Anna Comnena*) (Harmondsworth, England: Penguin Classics, 1969), 10.9.3; Constantine Manasses, "Journey to Jerusalem," in *Sources for the History of*

Cyprus VII: Greek Texts of the Fourth to Thirteenth Centuries, ed. Hans A. Pohlsander (Albany, N.Y.: Greece and Cyprus Research Center, 1999), 4.95–108; and in general John Haldon, "Humour and the Everyday in Byzantium," in *Humour, History and Politics in Late Antiquity and the Early Middle Ages*, ed. Guy Halsall (Cambridge: Cambridge University Press, 2002), 48–71.

12. Haldon, "Humour and the Everyday," 64. Compare the attitude of Kekaumenos quoted in Geanakoplos, *Byzantium*, 236–37.

13. G.E.R. Lloyd, *Greek Science after Aristotle* (London: Chatto and Windus, 1973). The subject is surveyed by K. Vogel, "Byzantine Technology," in *The Cambridge Medieval History*, vol. 4, *The Byzantine Empire*, pt. 2, *Government, Church and Civilization*, ed. Joan M. Hussey (Cambridge: Cambridge University Press, 1966–67), 299–305. For the classical background see K.D. White, *Greek and Roman Technology* (Ithaca, N.Y.: Cornell University Press, 1984); John G. Landels, "Engineering," in *Civilization of the Ancient Mediterranean: Greece and Rome*, ed. Michael Grant and Rachel Kitzinger (New York: Charles Scribner's Sons, 1988), 1:323–52; and Peter James and Nick Thorpe, *Ancient Inventions* (New York: Ballantine Books, 1994).

14. Anthony Bryer, "The Means of Agricultural Production: Muscle and Tools," in *The Economic History of Byzantium from the Seventh to the Fifth Century*, ed. Angeliki E. Laiou (Washington, D.C.: Dumbarton Oaks, 2002), 1:101–13. See further discussion in chapter 6.

15. J. R. Partington, *A History of Greek Fire and Gunpowder* (Cambridge: Cambridge University Press, 1960), 13. The story of the Hungarian engineer Urban, who sold his cannon-building expertise to Mehmet II after first offering it to the Byzantines, is in the same spirit.

16. See chapter 7.

17. Ships and their construction are discussed in chapter 5.

18. For a broadly conceived survey see K. Vogel, "Byzantine Science," in Hussey, *Cambridge Medieval History*, vol. 4, pt. 2, 264–305; and in general Wilson, *Scholars of Byzantium*. For the late period, Edmund Fryde, *The Early Palaeologan Renaissance (1261-c. 1360)* (Leiden, the Netherlands: Brill, 2000), 337–56.

19. Medieval descriptions of Theophilos's palace furnishings are in Cyril Mango, *Art of the Byzantine Empire, 312–1453* (Englewood Cliffs, N.J.: Prentice Hall, 1972; reprint, Toronto: Medieval Academy Reprints for Teaching, 1986), 160–65; and James Trilling, "Daedalus and the Nightingale: Art and Technology in the Myth of the Byzantine Court," in *Byzantine Court Culture from 829 to 1204*, ed. Henry Maguire (Washington, D.C.: Dumbarton Oaks, 1997), 217–30.

20. The slight evidence for Byzantine mapmaking is summarized by O.A.W. Dilke, "Cartography in the Byzantine Empire," in *The History of Cartography*, vol. 1, *Cartography in Prehistoric, Ancient and Medieval Europe and the Mediterranean*, ed. J.B. Harley and David Woodward (Chicago: University of Chicago Press, 1987), 258–75.

21. For the baked Zodiac as celebrated by a contemporary, see Paul Magdalino, "Cosmological Confectionery and Equal Opportunity in the Eleventh Century. An Ekphrasis by Christoper of Mitylene (Poem 42)," in *Byzantine Authors: Literary Activities and Preoccupations*, ed. John W. Nesbitt (Leiden, the Netherlands: Brill, 2003), 1–6.

22. Michael Psellos, *Chronographia*, trans. E.R.A. Sewter (as *Michael Psellus, Fourteen Byzantine Rulers*) (Harmondsworth, England: Penguin Classics, 1966),

5.19–20; Anna Komnene, trans., Sewter, *Alexiad* 6–7; Geanakoplos, *Byzantium*, 438–39. For background see Tamsyn Barton, *Ancient Astrology* (New York: Routledge, 1994); and Peter Whitfield, *Astrology: A History* (New York: Harry N. Abrams, 2001).

23. See John Scarborough, ed., *Symposium on Byzantine Medicine* (*Dumbarton Oaks Papers* 38, 1984). For comparison with western Europe see Katharine Park, "Medicine and Society in Medieval Europe, 500–1500," in *Medicine in Society*, ed. Andrew Wear (Cambridge: Cambridge University Press, 1992), 52–90; and Vivian Nutton, "Medicine in Late Antiquity and the Early Middle Ages," in *The Western Medical Tradition: 800 BC to AD 1800*, by Lawrence I. Conrad et al. (Cambridge: Cambridge University Press, 1995), 71–87.

24. Dioscorides, *De materia medica* 2.214, 4.65, adapted from an accessible older edition by Robert T. Gunther, *The Greek Herbal of Dioscorides* (New York: Hafner Publishing, 1968). For a detailed assessment see John M. Riddle, *Dioscorides on Pharmacy and Medicine* (Austin: University of Texas Press, 1985).

25. Timothy S. Miller, *The Birth of the Hospital in the Byzantine Empire* (Baltimore: John Hopkins University Press, 1997).

26. P. Allen, "The 'Justinianic' Plague," *Byzantion* 49 (1979): 5–20. For a vivid account of the plague and speculation about possible causes see David Keys, *Catastrophe: An Investigation into the Origins of the Modern World* (New York: Ballantine Books, 2000).

27. See Virgil S. Crisafulli, trans., *The Miracles of St. Artemios: A Collection of Miracle Stories by an Anonymous Author of Seventh-Century Byzantium* (Leiden, the Netherlands: Brill, 1997); and Matthew W. Dickie, *Magic and Magicians in the Greco-Roman World* (New York: Routledge, 2001), 293.

28. For popular beliefs see Peter Brown, "Sorcery, Demons, and the Rise of Christianity from Late Antiquity into the Middle Ages," in *Witchcraft Confessions and Accusations*, ed. Mary Douglas (New York: Tavistock Publications, 1970), 17–45; Dorothy de F. Abrahamse, "Magic and Sorcery in the Hagiography of the Middle Byzantine Period," *Byzantinische Forschungen* 8 (1982): 3–17; and Henry Maguire, ed., *Byzantine Magic* (Washington, D.C.: Dumbarton Oaks, 1995).

29. Pliny the Elder, *Natural History*, trans. H. Rackham, W.H.S. Jones, and D. E. Eichholz (Cambridge: Harvard University Press, 1938–62), 28.4.9 (trans., Jones).

30. See Richard Greenfield, "Sorcery and Politics at the Byzantine Court in the Twelfth Century: Interpretations of History," in *The Making of Byzantine History: Studies Dedicated to Donald M. Nicol*, ed. Roderick Beaton and Charlotte Roueché (Aldershot, England: Variorum, 1993), 73–85.

31. For common means of supernatural healing see Gary Vikan, "Art, Medicine, and Magic in Early Byzantium," *Dumbarton Oaks Papers* 38 (1984): 65–86. Further examples are in Eunice Dauterman Maguire, Henry P. Maguire, and Maggie J. Duncan-Flowers, *Art and Holy Powers in the Early Christian House* (Urbana: University of Illinois Press, 1989); and Maguire, *Byzantine Magic*.

32. These and other examples are in Hans Dieter Betz, ed., *The Greek Magical Papyri in Translation*, 2nd ed. (Chicago: University of Chicago Press, 1992); and Marvin Meyer and Richard Smith, eds., *Ancient Christian Magic: Coptic Texts of Ritual Power* (Princeton, N.J.: Princeton University Press, 1999), with the spells quoted here at 51 and 161.

33. For traditional views see Richard Blum and Eva Blum, *The Dangerous Hour: The Lore of Crisis and Mystery in Rural Greece* (London: Chatto and Windus,

1970); and Margaret Alexiou, *After Antiquity: Greek Language, Myth, and Metaphor* (Ithaca, N.Y.: Cornell University Press, 2002), 319–44. Compare Western concepts in J. B. Russell, *Witchcraft in the Middle Ages* (Ithaca, N.Y.: Cornell University Press, 1972); and B. Ankarloo and G. Henningsen, eds., *Early Modern European Witchcraft: Centres and Peripheries* (Oxford: Oxford University Press, 1990).

34. Augustine, *Confessions,* trans. Henry Chadwick (Oxford: Oxford University Press, 1991), 8.12.29.

35. Meyer and Smith, *Ancient Christian Magic,* 251–56.

36. G. Calofonos, "Dream Interpretation: A Byzantine Superstition?" *Byzantine and Modern Greek Studies* 9 (1985–85): 215–20; Maria Mavroudi, *A Byzantine Book on Dream Interpretation: The "Oneirocritikon of Achmet" and Its Arabic Sources* (Leiden, the Netherlands: Brill, 2002).

RULERS OF BYZANTIUM

Constantine I	312–37
Constantius II	337–61
Julian	361–63
Valens	364–78
Theodosius I	379–95
Arcadius	391–408
Theodosius II	408–50
Marcian	450–57
Leo I	457–74
Zeno	474–91
Anastasius I	491–518
Justin I	518–27
Justinian I	527–65
Justin II	565–78
Tiberius II	578–82
Maurice	582–602
Phokas	602–10
Heraclius	610–41
Constans II	641–68
Constantine IV	668–85
Justinian II	685–95
Leontios	695–98
Tiberios III	698–705
Justinian II (again)	705–11

Philippikos Bardanes	711–13
Anastasios II	713–15
Theodosios III	715–17
Leo III	717–41
Constantine V	741–75
Artabasdos	741–43
Leo IV	775–80
Constantine VI	780–97
Irene	780–802
Nikephoros I	802–11
Michael I	811–13
Leo V	813–20
Michael II	820–29
Theophilos	829–42
Michael III	842–67
Basil I	867–86
Leo VI ("the Wise")	886–912
Alexander	912–13
Constantine VII (Porphyrogennitos)	913–59
Romanos I Lekapenos	920–44
Romanos II	959–63
Nikephoros II Phokas	963–69
John I Tzimiskes	969–76
Basil II	976–1025
Constantine VIII	1025–28
Romanos III Argyros	1028–34
Michael IV ("the Paphlagonian")	1034–41
Michael V Kalaphates	1041–42
Zoe and Theodora	1042
Constantine IX Monomachos	1042–55
Theodora (again)	1055–56
Michael VI Stratiotikos	1056–57
Isaac I Komnenos	1057–59
Constantine X Doukas	1059–67
Eudokia	1067
Romanos IV Diogenes	1068–71
Eudokia (again)	1071
Michael VII Doukas	1071–78
Nikephoros III Botaneiates	1078–81
Alexios I Komnenos	1081–1118
John II Komnenos	1118–43
Manuel I Komnenos	1143–80

Alexios II Komnenos	1180–83
Andronikos I Komnenos	1183–85
Isaac II Angelos	1185–95
Alexios III Angelos	1195–1203
Isaac II (again) and	
Alexios IV Angelos	1203–1204
Alexios V Mourtzouphlos	1204
Latin Empire of	
Constantinople	*1204–59*
Michael VIII Palaiologos	1259–82
Andronikos II Palaiologos	1282–1328
Michael IX Palaiologos	1294–1320
Andronikos III Palaiologos	1328–41
John V Palaiologos	1341–91
John VI Kantakouzenos	1341–54
Andronikos IV Palaiologos	1376–79
John VII Palaiologos	1390
Manuel II Palaiologos	1391–1425
John VIII Palaiologos	1425–48
Constantine XI Palaiologos	1448–53

GLOSSARY

acheiropoietos/acheiropoietoi   Object, usually a religious image, of miraculous origin, "not made by human hands."

archon/archontes   Property owner who held an honorific title.

basileus (Rhomaion)   "Emperor (of the Romans)." Standard title of the Byzantine emperor during the medieval period, superseding the traditional titles Augustus and Autokrator used through late antiquity.

chiton   Basic tunic or undergarment of varying length worn, often belted, by men and women of all social levels.

chlamys   Long cloak or mantle fastened by a brooch or fibula at the front or right shoulder.

chrysobull   Official document certified by the wax impression of the gold seal of the emperor or patriarch.

didaskalos   Teacher or tutor of children.

diptychs   Hinged, decorated panels of ivory or metal originally intended for holding written texts.

dynatos/dynatoi   Civil or military member of the dominant social class.

ekphrasis/ekphraseis   Formal rhetorical description of a work of art, building, or city.

enkolpion/enkolpia   A small object, usually a protective amulet or *phylakterion*, that was worn around the neck.

enkomion   Formal rhetorical exercise praising a person or place.

eparch (eparchos)   Prefect of Constantinople, the city's highest-ranking government official, who was responsible for maintaining law, order, and public services.

ergasterion/ergasteria   Team, workshop, or commercial establishment.

eulogeion/eulogiai   The spiritual blessing derived from contact with a holy object, person, or place.

fibula/fibulae   Brooch or pin most commonly used to fasten a cloak at the shoulder.

follis/folles   Principal denomination of bronze coinage, worth 40 *nummi* and valued at 1/288 of a *solidus* for most of the Middle Ages.

Golden Horn (Chrysokeras)   Deep, naturally sheltered inlet on the north side of Constantinople; the commercial center of the medieval city.

grammatikos   Secondary or grammar teacher of older children.

gynaikeion   The area in a church or residence reserved for women and children.

hegoumenos (also archimandrite)   Abbot or leader of a monastery.

himation   A cloak or mantle worn draped in the classical manner, leaving the right arm free.

Hodegetria   Image of the Virgin with child as "Pointer of the Way," believed to originate in a painting done from life by Saint Luke.

icon   Religious image, usually painted in encaustic or tempera on wooden panels.

iconostasis   High sanctuary barrier supporting icons in medieval churches, superseding the low screens and open templons used in the early Middle Ages.

kastron/kastra (also kastellion or phrourion)   Fortified military garrison, castle, or town.

kataphraktos/kataphraktoi   Armored cavalry of the late Roman and medieval periods.

katholikon   The main church of a monastery or nunnery.

kollyba   Funeral cakes or meal usually consisting of boiled wheat, dried fruits, and nuts.

maphorion/maphoria   Shawl or veil worn by a woman to cover her head and shoulders.

martyrium/martyria   Chapel or shrine associated with a sacred place, event, or person; often located near the tomb of a martyr of the early church.

Mese   The main street, paved with marble and flanked by porticoes, of Constantinople.

metocheion/metocheia   Dependent outpost of a larger monastery.

modios/modioi   Unit of measure normally referring to a quantity of grain, or the surface area that could be planted with it (approximately 0.08–0.10 hectares).

naos   The nave or central part of a church.

nomisma/nomismata   Solidus, a gold coin.

oikos/oikoi   House, or more commonly household, including family members, servants, and slaves.

paludamentum   Military cloak worn by high-ranking officers.

Panagia   "All-holy." Epithet usually applied to the Virgin Mary as Theotokos.

panegyris/panegyreis   Civic or religious festival; particularly an occasional or periodic commercial fair or market.

Pantokrator   "All-ruling." Epithet usually applied to Christ.

paroikos/paroikoi   Peasant (*georgike*) who worked another person's land in exchange for annual rent.

Pascha   Easter, celebrating Christ's passion and resurrection (Anastasis); the culmination of the Orthodox liturgical year.

phylakterion/phylakteria   Protective amulet, commonly worn about the neck.

porphyrogennitos/porphyrogennitis   "Born in the Purple." Epithet applied to children born into the reigning family, particularly Constantine VII.

pronoia   Assignment of revenues from a property to a soldier (*pronoiar*) in return for military service.

proskynesis   Act of ceremonial greeting and submission before a figure or symbol of authority, ranging from a deep bow to full prostration.

solidus/solidi (or nomisma/nomismata)   Gold coin that formed the basic monetary unit of Byzantium; the "dollar of the Middle Ages" between the fourth and eleventh centuries.

strategos/strategoi   General or military governor of a provincial theme.

Synaxarion   Official church calendar with brief notes on religious festivals.

tagma/tagmata   Elite regiments of the Byzantine army, comprising the Scholai, Exkoubitoi, Vigla, Hikanatoi, and Athanatoi.

taxis   The Byzantine idea of order and stability as known on the cosmological, temporal, and domestic levels.

themes (thema/themata)   Administrative regions of the medieval empire; also the military units raised by each area.

tunic (also kamision)   Basic woven garment, usually of cotton, linen, or wool and of variable length in torso and sleeves, worn by all sectors of Byzantine society.

typikon/typika   Foundation charter for a monastery or nunnery; also calendar of liturgical observances.

xenon/xenones   Guest house *(xenodocheion)* or hospital *(nosokomeion)*, normally staffed by a trained medical staff.

SOME BYZANTINE AND CONTEMPORARY WRITERS

Aetius of Amida (mid-sixth century). Physician and medical encylopedist.

Alexander of Tralles (525–605). Physician and medical writer.

Amphilochius of Iconium (ca. 340/45–after 394) Church orator, theologian, and bishop of Iconium in Pisidia (from ca. 374).

Anna Komnene (1083–1153/54). Eldest daughter of Alexios I Komnenos and author of the *Alexiad*, a supportive history of the reign of her father.

Anthemius of Tralles (sixth century). Engineer, mathematician, author of mechanical treatises, and codesigner of Hagia Sophia.

Augustine (354–430) Bishop of Hippo in North Africa (from ca. 396) and influential Latin theologian.

Basil of Caesarea (ca. 329–79). Monk, bishop of Caesarea in Cappadocia (from 370), and author of important theological works as well as fundamental rules for Byzantine monasticism.

Christopher of Mytilene (ca. 1000–60). Court official and poet.

Constantine Manasses (ca. 1130–87). Court historian, poet, and writer.

Cosmas Indikopleustes (sixth century). Alexandrian merchant and later monk who wrote an interpretive account of his travels.

Demetrios Kydones (ca. 1324–98). Court official, scholar, translator, and writer.

Eusebius of Caesarea (ca. 260–339/40). Bishop, scholar, and author of an ecclesiastical history, a *Life* of Constantine, and other works.

Some Byzantine and Contemporary Writers

Eustathios Boilas (eleventh century). *Protospatharios* and wealthy Anatolian landowner who in April 1059 drew up a detailed will disposing of his estate.

Eustathios of Thessaloniki (ca. 1115–95/96). Archbishop, scholar, and writer.

George Pachymeres (ca. 1242–1308). Patriarchal official, scholar, and historian.

Gregory of Nazianzos (ca. 329–90). Bishop of Constantinople (380–81) and Nazianzos in Cappadocia (382–84) and prolific theological writer.

Isidorus of Miletus (sixth century). Mathematician, author of works on geometry, and codesigner of Hagia Sophia.

John Chrysostomos (ca. 345–407). Monk, patriarch of Constantinople (398–404), and influential theological writer.

John of Damascus (ca. 675–ca. 753/54). Monk, hagiographer, and scholar who wrote a number of influential theological works during the early years of Byzantine iconoclasm.

John of Ephesus (ca. 507–86). Bishop, hagiographer, and historian.

John Geometres (late tenth century). Court official and poet.

John the Lydian (ca. 490–565). Civil official, scholar, and author of a book on imperial administration and other works.

John Malalas (ca. 490–570s). Civil official and author of the first Byzantine universal history.

John Skylitzes (later eleventh century). Historian whose Chronicle of the ninth through eleventh centuries is best known from an illuminated manuscript today in Madrid.

John Tzetzes (ca. 1110–1180/85). Sometime teacher, poet, and writer.

Kekaumenos (ca. 1020–1070s). Civil or military official and landowner, who in retirement wrote the *Strategikon,* a book of moralizing advice.

Leo the Mathematician (also "the Philosopher," ca. 790–ca. 870). Scholar, teacher, and metropolitan of Thessaloniki (840–43), best known for his design of automata in the palace of Theophilos and a network of signal towers spanning Anatolia.

Leo of Synada (tenth century). Bishop, church diplomat, and writer.

Libanius (314–ca. 393). Orator, teacher of rhetoric, and longtime resident of Antioch.

Liudprand (also Liutprand, 920–72). Bishop of Cremona in Italy and emissary for the court of Otto I.

Manuel Philes (ca. 1275–1345). Court official and poet.

Maximos Planoudes (ca. 1255–1305). Monk, scribe, scholar, poet, and translator.

Michael Attaleiates (1020s–ca. 1085). Senator, legal scholar, historian, and founder of the monastery of Christ Panoiktirmon in Constantinople.

Michael Choniates (ca. 1138–ca. 1222). Writer and metropolitan of Athens (1182–1204).

Michael Psellos (ca. 1018–81). Civil official, intellectual, historian, philosopher, and writer.

Nikephoros Gregoras (ca. 1290–1360). Scholar, hagiographer, and historian.

Niketas Choniates (ca. 1155–1217). Palace official, historian, and theologian.

Odo of Deuil (ca. 1100–62). French monk and recorder of an expedition to Constantinople during the Second Crusade.

Oribasius of Pergamon (ca. 325–400). Physician and medical encyclopedist.

Pachomius (ca. 290–346). Early monastic leader whose letters, guidelines, and *Life* shaped the development of eastern monasticism.

Paul of Aegina (seventh century). Physician and medical encyclopedist, best known for a book on surgical procedures.

Paul the Silentiary (sixth century). Court official and poet, whose works include erotic verse and a florid *ekphrasis* of Hagia Sophia ca. 563.

Photios (ca. 810–93). Scholar, teacher, patriarch of Constantinople (858–67, 877–86), and author of various works, including the *Bibliotheka*.

Procopius of Caesarea (sixth century). Military official and historian of the reign of Justinian.

Symeon Seth (late eleventh century). Scholar, teacher, translator, and writer on scientific and pseudoscientific topics.

Theodore Hyrtakenos (early fourteenth century). Teacher and writer.

Theodore Metochites (1270–1332). Court official and prime minister (1305–28), scholar, bibliophile, and prolific writer on varied subjects.

Theodore Prodromos (ca. 1100–70). Court poet and believed author of satirical poems signed by Ptochoprodromos.

Theodore of Stoudios (759–826). Monk, abbot, theologian, and monastic reformer.

Theoleptos of Philadelphia (ca. 1250–1322). Monk, religious writer, and metropolitan of Philadelphia in western Asia Minor (from ca. 1284).

Theophilus (twelfth century). German craftsman and author of a book on medieval craft techniques.

Theophylakos (ca. 1050–1126 or later). Deacon, teacher, scholar, and archbishop of Ohrid (from 1088/89).

SELECTED BIBLIOGRAPHY

SOME BYZANTINE AND CONTEMPORARY SOURCES IN TRANSLATION

Brand, Charles M., ed. *Icon and Minaret: Sources of Byzantine and Islamic Civilization.* Englewood Cliffs, N.J.: Prentice Hall, 1969.

Thirty-seven well-known texts relating to Byzantium and its neighbors to the west and east.

Cameron, Averil, and Judith Herron, eds. and trans. *Constantinople in the Early Eighth Century: The Parastaseis Syntomoi Chronikai.* Leiden, the Netherlands: Brill, 1984.

Text and commentary on an early medieval guidebook to the wonders of the city.

Crisafulli, Virgil S., trans. *The Miracles of St. Artemios: A Collection of Miracle Stories by an Anonymous Author of Seventh-Century Byzantium.* Leiden, the Netherlands: Brill, 1997.

Text and commentary on a popular healing saint of early medieval Constantinople.

Dawes, Elizabeth, and Norman H. Baynes, trans. *Three Byzantine Saints: Contemporary Biographies of St. Daniel the Stylite, St. Theodore of Sykeon, and St. John the Almsgiver.* Crestwood, N.Y.: St. Vladimir's Seminar Press, 1977.

Three early saints' lives give a detailed view of life in Asia Minor, Cyprus, and Egypt in the sixth and seventh centuries.

Dewing, H. B., trans. *Procopius.* 7 vols. Cambridge: Harvard University Press, 1914–40; reprinted 1953–62.

The six-volume *Wars* constitute an official history of the reign of Justinian I (527–65), including fulsome accounts of campaigns against the Persians in the east, the Vandals in North Africa, and the Goths in Italy. An additional

volume, *On Buildings,* praises the emperor's construction and repair of fortifications, roads, bridges, churches, and monasteries across the empire.

Geanakoplos, Deno John. *Byzantium: Church, Society, and Civilization Seen through
Contemporary Eyes.* Chicago: University of Chicago Press, 1984.

Over 300 selected texts, ranging from official documents and historical
chronicles to personal letters. A number of excerpts deal with urban and
rural life, the family and household, and aspects of Byzantine culture.

Jeffreys, Elizabeth, ed. and trans. *Digenis Akritis: The Grottaferrata and Escorial
Versions.* Cambridge: Cambridge University Press, 1998.

Epic late-medieval legend of heroic life along the eastern frontier.

Mango, Cyril. *The Art of the Byzantine Empire, 312–1453.* Englewood Cliffs, N.J.:
Prentice Hall, 1972. Reprint, Toronto: Medieval Academy Reprints for
Teaching, 1986.

A selection of key writings dealing with major monuments, works, and
methods.

Odo of Deuil. *De Profectione Ludovici VII in Orientem: The Journey of Louis VII to the
East.* Ed. Virginia Gingerick Berry. New York: W. W. Norton, 1948.

A Westerner's view of Byzantium during the twelfth century.

Procopius. *Secret History (Anecdota).* Trans. G. A. Williamson. London: Penguin
Books, 1966.

A fascinating but problematic counterpart to his other works, the *Secret
History* offers a gossipy and darkly pessimistic view of Justinian and Theodora.
For a good assessment of these accounts see Averil Cameron, *Procopius and the
Sixth Century* (Berkeley: University of California Press, 1985).

Sewter, E.R.A., trans. *The Alexiad of Anna Comnena.* Harmondsworth, England:
Penguin Classics, 1969.

Famous chronicle of the life and times of the emperor Alexios I
Komnenos, as observed and recorded by his admiring daughter.

———. *Michael Psellus, Fourteen Byzantine Rulers* (the *Chronographia*).
Harmondsworth, England: Penguin Classics, 1966.

Historical chronicle of the lives and times of the Byzantine emperors and
empresses from Basil II (976–1025) to Michael VII (1071–78).

Talbot, Alice-Mary, ed. *Byzantine Defenders of Images: Eight Saints' Lives in English
Translation.* Washington, D.C.: Dumbarton Oaks, 1998.

The lives of eight saints of the eighth and ninth centuries. Available
online at http://www.doaks.org/.

———. *Holy Women of Byzantium: Ten Saints' Lives in English Translation.* Washington,
D.C.: Dumbarton Oaks, 1996.

Edifying accounts of 10 female saints who lived between late antiquity and
the thirteenth century. Available online at http://www.doaks.org/.

Thomas, John, and Angela Constantinides Hero, eds. *Byzantine Monastic Foundation
Documents.* 5 vols. Washington, D.C.: Dumbarton Oaks, 2000.

A comprehensive collection of monastic *typika,* ranging from the imperial Pantokrator complex in Constantinople to small rural monasteries.
Drawn up by the founders between the seventh and fifteenth centuries,
these 61 charters illustrate the range of monastic experience in the medieval empire. Available online at http://www.doaks.org/.

Wright, F. A., trans. *The Works of Liudprand of Cremona.* New York: E. P. Dutton,
1930.

Three outspoken accounts by the ambassador of the Ottonian court of his experiences in Constantinople in the later tenth century.

REFERENCE WORKS

Hussey, Joan M., ed. *The Cambridge Medieval History.* 2nd ed. Vol. 4, *The Byzantine Empire.* Part 1, *Byzantium and Its Neighbors.* Part 2, *Government, Church and Civilization.* Cambridge: Cambridge University Press, 1966–67.
Encyclopedic survey of Byzantium with a detailed historical narrative and topical articles.
Kazhdan, Alexander P., ed. *The Oxford Dictionary of Byzantium.* 3 vols. New York: Oxford University Press, 1991.
An encyclopedic compilation of over 5,000 short entries, alphabetically arranged, discussing all aspects of Byzantine culture. Particularly helpful for identifying historical personalities, geographic locations, and many objects used on a daily basis.
Laiou, Angeliki E., ed. *The Economic History of Byzantium from the Seventh to the Fifteenth Century.* Washington, D.C.: Dumbarton Oaks, 2002.
A milestone survey of economic activity during the medieval period. Available online at http://www.doaks.org/EHB.htm.
Strayer, Joseph R., ed. *Dictionary of the Middle Ages.* 14 vols. New York: Charles Scribner's Sons, 1982–89.
Comprehensive survey of medieval culture and history, including many useful articles on Byzantium.

INTRODUCTIONS TO BYZANTIUM AND THE ORTHODOX WORLD

Arnott, Peter. *The Byzantines and Their World.* New York: St. Martin's Press, 1973.
Popular historical introduction to the major cities and monuments.
Bowersock, Glen W., Peter Brown, and Oleg Grabar, eds. *Late Antiquity: A Guide to the Postclassical World.* Cambridge: Harvard University Press, 1999.
Eleven interpretive essays on aspects of late-antique history and culture, with alphabetically arranged entries on selected topics.
Brown, Peter. *The World of Late Antiquity A.D. 150–750.* London: Thames and Hudson, 1971. Reprint, New York: Norton, 1989.
An accessible introduction to Mediterranean and Near Eastern history and culture of the third to eighth centuries, paying special attention to the changing intellectual and spiritual experience of its inhabitants. This landmark study kindled popular and scholarly interest in a previously neglected historical period.
Browning, Robert, ed. *The Greek World: Classical, Byzantine, and Modern.* New York: Thames and Hudson, 1985.
Illustrated survey of Greek history and culture with essays by noted authorities in the field.
Foss, Clive, and Paul Magdalino. *Rome and Byzantium.* Oxford: Elsevier–Phaidon, 1977.

Illustrated introduction to Byzantine history, with particular emphasis on the contributions of archaeology and field research.

Hussey, Joan M. *The Byzantine World*. New York: Harper and Row, 1961.
Brief overview of Byzantine history and culture.

Kazhdan, Alexander P., and Giles Constable. *People and Power in Byzantium: An Introduction to Modern Byzantine Studies.* Washington, D.C.: Dumbarton Oaks, 1982.
Considers the difficulties of exploring Byzantine social history and the potential of new historical methods.

Kazhdan, Alexander P., and Ann Wharton Epstein. *Change in Byzantine Culture in the Eleventh and Twelfth Centuries*. Berkeley: University of California Press, 1985.
Explores the formation of medieval Byzantium with special emphasis on popular and intellectual society.

Kinross, Lord. *Hagia Sophia*. New York: Newsweek Books, 1972.
Well-illustrated introduction to the building and its history as church and mosque.

Laiou, Angeliki E., and Henry Maguire, eds. *Byzantium: A World Civilization*. Washington, D.C.: Dumbarton Oaks, 1992.
Seven essays on the place of Byzantium and Byzantine studies in the medieval and modern worlds.

Mango, Cyril. *Byzantium: The Empire of New Rome*. New York: Charles Scribner's Sons, 1980.
Selective survey of Byzantine culture, focusing on social, economic, and intellectual history.

———, ed. *The Oxford History of Byzantium*. Oxford: Oxford University Press, 2002.
Well-illustrated survey of Byzantine history between the fourth and fifteenth centuries.

Runciman, Steven. *Byzantine Style and Civilization*. Harmondsworth, England: Penguin Books, 1975.
Brief cultural survey by a leading twentieth-century interpreter of Byzantine culture.

Sherrard, Philip. *Byzantium*. New York: Time-Life Books, 1966.
Popular introduction to Byzantine history, art, and culture.

Talbot Rice, David. *The Byzantines*. London: Thames and Hudson, 1962.
Topical introduction to Byzantine culture with chapters on history, life-ways, and major monuments.

Ware, Timothy. *The Orthodox Church*. Rev. ed. London: Penguin Books, 1991.
Good introduction to Eastern Orthodoxy, its history, beliefs, and worship.

What Life Was Like amid Splendor and Intrigue: Byzantine Empire, A.D. 330–1453. Alexandria, Va.: Time-Life Books, 1998.
Popular introduction to Byzantine history and culture.

Whitting, Philip, ed. *Byzantium: An Introduction*. Rev. ed. New York: St. Martin's Press, 1981.
Seven chapters introduce the main periods of Byzantine history between the fourth and fifteenth centuries.

DAILY LIFE AND MATERIAL CULTURE

Angelidi, Christina, ed. *He Kathemerine Zoe sto Vyzantio: Tomes kai Synecheies* (Everyday life in Byzantium: Breaks and continuities). Athens: Center for Byzantine Research, 1989.
Fifty conference papers on a wide range of related topics.
Bass, George F., and Frederick van Doorninck Jr. *Yassi Ada I: A Seventh-Century Byzantine Shipwreck.* College Station: Texas A&M University Press, 1982.
Comprehensive report on the underwater recovery of an early merchant vessel. Individual chapters discuss aspects of the ship's construction and associated finds.
Bass, George F., et al. *Serçe Limani I: An Eleventh-Century Shipwreck.* College Station: Texas A&M University Press, 2004.
Monumental report on the excavation of a medieval merchant ship and some of its artifacts.
Cavallo, Guglielmo, ed. *The Byzantines.* Trans., Thomas Dunlap, Theresa Lavender Fagan, and Charles Lambert. Chicago: University of Chicago Press, 1997.
A composite overview of some of the most important groups that made up medieval society, with 10 prominent scholars contributing incisive essays on the poor, peasants, soldiers, teachers, women, businessmen, bishops, bureaucrats, and emperors.
Charanis, Peter. "Some Aspects of Daily Life in Byzantium." *Greek Orthodox Theological Review* 8 (1962–63): 53–70.
Reprinted in Peter Charanis, *Social, Economic, and Political Life in the Byzantine Empire* (London: Variorum, 1973). Introduction to medieval written sources for exploring Byzantine lifeways.
Dalby, Andrew. *Flavours of Byzantium.* Totnes, England: Prospect Books, 2003.
Authoritative overview of Byzantine food and diet, their historical sources, and culinary legacy.
Dark, Ken. *Byzantine Pottery.* Charleston, S.C.: Tempus, 2001.
Introduction to an essential facet of medieval daily life, covering manufacturing methods, historical development, and significance of pottery for understanding trade. Individual chapters cover the most important traditions of pottery making, from late antiquity into the sixteenth century.
———. *Secular Buildings and the Archaeology of Everyday Life in the Byzantine Empire.* Oxford: Oxbow Books, 2004.
Five essays address aspects of residential, commercial, and religious life.
Grierson, Philip. *Byzantine Coins.* Berkeley: University of California Press, 1982.
Authoritative survey of Byzantine coinage and monetary history.
Grünbart, Michael, and Dionysios Stathakopoulos. "Sticks and Stones: Byzantine Material Culture." *Byzantine and Modern Greek Studies* 26 (2002): 298–327.
Critical review of recent publications relating to questions of daily life.
Haldon, John. "Everyday Life in Byzantium: Some Problems of Approach." *Byzantine and Modern Greek Studies* 10 (1986): 51–72.
Introduction to the challenges and potential contribution of written sources, with special reference to the limits of socially acceptable behavior.
Koukales, Phaidon. *Vyzantinon Vios kai Politismos* (Life and culture of the Byzantines). 6 vols. Athens: French Institute, 1948–57.

Fundamental topical collection of Byzantine texts covering all recorded aspects of medieval life.

Magdalino, Paul. "The Literary Perception of Everyday Life in Byzantium" *Byzantinoslavica* 48 (1987): 28–38.
Evaluates the unstated potential of late-medieval written sources for understanding daily life.

Mango, Cyril. "Daily Life in Byzantium." *Jahrbuch der Österreichischen Byzantinistik* 31, no. 1 (1981): 337–53.
Reviews problems of method with special reference to public bathing and popular entertainment.

Parani, Maria G. *Reconstructing the Reality of Images: Byzantine Material Culture and Religious Iconography (11th–15th Centuries).* Leiden, the Netherlands: Brill, 2003.
Comprehensive study of costume, jewelry, tools, and weapons based primarily on medieval manuscripts and wall paintings.

Prinzing, Günter, and Dieter Simon, eds. *Fest und Alltag in Byzanz.* Munich: C. H. Beck, 1990.
Eleven essays discuss diverse aspects of the Byzantine experience.

Talbot Rice, Tamara. *Everyday Life in Byzantium.* London: B. T. Batsford and New York: G. P. Putnam's Sons, 1967.
Popular introduction to selected aspects of Byzantine culture, with chapters on civil and religious administration, social groups, and urban and rural life.

Veyne, Paul, ed. *A History of Private Life.* Vol. 1, *From Pagan Rome to Byzantium.* Trans. Arthur Goldhammer. Cambridge: Harvard University Press, Belknap Press, 1987.
Stimulating surveys of family structure and domestic affairs in Roman times by Paul Veyne and Yvon Thébert. Peter Brown and Evelyne Patlagean contribute essays on late antiquity and Byzantium in the tenth and eleventh centuries.

Walter, Gérard. *La vie quotidienne à Byzance au siècle des Comnènes (1081– 1180).* Paris: Hachette, 1966.
Popular account of medieval society and culture.

Whitting, Philip D. *Byzantine Coins.* New York: G. P. Putnam's Sons, 1973.
Well-illustrated guide to Byzantine coins.

MUSEUM CATALOGS AND EXHIBITIONS

Acheimastou-Potamianou, Myrtali, ed. *From Byzantium to El Greco: Greek Frescoes and Icons.* Athens: Greek Ministry of Culture, 1987.
Over 70 examples of paintings in the Byzantine tradition from the thirteenth to seventeenth centuries.

Buckton, David, ed. *Byzantium: Treasures of Byzantine Art and Culture from British Collections.* London: British Museum, 1994.
Major exhibition of over 250 works from private and public collections.

———. *The Treasury of San Marco, Venice.* Milan: Olivetti, 1984.
Exhibition of nearly 50 celebrated works of medieval Byzantine art, many of which were taken to Venice at the time of the Fourth Crusade.

Byzantine and Early Mediaeval Antiquities in the Dumbarton Oaks Collection. 3 vols. Vols. 1 and 2 edited by Marvin C. Ross, vol. 3 edited by Kurt Weitzmann. Washington, D.C.: Dumbarton Oaks, 1962–72.
> Comprehensive catalog of an important collection of Byzantine and Western medieval art.

Byzantine Art, An European Art. 2d ed. Athens: Department of Antiquities and Archaeological Restoration, 1964.
> This huge exhibition, one of the first devoted exclusively to Byzantine art, assembled over 700 objects in Athens under the sponsorship of the Council of Europe. The exhibition, catalog, and accompanying volume of essays reflect growing interest in Byzantine art and culture around the middle of the twentieth century.

Durand, Jannic, ed. *Byzance: L'Art byzantin dans le collections publiques françaises.* Paris: Musée du Louvre, 1992.
> Major exhibition of more than 400 works of Byzantine art held by French museums.

Evans, Helen C., ed. *Byzantium: Faith and Power (1261–1557).* New Haven, Conn.: Yale University Press, 2004.
> Major international exhibition of 355 works from the late Byzantine period mounted by the Metropolitan Museum of Art.

Evans, Helen C., and William D. Wixom, eds. *The Glory of Byzantium: Art and Culture of the Middle Byzantine Era, A.D. 843–1261.* New York: Metropolitan Museum of Art, 1997.
> Monumental international exhibition of over 300 objects from the apogee of the medieval empire, with particular emphasis on Constantinople and its influence on neighboring states. Lavishly illustrated catalog includes essays on the arts of Bulgaria, Armenia, Georgia, Russia, the Islamic East, and the Latin crusaders.

Gonosová, Anna, and Christine Kondoleon, eds. *Art of Late Rome and Byzantium in the Virginia Museum of Fine Arts.* Richmond, Va.: Virginia Museum of Fine Arts, 1994.
> Comprehensive catalog of an important collection of Byzantine art and artifacts.

Kalavrezou, Ioli. *Byzantine Women and Their World.* New Haven, Conn.: Yale University Press, 2003.
> Exhibition of nearly 200 objects from North American collections with accompanying essays on the expectations and experiences of medieval women.

Maguire, Eunice Dauterman, Henry P. Maguire, and Maggie J. Duncan-Flowers. *Art and Holy Powers in the Early Christian House.* Urbana: University of Illinois Press, 1989.
> Illustrated catalog of over 150 objects from North American collections illustrating the variety and meaning of domestic furnishings in late antiquity.

Papanikola-Bakirtzis, Demetra, ed. *Kathemerine Zoe sto Vyzantio* (Everyday life in Byzantium). Athens: Ekdoseis Kapon, 2002.
> Monumental international exhibition of over 800 objects, with beautiful illustrations of both the exotic and mundane.

Piatnitsky, Yuri, et al. *Sinai, Byzantium, Russia: Orthodox Art from the Sixth to the Twentieth Century,* eds. London: Saint Catherine Foundation, 2000.
   Major exhibition exploring the connections between medieval and modern Russia and the Holy Land as seen in the decorative, devotional, and pilgrimage arts, especially icons.
Post-Byzantium: The Greek Renaissance; 15th–18th Century Treasures from the Byzantine and Christian Museum, Athens. Athens: Hellenic Ministry of Culture and Alexander S. Onassis Public Benefit Foundation (USA), 2002.
   Exhibition of 54 Greek devotional and liturgical works in the Byzantine tradition.
Vassilaki, Maria, ed. *Mother of God: Representations of the Virgin in Byzantine Art.* New York: Abbeville, 2000.
   Major exhibition of a central cultural image as depicted in all media, organized by the Benaki Museum.
Weitzmann, Kurt, ed. *Age of Spirituality: Late Antique and Early Christian Art, Third to Seventh Century.* New York: Metropolitan Museum of Art, 1979.
   Monumental international exhibition of more than 600 objects from the early centuries of Byzantine history. The 1977 exhibition, together with a volume of symposium essays, played a key role in stimulating public and scholarly interest in the period of late antiquity.

SURVEYS OF BYZANTINE ART AND ARCHITECTURE

Beckwith, John. *Early Christian and Byzantine Art.* 2nd ed. Harmondsworth, England: Penguin Books, 1979.
   Historical survey of the figural and decorative arts between the third and fifteenth centuries.
Cormack, Robin. *Byzantine Art.* Oxford: Oxford University Press, 2000.
   The development of the visual arts from the fourth to fifteenth centuries.
Elsner, Jas. *Imperial Roman and Christian Triumph: The Art of the Roman Empire, A.D. 100–450.* Oxford: Oxford University Press, 1998.
   Introduction to late-antique society and the visual arts.
Harrison, R. Martin. *A Temple for Byzantium: The Discovery and Excavation of Anicia Juliana's Palace-Church in Istanbul.* Austin: University of Texas Press, 1989.
   Well-illustrated popular account of the recovery of one of the great, forgotten monuments of Constantinople, the sixth-century church of Saint Polyeuktos.
Kitzinger, Ernst. *Byzantine Art in the Making: Main Lines of Stylistic Development in Mediterranean Art, 3rd–7th Century.* Cambridge: Harvard University Press, 1977.
   Stylistic survey of figural and decorative arts in late antiquity.
Krautheimer, Richard. *Early Christian and Byzantine Architecture.* 4th ed. Harmondsworth, England: Penguin Books, 1986.
   Historical survey of church building from the third to fifteenth centuries.
Lowden, John. *Early Christian and Byzantine Art.* London: Phaidon, 1997.
   Survey of visual arts from the third to fifteenth centuries, with particular emphasis on illuminated manuscripts.

Mango, Cyril. *Byzantine Architecture.* New York: Harry N. Abrams, 1976. Reprint, New York: Rizzoli, 1991.
  Well-illustrated historical account of Byzantine building.
Mathews, Thomas F. *Byzantium: From Antiquity to the Renaissance.* New York: Harry N. Abrams, 1998.
  Thematically organized introductory survey of art and architecture.
Ousterhout, Robert G. *Master Builders of Byzantium.* Princeton, N.J.: Princeton University Press, 1999.
  Systematic investigation of the people, materials, and methods of Byzantine architecture.
Rodley, Lyn. *Byzantine Art and Architecture: An Introduction.* Cambridge: Cambridge University Press, 1994.
  Historical survey of major monuments from the fourth to fifteenth centuries.
Safran, Linda, ed. *Heaven on Earth: Art and the Church in Byzantium.* University Park: Pennsylvania State University Press, 1998.
  Eight introductory essays on Byzantium and its liturgical arts.

HISTORICAL NARRATIVES

Angold, Michael, *Byzantium: The Bridge from Antiquity to the Middle Ages.* New York: St. Martin's Press, 2001.
  Popular historical introduction to Byzantium.
Browning, Robert. *The Byzantine Empire.* London: Weidenfeld and Nicolson, 1980.
  Comprehensive historical survey.
Gregory, Timothy E. *A History of Byzantium.* Oxford: Blackwell, 2005.
  Historical overview paying particular attention to the contribution of material sources.
Haldon, John. *Byzantium: A History.* Charleston, S.C.: Tempus, 2000.
  Concise survey of the fourth to fifteenth centuries, with special attention to the empire's physical setting, political apparatus, and economic productivity.
Norwich, John Julius. *Byzantium.* Vol. 1, *The Early Years;* vol. 2, *The Apogee;* vol. 3, *Decline and Fall.* New York: Knopf, 1989–96.
  Lively narrative of political affairs and military history. An abridged version of all three volumes was published as *A Shorter History of Byzantium* (New York: Random House, 1998).
Ostrogorsky, George. *History of the Byzantine State.* Trans. Joan M. Hussey. New Brunswick, N.J.: Rutgers University Press, 1968.
  Fundamental historical survey of political history and organization.
Toynbee, Arnold. *Constantine Porphyrogenitus and His World.* London: Oxford University Press. 1973.
  Landmark survey of the tenth-century empire.
Treadgold, Warren. *History of the Byzantine State and Society.* Stanford, Calif.: Stanford University Press, 1997.
  Sweeping institutional assessment spanning the fourth to fifteenth centuries. For a shorter version, see *A Concise History of the Byzantium* (New York: Palgrave Macmillan, 2002).

Whittow, Mark. *The Making of Byzantium, 600–1025.* Berkeley: University of California Press, 1996.
> Reassessment of the early medieval period, from the wars of Justinian through the reign of Basil II.

TRAVEL GUIDES

Ash, John. *A Byzantine Journey.* New York: Random House, 1995.
> Travels in western and central Turkey with historical commentary.

Freely, John. *Istanbul.* 3rd ed. New York: W. W. Norton, 1991.
> *Blue Guide* handbook to the city's history and sights, with maps, plans, and atlas, written by a local authority and longtime resident.

———. *Istanbul: The Imperial City.* New York: Penguin Books, 1998.
> Historical overview of the Byzantine and Ottoman capital.

Hetherington, Paul. *Byzantine and Medieval Greece: Churches, Castles, and Art of the Mainland and the Peloponnese.* New York: J. Murray, 1991.
> Descriptive guide to historic sites and buildings.

———. *The Greek Islands: Guide to the Byzantine and Medieval Buildings and Their Art.* London: Quiller, 2001.
> Descriptive guide to historic sites and buildings.

Kelly, Laurence. *Istanbul: A Travellers' Companion.* London: Constable, 1987.
> Anthology of literary accounts and travel writings.

Sumner-Boyd, Hilary, and John Freely. *Strolling through Istanbul: A Guide to the City.* 2nd ed. Istanbul: Redhouse Press, 1972.
> Classic walking guide to the monuments, great and small.

ELECTRONIC RESOURCES

Documents, Texts, and Studies

Dumbarton Oaks Research Library. http://www.doaks.org/.
> Selected monastic foundation accounts, saints' lives, and publications.

———. "Byzantine Online Resources." http://www.doaks.org/byzrelatedsites.html.
> Byzantine-related resources.

Levantia: Social History of the Levant, ed. Timothy Dawson. http://www.levantia.com.au.
> Aspects of east Mediterranean culture in the ninth to thirteenth centuries, with an emphasis on social history, reconstruction, and reenactment.

Medieval Sourcebook for Byzantium, ed. Paul Halsall. http://www.fordham.edu/halsall/sbook1c.html.

ORB: On-line Reference Book for Medieval Studies, ed. Kathryn Talarico. http://www.the-orb.net/.

Suda On Line, ed. David Whitehead. http://www.stoa.org/sol/.
> Collaborative, open-source edition of a tenth-century historical and literary encyclopedia.

Excavations and Sites

American School of Classical Studies. http://www.ascsa.org/.
> Includes ongoing excavations at Athens and Corinth.

British School at Athens. http://www.bsa.gla.ac.uk/.
Constantinople home page. http://www2.arch.uiuc.edu/research/rgouster/.
    Information about monuments, images, and reports of research work.
French School at Athens. http://www.efa.gr/.
German Archaeological Institute. http://www.dainst.org/index.php?id=26.
        Includes research departments in Athens, Cairo, Istanbul, Rome, and
    elsewhere.
Greek Ministry of Culture. http://www.culture.gr/2/21/toc/arch_mus.html.
    Includes archaeological sites and museums.
Institute for Nautical Archaeology. http://www.tam.ina/.
Long Walls of Thrace. http://www.museums.ncl.uk/long_walls/index.html.

Libraries and Museums

Benaki Museum, Athens. http://www.benaki.gr/.
British Museum, London. http://www.britishmuseum.co.uk/.
Byzantine Museum, Athens. http://www.culture.gr/2/21/214/21404m/
    e21404m1.html.
Dumbarton Oaks Research Library, Washington, D.C. http://www.doaks.org/.
Louvre Museum, Paris. http://www.louvre.fr/.
Metropolitan Museum of Art, New York. http://www.metmuseum.org/.
Walters Art Gallery, Baltimore. http://www.thewalters.org.

INDEX

Agriculture and agricultural
  equipment, 172–83, 251, 291
Akritis, Digenis, 16, 132, 278
Alexandria, 282, 294, 299
Alphabet, 282–84
Amulets, 50–52, 217, 263, 299, 303–7
Animals: as companions, 54, 56;
  as entertainment, 80, 110, 115. *See
  also* Dogs
Ankara, 127–28
Antioch, 282, 294
Aqueduct of Constantinople, 73
Arabs, 16, 70, 85, 200, 208–9, 218–19,
  268, 290, 296
Archaeology, 9, 62, 159
Archery, 207
Architecture, 270–76
Aristotle, 54, 288, 294
Armies, 202–9; cavalry, 207–9;
  infantry, 204–7
Armor, 201–2, 204–6, 208
Astrology, 7, 296–98
Astronomy, 284, 294, 296–97
Athens, 138–39, 182–83, 267, 281–82,
  294; Academy of, 282, 294
Attaleiates, Michael, 289

Backgammon, 57, 104
Bakers and baking, 75, 102–3, 251–52.
  See also Bread; Ovens
Bandits and brigands, 29, 147, 153,
  161, 242
Banners and flags: hippodrome, 112;
  military, 211, 215–17; street, 79
Baptism, 43–44, 54
Barley, 102, 172–74, 177, 214
Basil of Caesarea, 229, 234, 254,
  281, 288
Baskets and basket making, 22, 193
Baths and bathing, 41, 47, 76–77, 87,
  123; in monasteries, 247
Beards, 47, 240
Beds and bedding, 92–93, 132,
  168, 186
Beer, 104, 214
Bees and beekeeping, 177, 186, 191
Beirut, 282, 294
Bible, 54, 269, 306–7
Birds, 5–6, 12, 59 n.20. *See also* Poultry
Boilas, Eustathios, 22, 289
Book of Ceremonies, 87, 108, 276
Book of the Eparch, 30, 98–100, 105–6,
  170, 262

Books, 243, 247, 254, 267, 287–89; and divination, 306–7; production of, 247, 254, 267–70, 284–85. *See also* Libraries

Bread, 75, 102–3, 174, 214, 251–52

Bricks and tiles, 137–38, 166, 191–92, 270–72

Bronze, 34–35, 263

Building materials and trades, 100, 107–8, 137–39, 166–67, 223, 270–74, 292

Bureaucracy: of church, 23–24; of state, 86–90

Burial traditions, 10–12, 45–46, 78, 163–64; monastic, 242, 247–48

Butchers, 101, 103

Calendar, 6–8

Camels, 145, 148–49, 183, 214

Candles, 4, 105–6

Cannons and gunpowder, 220–21, 291

Carpentry and woodworking, 187

Carts and wagons, 147–48, 183–84, 214

Castles *(kastra)*, 127–29, 223

Castration, 27–28, 55–56

Catapult (trebuchet), 218–20, 225

Cattle, 79–80, 103, 185–86

Celibacy, 40, 234, 239; clerical, 23

Cemeteries, 11, 29, 78, 163–64

Cereals and grains, cultivation, 172–74. *See also* Harvesting; Mills and milling

Chariots and chariot racing, 110–113, 123

Charity, 21, 27, 77, 97, 234, 247

Cheese, 95–96, 115, 185, 252–53

Chess, 57

Childbirth, 52–54, 306

Children and childhood, 8–9, 43, 54–56, 281–82; abandonment of, 52; mortality, 9, 39, 54. *See also* Education and schooling

China, 98, 105–6, 137, 148, 268, 296

Church: buildings, 25, 82, 128, 244–46, 274–76; organization, 23–24, 89

Cisterns of Constantinople, 73–75

Cities and towns, 119–21; economy of, 97–98, 120–21, 134–37; fortification of, in late antiquity, 121–27; in Middle Ages, 127–33

Clergy, 23–24, 89

Climate, 157

Cloth and cloth making, 22, 26, 106, 192–93, 267. *See also* Dyes and dyeing

Clothing, 48; elite, 88; clerical and monastic, 240–42

Coins and money, 31–5, 99–101, 262–63; "Charon's obol," 11

Communication, 216–17

Constantine I (emperor), 40, 65, 216

Constantine VII (emperor), 87, 108, 217, 269

Contraception, 43, 51–52

Cooking and food preparation, 95–96, 169

Corinth, 135–36, 139

Indikopleustes, Cosmas, 105, 144, 296

Cosmetics, 47

Cotton, 106, 192–93

Crafts and trades: in Constantinople, 97–108; in villages, 186–95. *See also* Guilds

Crime and punishment, 29–31, 68–69

Cross, depictions of, 125, 216, 259, 263

Crossbow, 218, 291

Curtains, 92, 130–32

Dancing, 27, 42, 56, 94, 104, 113–15, 277, 293

Day: days of the week, 3–5; monastic, 249–51

Death, 9–10, 45–46, 247

Demons, 43, 45, 50, 306

Diet and food, 46; military, 214; monastic, 251–53; rural, 169

Dining traditions, 46–47, 92, 94–96; monastic, 246–47

Dioscorides, 50–51, 288, 298–300

Disabilities, 56, 194

Divination, 306–7

Divorce, 42, 95

Dogs, 12, 56, 80, 141, 158, 184, 214, 298, 305

Donkeys, 148, 183, 212, 214
Doors, 262–63
Dowry, 40–42, 263
Dreams and dream interpretation, 51, 83, 303–4, 306–7
Dyes and dyeing, 125, 192–93, 267, 273

Easter Lent, 109, 115, 252–53
Economy, 31–35; rural, 159–60; urban, 97–98, 134–37
Education and schooling, 54, 254–55, 281–84. *See also* Literacy; Writing
Elites, 20, 90, 120–21
Emperor, 18, 20, 108–9
Enamel and enamel working, 264
Environment. *See* Weather
Eparch of Constantinople, 68, 90, 98–100
Ephesus, 140
Estates: monastic, 165–66, 235; rural, 164–65
Eunuchs, 27–28, 55–56, 88–89
Eustathius of Thessaloniki, 92, 153, 235, 286

Fairs and markets, 115, 140–41
Family, 18–9, 39–44; rural, 160
Farmer's Law, 29–30, 158–59, 171, 182
Fasting, 115, 253
Festivals: of Constantinople, 108–9, 114–15; liturgical, 7
Financial services, 98–101
Fires, 69, 158, 225
Fish, seafood, 95, 100, 103, 172
Fishing, 171–72, 177, 212
Flowers, 12, 79, 92, 176, 259
Forks, 47, 94, 262
Fortifications, 122–23, 127, 223, 242. *See also* Castles; Land walls of Constantinople
Forum of Constantine in Constantinople, 66, 80–81, 109
Fountains, 75, 96, 245
Frescos and wall paintings, 87, 92, 132, 272–73
Friendship, 18, 51, 185–87
Fruit and nut trees, 12, 92, 96, 135, 176

Funerary traditions, 10–12, 45–46; monastic, 247–48
Fur, 107, 137, 194
Furniture, 92–93, 132, 168, 272. *See also* Beds and bedding; Tables

Galen, 50–51, 298–99
Gambling, 57, 79, 104, 149
Games, 54, 56–57, 149, 225
Gardens, 12, 75, 82, 91–92, 135, 175–76
Gender roles, 25–28
Geoffrey of Villehardouin, 144
Geography, 295–96. *See also* Ptolemy
Geoponika, 5, 12, 76, 95, 102, 158–59, 165, 170–71, 174, 181, 188, 195 n.3, 288
Glass and glassmaking, 265–67
Goats, 79, 103, 185
Godparents, 44
Gold, 32–34, 247, 261–64
Golden Gate of Constantinople, 66, 71–72, 109
Golden Horn of Constantinople, 16–18, 62, 68, 85–86, 101
Goths, 16, 54, 69–70, 85, 157, 264, 290
Government, 20, 86–90
Grain supply of Constantinople, 75, 153
Grapes and vines: cultivation, 174, 177; pressing, 180–81
Grave robbing, 69, 78
Great Palace in Constantinople, 86–87
Greek (language), 16
Greek Fire, 210, 221–23, 291
Grooming, 47–50
Guidebooks, 81, 142–45
Guilds, 98–108

Hagia Sophia in Constantinople, 23–24, 31, 33, 83–85, 271–75, 292
Hair, 47–48
Harbors, 72, 101, 148–49
Harness, 148, 291
Harvesting, 173–74, 178–79, 291
Hats and headdresses, 48
Healing, spiritual, 83, 302–4
Health care, 50, 83, 247, 298–304. *See also* Hygiene; Medicine

Helmets, 205–6, 208–9
Herbs, 76, 104–5, 170; medicinal, 198–99. *See also* Spices and seasonings
Hippodrome in Constantinople, 110–13
History, idea of, 1–3
Homer, 54, 255, 282–82, 288
Honey, 52, 104–5, 186. *See also* Bees and beekeeping
Horses, 146–48, 204, 207–9, 212–14, 298
Hospitals, 77, 83, 299–301
Household, 43–45
Houses and housing: elite, 90–93; rural, 167–69; urban, 96–97, 123, 125–34
Humor, 289–90
Hunting, 95, 170, 214
Hygiene, 49–50
Hyrtakenos, Theodore, 283, 286, 288

Iconoclasm, 258–59
Iconostasis, 2, 23, 25, 245–46, 276
Icons, 82–83, 110, 153, 218, 243, 245, 264; icon making, 260
India, 98, 105–6, 144, 296
Inns, 146. *See also* Tavernas
Iron, and ironworking, 187–88
Irrigation, 162, 166, 178
Ivory and ivory carving, 264–66

Jerusalem, 142, 295
Jewelry, 48–49; jewelry making, 263–64
Jews, 8, 16–18, 85, 144
Justinian (emperor), 24, 29, 83, 112, 294, 307

Kekaumenos, 18, 26, 45, 164, 171, 287–88
Knives, 46, 94, 262
Komnene, Anna, 26, 55, 57, 199–200, 203, 218, 221, 298

Lamps and lighting, 4, 79, 105–6, 175, 246, 266
Landownership, 31, 120–21, 159–60, 164, 235

Land walls of Constantinople, 67, 70–72
Lombards, 157
Languages, 15–16, 85
Latin (language), 85, 200, 298
Latins, 68, 70, 72, 200, 290
Laundry, 49–50, 106, 125
Law, and order, 29–31, 68–69
Leatherworking, 107, 193–94
Legumes, 95, 105, 176
Leo the Mathematician, 217, 284, 287, 291, 294–95
Letters, 267–68, 285–87
Libraries: monastic, 254, 287–89; patriarchal, 284, 288; private, 269–70, 289
Life expectancy, 9, 302
Linen, 106, 136, 192–93
Literacy, 281–89. *See also* Education and schooling; Writing
Liturgy, 24–25, 249–51, 276; liturgical drama, 114; liturgical equipment, 262
Liudprand of Cremona, 87, 262
Long Walls of Thrace, 69
Looms, 106, 192–93

Magic and sorcery, 113, 304–7
Manure, 175, 179
Maps, 142, 295–96. *See also* Ptolemy
Marble, 108, 138, 270–72
Marriage, 40–42; ceremonies, 41–42; minimum age, 40, 55; rings, 41–42
Mathematics, 294–95
Meat, 95–96, 103, 169
Medicine, 298–304; household, 50; medical training, 299; military, 226–27
Mese of Constantinople, 66, 78
Metals and metalworking, 187–88, 261–64
Meteora, 236
Metochites, Theodore, 92, 289, 294, 297
Middle classes, 21
Midwives, 52–54
Military organization, 89–90, 202–9; veterans, 228–29
Millet, 102, 172–74, 177, 185, 214

Mill game, 57
Mills and milling, 158–59, 181–83, 291. *See also* Watermills; Windmills
Mines and mining, 32; in siege warfare, 225
Mistra, 129–32
Monastic clothing, 240–42; organization, 237–40
Monasticism, 233–34
Mosaics, 86–87, 266–67, 272–73
Mosques, 86–87
Mount Athos, 28, 236–37, 288
Mules, 148, 183, 212, 214
Music and musical instruments, 113, 249–50, 276–78, 293
Muslims, 144, 218

Names, 19–20, 43
Nature, attitudes toward, 12–13
Navy, 72, 209–12
Nicaea, 122, 224
Numbers and numerals, 284. *See also* Mathematics

Oats, 173, 177
Odo of Deuil, 75, 79, 147
Old age and retirement, 9, 229, 240, 247
Olives: cultivation, 174–75; pressing, 180–81
Organ, 276, 293
Orphans and orphanages, 52, 77
Ovens, 102, 168–69; in monasteries, 247–48. *See also* Bakers and baking; Bread
Oxen, 185–86

Pachymeres, George, 153, 294–95
Paper, 268
Papyrus, 267
Parchment, 107, 268
Paul the Silentiary, 51, 91
Perfume, 99, 101–2
Pergamon, 132–34, 139
Persians, 207
Peutinger Table, 142, 295; illustrated, 17, 63, 143
Philanthropy, 21, 75, 77, 97, 234
Photios (patriarch), 272–73, 288

Physicians, 298–304. *See also* Medicine
Pigs, 79, 103, 170, 185, 226
Pilgrimage, 81–83, 144–45, 234–35, 264. *See also* Travel and transportation
Plague, 3, 68, 78, 225, 302
Plato, 54, 294
Pliny the Elder, 32, 49, 174–75, 262, 290, 304
Plow, 178–79, 291
Pottery and pottery making, 22, 136, 139, 169; amphoras, 103–4, 189–90; cooking, 190–91; storage, 133, 188–89; table, 190–91
Poultry, 103, 186
Poverty and the poor, 21, 27, 97
Prayer, 25, 217, 249, 253, 305
Presses, 180–81
Prices, 34; of books, 35, 269–70, 288; of icons, 260; of slaves, 34
Priests, 23–24
Prisoners of war, 21–22, 228
Prisons, 30, 69, 77. *See also* Crime and punishment
Privacy, 26, 44–45, 290
Procopius, 85, 302
Prostitutes, 27, 77, 79, 114
Psellos, Michael, 28, 54, 90, 173, 218, 294, 298, 302
Ptolemy, 4, 8, 142, 290, 294–97

Relics, 82–83, 217; reliquaries, 153, 263–65
Roads, 146–47. *See also* Travel and transportation
Rus, 16

Sailing and seafaring, 142–44, 148–54, 179, 291–92
Sanitation, 76, 79, 96, 302. *See also* Hygiene
Sardis, 16, 123–27
Science, 293–94
Seals and sealings, 24, 287
Seasons, 5–6, 297
Sex and sexuality, 50–51, 305–7
Sheep, 79, 103, 179, 185
Shields, military, 205–8
Ships and shipbuilding, 150–51, 292
Shoes and footwear, 107, 194

Shops, 79, 101, 105, 124–25. *See also* Fairs and markets

Sieges and siege equipment, 218–20, 223–26

Signal towers, 217, 291

Silk, 48, 88; silk production, 106–7, 186

Silver, 32–34, 162, 261–64

Singing, 42, 56, 276–78; liturgical, 24–25, 217, 249–50

Skylitzes Chronicle, 202, 269; illustrated, 110, 209, 222, 226, 271

Slaves and slavery, 21–22, 50, 137; prices of, 34

Slavs, 16, 69, 209

Soap, 49–50, 170

Social structure, 18–25

Soldiers, 104, 202–18, 226–29, 240

Soul, concept of, 2, 10

Spices and seasonings, 95, 105, 137

Spinning and weaving, 106, 192–93; as female activity, 26, 45

Spoons, 46–47, 262

Sports, 109–13

Statues, 71, 77, 80–81, 111

Stirrup, 147, 208, 291

Streets and porticoes, 78–80, 102, 122

Surgeons and surgery, 301–2. *See also* Medicine; Physicians

Swords, 205–8

Synagogues, 85–86, 124

Tables, 92, 94, 104, 132, 272

Tableware, 46–47, 87, 94, 262. *See also* Forks; Knives; Pottery and pottery making; Spoons

Tanning, 107, 193–94

Tavernas, 100, 104–5, 125, 146

Taxes, 32, 100, 160–61

Teachers, 54, 281–84. *See also* Education and schooling

Technology, 290–93

Teeth and dental care, 49, 174, 299

Theater and theatrical performances, 112–14, 123

Thebes, 18, 137, 267

Thessaloniki, 135, 138–39, 267; Festival of Demetria, 141

Time and timekeeping, 3–4, 297

Titles and dignities, 20, 31, 87–88, 90, 203–4

Tools, 178–80, 187–88, 291

Toys, 54–57

Trades: in Constantinople, 97–108; in towns, 134–41; in villages, 186–94

Travel and transportation, 141–54, 183, 291–92

Turks, 16, 132–33, 200, 291

Vegetables, 46, 76, 95, 176

Varangians, 69, 88, 203, 206

Villages and village life, 161–64, 194–95, 159–60; organization, 159–64

Vinegar, 97, 104, 169

Water supply of Constantinople, 72–75, 292. *See also* Aqueduct of Constantinople; Cisterns of Constantinople

Water, 96, 162, 212, 243–44

Watermills, 182–83, 291

Weapons, 205–8

Weather, 5–6, 153, 210

Week, 4–5

Weights and measures, 98, 102

Wheat, varieties of, 102, 176

Windmills, 183, 291

Windows, 91–92, 130–32, 266

Wine, 96, 103–4, 115; varieties, 103–4, 174; wine making, 180–81

Women, social roles, 25–27, 45–46, 306

Wool, 106, 136, 192–93. *See also* Cloth and cloth making

Worship, 24–25, 234; military, 217; monastic, 234

Writing, 268–69, 284–85

About the Author

MARCUS RAUTMAN is Professor and Department Chair of the Department of Art History and Archaeology, University of Missouri, Columbia.